FAMILIAR EXPLOITATION

Feminist Perspectives

Series Editor: Michelle Stanworth

Published

Forthcoming

FAMILIAR EXPLOITATION:
A New Analysis of Marriage in Contemporary Western Societies

CHRISTINE DELPHY and DIANA LEONARD

Polity Press

First published in 1992 by Polity Press
in association with Blackwell Publishers

Editorial office:
Polity Press
65 Bridge Street
Cambridge CB2 1UR, UK

Marketing and production:
Blackwell Publishers
108 Cowley Road
Oxford OX4 1JF, UK

3 Cambridge Center
Cambridge, Massachusetts 02142, USA

ISBN 0 7456 0858 2
ISBN 0 7456 0985 6 (pbk)

A CIP catalogue record for this book is available from the British Library and the Library of Congress.

Typeset in 10 on 11 pt Times
by Graphicraft Typesetters Ltd., Hong Kong
Printed and bound in Great Britain by
Biddles Ltd, Guildford and King's Lynn

This book is printed on acid-free paper.

CONTENTS

ACKNOWLEDGEMENTS

Many people have given us help and support in writing this book. We should like to thank in particular Lisa Adkins, Françoise Armengaud, Alice Barthez, Leonore Davidoff, Meghnad Desai, Peter Gidal, Mavis Maclean and Michelle Stanworth who all commented on the final version of the manuscript.

1

INTRODUCTION:
FEMINISM AND THE FAMILY

In this book we develop a new approach to understanding the subordination of women in western societies. It is an approach which focuses on the family, which many have recognized as one of the main sites of inequalities between the sexes; but it is different in that it highlights the family *as an economic system*. It stresses that domestic groups are not just random sets of people united by bonds of affection and kinship who live together and share out the jobs that need doing so as to offer each other practical support in a joint endeavour to get along in the world. Rather they are also (indeed they are primarily) part of a system of *labour relations* in which men benefit from, and exploit, the work of women – and sometimes that of their children and other male relatives too.

Our approach to understanding women's subordination starts, therefore, from a recognition that in the West, domestic groups are characterized by a male head maintaining a number of dependants (one woman at least, his wife, and often his children and possibly a number of male and female relatives) whose labour he appropriates and uses in various ways. We stress that domestic groups are hierarchically structured and that there are 'relations of production' between particular family members. But we also stress that what is 'exchanged' for what, and how, within family relations differs from what is exchanged and the form of exchange within the market relations of production which exist alongside the domestic domain.

Other people who have approached the family as an economic system have got lost on this last point because they have simply compared the family and the market – or rather they have only compared the family to the market. That is, they have not explored family economic relationships in and of themselves. They have used the market as the standard, and applied terms relevant to capitalist labour relations to family labour relations.

This has meant that all the bad things about family labour have kept getting lost. For instance, in asking if wives get more or less for their work in the family than they would on the labour market, it gets forgotten that the 'wage rate' is not the point at issue in family labour. Family oppression is about family subordinates being personal dependants. It is about their not being able to change to another husband/father easily (or their not being able to change at all), and their having to do whatever their husband / father requires rather than specific tasks, and his being able to be violent or sexually abusive towards them with relative impunity. Family dependants do not own their own labour power in the same way as heads of households own theirs, and if dependants sell labour they do so under different conditions from heads. Dependants either do not have any money at all except what their head 'gives' them, or if they earn money, they do not own it in the same way as their household head owns what he earns.

If the bad things about family labour keep getting forgotten, the bad things about wage work, on the other hand, are nearly always recalled. Hence, not surprisingly, people end up saying that family labour is not as bad as wage labour. They then cannot understand how the family contributes to the continuing subordination of women generally, or why women, when given the choice, generally opt for paid employment rather than for being 'kept women'.

Our approach to the family may therefore shock some people because, like other feminists, we focus upon what is bad as well as good about the family: in this instance, the bad (and the good) aspects of family labour. This violates the general social consensus that one should concentrate only on good things about the family: how it is different from and better than the rest of the world. We may also upset some people because we do not explain family relations either in terms of the physiological or psychological characteristics of male and female human beings, or in terms of the desires felt and the choices made by individuals. This violates the consensus that the family is particularly valuable to society because it is one area at least where human behaviour is still nearly natural and where primacy is still given to the needs of the individual. We believe, on the contrary, that the family is every bit as social a structure as, say, industrial capitalism, and that 'choices' in and around family life are every bit as constructed and constrained as they are in, for example, the labour market. Families too need to be analysed as social institutions – and as *socio-economic* institutions: as structured hierarchical systems of social relations around the production, consumption and transmission of property. Family relationships can and do involve *economic exploitation*, even though ideologically such harsh words as 'economic' and 'exploitation' are supposed to be kept apart from the nice cosy world of the home.

Our approach may also surprise those familiar with recent feminist scholarship in that it is radical feminist and yet it uses marxist methodology. Radical feminism and marxism have often been presented as antithetical to one another, but we believe not only that men are the primary beneficiaries of the subordination of women in western societies, but also that a marxist approach is the one which best helps us to understand why and how men oppress women.

Historical materialist analysis was developed by Marx as a means of understanding different forms of exploitation. His point of departure was the different forms of oppression suffered by different groups in different societies, and he described and accounted for the genesis and continuation of the varying socio-economic systems which produced these experiences. His genius lay in recognizing the importance of the work people do and the relations within which they do it, and how these have changed over time, in explaining people's situations and their experience of their situations.

Marx's concern to understand forms of exploitation derived from his involvement in political movements struggling to change the lot of subordinate groups. His particular concern was to understand the nature of capitalist exploitation so as to change the world and improve the position of the poor in mid-nineteenth-century Europe – as part of his involvement in the international workers' movement of his time. He emphasized that the dynamic for social change would come in future, as it has in the past, primarily from the 'class antagonisms' which are at the heart of capitalist relations, and from changes in the technology associated with production.

Women have often been studied, and historical materialism is well established, but using marxist methodology to study something it has ignored, sex / gender relations and women's oppression, enables us to understand better whole areas of experience where idealist and individualistic views have been relatively unchallenged, i.e. relationships based on 'love'. A materialist approach enables us to see and understand the previously unrecognized 'class' relations which exist between men and women (as socially not biologically defined actors), and it helps us start to rethink family history as a process of continuing gender and generational struggle.

Unlike some radical feminists, we do not believe that men have always and everywhere dominated women, and in the same ways and for the same reasons as today; especially if this includes a suggestion that this is to do with the good or bad 'natures' of men and women. What we offer here is a radical feminist analysis developed to understand the position of women in contemporary western societies, which may or may not also be applicable to other times and places, which recognizes the advantages which men (as a socially constituted group) derive from using and abusing women.

But we are equally critical of marxist feminists who continue to produce male-centred marxism (as we shall show in the next two chapters). We believe our work shows yet again, in a new field, how productive marxist methodology can be. But neither we nor anyone else can stick to the letter of Marx's own writings if we want to understand the oppression of women, since this did not concern him.

Aiming to do so much, and threatening so many sensibilities, explains why this is a long book – and why it has taken us a long time to write it. We are saying something original and we therefore need to develop and explain the language in which we can express it. We have to outline things and then to circle back and develop them: to say certain things before we can say others, aware that the things we say first will only be fully explicated after other things have been explained. And we have constantly to clarify how and why we differ from previous writers.

We shall therefore spend the rest of this chapter and chapters 2 and 3 showing what in the past has most concerned radicals and feminists about the family, and the sorts of explanation they have produced – and when, where and why we disagree with them. This gives a first outline of our ideas and enables us to define and clarify our use of various concepts. We then go on in chapters 4, 5 and 6 to develop our own analysis, and to sort out some of the misconceptions which have developed since we first started publishing in this area 20 years ago. And finally we apply our analysis to other people's accounts of families and households in chapters 7, 8 and 9.

First, though, we need to define some of the terms we have already used, namely 'the family' and 'household'. The term 'family' as used in contemporary western societies refers either to a group of people who live together and have some degree of shared housekeeping (which is strictly speaking a 'household'), or to those who are seen as related by marriage or descent from common ancestors (which anthropologists would refer to as a 'lineage').[1] The context usually makes it clear who is supposed to be included in the term when it is used in the second way, but it can range from just someone's children, to all their grandparents and parents and brothers and sisters and aunts and uncles and all of *their* spouses and children. 'The family' most commonly, however, and as a social ideal, refers to a combination of the two meanings: to a group which lives together and is related by marriage and close kinship, and specifically a domestic group made up of a man and his wife and their children.

Both households and lines of descent can equally be called 'families' because almost all domestic groups today actually do consist of people who are related by marriage or descent. In addition, the various members of the short line of descent referred to as 'close family' – grandparents, parents and children and their spouses – have generally lived together in changing household groups at different points in their lives.

Relatively few people in our society (only about 3 per cent of the population) live outside private households, in hostels, boarding houses, residential homes, boarding schools, colleges, barracks, hospitals and prisons. Of those who live in private households, only about 10 per cent live on their own (many of them being elderly and widowed), and less than 10 per cent live in households with people to whom they are not related. Thus more than 80 per cent of people in western countries at any one time live in households with people to whom they are related by marriage and / or descent (that is, with their spouse and / or their parents or children), and the rest will live, or will have lived, in such households for most of the rest of their lives.

In this book we are therefore following common usage when we use 'the family' to refer (unless otherwise specified) to the domestic residential group based on a man and his wife and children (the family in space), though we do also sometimes talk of the family line (the family in time). We know of course that there are arguments for referring to domestic groups as 'households' because this recognizes that domestic groups are not necessarily composed of people related to each other by kinship and marriage: that some adults live alone or with friends or in homosexual couples. But we ourselves generally only use the term 'household' when we want specifically to signal recognition of this fact or to distinguish the family in space from the family in time.

We are wary of calling domestic groups 'households' rather than 'families' because the distinction has sometimes been used as a means to downplay the significance of family relationships (and their gender and generational hierarchies) in structuring people's lives in contemporary western societies.[2] That is to say, the distinction has been used by some writers as a way of suggesting that households are only sometimes, contingently, or as a matter of choice, based on family relations. But in fact they are so based as *part of our social system*. Domestic groups nearly always consist of men / husbands and women / wives and their children, and most of the single or two (unrelated) person households which do exist are part of the cycle of the nuclear family – that is, they consist of people who have not yet reached or or who have passed the marriage-and-children stage of the life-course – rather than being alternatives to family-based households.

We see the familial basis of domestic groups as an important element in continuing the patriarchal nature of our society: that is, in the continuance of men's dominance over women and children in the West (and in many other parts of the world too). It is therefore a social structure which we must recognize if we want to understand gender divisions; not something we should hide by spuriously 'scientific' definitional distinctions. Equally, of course, we must always be conscious that not all domestic groups are so constituted, and we must look to see how, why and when 'deviant' households come into being and how they fare.

Views of women and the family in three periods of feminism

Mainstream social and political thought in the West over the past two centuries has taken the structure and functioning of the western family for granted. Virtually everyone who has described the structure of such societies and proposed changes has assumed that the 'basic unit of society' is and should be a man and his wife and children, and that property should pass from parents to children. They have generally not even discussed such matters. The inevitability and importance of the family has been deemed self-evident.

Such general criticism as there has been of the family has said either that the family can be bad for individual members because of its closed, intensive, exclusive relationships; or that the family can be bad for society as a whole, or a subgroup within society, because it encourages insularity. The former line of criticism can be seen, for instance, in Strindberg's plays or D. H. Lawrence's novels about women restricting and emasculating men, or (in a much less common form) in Ibsen's play *The Doll's House* about family life stifling wives. It can also be seen in R. D. Laing's work on how families can precipitate schizophrenia in individual members. The second line of criticism, that of family insularity, suggests that because individuals usually owe their primary allegiance to their family (domestic group or line), they devote too much time and energy to it to the detriment of some other interests, objectives or groups (for example, instead of devoting time to the glory of God, or to fighting for the revolution or the nation). Hence religious communities, political cadres and armies (amongst others) have often established alternatives to family life for their members.

But these critiques of family intensity or insularity have not always specified differential effects on men and women, nor have they suggested the family presents specific problems for women and children, much less that it needs to be changed to improve their situation. For this we have to look to more radical writing, mainly by women, and within such feminist work we can differentiate three historical periods.

The first wave of feminism: 1850–1920

Relatively few nineteenth-century and early-twentieth-century thinkers proposed changes to the family in their political analyses, but those who did included individualists, socialists, anarchists and communists as well as feminists. None contested, however, that 'the union of one man and one woman voluntarily entered into for life' was fundamental to civilized society. Not only did they accept marriage, or at least heterosexual monogamy, they also accepted a division of labour within marriage, and that men should be the superior partners. What concerned them was rather that *certain* families were oppressive for those who were subordinates within them, so reforms were needed to protect women and children.

Some explained the existing oppression of women and children as simply a matter of a few unfortunate instances: of occasional bad husbands and fathers abusing their power. But most feminists argued instead that it was a question of the existing form of the family as an institution being oppressive because it prevented women from having an independent life and income, from having the right to control sexual access to their bodies, from having the protection of the law as an individual, and from having full rights and performing their full duties as citizens. The institution itself therefore needed to be reformed, rather than just help offered in individual cases where things 'had gone wrong'.

One common nineteenth-century radical view suggested that the family had changed over time – that it had moved from natural equity to male domination – because of pressures from outside. These pressures were variously identified as the establishment of private property, the forces of urban life, the effects of industrialization in separating home and 'work', and / or the ubiquity and power of commercial values. If these outside influences were modified, it was argued, the family itself would return to its (supposedly) natural equality and harmony.

Although they varied in their analysis, many people of all shades of political opinion therefore worked for changes in the family in the nineteenth century. Their particular focus was often on aspects of family law relating to property and divorce, where changes were sought to curb husband / fathers' powers and to give dependants protection. Efforts were also directed towards achieving a higher valuation of women's work and women's proper sphere, the home. Some sought to mitigate the plight of women who could not marry or who were widowed, by offering direct help and alternative places to live; while others gave support to victims of domestic violence, marital rape, and incest. Many fought for changes in women's involvement in public life and the improvement of women's education and for the opening up of occupations to women and the availability of paid employment for unmarried women of all classes. Some argued for the reform of men's sexual behaviour, for improving police treatment of prostitutes, against 'white slavery', and for raising the age of sexual consent. Those who thought there would be a changed, renewed, perfect family life to look forward to once other aspects of society had been changed, that is, after the (anticipated, class-based) revolution, worked for revolution. And a few argued for domestic reform and set up actual reformed communities providing houses for many families living together, with communal facilities (kitchens, laundries, childcare) run by women. If there was little discussion of the division of labour between men and women, this was largely due to most routine domestic work and childcare in middle class and artisans' homes being done by servants.

Through all this activity, the future perceived for marriage and the gender division of labour was not all that different from what currently existed among the middle classes. Equality between men and women was equated with husbands and wives (or more rarely men and women in 'free unions') choosing each other without family or economic pressures, being companions, and having personal and economic autonomy. But each was to have their different role, and (European, middle class) masculinity and femininity were to remain unthreatened. Thus William Morris, in his 1890s vision of a future utopia, *News from Nowhere*, has men and women still in monogamous marriages, with men continuing to talk while the women wait at table, but he suggests women will no longer be doing this out of wifely duty but because they are better at housework, because it has become more highly valued, and because they enjoy it. Blatchford in his utopia of the same period, *Merrie England*, has the drudgery taken out of the cooking, cleaning and rearing of children by the collective, communal performance of these tasks – by women; while the anarchist Kropotkin argued that technical progress would eliminate the drudgery of housework and thus liberate women.[3] In the American feminist Charlotte Perkins Gilman's utopia, *Herland* (1915), both men and women leave their homes each day to do 'world work', which could be housework in someone else's house as a public (that is, paid) activity 'by those who chose to do it'; but children were still raised (collectively) by women, who were the nurturers, and each nuclear family was reunited at the end of the day in its own home, which has become a place of love and relaxation.

Even women who were themselves active in public service in Victorian times, or campaigners for the vote, or active in establishing, for instance, the Women's Labour League, subscribed to the view that marriage and the family were women's most important responsibilities. They often campaigned within separate women's organizations on 'women's issues' (for example, for maternal and child welfare, and against unwanted child-bearing) precisely because they accepted the immutability of sexual differences. And although some feminists sought recognition for the merits of single life, arguing that marriage should not be the only possible or desirable career for a woman and that single women could make a useful if different contribution to society and were not necessarily unhappy or frustrated or the appropriate people to care for elderly parents and unmarried brothers, the ideal of (married or single) women *combining* employment and family responsibilities was only rarely represented. It was never strong and declined towards the turn of the century.

What most first wave feminists were seeking was not to undermine the family, but rather to raise the quality of all family life to that of their own: to the level where members were mutually responsible and self-reliant as a unit, under the continuing beneficent direction of the husband / father. Such women acted mainly philanthropically, seeking change not for themselves but for other less fortunate women. Indeed, they often cited this fact to show the justice of their cause. They did not question the division of family responsibilities or the possibility (indeed the general prevalence) of good and happy marriages. Rather their actions in supporting those without families and in modernizing family law and in spreading Christian marriage overseas through missionary activities, both presumed the centrality of the family for all women's lives and aimed at actually preserving and strengthening marriage.

From the 1890s, as the leadership of the women's emancipation movement concentrated more and more on getting the vote, seeing parliamentary representation as the cure-all for women's problems, there was in fact an increasing tendency (especially marked in America) to retreat to a position where differences in capacity for logical thought and in morals between men and women, as well as differences in their social situation and interests, were not only accepted by feminists, but formed the very basis of their demands. Arguments for enfranchisement in the early twentieth century were often specifically in terms of the need for white middle class women to have the vote so as to ensure that the needs of their specific and proper sphere – the running of (white, middle class, western) households, the care of children, philanthropic endeavours, temperance and other moral issues – were recognized by the legislature. In other words, women were to have the vote so as to support and strengthen the bourgeois home and family.

Between the two waves: 1920–1968

After the First World War even the previous limited discussion of the family disappeared from western socialism. Until the turn of the century some radicals, anarchists and communists had really believed they were preparing for a new world and so any and everything should be called into question. But since then the concern of the Left has been mainly with questions of redistributing the benefits of the existing order. Those who have planned for revolution have had a much narrower focus, seeing workplace struggles and the establishment of a vanguard party to organize and politicize the (male) industrial proletariat against capital as the primary issue. They have either supported the working class family as a bastion of class resistance and communal values, or attacked it because its demands on men for attention and money deflect them from revolutionary politics or make them unable to undertake industrial action. Feeling itself to be generally in a defensive position, the Left has certainly not been willing to be seen to attack the family or to advocate 'free love' – given the extent to which this was used to pillory earlier revolutionary socialists and free-thinkers from Mary Wollstonecraft onwards. Although this unwillingness is perhaps not surprising, it has nevertheless constituted a continued selling out of the interests of women. It has been a means to buy support by accepting patriarchal family structures and male advantage in the workplace (better jobs and better pay), and as such it has been justly criticized.

Throughout the period from 1920 to the late 1960s, however, despite the demise of feminism as a large-scale movement, some women's organizations and many individual women continued to press for improving women's employment situation and for their civil and marital rights. They continued to seek equality in education and training, to encourage ambition and the opening up of new fields to girls (because women continued to be largely restricted to a narrow range of occupations and to the bottom of the hierarchy within each occupation), to 'endow motherhood' (that is, to get family allowances paid to women), to make contraception available to married women so they could 'plan' their families, to equalize the grounds for divorce between men and women, to make divorce more accessible to the poorer sections of society, and to get better economic support for women who lost their husbands through death, divorce or desertion. Research and the collection of information on women was encouraged to pressure government agencies, doctors, employers and trade unions to recognize women's special needs, and to make women's contribution to society generally, and to marriage specifically, recognized as different from, but equal to, the contribution made by men.

But these organizations were numerically weak, individuals were often isolated, and there was a general fear of the label feminist: of being seen to be extremist or militant. (This did not of course stop the women involved being labelled as warhorses, frustrated spinsters and lesbians – or as at best having some very odd and tiresome bees in their bonnets.) In addition, the 1920s and 1930s saw moves which made the choice of non-marriage – of spinsterhood or celibacy or close relationships with women – even less acceptable for women. The sex reformers of the period promoted heterosexual intercourse as necessary to both sexes, and although this may have allowed women to take pleasure in heterosexual intercourse, its negative side was the suggestion that women who remained unmarried or who did not want to engage in heterosexual intercourse suffered from repression. If not married, then free love and non-monogamy were both preferable to women not relating sexually to men at all. For women to have their primary relationships with other women was evidence of immaturity, deviance or failure.

The 1930s also saw the growth of right-wing and nationalist arguments (articulated in vigorous National Socialist parties in many European countries) about the importance of the family, women's role as wives and mothers, and the authority of parents in bearing and training children for the nation. These have had continuing and extremely important church support, as have anti-feminist and anti-homosexual backlashes.

The period from the end of the First World War to the 1960s is therefore remembered as one where there was little criticism of marriage and the family and considerable prejudice against homosexuality. And by the end of the Second World War the concern was simply whether the family was in decline; and if it was, how best to support it. At this time any and every social change was liable to be scrutinized for its possibly weakening influence on the family. For example, whether the provision of free school milk, cheap school dinners, and retirement and health insurance might be undesirable if they reduced men's feelings of responsibility for their dependants; and whether the decline of religion, and the increase in women's paid employment might not encourage divorce. The pessimists' claims that social changes had weakened the family and that this was a bad thing, were just about balanced by the optimists who said they had actually strengthened it, which was all to the good. No one said the family was declining and that this was a good thing.

However, during the 50 years from 1918–68, important critiques of women's situation were produced, even if they lacked a wide women's movement audience. Most notable was Simone de Beauvoir's angry and courageous protest in *The Second Sex* (1949). Both the book and its author personally were seen as monstrosities by the Right, and (to her surprise) also viewed with ambivalence and disfavour by the Left. But the book's abiding importance, along with the work of others, including, for instance, Margaret Mead in the USA (from the late 1920s to the 1950s), Viola Klein in Britain (from the 1940s to the 1960s) and Andrée Michel in France (in the 1960s and 1970s), lay in its stress on the social construction of masculinity and femininity and the arbitrary and variable nature of the division of labour between men and women. These existentialists, anthropologists and 'role theory' sociologists laid the foundation, in a very inauspicious intellectual climate, for the later feminist concept of 'gender'.

In addition, during these 50 years there were also major changes in the internal worlds of rural and urban middle and working class families throughout northern Europe and North America. (Changes were even more marked, of course, for those who emigrated into these areas from other parts of the world.) Fewer men were self-employed (though there remains considerable variation by region) and fewer worked in or near their homes. Domestic life was increasingly separated from town centres into suburbs and housing estates, and families were less likely to live near kin. Fewer families had servants or nursemaids (especially in Europe after the 1930s). Women married younger and had fewer children, but they devoted more time to childcare, and despite new household technologies (such as running water, electric or gas stoves, washing machines and telephones) the hours wives needed to work to attain the required level of housewifery remained the same because standards rose and more work was concentrated in one woman's hands in each household. Consequently women of all social classes, including for the first time servantless middle class women, found themselves increasingly on their own for most of the day, or with only the company of small children or sick and elderly relatives. They were tied to their houses and performed repetitive 'invisible' housework, or did voluntary good works in the suburbs.

Some of these women had received an education and training for interesting paid jobs, and most had experienced a period of employment and financial independence between leaving school and marriage or the birth of their first child. They entered marriage expecting a partnership, including mutual sexual fulfilment, but instead found themselves miserable when surrounded by all the things they were told would make them happy: a nice house, a loving husband and pretty children. They felt frustrated at being a *Captive Wife* (Gavron 1966). They saw their fathers, brothers, husbands and sons doing things: going to workplaces, developing leisure activities including sports, meeting people and making things which, unlike meals and clean floors, did not seem to have vanished at the end of the day. Men earned money, ran political movements, drove cars, and went to bars and football matches. Men were the ones who took sexual initiatives, got most pleasure out of sex within marriage, and could sow wild oats. Women knew that most things they did were said to be uncreative and trivial, though they seemed necessary and were certainly time-consuming. They knew too that although lip service was paid to motherhood, it was actually little valued; and that although they were men's 'partners', they were definitely not their equals. But they could not work out why, nor what to do about it.

The second wave of feminism: 1968–1990

The dissatisfaction such women felt with their lives was the 'problem which has no name', *The Feminine Mystique* which Betty Friedan sought to pin down in 1963. Combined with some women's experience of the so-called sexual revolution of the late 1960s and the student revolt and direct action of social welfare movements (squatters' and claimants' unions, etc.) of the same period, it produced the explosion of anger which launched the second wave of feminism, the Women's Liberation movement, in 1968. Middle class women's particular dissatisfaction with both their post-war domestic role as 'eroticized housewives' and their 1960s 'libertarian' sexual role, ensured that much of the feminist critique published in the early 1970s focused on the private sphere, on life within quite affluent domestic groups and on interpersonal and sexual relationships, as well as on the labour market, the education system, the media and conventional political life.

Given the previous history of implicit acceptance and support for family life, and first wave feminists' relative silence on marital sexuality (except in relation to unwanted pregnancies and the risks to wives of contracting VD if their husbands used prostitutes), the attacks launched by the second wave of feminism on the division of labour and power within economically secure and prosperous homes, on consensual sexual relations between men and women, and on the constitution of masculinity and femininity, were startling and genuinely radical – and threatening. They constituted a marked break with what remained of past feminism and with other contemporary political movements. The WLM introduced new ways of gaining an understanding of women's situation – via consciousness raising – and developed forms of political action drawn from anarchism and the Black Power movement, such as the use of direct action and only allowing the oppressed group (women) to participate.

From the start, second wave feminism recognized women to be not a 'second sex', different from men by nature or because so moulded from birth, but a secondary social group, oppressed and dominated by men. Women were seen to be both a super-exploited section of the labour force, and unpaid domestic and sexual servicers. Further insights and new understandings came over the years – but not always quickly or easily. For instance, it was only over the course of ten years that the incidence and causes of violence in the home, of rape, the sexual abuse of children, and sexual harassment at work came to be recognized and set as items on the political agenda. And it required sustained pressure by lesbians, working class and Black feminists to get those who felt they were the mainstream of the women's movement to accept that what they had initially focused on were the particular forms of oppression which most concerned heterosexual, middle class, white, western women, whereas the modalities of women's oppression vary with their sexual practice, class, race and nation, and all these diverse forms need to be confronted.

In the process, terms such as 'sexual politics', 'sexism', 'patriarchy' and 'heterosexism' were introduced and their meanings gradually refined and sharpened. 'Patriarchy' in French, for instance, had been little used previously outside the literary context, where it was used chiefly as an adjective in the phrase 'patriarchal virtues'. Feminists turned its sense of peaceful, cohesive, traditional, communal society upside down, by stressing that such utopian, golden age, family-based societies were certainly not egalitarian. They were systematically exploitative of women.

How the new terms are used still varies, however. 'Patriarchy' itself always means 'a system of rule by the *pater*', but some (including ourselves) take this to mean specifically the rule of heads of households (husbands, fathers, masters) over their dependants in western families, while others use it much more generally, to indicate dominance by (older) men in all parts of society and in all societies, past and present. In addition, our analysis of the family clearly shows a generational as well as a gender dimension to the authority of heads of households, but some would argue for using 'patriarchy' to refer only to men's dominance over women. Despite these disagreements, feminists' use of this term has always implied that we suffer not a series of haphazard, piecemeal oppressions, but rather that our diverse forms of oppression are interconnected and mutually sustaining. That is to say, use of the term implies a recognition of a *system* of male domination.

From the start of the second wave of feminism there was a clear recognition that marriage and heterosexual couple relations generally were an important element within this system. Marriage exists legally only between a man and a woman in western societies (even if a few nations, for example, Denmark, now purport to have extended the institution to same-sex couples). It is therefore never a contract between equals, since men and women are not equals. Men are individual adult citizens in a way women are not. They have civic rights as contracting individuals and many customary rights which are denied women. They usually have more money and property, and it is accepted they 'need' more money – not only because they may have dependants, but also because they 'need' more food, they 'need' to have their domestic work done for them, and they 'need' to have various pleasures catered for, etc. Men may feel they are oppressed by marriage too, and some try to resist it – even though feminists would argue that overall men benefit from heterosexuality as a system. But men are constrained by different things, and from a quite different location *vis-à-vis* generational and couple relationships than women.

Women (and men) cannot in any case avoid the consequences of heterosexual coupledom simply by remaining unmarried. Women who cohabit with men rather than marrying, or who live as single women, find that things for them are different but not by any means necessarily better than for married women. Women are usually much worse off economically if they are unmarried, especially if they have children. Those who experienced communal living in the 1960s found that it often meant complete freedom from all domestic responsibility for men; while the 1970s search for self-fulfilment and autonomy in collective houses, with individuals always free to leave, created greater insecurity and tension rather than companionship and a freer sex life for women. Lesbians know that Gay Liberation brought little concern for the situation of women; and Black women note that different household patterns can be just different modalities of 'marriage'. Traditions of either low rates of marriage and transient heterosexual relations (Afro-Caribbeans and Afro-Americans) or extended families and arranged marriages (South Asians, Cypriots and others) are but varying forms of similar underlying family-based sex inequalities.

Domestic responsibilities fall to women whether they are married or cohabiting or single. In the absence of a wife or female cohabitee, such work can fall to daughters, daughters-in-law and sisters, living inside or even outside a particular household. Forms of masculinity and femininity and appropriate sexual behaviour for males and females may vary from class to class and one ethnic group to another, but they are always defined as opposites of each other within each group, with women always the subordinate and less valued half.

The new feminism has thus produced a lot of new information about the variety of forms of women's subordination and, in the late 1960s and 1970s at least, family and sexual relationships were always stressed as key sites of oppression and in need of radical change. This new interest and concern not surprisingly produced a diversity of explanations – of possible reasons for the existence and continuation of women's secondary status – and there have been plenty of vigorous disagreements about what action should be taken to change individuals' lives and society as a whole. We therefore need now to show where our argument is located within such debates.

Explanations of women's subordination

For centuries in Europe the family and women's subordination within it were justified as Christian institutions: as a grouping and a relationship established by God the Father with Adam and Eve. It was He who decreed that wives should honour their husbands, just as children should honour their fathers and mothers, the poor and lowly their betters, and subjects their sovereign. Patriarchy, in which the power of the king over his people was the mirror of that of husband / fathers over their wives, children and servants, was held to have been present and divinely ordained from the beginning of time.

Today science carries greater weight than the church in determining that what is, must and should be. If the naturalness of heterosexuality – or monogamy, or the need to know one's legitimate biological heirs for the purposes of inheritance, or why it should be biological mothers who care more or less exclusively for their own offspring – is ever questioned or alternatives proposed, recourse is made to the 'facts' established by biology, psychology and anthropology. The social organization of other animal species, the evolution of 'man the hunter', the universal needs of developing children, the natural differences in physique, physiology, aptitudes or interests of men and women, or the universal functions established for the family, are all called upon as evidence that what exists in the West is natural, normal, and the best way of doing things. Feminists have therefore had to contest each and every one of these 'facts' within the various sciences – even though in fact, as we shall show, a number of feminist accounts themselves incorporate these selfsame assumptions.

Feminists have also asked why academics seem so willing to leap to generalizations in this field. Why are they so prepared to abandon the precepts of their disciplines and scientific methodology – to fail to produce definitions, to be anthropomorphic, to talk of 'necessity' or of things being 'obvious' – in this area when they are so loath to do it elsewhere? Why do writers so often focus on the question of the universality of the family or the differences between the sexes, rather than the variability of gender, domestic units and kinship structures, or the physiological overlap between the sexes? Could it be that many scientists themselves are concerned (consciously or unconsciously) to contribute to the legitimation of certain social structures and divisions, and hence to maintain the status quo in their own society?

In constructing biological, psychological and anthropological 'facts' which are then treated as extra-social explanations of the social, scientists and social scientists produce 'knowledge' which bases a social hierarchy and its key institutional locus, the family, in a principle of the natural order. This naturalistic discourse then hides: (1) the social nature of gender, kinship, marriage, parenthood, heterosexuality, etc.; (2) the variability of these social facts; and above all (3) the oppression and exploitation which is associated with them. It makes it seem undesirable, hopeless and even dangerous to try to undermine and change them. This justifies and hence helps continue sexual divisions generally, and within the family in particular.

While broadly agreed in their critique of the church and the scientific disciplines, and while also agreed that there must be some reason(s) for the continuance of sexual divisions in society, feminists have, however, disagreed among themselves as to what the reason (or reasons) may be. There are various views on whether any group benefits from the divisions (or whether it is a case of everyone suffering because of them); and, if one group does benefit, how it benefits.

Early second wave feminists in America suggested, for instance, 'that the purpose of male supremacy is primarily to obtain psychological ego satisfaction' (N.Y. Radical Feminist Manifesto, 1970: 214), while Ti-Grace Atkinson spoke of the psychological advantages men get from devaluing women as 'metaphysical cannibalism': as the psychic devouring of women. She suggested men achieved 'manliness', their sense of power and confidence, by overcoming the egos of women. She felt women were oppressed because men needed women as subservients so as to feel superior – in the family, in the labour market, and in all other institutionalized roles (Atkinson 1974).

Many still go along with this sort of argument. Even some marxist feminists see women's oppression as different from that of other groups (for example, the working class, Blacks or slaves) in being not primarily material or economic, but rather almost entirely psychological or ideological. They suggest that the basis of men's oppression of women is men's need for respect or love or feelings of power; and that it just so happens that to show their love, etc., women do menial work, abnegate themselves, and are sexually 'responsive' rather than assertive. Or they suggest that men devalue whatever women do in order to feel superior, and sexually objectify women so as to get the necessary boost to perform the (supposedly) difficult male part in sexual intercourse.

We think such analyses are upside down. They need turning around to stand them on their feet. It is primarily the *work* women do, the uses to which our bodies can be put, which constitutes the reason for our oppression (that is, which explains why we are kept in relationships which enable men to profit from our labour). Women's material oppression, like various other material oppressions, also produces a psychological advantage for the oppressor, but this is a product of, and forms part of, an ideology which maintains the appropriation of the subordinates' labour. Material appropriation of work is, in our view, what is most important, and most often forgotten. Hence our stress on it.

Slaves, for instance, may sometimes respect or even love their owners, and servants often admire and live vicariously through their masters and mistresses. Owners and masters enjoy this love and feel they deserve the concern shown for them by their subordinates. But the key feature in understanding such interactions is the labour relationship involved, not each side's feelings about or images of the other.

The devaluation of what women do, and the belief that what men do is what particularly counts in society, is to us not the cause of women's oppression, but rather part of the mechanism by which the appropriation of our labour is continued. That is to say, we believe that women's work is used by men, and that the low value set on women, the self-denial and masochism we are encouraged to develop, and each woman's identification with 'her man', etc., exist because our labour is appropriated by men. Ideas and values are the effect of, and not the reason why, we do the work we do, though they are part of the means whereby the exploitation is continued.

Women do not work for their husbands because they love and respect them, they work for them because they are their wives. An individual woman may choose a particular man as her husband because she loves *him* (rather than the rest of the bunch); and working for him as a personal dependant will certainly encourage her to respect and identify with him. But the emotion and the work are separate, and familiarity can equally breed contempt. Some wives have a hearty disrespect for their husbands and distance themselves emotionally – but they still work for them. However, when present (as it usually is) the love and respect given to husbands by wives is an obvious satisfaction and reward in its own right. And it is also, and as importantly, a means to continue to get other benefits, for example, more work from the wives in question, since the love, respect and identification veils the very fact that labour is being extorted. Labour seems to be being freely given to someone who deserves it. Love hides the exploitation; and it also allows the work appropriated to take various forms (whatever the individual man needs and wants) – as we shall show in later chapters.

Although in the analysis of other forms of oppression, be it slavery or class oppression, the importance of labour is generally recognized, until recently, very little attention was paid to either the division of labour between men and women or to the actual work women do in western societies. This was largely because it was believed that women in all societies, and especially in our own, do less work, and less important work, than men. It used, for example, to be suggested, and accepted, that full-time housewives 'did nothing' when at home all day, and that this was why they were subordinates. If nowadays it is recognized that women often work longer hours and contribute as much if not more than men to production in all cultures, this has only come about after a struggle and thanks to a lot of academic research and a political movement.

But what has not generally been clearly recognized in this research nor by the women's movement generally, is that women characteristically do not own or profit from what they produce in society. This is, however, central to our analysis. It is not just a question of women in our society doing most of the boring and arduous tasks within households and having a disadvantaged position in the labour market, but of our not owning the products of the work we do as wives and daughters. We get what we do get for our labour only indirectly. Men are not only exempt from doing particular household tasks and advantaged in the labour market, they also own most of the valued resources coming into the family as well as their dependants' labour within it. Men personally consume much of what they own, namely, a major part of the family's resources and the labour of their dependants; and the rest they use to 'maintain' 'their' wives and dependants.

Women are told that men do what they do, and get what they get, because men need more and are better at doing (what our society sees as) the more important tasks. But in fact men do what they do and get what they get because women work for them, across classes and races; and women do this because men dominate them. Men own the productive forces in societies and have the ability and right to coerce women to do as they wish in various ways. This, not men's physical or mental superiority or the things they do, is what enables men to take more of the family's resources and to maintain their self-importance. **Within the family in our society, women are dominated in order that their work may be exploited and because their work is exploited.**

Our concern is to analyse the mechanism of this particular form of extortion and the dynamics of its continuation. We therefore look in this book at the western family in terms of the different work done and the rewards enjoyed by its various members, and explain the hierarchy of the sexes and their behaviour in terms of the work relationships they have with one another: their relations of production. Others have also sought to do something along the same lines, that is, to analyse women's oppression in the home from a materialist perspective. But they have almost all concentrated on trying to show that it is 'the system' or 'capitalism' which benefits (see chapters 2 and 3), whereas we show that although capitalism may benefit indirectly, it is men who are the major, direct beneficiaries of the familial oppression of women. In addition, the others have almost all taken account only of housework or childcare, whereas we are concerned with all the work that women do for their husbands within the family-based household.

It has not been easy for anyone to develop an economic analysis of women's domestic work. It was indeed quite a triumph for the WLM to establish the very fact of the existence of housework: to get it agreed that a lot of housework is done, that it is work, and that it is mainly done by women. It has certainly been a struggle to get it accepted that there is (still) a hierarchy within the family, and even more to get it accepted that there is exploitation. Exploitation is supposed to be what happens outside the family, in the labour market, and to affect the family only as a unit. Relations inside the family are supposed to be non-calculative and therefore (it is said) non-exploitative.

However, when we look at 'the role of the housewife', what we see is the way most women make their living. Wives' (or cohabitees', or sometimes daughters') relationships with their husbands (or lovers or fathers) need, therefore, to be analysed in the same sorts of ways as wage earners' relationships to their employers. The nature of the two sorts of relationship are different of course, as we said earlier, and many women work for both husbands and employers. But the fact that the two labour relationships are different does not mean that a wife's relationship to her husband is not a work relationship. Nor does the fact that a husband loves his wife and that the relationship is not calculative mean that it is not exploitative (as we shall show in chapters 4 to 6).

In studies of factories or businesses or farms there is as much concern with how things are produced within an enterprise as there is with the economic relationships the enterprise has with the wider market. But studies of the family (or households) still treat these units as if their only economic relationships were with the outside; as if families were economic unities, within which everyone is equal and everyone does the same sorts of things and gets the same share of resources. In other words, households are taken as the basic units from which one starts – as if they had no prior internal structures. Against all the evidence, people start using the term 'spouses' instead of 'husbands' and 'wives' when talking of who does what domestic work or who makes 'household' decisions – as if husbands and wives had interchangeable and equivalent roles. They stress 'collectivity', 'equal participation', 'co-operation' and 'functional complementarity' with an almost desperate fervour.

Now of course family members do share certain interests, just as the soldiers and officers within an army share an interest in winning a war, or the workers and owners of a company share a concern for its commercial success. So there *are* occasions when it is appropriate to treat family households as units. But there are also many oppositions of interest within families and occasions when households should not be taken as units – and when we seek to understand the relationships of men and women is precisely such an occasion. We cannot understand the overall subordination of women in western societies without understanding their relations of subordination within domestic groups and lines of descent. Hence any sociologists' or historians' accounts which focus on families mainly or only as units, inevitably minimize the differences of interest of men and women. They are therefore political statements. They contribute to the ideology that says there is an identity of family interests. And this ideology helps to maintain men's supremacy.[4]

Similarly, although members of working class families and Black families have things in common because of their common class and race location and experience of oppression, there is nevertheless inequality between men and women within such households. Those involved may judge class or race oppression to weigh much more heavily on women in such circumstances than working class or Black men's oppression of 'their' women. And certainly the modalities of women's oppression do differ in very important ways. But that is not to say that the family does not play much the same role in Black women's oppression as women as it does in white women's.

Afro-Caribbean women in Britain, for instance, often spend less time in unpaid domestic labour and more in unpleasant, low-paid waged labour than white women because their earnings are even more essential to their (lower income) households than white women's earnings are to theirs. In addition to such indirect (structural) racism, Black women also suffer direct racist abuse and specific oppressions. For instance, they not only suffer (as white women do) when they watch their adolescent sons turning into misogynist young men, they are also afraid their sons will be arrested or even killed before they reach manhood at all.[5] But despite important differences, Black women have in common with white women the responsibility to do unpaid domestic work, to provide childcare (individually or collectively with female kin), and to service men emotionally and sexually. To suggest, as some do, that because Afro-Caribbean women are 'economically independent' they are able to take less lip from men and to have a freer sex life, and that family life is unequivocally a support for Black women in a racist society, seems to us unjustified.

Women's family work and labour relations

We are not, of course, suggesting that in looking at work, hierarchy and economics in the household and at relations between spouses and kin, we are describing and explaining each and every feature of family life; nor that in looking at domestic groups and inter-generational relations we are describing and exploring each and every feature of women's oppression in our society. We are simply saying that an understanding of the work women do in the family, and the relations within which they do it, are key elements in understanding male domination in western societies today. We must, therefore, before going further, establish what we mean by 'work'.

In its common usage, 'work' has a very masculine and capitalistic bias. This has had to be modified to make the concept useful in understanding gender and domestic relations. 'Work' commonly refers to paid employment: the something which people go out to do for a fixed number of hours each day, and which people are either in or out of from the time they leave school to retirement. It is seen as characteristically to do with producing things, often in large workplaces like factories or mines, or to be management or financial activities associated with such production, done in offices.

As many have pointed out, this does not characterize women's paid employment at all well. Women's jobs are often part-time, to do with caring for people or providing services (including sexual or quasi-sexual services), and located in diverse small work-places – clinics, schools, cafés, shops, residential homes or other people's homes, or even the woman's own home (for example, with child-minding, homework or taking in lodgers). Women may in addition move in and out of the labour market at several points in their lives between school and retirement. Because of this lack of fit with the male-stream definition, women's employment is often seen as somehow less real work than men's.

Feminist concern with women's work in the 1970s and 1980s led both to a reconceptualization of the labour market and to a stress on the quantity of work that is done unpaid in the home and local community. It pointed especially to the huge quantity of paid and unpaid service and caring work performed in contemporary western societies (that is, work done for or on people, as opposed to producing things).

This feminist critique occurred shortly after, and has fed into, a problematizing of the western concept of 'work' (and the related marxist concept of 'productive labour') by those concerned with relations between the West and the Third World (see especially the work of Gunder Frank in the 1960s). It also related to attempts to refine and develop ideas about changes in the class structure in the West, notably the postwar growth of the tertiary sector; the increase in the informal economy, including various forms of work done within the household as a consequence of rising male unemployment in the 1980s; and accounts which focus on work directed to producing social and cultural capital rather than just economic capital: which stress that individuals are concerned not only with having money and property but also status, attention, fame, a reputation for generosity, etc.

The discussion has therefore moved on from a definition of work as directly or indirectly materially productive labour – from just the production for exchange of goods or tangible services. But it has not moved far enough, because the only non-waged work involved in servicing humans which has been included has been the provision of physical care, and a lot of the important servicing of humans is emotional work.

Emotional work is work which establishes relations of solidarity, which maintains bonds of affection, which provides moral support, friendship and love, which gives people a sense of belonging, of ontological strength, of empowerment, and thereby makes them feel good. This too requires effort and skill. It is not just a question of thinking about someone, but doing actual activities: talking to them about things that interest them, fetching them things that give them pleasure, smiling at them, cuddling them, and stroking their bodies and their egos. This has occasionally been recognized in accounts of waged work, see for example Arlene Russell Hochschild's work on air hostesses where she shows how they 'manage emotions'. But it is an especially important component of women's domestic work. Emotional work needs therefore to be included alongside other forms of paid and unpaid labour.

We therefore include within our definition of 'work'

- economically or practically productive work (on objects or on people),
- cultural work (for display), and
- emotional work.

All of these can be done either for self-consumption or for exchange, and as unpaid or paid labour. And any one task can involve elements of all three types of work. For instance, a mother may feed her children nourishing food, carefully served at the temperature each prefers, from specially patterned expensive bowls.

To these three types of work we need also to add sexual work and reproductive work (the production of children). Marriage is defined by sexuality and often also by reproduction. For a marriage to be consummated (that is, for the contract to be fully and finally sealed) requires a particular kind of sexual intercourse to take place, and the whole weight of the culture makes clear that having sex and having children (sons in particular) are things wives owe their husbands. However, to say directly that having sexual relations and bearing children is work women do in the family is iconoclastic, since our cultures see sexual activity and having babies as very special areas of life. Many resist seeing the pleasure and 'fulfilment of human needs' in sexuality (which is seen as at the core of the person of both men and women) and motherhood (which is seen as the fulfilment of the person for women) as having anything to do with the mundane obligations and calculative exchanges associated with work. This discomfort may lead them to argue for sticking to a narrow definition of work – as just paid labour producing goods and services. In this way they hope things like sex and reproduction will be kept well clear. But of course it simply means they do not recognize prostitution and surrogate motherhood as work – even though these are productive activities and done for pay.

We do not accept, however, that because certain activities are seen as mystical and others as morally repugnant, they should not be demeaned or graced with such a workaday, positive term as 'work'. We must use logical not moral categories in our analysis.

Nor can we accept the argument that sex and reproduction are not work because women enter heterosexual relationships and bear children willingly and get pleasure from these activities. After all most people could be said to enter paid employment willingly within our society, and some get considerable pleasure from it. Choosing to do something and benefiting from doing it does not preclude its being work; nor does it guarantee it is not work done for someone else, as part of an inequitable exchange.

All too many feminists unfortunately follow the dominant ideology and take for granted that sexuality, child-bearing and child-rearing are mystical and special activities. Some continue the error by arguing that women's oppression is specific and special in that it concerns 'the body'; which is often accompanied by the assertion that men's power is especially, overwhelmingly, concerned with the sexual and reproductive use and abuse of women (which means they neglect all the other work women do for men).

But the fact that women's oppression concerns their bodies, or that women's whole identity becomes tied up in being a mother, is not specific to women's oppression only. The oppression of wage workers also concerns their bodies and their whole personalities. Men and women employees' bodies are used and exhausted and maimed and objectified (though men and women workers' qualitatively different bodies are sometimes used qualitatively differently), and their possibilities for creative work are alienated from them, while their sense of self and self-worth becomes tied up with being a coal-miner (or a prostitute, or a solicitor, or a nurse, or an academic).

So for the moment we will leave open the question of whether sexuality is reducible to (is exactly the same as, is no more than another form of) work. We recognize that the culture does not see it as such; but equally none of the reasons given for treating it apart from work, as not work, and as quite different in kind from work, seem valid. And we will also leave open what men get from women's bearing and rearing of children within marriage, although in an earlier paper (Delphy 1976a) we suggested that perhaps childcare is analytically (though not empirically) different from the rest of domestic work. The obligation on women to provide unpaid childcare may perhaps not stem from marriage and family relations. It may even be one of the factors that makes possible men's appropriation of wives' domestic labour within marriage. That is to say, women's responsibility for children is antecedent to marriage. It is usually carried on in marriage, but it exists even if marriage has not taken place and it continues after separation, divorce or widowhood. It is a collective exploitation by men of women; a collective exemption of men from responsibility. In a particular marriage an individual man appropriates a woman's labour and in return contributes to her and the children's upkeep. He thus 'lightens' her burden by partially assuming a responsibility from which society exempts him. After divorce his appropriation of her labour could be held to cease partly or completely, depending on whether he continues to benefit from the children or not. Marriage with children may therefore be the meeting point for the institution of women's exclusive responsibility for childcare with the institution of husbands' appropriation of wives' labour power.

In this book we shall however simply treat sex, procreation and child-rearing as being among the various forms of labour women perform for men specifically within the family. **Our focus is, therefore, the practical, emotional, sexual, procreative and symbolic work done by women for men within family relationships**. This includes housework, work for men's occupations, emotional servicing of family members, childcare, the care of sick and frail family members, sexual servicing of husbands and the bearing of children.

We are therefore not claiming to be giving a total account of even the material oppression of women – of *all* the ways in which women's work is exploited – since we are not going to deal with the labour market (even though our analysis gives new ways of looking at women's and men's involvement in paid work). Still less do we claim to be describing and explaining women's overall oppression even in western countries today. The full extent of the diverse forms of women's oppression, and how these forms affect and reinforce each other, and how and why some of them have the same framework and institution, the western family, have yet to be established. This remains a primary theoretical goal of the women's movement.

But if our restricted area of concern is a shortcoming for some people, for us the limitation of our focus of analysis is a strength, a quite deliberate choice. We distrust theories which set out to be general explanations of each and every aspect of women's oppression today.

We distrust them firstly because they have to stick so much to the oppression of women and to what is specific to it that they cannot locate it among other oppressions, and so they cannot compare it with anything else. They therefore lose any real insight into it. They describe women's oppression but they cannot explain it. Because they are held so tightly to the way things are perceived, they are also held tightly to the dominant ideology.

We also distrust general theories because in wanting to explain everything they look for single causes – and in the case of theories of women's oppression, this search for a single cause leads authors time and time again straight into the arms of naturalism, that is, into supporting a variant of the very ideology usually used to justify women's subordination.

We believe, on the contrary, that the power of a theory to explain something lies precisely in its capacity to find out what is common to several phenomena of the same order – that is, in its ability to go beyond what is immediately apparent in each case to show how each is an instance of a common kind of thing. This is why we adopt a structural approach to understanding women's oppression rather than working from within women's experience – despite the advocacy of the latter by many recent writers on feminist methodology. If we want to understand women's oppression, we have to start by breaking it down into pieces, to see the way in which it contains different instances of the general phenomena of one group subordinating another. We can then later reassemble the bits to produce, not the reality we experience or observe, but a model of women's subordination which is comparable to models of other types of class subordination.

What we want to do in this book is, therefore, not so much to describe women's subordination in the family as to explain it, using concepts which are not specific to it alone. We do not deal primarily with women's (or men's) experience or ideals of family life, but instead try to explain women's subordination as an instance of economic exploitation. This is not at all an obvious way of thinking about the family, as we have said; but then it was not an obvious way of thinking about any phenomena whatsoever a few centuries ago – even those which form part of what our language now calls 'the economy', or institutions which are now generally unproblematically accepted as exploitative, such as slavery.

Notes

1 Historians have studied the changing meanings of both aspects of the family, including showing clearly how it involves household labour relations.

In Roman times, the *familia* consisted only of slaves; then of slaves and servants and the wife and children of the *pater familias*. He himself was only included in the term later. In early modern English (seventeenth century), the 'family' meant a man's servants and apprentices (and the servants' wives and children) as well as his wife and children. All were under his authority. By the nineteenth century it had come to mean 'everyone in the household except the servants', who were by then waged workers. See for example Kussmaul (1978) and Flandrin (1979).

2   See Chester (1986) for various examples, including such feminist writing as Barrett and McIntosh (1982) and Segal (1983).

The common argument is along the lines that 'the household of married couple and children ... is already not the "norm" in Britain, and American research suggests it will be very much a minority in that society by the 1990s' (Bechhofer 1986: 229). But to say 'the nuclear family is a minority form' is true only if a very narrow definition of the nuclear family is used, as consisting only of a breadwinning father with a full-time housewife mother and dependent children. If we enlarge the definition to include households where the wife has part-time employment, and where there are children over as well as under the age of 16, the picture changes drastically.

In Britain in 1989:

27 per cent of households consisted of married couples
 9 per cent of households consisted of couples plus children over 16
26 per cent of households consisted of couples plus dependent children
 9 per cent of households consisted of a single parent plus children.

Thus 71 per cent of households consisted of husbands, wives and children (*Social Trends*, 1991 edition, table 2.4).

Further, if we look at where people live, that is, if we take individuals not households as our units, we find 82 per cent of people in Britain in 1989 lived with a spouse and/or their children (*Social Trends*, 1991 edition, table 2.7).

In 1989:

10 per cent of people lived alone
22 per cent lived in a household with just their spouse
42 per cent lived in a household consisting of parents and dependent children
11 per cent lived in a household consisting of parents and children over 16
 6 per cent lived in a household consisting of a single parent plus children
 8 per cent lived in other sorts of household.

3   We are grateful to Rodney Barker for these examples. See W. Morris (1890: 69–71), Blatchford (1894), and on Kropotkin, Woodcock and Avakumovic (1950: 321).

4   Ray Pahl, for example, in his *Divisions of Labour* (1984) provides valuable material on contemporary households on the Isle of Sheppey in Kent. He makes many interesting points about how the family household 'continues to be the basic social unit around which people conduct their lives' (p. 13) and how such households have in the past and continue today to 'get by' economically in a whole variety of ways.

However, since he endlessly stresses 'household' strategies, and that 'work ... done by members of the household [is] for the collective well-being of household members' (pp. 19–20) as part of an 'economic partnership between men and women and other household members', he in effect minimizes the differences of interest of men and women. It is not that he does not see the differences in the work they do – he has a whole chapter on them. But he does not consider the possibility that men *use* women's work – that is, although he recognizes a 'division of labour', he does not recognize the hierarchy which is part and parcel of this division of labour. This means his work ends up supporting the ideology that what is good for men is good for women.

5   The example is taken from Audre Lorde (1984).

PART I
CRITICAL
PERSPECTIVES

2

PART OF CAPITALISM: ACCOUNTS OF WOMEN'S OPPRESSION IN THE FAMILY BY TRADITIONAL MARXISTS

Our argument that women's continuing subordination in western society is due in large measure to men's exploitation of women's domestic labour is a materialist explanation. It sees the production of material life as of primary importance in determining the structure of a society, oppression as fundamentally related to the appropriation of labour, and social categories as deriving from and maintaining exploitative social relations. We believe our culture sees the world in terms of a binary opposition between men and women (that is, as gendered) because of a labour relationship which exists between these two social groups. Gender categories arose with this exploitative labour relationship and ensure its continuation. If we want to understand women's oppression we must therefore look, not at the supposed physiological or psychological characteristics of women and men (or rather the supposed differences between men and women), but rather at who appropriates women's labour, and how.

As was made clear in chapter 1, this approach to understanding the family via its relations of production uses a methodology for understanding oppression which was largely developed by Marx and Engels in their analysis of the oppression of workers within the capitalist mode of production. However, our ideas are far from generally accepted by many who see themselves as the custodians of marxism.[1] We, on the other hand, think that many accounts of women's oppression which call themselves marxist or marxist feminist are not in fact true to the spirit of marxism. Instead they have taken over a series of dogmas developed since Marx's death which have become marxist orthodoxy (or orthodox marxism), and tried to develop these in various ways to explain women's oppression by connecting it to capitalism.

Jean Gardiner distinguished three sorts of marxist and marxist feminist theories in an article published in 1978:

Traditional marxist theory This argues that women's oppression is a form of class oppression. The only material relationships within contemporary society which are important are those around wage labour; and women are only materially oppressed when they are waged workers. What women experience is different from what men experience because their biology and social roles are different, but both sexes' experiences are due to class divisions and not sex antagonisms. In so far as women as a whole, and not just working class women, are oppressed, this is due to ideology: to sets of ideas and related institutions which will disappear more or less automatically when the economic changes involved in the establishment of socialism are brought about (when true socialism is established, that is, not what has passed for socialism in eastern Europe). A separate women's movement is therefore not necessary, indeed it is diversionary, because women's problems will be resolved when class divisions are ended.

Revised traditional marxist theory This sees women's oppression as twofold. Many women suffer economic oppression as (particularly disadvantaged) wage workers; and all women are oppressed ideologically. Two separate struggles are therefore needed: men and women workers together against economic oppression; and women against ideological oppression. But the women's struggle is secondary in importance to the class struggle.

Marxist feminist theory This sees class oppression and sex oppression as distinct but linked. The working class experiences material and ideological oppression as a class; and women experience certain common material and ideological oppressions which are not directly related to class but which derive from their experience as a sex and their productive and reproductive roles within capitalist society. Capitalism plays men and women off against each other.

Some marxist feminists go further and recognize non-market production occurs in households and that this domestic production and motherhood specifically oppress women. But they see this reproductive production as dominated by and contributing towards the capitalist mode of production within western societies.

For marxist feminists, since class and sex oppression overlap, what most women experience derives from their being both women *and* members of the working class. (They are not very concerned with the problems of 'bourgeois women', despite often being middle class themselves.) They therefore see an independent women's movement as necessary, but they stress it must be part of the anti-capitalist class struggle since neither of the two oppressions can be resolved without some kind of combined struggle. The question marxist feminist intellectuals have to answer to make their contribution to the struggle, is how women's oppression generally, and household production and motherhood specifically, is functional for capitalism.

At first sight these look like three different theories, but in fact they are differences of degree. They are various points of retreat, various points to which feminism had pushed orthodox marxism by 1978 from its 1960s position that there was no specific (problem of the) oppression of women. They see capitalism as either (1) the sole, or (2) the most important, form of oppression to which women's oppression must be related, or (3) as the system which dominates and overarches whatever additional system may be responsible for sex oppression. They are, moreover, none of them *materialist* explanations of gender divisions since they all incorporate gender categories within their premises. They all see 'sex roles' or 'gender differences' as cultural variations built on underlying biological (sexual and reproductive) divisions.[2]

It is none the less worth giving these theories some initial attention because they are the ideas closest to our own which have found their way into what is now established as Feminist Theory. They are also worth unpacking because the sort of circular thinking they involve is common – and because evaluating other theories is a fruitful way of starting to explain and develop our own (see also chapter 4).

We shall therefore try to show in the remainder of this chapter the problems with explanations which suggest that 'women's oppression is due to capitalism because it's a capitalist society', and that 'women are oppressed but not exploited'. In the next chapter we shall look at more sophisticated accounts of the ways in which women's oppression and/or the family is seen as 'functional for capitalism' which have been developed since the mid 1970s.

'Women's oppression in the West is due to capitalism because these are capitalist societies'

At first sight such an argument might appear unanswerable, but it is actually tautologous – and in fact rarely put forward quite as baldly and naively as this. Usually it is wrapped up in a more elaborate (but still circular) argument. For instance, it is said that the 'pre-capitalist form' of the family was taken over by capitalism; that the previously existing subordination of women in the family was exacerbated by the separation of home from work resulting from industrial capitalism; that the form of private family household which came into existence with the industrial revolution serves capitalism and is necessary for capitalism; and that the family household can therefore be described as a capitalist institution, and women's oppression in the family is thus due to capitalism. Such arguments involve at least three logical (as well as empirical) errors.

First, there is a play on the word 'capitalism'. It is used in both a specific and a general way, as both the totality of the social system within which we live, and as a particular part of that system (that is, to refer to the very extensive wage labour system and the private ownership of productive property in our societies).

If we define the totality of the social system within which we live as 'capitalism', then any evils, any oppressions which exist, can be said to be due to capitalism; and it can also be argued that to combat these evils we must combat 'the system'. Of course, it also means that any good things present are also due to capitalism. But in fact neither bad nor good things can really be argued to be *due* to capitalism, since if the elision is made both good and bad things are *part* of it. Capitalism cannot have a causal role *vis-à-vis* any of the parts within it if it is itself the sum of all the parts. If it is argued that capitalism changed or integrated the family to the extent that the one becomes an integral part of the other, they must both have lost their specificity and the one cannot have relations with, or cause anything in, the other. Women's oppression cannot be due to capitalism if it is part of it.

If on the other hand what is being said is that women's oppression is due to a particular part of our social system, the capitalist labour process, then how and why needs to be demonstrated. It cannot just be asserted as an article of faith (especially since women were oppressed in Europe before the advent of widespread capitalism).

The second logical and epistemological error in such arguments is this suggestion that something which came later caused something which existed before it. Even if the family and women's oppression are now necessary for capitalism, it cannot be argued that the family and women's subordination are due to capitalism. Rather capitalism developed in a society based on the family (household and line). *Prima facie*, capitalism is familistic and gendered, rather than gender and the family capitalistic.

The third logical and epistemological error is the suggestion that because two things coexist and interact there is a causal relationship between them – that capitalism causes the oppression of women in the family rather than that capitalism and patriarchy exist alongside and interrelate with each other.

Against such criticisms it may be countered that although the family pre-dated capitalism, the form of family which exists today is very different from the form of the family found in eighteenth-century England or nineteenth-century France. Further, it may be argued that these differences were produced by capitalism: that capitalism built on and then modified and used for its own advantage what it inherited from the past.

But for this argument to hold water it would have to be shown, first, that the pre-capitalist internal relations and forms of the institutions (the family and women's subordination) have not only been altered, but altered very substantially, and altered predominantly by capitalism. (We might then want to ask why we go on using the same terms to denote two realities if indeed they have so little in common as to justify calling the family household structure that now exists 'capitalist'.)

It would also need to be shown that nowadays the family has virtually no major features or functions other than those needed by the capitalist mode of production. This would include showing that the sexual division of labour within the family serves only capitalism.

And as final proof it would be desirable to be able to argue that had the inherited institutions not existed, capitalism would have had to create them in at least their main essentials. Otherwise it can better be argued that what we see are simply pre-capitalist (or non-capitalist) institutions continuing alongside capitalism.

So far as we can see, the accumulating historical evidence shows that the social relations and structure of both the family household and the family line remained very similar pre- and post-capitalism in Europe, despite the development of wage labour for various family members and the industrial production of many goods and services. Also, while the capitalist mode of production needs a supply of workers who are free to sell their labour, there seems no evidence that it needs them to be produced by the particular form of domestic group we know in Europe today. It therefore seems to us unjustified to label western family-based households and inheritance patterns and women's oppression within them, 'capitalist'.

The capitalist mode of production is powerful, but that does not mean it transforms everything it touches. The fact that the family continues to coexist with a capitalist economy does not prove it serves the latter, still less that it serves only the latter. All their coexistence proves is that the prior institution, the family, and the wage labour system, etc., are compatible. What does need to be stressed, however, since it seems not to be evident to many authors, is that compatibility is necessarily mutual. Coexistence does not imply a hierarchical relationship, still less a one-way causality. There *may* be hierarchical relations between capitalism and the family: the structure of one *may* determine the other. In which case, a priori it would seem likely that the pre-existing, established institution (the family) had, at least initially, the determining influence. But over a long period of coexistence there has been a lot of mutual influence and mutual accommodation, so 'disentangling' is usually an idealist project anyway. In any event, interactions, influences and determinations need to be studied historically, not presumed dogmatically. And when looking to see how capitalism has influenced the family and women's subordination, we should also look to see how the family (that is, its characteristic relations of men and women and between generations) has influenced capitalism, including the structure of the labour force, and other aspects of society.

So far we have treated marxists' use of 'capitalism' in both a broad and a narrow usage as if what was at issue was an intellectual error, as if it were a case of a bit of sloppiness on their part in their attempts to link one specific institution (the family) to another institution (capitalism). But of course what is at issue is politics and not philosophy.

Authors say in the same breath that capitalism is both the whole social system and the determinate element in the social system, that all concrete forms of oppression derive from capitalism while also saying capitalism is the precise mechanism of a particular form of exploitation (that is, a particular mode of production), because they are not actually aiming to establish the nature of the links between particular forms of oppression and capitalism (narrowly defined). They have other ends in view. They call all institutions which they deem oppressive (including the family and women's subordination) 'capitalist institutions', while also using 'capitalism' to refer to the labour process alone, in order to assert the predominance of capitalism and to legitimate a focus upon the protagonists (or rather on some of the protagonists, the 'main protagonists') in this system, that is, to justify their continuing to be concerned primarily or exclusively with men.

Men have to date been the main protagonists on the commodity and labour markets. Indeed (as we shall argue in chapter 5) the actors in these arenas have been men by definition: the quality of being a full economic subject, of having full access to the market, is something which distinguishes men (as a gender and age group) from women, children and the elderly. It has been an important element in what constitutes men as men. Only with the recent profound changes in capitalism and the massive rise in male unemployment and the associated (re)growth of men's involvement in non-market activities, or when they have been looking at Third World societies, have marxist (and other) theorists been or become concerned with the 'informal' sector and the domestic economy. Only under such circumstances do they recognize the scale and importance of the 'non-market' sector.

Another reason why some writers have sought to attach women's oppression to capitalism is because for them unless it is so attached they really cannot understand why women should be oppressed – other than because of our biology (our weak muscles, incapacitation by child-bearing, brains which cannot cope with engineering, or whatever). For these theorists, women really do not have anything social worth exploiting. So to the extent that women *are* oppressed, and for other than natural reasons, it *must* be to do with the system of exploitation in contemporary developed societies, the mode of production of our society – in a word, to do with the oppression which affects (most) men. Capitalist oppression is for such people real, social, important, systematic and to be taken very seriously. It involves people – men – who are worth oppressing and whose oppression is fully social. Therefore, if they can attach women's oppression to capitalist exploitation, women's oppression will have to be taken (reasonably) seriously. It will at least have a reason for existing.[3]

Thus arguments which seek to see women's oppression as due to capitalism may derive from either a straightforward political belief that the anti-capitalist struggle should remain pre-eminent and in no way be compromised by relatively trivial 'sex antagonisms', or it may derive from an even more insidious and anti-feminist belief that women are too worthless to be worth oppressing in and of themselves. (The two beliefs are anyway quite mutually compatible.) The only possible reason for women being oppressed must be that it furthers / enables / increases the oppression of men. The belief that the class struggle is primary will at least ensure that proletarians, that is, men, are certain to be liberated before women. (And that until they are, they will at least each have a woman to oppress.) The belief that women are not worth exploiting in their own right is simply another affirmation of the lesser worth of women and our lesser humanity.

Women's oppression is, however, fully social and important in and of itself. Women's work is worth exploiting and is indeed exploited. We can be concerned with what happens to women even if what happens to us does not contribute to, even if it is not linked to, the exploitation of male proletarians. Furthermore, we believe women's oppression is directly beneficial to men and perhaps only indirectly beneficial to capitalism. If women's oppression is to be ended, we must therefore direct attention first to the relations between men and women, and only later to how these connect with capitalism.

'Women are oppressed but not exploited'

Arguments about the relationship of women's oppression and capitalism may also involve the assertion that women are 'oppressed' by capitalism and / or by men, but not 'exploited' by either.[4] This might appear to relate to a precise conceptual difference between the situation of women and other groups; to be a suggestion that what women suffer is due to their being in a particular type of situation – oppression (to be defined), while other groups are in a different type of situation – exploitation (also to be defined, but mutually exclusive of oppression).

As generally used, however, the terms do not have specific and opposed denotations: they do not relate to explicit, mutually exclusive structural situations. But they do have different connotations: they do carry an implicit message extra to the obvious one. That is to say, oppression and exploitation are generally used as different points on a single scale – that of the degree of political importance attached to the group and its suffering. To the Left in particular, oppression is something less important, something less serious than exploitation. Exploitation connotes greater political urgency, something which should be of primary concern to everyone, whereas oppression, what women (and especially what middle class women) suffer, is less pressing and less onerous. Exploitation is thus a plus. Every exploitative relationship is presumed to involve heavy oppression, but not all oppression is exploitation. Whether a writer describes a group (be it Blacks, women, or Third World nations) as 'exploited' or 'oppressed' therefore usually indicates merely the political importance he or she attaches to their struggle: whether what they suffer is rated as being as serious as, or less serious than, what wage workers suffer (the proletarian being taken as the yardstick for measuring exploitation). To say that women are oppressed but not exploited is therefore generally not to say anything precise, but merely that their situation is less serious than that of the proletariat. It is just a refined put-down.

Sometimes, however, writers do use 'exploitation' with a quite specific meaning. They restrict the term to situations where what is done by one group to the other is economic in character; or they define it even more narrowly to refer to just the economic oppression characteristic of capitalism. 'Oppression' is for these analysts a blanket term for any sort of weighing down, any sort of ill-treatment, other than the suffering due to economic, or specifically capitalist economic, systems. Oppression is then often presented as 'ideological' or 'psychological'.

Although these narrower usages are more clearly defined than the broader one, it is still very unclear whether what writers refer to as the 'exploitation' of a group is economic in its *means* or in its *ends*. For instance, when people say that women are oppressed but not exploited (in the restricted sense), do they mean

• that women do not suffer from economic inequality in relation to men, but only from being demeaned by sets of ideas (ideologies) (that is, that exploitation refers to *an economic end result*);
• or that women do suffer from economic inequality in relation to men (it being hard after all to deny this), but for non-economic reasons – that nobody derives economic benefit from it (that is, that exploitation refers to *an economic mechanism*);
• or, more restrictively, that women do suffer economic inequality, but capitalism derives no economic benefit from it (that is, that 'exploitation' refers only to *the economic mechanism of capitalism*).

In the last case it would mean that feudalism and slavery could not be regarded as exploitative, and some do indeed argue this. But it seems to us to be an odd use of the term.

Unfortunately we have again to work through this muddled thinking if we want to understand what Left writers really mean by the term to which they attach such political pre-eminence. Indeed, since their definition of exploitation relates to their definition of the economy, we must start by looking at the latter first. This opens up a much larger can of worms, for the problem of what is and what is not exploitation is in fact part of a much more general problem in contemporary marxist analysis. This problem is the permanent and often virtually exclusive occupation of the centre stage by capitalism (to which we referred in the previous section) and the consequent inversion of the priorities of Marx's methodology: of historical materialism.

According to materialist theory, economic aspects of society are of special importance only because relations of production are the source of social hierarchy and because those at the base of the hierarchy suffer oppression. It is the oppression which is experienced that matters. It is this that has to be analysed so that what causes it can be changed and the suffering alleviated. In other theories the economy may be important in itself, or important for other political reasons, but in materialist theory it is social inequalities which are the object and focus of research. This centring on inequality is what leads to the investigation of causes, and it is as the (presumed) cause of an important phenomenon that economic factors acquire importance. They are not important in and of themselves for socialism.

Marx and Engels started with a concern for the condition of the poor in mid-nineteenth-century Europe, and it was this which led them to investigate and 'discover' capitalism (that is, to recognize it as a system of exploitation, and to understand and interpret it to others). It was their concern to understand the exploitation of the working class – and essentially the exploitation of working men (adult married males) – which required the analysis which led Marx to write *Capital*.[5]

In orthodox marxism, however, this ordering of priorities has been stood on its head and the reasons why the economy is important have been lost sight of. People forget that Marx and Engels's point of departure was a concern for the oppression of the proletariat. They forget that the economic realm is only a means to the capitalists' ends. All they retain is the link between 'the economic' and 'oppression', and some even go so far as to say that it is the particular economic character of a situation which determines whether the oppression endured is serious or not, or even if it exists at all. For them, if an oppression is economic, especially if it is due to the economics of capitalism, it is serious, it is exploitation. But if it is not capitalistic, it is not exploitation, it is not serious. Even some feminists have actually argued that because the oppression of women is not (in their view) economic, or not primarily economic, but rather ideological, it therefore cannot be particularly severe or important; and that if women's oppression does not provide surplus value for capitalism, it is not exploitation, so it is therefore only a secondary cause for concern.

Marx, however, discovered the importance of the economic arena only as a result of the study of a specific inequality – that between owners and workers. He did not deduce the oppression of the workers from what he analysed as its cause. He obviously could not have done because the cause was precisely what he was trying to uncover. Reaching an understanding of the mechanism by which this inequality was produced and reproduced took genius and years of dedicated study. He looked for the cause, for the mechanism of the exploitation, because he was concerned with the lives of the working class, because he considered their oppression important and their sufferings evil, and because he was involved in and wished to contribute to forwarding the actions of the international workers' movement.

The specifications of the last sentence are crucial because before a phenomenon can be considered important it must first be recognized.

Before being judged significant an oppression must first be seen to exist, and evidence to support the fact that it is there and important must be assembled. This is not always an immediate or obvious process. One of the means by which a system is continued is through both sides (lords and vassals, owners and workers, whites and Blacks, men and women) seeing the inequalities between them as insignificant and / or as inevitable because they are due to innate differences between them; or because each individual considers his or her biography and situation to be unique or the result of individual choice.

Political movements are necessary precisely to collect evidence of the existence and forms of inequalities, to awaken people to their situation, and to make them see that it is due to *structured* inequalities. Only when an oppression has been declared can an analysis of its causes begin. Establishing the existence of an oppression thus precedes, in logic and in time, the investigation of its causes. And the oppression's existence is separate from the analysis of its causes. That is to say, if Marx's whole analysis of capitalism were wrong, this would not alter the fact that the workers are oppressed. On the other hand, if it were shown that the workers were in all ways as well off as the owners, his analysis would have no object and be worthless.

Marxist orthodoxy has, however, absurdly and seriously inverted his methodology – at least so far as the oppression of groups other than the proletariat is concerned. It has become acceptable to reason as if oppression were not obvious, as if it did not declare itself via political movements but rather had to be discovered and proved by intellectuals rummaging through the works of Marx and Engels to emerge with selected quotations which suggest this particular oppression can be accepted to exist because it can be tied to what Marx and Engels had to say when analysing the causes of another oppression. Marxist orthodoxy is so befuddled by capitalism that some deny the existence of an oppression when they cannot attribute it to the 'usual cause' – that is, when they cannot see it as of benefit to capital.

The early Women's Liberation movement had therefore not only to establish the existence of women's oppression and its various forms – or rather to re-establish their existence, since much of what was 'discovered' in the late 1960s was common knowledge to feminists of the 1890s. It also had to run the gauntlet of the Right *and* the Left. Socialists might have been expected to be the allies of feminists, but in fact many denied the possibility of the existence of women's oppression if it was not tied to capitalist oppression. Many still deny women's oppression is economic in its own right, and that it is exploitation; and they therefore rule out the possibility of using marxist methodology to analyse the causes of this oppression.

A similar though less general inversion of marxist methodology occurs when writers confuse the economic sphere as a means and an end, and then present the means as more important than the ends. That is, they confuse (1) the ownership of productive property as a means to extort surplus value, and wage labour as a mechanism which oppresses the workers; with (2) the extortion of surplus value as an end for capitalists, and alienated labour as a result for the workers. What really matters is (2): the ends, the results, what some gain and others suffer.

Put at its most basic, the cause for concern with capitalism is that 7 per cent of the population own 84 per cent of the income and wealth and live lavishly, while vast numbers of people live in poverty and insecurity and have to do debilitating and soul-destroying work, and the environment is destroyed in pursuit of profit. The mechanism through which this inequality is achieved is in itself unimportant. Or rather, it is important only in so far as it leads to this result, and because we need to understand it if we want to change the situation.

The private ownership of factories, for instance, is important only in so far as it forms part of the mechanism (within a certain system) whereby some people extort labour from many others and make self-interested decisions in pursuit of profits – decisions which affect the quality of life of all members of entire communities.

Many marxists, however, having identified private ownership as the (presumed) cause of capitalist exploitation, first assimilate the two into each other, and then treat them as synonymous:

> private property = exploitation;
> exploitation = private property.

If they kept the distinction between means and ends clear they would remember, however, not only that private property is but *one* means to extort labour, but also that as a means it can be replaced. (That it is, indeed, only the means of a means: that it is only one of the forms that the control of the means of production can take.)

Each of these stages of reification represents a regression from historical materialism – and a bourgeois regression at that, as is shown by the reification of private ownership. For it is bourgeois ideology which identifies legal property and control. The same sort of mistake is also found in many current 'marxist' definitions of the economy and in marxists' concentration on the monetary system and the production and consumption of substantial goods.

The fact that many have not remembered that private property is only one means to extort labour has had considerable political consequences. For instance, it meant that it took 40 years for western intellectuals to realize that Russian workers were exploited even though there was no private ownership of farms, factories and shops in the Soviet Union. Having established private property as an absolute and quasi-natural cause of exploitation, these intellectuals could not conceive of control taking other forms. They could not see that in the case of the USSR, control actually had taken other forms. Having globally reified the means (private ownership of the means of production), and having identified these means with the results (exploitation of the workers), when they no longer saw the means they no longer saw the results – nor the facts. They did not see the long hours, lack of food, poor housing, alienating work and environmental pollution, nor the complete absence of political power and civil rights which existed and which were just as visible in the 1930s and 1940s as they were in the 1980s. They did not even see the forced labour camps.

The same holds for their approach to familial exploitation and the oppression of women. Since they do not see wage labour in the family, they have not realized that there are other means to control production and to exploit labour. And it took years for them to begin to see the results of this alternative system for women. They did not even see the systematic violence and sexual abuse inflicted on women and children in the home.

To explore this further we need to return to our earlier distinction between

- the cause of the proletariat's oppression (the wage labour system) and its effects on them (poverty, insecurity, alienated labour); and
- the capitalists' means of oppression (the extraction of surplus value) and their ends (higher consumption and investment, and use of state agencies to ensure their continuing control).

All too often these become so elided that the exploitation of the workers is reduced to the apparently monetary benefit for the employer (or the sum of money, the surplus value 'stolen' from the employee). What workers suffer is much more than, and different from, this.

The means and ends of exploitation

The ends of exploitation for an exploiter

In the capitalist system, the owner of the means of production benefits via the monetary system. He has more money. But this does not mean that the possession of money constitutes the essential element, much less the essence, of his advantages. People who merely hoard money – misers – are regarded as crazy. Sane people know that, providing one reinvests adequately, it is the (material and symbolic) things money can buy which count. What is at issue is rather that capitalism is a complex system for exploiting other people's labour which involves money at various stages.

At its simplest, capitalism involves one person owning a field or factory or shop and employing labourers to work on or in it. He pays them a wage which is worth less than the value they add to his crops, goods or services by their labour, and when he sells the crops, etc., he pockets the difference: the surplus value. In other words, the exploitation of labour in the capitalist system takes place indirectly, through the appropriation of surplus value embedded in a product, which is realized when the product is sold. The surplus from the labour is harvested by the capitalist in the form of money.

He does not use the labour directly for his personal needs. He may then invest the money, or he may decide to go through a further monetary transaction and either buy some labour directly (for example, he may decide he wants a massage and pay a masseur to give him one), or he may buy a product which has been produced by other people's labour (for example, a house), or he may take an attractive wife and 'allow' her to be conspicuously leisured.

In non-capitalist systems, however, the extortion of surplus labour does not necessarily go through an initial monetary transaction (that is, the sale of products incorporating surplus labour). Labour may be used directly by whoever extorts it. For example, a slave owner can directly consume the labour of a slave by requiring the slave to give him a massage or build a house. Nor are labourers necessarily given a wage with which to pay for their upkeep. They may be given 'protection' and land on which to grow their own food (as in serfdom), or food, housing and clothing directly and with little or no choice in what they consume (as in slavery and, though it is less apparent, in the family).

The monetary form disguises the ultimate nature of the capitalist's benefits because at the point where the tale ends in much marxist theorizing, he has only money, and no clue is given as to what he uses it for / converts it into. (There is even a tendency to suggest it is *all* reinvested to enable him to go on making more money.) Marxist and other economists' obsession with the monetary economy makes them forget that some of the ultimate benefits (some of the things which the individual finally consumes) can, in another system, be appropriated directly, without going through a double set of monetary transactions. And their focus on products can also make us forget that a great deal of what the bourgeoisie (and everyone else) consume is not 'material' in the narrow sense. It does not consist of *objects* which have been produced, but of non-tangible goods and services, and of things used for display or pleasure rather than instrumentally (see chapter 1 pp. 21–3), even if to get these non-material benefits the economic good *par excellence*, money, has to be spent. This is particularly obvious in the case of conspicuous consumption, where what is being bought is not what is seen in that society as a functional necessity, but an expensive, ostentatious luxury. The wish to conform and gain prestige, etc., accounts for an important part of our total consumption. Material goods and services for symbolic status must be included as economic, alongside instrumental objects. For example, a first class seat on a train not only ensures one's body is moved from A to B, but assures that same body comfort and peace and quiet – and the respect of second class passengers. Having a house in Provence is, of course, a material possession, but it is also the enjoyment of a particularly beautiful landscape and spending the summer near to a number of (American, Dutch or English) people similar to oneself. Having a Porsche means owning a fast, (un)reliable car, but Porsches are more usually bought to enable the owner to show off to the world.

From the point of view of the ultimate benefits for exploiters, therefore, any distinction between essentials and 'non-essentials' is arbitrary, and we must work with a wide definition of consumption and material benefits. This is especially important when we come to look at the benefits men receive from marriage, since many argue that a husband getting certain things (for example, someone to look interested while he tells his stories over and over again, or to make sure the food he gets on holiday does not upset his stomach, or to keep the children quiet when he wants to catch up on his sleep, or to make sure all the trousers bought for him have back pockets for his golf tees) is not exploitation because these benefits are not material goods, so appropriating or 'consuming' them cannot be an economic gain. It is love, not work that is involved. However, the 'end' of exploitation can be, and often is, non-material things. This applies both to capitalist exploitation and (as much if not more) to familial exploitation. The benefits of exploitation are also not necessarily obtained in a classically economic fashion, that is, via purchase, they can be obtained directly, and are so obtained within the family.

The means of exploitation: the variety of mechanisms and the social rules involved

Having established that the 'ends' of exploitation can be the direct appropriation of non-material benefits, we can now turn to consider the 'means' by which they are achieved. That is to say, we can look at the argument we referred to above, that only the capitalist form of appropriation of labour is strictly exploitation. We have already shown that there are problems with this assertion because, as with the example of the slave 'giving' a massage, things produced by the labour of one person and consumed by another person in a very unbalanced 'exchange' may not be economic in the narrow sense of wage labour and purchase. There are other means than the capitalist system to obtain the things the more powerful 'partner' consumes. We think it appropriate to use the emotive and political word 'exploitation' for *all* such unequal transactions.

We are in fact back with the problems of current marxist definitions of the term 'economic', for it is frequently used to connote some sort of autonomous process; something having its own logic and functioning, independent of human agents and social rules. This sort of thinking reifies the economy and is simply a repetition of the error of the nineteenth-century bourgeois economists in opposition to whom Marx and Engels constructed their theories.

We can illustrate this by again taking the example of private property. Classical economists had discovered well before Marx that certain forms of private property give a right to use other people's labour. The actual ownership of something means next to nothing when the thing is a means of production. Owning a factory or a field or a shop carries little in itself.

You can walk around it or look at it, but you cannot eat it or live in it or indeed keep it going through time. It is useful only in so far as labour is applied to it. Ownership of such property concerns rather ownership of the goods and services created by the labour applied to the machines or fields or customers. The important convention of our form of 'ownership of property' is that the fruits of the labour applied to the means of production belong to the person who owns the thing on which the work is done, and not to the person who does the work. This social rule means that the owner of the thing can appropriate at least part of someone else's labour.

A concept of private property does not have to exist to guarantee that you harvest the fruits of your own labour. All that is necessary for this is a social rule that whoever does the work gets the fruits: that whatever you make, whatever is produced with your labour, belongs to you. (This is of course always providing that you own your own labour, which can in no way be taken for granted.) If you own your own labour, and products belong to the producer, 'owning' a machine, etc., would be of no additional advantage, if you had access to using it, since you would profit from the fruits of your own work anyway. Owning something is only useful when someone other than the owner works on it and the product belongs to the owner. Owning a tree does not help to guarantee that you harvest the fruits of the labour *you* apply to it. On the contrary, what it does is allow you to profit from labour you have *not* provided. Private property is thus a convention which undoes a logically prior convention – that the fruits of labour belong to the labourer. It undoes it, but it also presupposes it. If labour must be 'stolen' in this way – by appropriating the products – it is because the labour belongs to the labourers.

This prior convention (that the fruits of the labour belong to the labourer) is, however, itself neither 'natural' nor universal. **The products of your labour may be denied you, not because the factory or field in which you work belongs to someone else, but more simply because your labour belongs to someone else – because you do not own your own ability to work (your own labour power).** Appropriating the products of other people's work via owning the means of production is a subterfuge to steal indirectly (part of) the labour owned by its purveyor. But this labour can be, has been in past economic systems, and is still in various existing systems, 'stolen' directly. Owning the means of production is unnecessary if you own slaves or serfs or wives and children.

The convention of owning the means of production is part of the complex system of capitalist exploitation, but as Marx stressed, there is nothing natural about it and there is no technical reason for it. Like any other social rule it is arbitrary, hence fragile, and in the last resort imposed by force. One of its advantages, however, is that it makes potentially possible the extraction (or theft) of surplus labour from vast numbers of labourers. Hence it can lead to massive inequalities in wealth and standards of living; and the flexibility of money, realized when the goods are sold, allows great choice in consumption.

Unless we call this whole complex convention of capitalist exploitation 'economic', we cannot talk of society as being 'determined in the last instance by the economic', since the economic itself is based on social and political (that is, on arbitrary) conventions upheld by most people's accepting them, and those who do not being coerced. The 'last instance', the one on which the conventions which create the relations of production rest, is power (ideological and physical control). To talk of 'the economic' as a factor or level distinct from political/power relationships between groups, and as determining the latter, is to deny the social character of social relations – social relations of which relations of production are but one (albeit an extremely important) part.

When 'marxists' talk in this way they follow the selfsame lines as the classical economists Marx himself directly criticized. They reify the economy, making it a thing, of the same order as 'natural things': a thing having its own laws just as nature has laws. They suggest these laws are outside society and unchangeable by human action. Now obviously we are not suggesting that an individual, or even a group of individuals acting together, can change the economic laws of their society at will. It takes more than a revolution. Rather we are suggesting that the 'laws' economists have established are based on social conventions. They are based, for example, on the notion of ownership, and rights in relation to others which this notion subsumes (of disposal of one's labour, of disposal of the fruits of property one owns, etc.), which derive from western (Roman) law. But to suggest that social rules are natural laws is a classic ideological process. It involves social laws being projected outside society, and then 'discovered' to be there, outside the social system; hence to their being declared non-social, natural constraints, and therefore binding on society. Materialism is supposed to consist precisely in the demystification of such idealism. Marx showed so-called economic laws to be no more than what they are – products of human laws and conventions.

The effects of exploitation on the exploited

This discussion has established that no exploitation is economic in its means (or at least not 'in the last instance') if by 'economic' is meant a level which is distinct from the socio-political and which functions autonomously. It has also established that the capitalist means of extortion is only one means, only one form or mode among others, to extort labour or gain profit from the labour of others. Only muddled thinking identifies exploitation exclusively with the extraction of surplus value. There may be other, and worse, forms of exploitation, such as slavery.

The discussion has also stressed that the capitalist system of exploitation rests on two conventions: private property (the ownership of the means of production), and free labour (workers owning their own labour). Under capitalism labour belongs to its purveyor. It is not appropriated directly (and simply), but by the 'subterfuge' of the appropriation of products. Consequently the process of appropriation seldom resorts to direct physical coercion, and in addition the labour is not totally appropriated – it must be bought and paid for. As a result only part of the workers' labour is stolen, and under conditions of strong collective bargaining and labour shortage only a relatively small amount may be taken from each individual. (Of course the converse is also, and probably more often, true.) In addition, each worker has a wage and a certain freedom of consumption – though capitalists will certainly exercise pressures on him or her to consume particular things (for example, via advertising) since they can only realize the surplus value embodied in the products of their factories, fields, etc., when the goods are sold. These conditions can mitigate super-exploitation, however, which is why, when people have the opportunity to move from other forms of exploitation to capitalist wage labour, they often do so.

Against this we must stress, and it is a point which tends to get lost more than any other, that while surplus value (the stolen part of the workers' labour) represents what capitalists gain, it in no way represents what workers suffer as a result of the exploitative relationship. The gains and losses of the exploiter and the exploited are not identical, not commensurable (that is, the things involved do not have a common measure) and are not even comparable. Workers' involvement in the wage labour system loses them far more than the equivalent of a few hours of labour a day (that is, the monetary value of their surplus labour). Surplus value is the result for the capitalist of the exploitation of the proletariat, but this result, like any result, does not describe the processes which lead up to it and make it possible. The conditions of life inflicted upon the proletariat to make them work for their boss each day and make the capitalists' profit possible, are what constitute the exploitation for the workers. These conditions include economic insecurity, doing alienating, boring, dirty, dangerous work, and obeying orders. To identify the gains and losses in terms of surplus value alone is to take the point of view of the exploiter.

This is also an essential point to stress in relation to familial relations. The gains and losses of exploiter and exploited are not zero-sum. Women / wives lose and suffer far more and in various ways from the processes which ensure the continued appropriation of their (productive, emotional, sexual and reproductive) labour than just the benefits men / husbands gain. This is clear when we reflect on the regulation of women's sexuality, or the relative experience for husband and wife of economic dependency, or the use of physical violence in the home.

If one social group uses another for its purposes, it must mould its subordinates: it must shape them as human beings and not just control their work. And it must leave the subordinates no choice but to do the work. This can include putting them into double-bind situations where there are few options. All the options expose the subordinates to penalty, censure and deprivation, but overall they are arguably better off co-operating than kicking against the traces.[6]

Conclusion

It is obviously no accident that those whose overwhelming goal has been the overthrow of capitalism have had a theoretical analysis in which there is only one system of oppression and exploitation: capitalism. Such an analysis denies the very existence of other systems of oppression and exploitation and consequently disposes of them theoretically. Likewise the political groups from which such analyses derive have long denied the practical possibility of struggles outside the labour movement. They were certainly not concerned with the ethics of deflecting women from struggles against men to the anti-capitalist struggle, since the possibility of the latter not being in women's interests is ruled out by both their theoretical analysis and their gut presumptions. For them, women's interests were both bound up in and unimportant compared with the interests of 'the proletariat as a whole'. Heidi Hartmann expressed this by beginning an essay, 'The "marriage" of marxism and feminism has been like the marriage of husband and wife depicted in English common law: marxism and feminism are one and that one is marxism' (in Sargent 1981: 2).

Such is their reluctance to conceive of women as the subjects of oppression in their own right that some marxists, including some marxist feminists, go so far as to say that unless the oppression of women is linked to capitalism, the only alternative left is an explanation in terms of men's nature (as males). These are the only two alternatives they can see. Either one must reason in terms of a social system and therefore in terms of capitalism, or in terms of a non-social (natural) system and therefore in terms of men being inherently aggressive and exploitative.[7]

While men as existing adult actors in western societies are undoubtedly collectively more violent, selfish, destructive, etc., than women, human males are not naturally bad and are intrinsically very little different from human females. Actually existing differences are a result of cultural divisions. (Conversely human females are not intrinsically good – empathetic, peace-loving, unselfish, constructive, etc. – though actual women certainly often show these admirable qualities.)

But one can challenge biologism without thinking that women's oppression must therefore be linked only to capitalism. That marxists cannot see this shows simply that they cannot conceive of any social system other than capitalism; and that they are unable to conceive of the oppression of women (of patriarchy) as forming a social system – in part because they ignore what is specific about women's oppression.

We think this limited thinking reveals that those who so argue in fact see only half the human species as social beings. If the only way they can refute the biologistic thesis is to associate women's oppression with capitalist oppression, which they recognize as social and which is essentially to do with the oppression of men, it is because for them women only acquire the status of social beings (they only become part of the social as opposed to the natural division of labour) by association with men.

Scratch *this* thesis and one again finds biologism close beneath the surface. For according to these marxists, to what is the difference between men and women due? Why to biology of course: to differences of role in biological reproduction or to psychological sex differences. Thus these efforts to refute biologistic theory (when it is in danger of being used against men), in fact support it: they require and are themselves a form of it. Biologism is thus part of the refutation of anti-male biologism! Biologistic premises are used to challenge (they are the only ones seen as able to challenge) the anti-male thesis.

Such incapacities are not, of course, exclusive to the defenders of the school connecting women's oppression with capitalism. They characterize the whole society. Wherever women are oppressed there is an ideology representing them as worthless. What runs like a watermark through all these arguments, even if it is never said explicitly, is the question 'why should anyone bother to oppress women if not in order to oppress men?' In linking women's oppression to an oppression which affects men, authors feel they give a meaning to women's lives. This shows that if women's oppression were not so connected, if it did not have this ultimate end, it would (to them) be absurd and pointless, for women are not even worth exploiting.

Here we can recognize the dominant ideology which Janice Raymond calls 'hetero-reality': the world-view that women always exist in relation to men, that woman was made for man, and that heterosexual relations are normality (Raymond 1986: 3). The life of women has reason only in so far as it is useful to the male part of humanity. Women are part of humankind only in the sense of being complements, instruments, in brief, the possessions of humanity (of the groups that constitute societies and the individuals that constitute these groups). And at the level of representation of humanity as a biological species, this can lead to a truly crazy vision, where the female of the species is a sort of physiological attribute of the male: where women, though physically separate from men, are seen as really just sexual receptacles for penises or the detached reproductive organ of the male body – just cunts or wombs on legs.

Our analysis starts, however, from the premise that women are oppressed and exploited in and of themselves, and that patriarchy and capitalism are distinct, and equally social, systems which are empirically and historically intertwined. We do not think capitalism dominates patriarchy, but rather that they influence and structure each other. We must consider the possibility that women's liberation can be achieved under capitalism, and that capitalism can be overthrown without patriarchy being weakened. We may wish for a change in both systems, but this does not justify a short-circuiting of the analysis of the possibility of independent change. It is no more justifiable to assert, a priori (for that is what it is, in the absence of substantiation), that capitalism today is the major cause of women's oppression than it is to assert that patriarchy produced capitalism and all other class systems. There are two systems. The Women's Liberation movement has made many conscious of this.

Notes

1 Some of the responses to our ideas in the past have been surprisingly hostile (See Barrett and McIntosh 1979; Molyneux 1979; O. Harris 1981), which Mica Nava (1983) suggests may partly be due to our calling ourselves radical and not socialist feminists. She points out that Heidi Hartmann's ideas, which are not very different from ours, though developed less fully (see chapter 3), are attacked less often and less personally.
2 For further development of this point see Freidman (1982) and Delphy (1984: Introduction; 1989a).
3 For further development of these points, see Delphy (1977) and Delphy and Leonard (1986).
4 A whole pamphlet commissioned from Claude Alzon by the radical publishers Maspero (Alzon 1973) is based on this distinction, though Alzon does not define either term nor does he even try to justify the distinction (see Delphy 1977).
5 Marx recognized women and children as a sector of the proletariat and as the dependants of fully fledged proletarians. But they were not the origin of his concern, nor were they the focus of his and Engels's attention (even in the sense of being given a proportionate share of their attention). Women and children were a lumpen sector, undercutters of 'proper' wages, a reserve army ... the part, the specific, the other.
6 This point has been made in relation to women by, among others, Frye (1983) and Mackinnon (1987). It is used as an argument against feminism by many right-wing women, see Dworkin (1983).
7 To add insult to injury, they then time and again accuse other feminists of biologism! See for example Barrett (1980), Beechey (1979), Rowbotham (1981) and Eisenstein (1984).

3

STILL PART OF CAPITALISM? MARXIST FEMINIST ACCOUNTS OF THE FAMILY

In the accounts of women's oppression produced by marxist feminists from the mid 1970s to the mid 1980s, the analysis changed considerably from the positions discussed in the previous chapter. Writers tried to specify the ways in which capitalism shapes women's oppression within society as a whole, and in particular within the labour market. They also, though to a much more limited extent, provided explanations for why capitalism maintains the nuclear family household and women's oppression within it. All the writers recognized the need for an autonomous women's movement, but they differed in the extent to which they saw women's oppression as indissolubly interlocked into, or as a separate system intertwined with, capitalism; and in how far they saw patriarchy as materially based. The majority continued to see patriarchy and capitalism as fused, and all saw capitalism as unquestionably the dominant partner. Consequently most of those who call themselves marxist feminists or socialist feminists have continued to explain women's oppression and/or the family either mainly in terms of how these institutions contribute to the maintenance of capitalism, or in terms of patriarchal ideologies. A whole range of ways in which the family supposedly supports capitalism have been proposed over the last 50 years.

1 For instance, it has been suggested that women in the family socialize children into submissive personality structures and bourgeois norms generally (and bourgeois sexual norms specifically), making them accept existing authority structures, their allotted place in society, and alienating waged work.[1]

2 It is said that the nuclear family is supported by capital because it undermines the class struggle. The values the family represents (privatized domestic life and the husband's over-riding responsibility to his dependants) conflict with his class solidarity. Also women are more conservative than men and push husbands who are on strike back to work.[2]

3 It is claimed that wives absorb the anger of their alienated (pro-

letarian) husbands. They provide an emotionally supportive retreat for workers and so muffle the discontents of the workplace. The home is at least one place where men oppressed by capitalism can feel they are the boss and be in control.[3]

4   Alternatively it is suggested that capitalists support the existence of lots of separate, small, nuclear family households (rather than large, communal households) because each family purchases its own consumer durables, enabling producers to sell goods in large quantities. It is also pointed out that housewives, especially full-time housewives, are important consumers and a target for advertisers.[4]

5   The fact that women are maintained by their husbands is said not only to tie down their husbands (see above), but also to mean women themselves can provide a 'reserve army' of wage workers who can be easily recruited and dismissed, and paid below subsistence wages. Married women constantly threaten to undercut 'proper' (male) wage levels.[5]

6   Women's unpaid labour in the home is said to be used by capital to lower the cost of reproducing labour power. Women's contribution to household work allows lower wages to be paid to their husbands because the breadwinner's wage does not in fact have to pay for all essential goods and services. Some things do not have to be purchased because they are produced at home.[6]

7   It is also argued that as a result of a working class struggle to limit the grosser exploitation of early capitalism, later capitalists and / or the capitalist state have settled for supporting the working class family, with wives at home and a family wage for men, as the best means to ensure the reproduction of the working class as a whole and to maintain social stability. Support for the family is a compromise between (a) working class concerns for reducing the total hours worked by all members taken together, and thereby ensuring good care for the young, sick and elderly who cannot work and the physical and mental health of adult workers; and (b) capital's concern for a healthy workforce and minimal worker unrest.[7]

Such accounts of the interrelations of the capitalist mode of production, the state, the family and the sexual division of labour (each of which exists in several variants) are all valuable functionalist hypotheses which merit further investigation. However, at present they are often teleological and ahistorical because they are constructed around the assumption that the form of oppression to which all other forms of oppression must be attached (directly or indirectly) is capitalist oppression. Even when they do not imply that all production occurs outside the household (see chapters 1 and 4), or that the only form of exploitation is the extortion of surplus (value or labour) by capital (see chapter 2), they still believe that the way to understand any oppression is by finding the link between the institution in which the oppression occurs and the capitalist mode of production. They work backwards from this.

We can illustrate this by considering two forms of such arguments in detail: what has become known as the domestic labour debate, and the dichotomy frequently drawn between production and reproduction. The DLD flourished from the mid to late 1970s in the UK and Canada, with contributions also from authors in (at least) France, Germany, Italy and the USA. Some authors claim we have moved beyond it (for example, Maxine Molyneux in 1979), but hapless students still flog their way through it, and it frequently reappears, repolished, in conference papers. The analysis based on opposing production and reproduction, on the other hand, has surfaced and resurfaced many times in the last 20 years, and it is certainly currently alive and well.

These two particular attempts to link women's oppression in the family to capitalism reveal some of the worst features of putatively marxist accounts of the family. In the DLD there was an attempt to restrict 'proper marxist theorizing' to a mechanistic use of a 100-year-old terminology, as if it were timeless and essential. In contrast, the production / reproduction debate is characterized by extreme vagueness about the definition of terms, and confusion about what in capitalism causes what and how. In addition it reintroduces patriarchal ideologies right into the heart of the analysis.

The domestic labour debate

The domestic labour debate is an interesting phenomenon which can really only be approached by looking at its political implications, otherwise one rapidly gets lost in what seems (and is) an internal squabble about marxist terminology. The remarkable, contradictory and paradoxical thing about the whole interchange was that while it was going on (and still today) everyone knew it was of great political importance, and that passions surrounded it, but equally almost no one understood what the heck it was actually about. Most of the literature is unreadably abstruse.[8]

The basic political importance of the debate, and the reason why it took place, was to try to establish whether in fact the oppression of women could be analytically (and therefore strategically) incorporated within the Left's accepted analysis of capitalism, or whether it was part of a different system – and thus necessitated a distinct and separate explanation and a distinct and separate political struggle. The latter did not, of course, rule out the possibility of a tactical alliance between the anti-capitalist movement and the women's movement at particular points – though the debate never got as far as that. It merely put radical feminists (who were arguing the 'different system and autonomous struggle' line) on the defensive.

The earliest papers which sought to discuss the economic significance of housework in marxist terms, published three to five years before the

DLD began,[9] emphasized what they saw to be special about the relations of production of wives. That is, they analysed housework from a feminist point of view and said (either in an elaborate way or quite simply) that housework is work, that it is work which is extorted from the person who does it (that is, it is exploitation), and it is nearly always done by women. It is therefore an important form of economic exploitation of women.

But another current which was around at the same time (see chapter 2), said that housework cannot be exploited work because exploitation is something capitalistic, something specific to the proletariat. Women as women cannot be exploited, so there is no need to make room for them within the sacred realm of marxist economic theory, nor can they be part of the vanguard of the revolution. The fact that they have always been in the vanguard of every revolution which has actually taken place had no effect on such theories. This strand effectively dismissed housework with the phrase (which in itself does not say much, but which has a lot of political mileage in it)[10] that while housework is work, it is not productive work. It is rather (or only) reproductive work.

We see this as a cop-out via a pun. It had become difficult at that point in political time to go on saying that housewives did nothing (as people had before), so housework was accepted as work, but it was contrasted with real work, with productive work (that is, with work within the capitalist mode of production) by tying it to the naturalizing idea of women as reproducers of the human species. It was certainly a loaded way of putting things, but many, even feminists, seemed quite happy with it.

But then the debate became narrowed down and theoretically reorientated by Mariarosa Dalla Costa's paper on 'Women and the subversion of the community' (1972). This paper elaborated upon the idea of the importance of women in the anti-capitalist struggle, again saying women had an important reproductive role (that they played an important part in the reproduction of labour power), but also claiming that since women were not physically present in the factories, etc., where their husbands worked, they had possibilities for subversive action denied those more under the bosses' thumbs. As a result of this paper, the current which said women do reproductive work began to take cognizance of the arguments of the current which said housework is economic exploitation, but in a bizarre and ambiguous way.

Dalla Costa had produced a non-feminist analysis which nevertheless had feminist implications. She said, like many feminist writers, that housework was work and that it did indeed produce something; but then she concentrated exclusively upon the one thing it produced which (she thought) was of benefit to capitalism. That is, she argued that housework was of benefit to capitalism because it reproduced the labour power of workers (implicitly assumed to be male and married to the aforementioned housewives). It therefore contributed to the production of surplus value. In other words she narrowed down all the work which women do in the home to just that bit which is necessary to produce the labour sold by married male wage workers – and the whole debate came to hinge around this. It approached housework (1) through its supposed use outside the home; and (2) through only one of its supposed uses, since not all housewives are married to male proletarians, nor are all wage workers men, nor for that matter married to women. And it did this (that is, it focused the argument in this way) because its primary concern was not women's work, but tying housework to capitalism (which is why we say it is not a feminist analysis).

But other implications of Dalla Costa's analysis *were* feminist, and she developed them at length. She asserted that women were part of the working class and, furthermore, that they were in it on at least an equal footing with men since not only were they exploited, and by capitalism, but they were as exploited as men (or even more so), and in addition they had a freedom of manoeuvre which could allow them to form a new vanguard. The first part of this was welcome to the Left, but the rest was much less well received. In fact it was probably an angry reaction to the suggestion that housewives in the community were equal to or ahead of men as members of the working class which triggered the articles which followed and which sought to answer her.[11] For what she was saying was really sacrilegious, and in this respect her position is paradoxical – but paradoxical only to the extent that the male Left position is paradoxical.

The male Left wants women to be recognized as part of the working class because they do not want women to wage a separate (anti-patriarchal) fight. And quite a number of feminists work in the Left with men because they see the anti-capitalist fight as extremely important and the Left as having an important revolutionary role. They therefore want to reform, not to leave it. But at the same time neither the men nor actually most of the women want women to be ranked on exactly the same level as the cultural heroes: the male proletariat.[12] So some way has to be found by which women can be included in the working class with men, but backing them up, not alongside them, and certainly not in front of them.

This, then, is the politics which informed the ensuing debate – and it seems the best way to understand it, because, as we said, the analyses themselves, if they are read carefully (which is a difficult and unenviable task), do not make much sense. They produce models which are very strange even to connoisseurs of economics, whereby surplus value is transferred from one sector of the economy to another, figures about what would be most cost-effective for capitalism are pulled out of the air, and incomparable things are compared – like apples being evaluated against carrots. But they do make political sense.

The accounts say that housework is work, and that it benefits capitalism; and they also stress the primacy of domestic labour in the analysis of women's oppression. But the participants in the debate never considered whether domestic work might also benefit other parties – because if they had they might (they would) have had, on the one hand, the working class split and divided, and on the other, 'bourgeois women' recognized as oppressed.

However, the papers in the debate also say, very clearly, that housework cannot be as oppressive or as important as wage work to capitalism. This is a difficult line to argue. Housework (done by working class women) must benefit capitalism, but at the same time it must not be 'exploitation'. Hence models were produced where housework benefited capitalism because it lowered the level of the wage, or did or did not produce value / surplus labour / surplus value, and there were erudite discussions of the value of labour power 'according to Marx and Engels'. But in the end the whole business got impossibly intricate and the authors could not get out of their models. So the English protagonists just abandoned the area and let it collapse (though a group in Toronto continue to revisit it);[13] and most writers moved (back) into the even trickier business of production and reproduction.

From a feminist point of view, what was wrong with the whole debate was simply that it did not (because it could not) account for, nor was it concerned with, house*wives* – with gender relations. It was (and is, since these analyses are still in play) 'gender-blind'.[14]

First, none of these theories explains why a particular sub-group of the working class, women, do virtually all the housework. They do not in fact actually require a person separate from the wage earner whose labour power is being maintained, to do it (the wage earner could do it in his leisure time), let alone a distinct category of persons. Housework is just another modality for the extortion of surplus labour. The DLD empirically differentiated the working class housewife and the wage worker, but theoretically gave no explanation for their separateness.

Second, it neither provides nor allows for a definition of housework. If housework is 'everything necessary for the reproduction of labour power', then any and all personal services for a wage earner, even those he does for himself, must count, and the theory of value has to cope with the remuneration of this (boundless, indefinite, culturally and individually variant amount of) household work in the wage. However, from the point of view of the wife as a separate individual whose work contributes to the reproduction of the labourer, the boundary of family work is work done for someone else (as we shall argue in chapter 4) and this is in no way restricted to work done for family members as wage workers, nor is it limited to housework as a list of concrete tasks. In addition (see chapters 7 and 8) it varies between husbands according to their individual 'needs' even when the men have the same occupation and earn the same wage.

Third, an essential feature of the approach to housework through the concept of 'the reproduction of labour power' is that it excludes enormous amounts of domestic work. Not only does it exclude 'housework' done in the homes of proletarians which is dubiously necessary 'to reproduce their labour power', it also excludes all the work done in homes where the husband is not a wage worker – where he is a self-employed small businessman or craftsman, or the owner of a large enterprise, or an executive of a corporation. It also means that if a man changes his job situation, his wife's work can just disappear from sight. This 'disappearance' may or may not be valid from the point of view of capital, but it certainly is not true from the point of view of the woman.

It is also assumed in most of the DLD literature that wives are not employed. All the calculations about the surplus labour extracted from the wife via the husband were premised initially on the presumption that all she consumed was taken out of his wage. Later writing tried to take account of the fact that many housewives also earn wages and do the housework on top of paid work, but this did not materially change the argument. The premise was still that wage workers need domestic workers to do housework for them. This is most clearly seen in those articles which conclude that capital supports the form of the family we know, where a dependent wife (or semi-dependent wife, if she has a part-time job) does housework and childcare, because this keeps down the level of male wages. This is, of course, debatable (that is, it relies on certain assumptions about costs). But even leaving this aside, in order to make this presumption one has to assume (though it is never made explicit):

1 that what authors call the 'socialization of housework' (but which we would prefer to call its commercialization), that is, that taking housework outside the home and putting it into public (capitalist or socialist) industry, would be more expensive / less profitable for capital; and
2 that domestic servicing is part of what the proletariat is owed by capital: that in order to get men to go on turning up for work, they must either get their washing and cooking and childcare done for them by their wives, or have these services provided for them directly by their employers, or be paid a larger wage so as to enable them to buy them for themselves.

These are audit arguments. They say that things that are part of the essential costs of reproduction of labour power and therefore necessarily part of the wage-packet, are provided more cheaply by wives (hence, thanks to wives, a lower wage can be paid). Given the absence of even hypothetical figures the arguments might seem just mildly vague – maybe it would cost capital more, maybe not – were it not for the fact there has always been a control population to disprove the very premises of the argument.

There are in fact many people who are wage workers, some of whom have children or care for the elderly, who do not get domestic help. They make up half the workforce: they are young men, unmarried women, and employed married women themselves. They earn wages which are not high enough to enable them either to have 'wives' or to purchase a full complement of commercial substitutes, but nor are their needs provided for directly by their employers. So domestic servicing is not something capital 'owes' to the whole, but only to part, of the proletariat.

Neo-marxist arguments about 'the value of labour power' or 'the subsistence level as historically determined' therefore apply differently to adult males than to young males and all female employees. Only adult male members of the working class are apparently owed domestic services in their wage-packets by employers. But if the value of labour power is not the same for all workers (doing the same type of work at the same historical period), it can no longer play the key role it does in marxist theory of wage levels and surplus value.

A further major shortcoming for feminists of the domestic labour debate was that it looked not at the actual relations of production of housewives, but only at what happens before or after their work. That is to say, it looked at the sources and level of the remuneration received by their husbands (that is, at what determined their husbands' wage levels) and / or the uses to which their products were put (for example, the sale of their husbands' or children's labour).

This is indeed a remarkable, though a not often remarked, feature of all too many who claim to be talking about women's work in the home. Time and time again the actual work done, or the conditions of economic dependency and isolation under which it is done, or women's own feelings about it, are skipped over. Instead writers concentrate upon what use the work women do has for other people and for another system of oppression. For instance, we know relatively little about the actual day-to-day work of the wives of middle class men, but much is asserted about the significance of the child care they provide (and its difference from that provided by the wives of working class men) in ensuring their children's success outside the family, that is, in reproducing their class position via the education system.

Some writers on domestic work go even further. Not only do they ignore the work women do in favour of looking at the uses to which the work is put, they even suggest that the fact that the work middle class wives do helps in various ways to perpetuate the class system, shows that the women concerned are not themselves oppressed.

However, the fact that the labour of certain men's wives is used in certain ways, for example, helping children with homework or hostessing cocktail parties (which people choose to get very moralistic about), of course neither proves nor disproves these women's oppression. It does not even touch on it. It is quite a different issue. Middle class (or bourgeois) wives' labour is appropriated. The uses to which it is put is a different question. Not to recognize this is equivalent to talking about the exploitation of workers only in relation to what they produce. It is like taking two groups of workers, one which produces flour and one which produces bullets, and evaluating whether or not they are oppressed in terms of moral approval or disapproval of their products. If they produce useful things like flour we will accept they are exploited, but if they produce things we do not approve of, like bullets, we will not recognize that their employers use their labour. It suggests we can measure whether people are exploited or not in terms of their employers' decisions.

A feminist analysis must stop and focus on the relations of production of women themselves – and not be always upstream or downstream of them. It must not look (just) at the nature of the products of women's labour and the use to which these are put, but rather at the actual processes of production. It is very striking that in the whole domestic labour debate not only was the actual nature of the work performed by women ignored, but the fact that housewives are not paid, that they are dependent on their husbands, was noted as some sort of an aside to the fact that capital benefits from their work. It certainly was not seen as a central problem, or even a problem. Yet for women it is a problem. For women the problem of housework focuses around doing certain tasks in a situation of personal dependency on their husbands (that is, it is about their status in relation to men).

Likewise the papers in the debate almost never discussed the level or form of upkeep which wives get from their husbands. When they did occasionally mention it, they (implicitly) compared upkeep to a wage, missing the very fact of its specificity: that it is *not* comparable to a wage. (Stranger still, one author, Wally Seccombe (1974), compared wives to petty commodity producers, which could be taken to suggest wives go onto the labour market and sell their husbands' labour!)

In all these analyses the two individuals in the ideal working class couple appear interchangeable. This is just not true, and everyone with an interest in the position of women or in gender knows it. But this assumption was never explored or explained, and instead the account of why men are breadwinners and women 'only housewives' was switched to an account of differential wage rates between men and women – that is, an explanation was sought outside the home. But differential wage rates derived historically from the prior existence of family relationships. They were not *the cause of* gender and generational divisions within households.

What the debate did accomplish, however, was to emphasize the solidarity of husband and wife – how both were exploited by the same institution: capitalism. This is not surprising, since that is precisely what it set out to do. It set out to show how capitalism benefited from housework – and, having spilt a small lake of printers' ink, it concluded that it did benefit. What was excluded from the start and stayed lost was the possibility that men benefit from women's labour; that is, that men comprise an exploitative class.

Production and reproduction

The second type of marxist feminist account of the family we shall consider is almost harder to come to grips with than the domestic labour debate, not because the arguments are abstruse and the language complex, with protagonists constantly accusing each other of improper usage, but quite the reverse. When writers compare and contrast men and women and production and reproduction, everything looks simple and agreed. But appearances are deceptive, for different authors use the words in different ways – but their differences are not made clear. Thus what looks like a school of thought is in fact an intellectual confusion. We can detail only a few of its variants here, but what they all have in common is that they reinject patriarchal, naturalizing, ideology into the concept of patriarchy itself.[15]

Analyses in this genre often start by quoting two sentences from Engels's preface to the first edition of *The Origins of the Family, Private Property and the State* (1884):

> According to the materialist conception, the determining factor in history is, in the final instance, the production and reproduction of immediate life. This, again, is of a twofold character: on the one side, the production of the means of existence, of food, clothing and shelter and the tools necessary for that production; on the other side, the production of human beings themselves, the propagation of the species. (Leacock edition 1972: 71)

We read this to mean that since things are continually used up and people die, if society is to continue, the individuals within it have to do again tomorrow what they did today. We produce, then we produce again, and then again . . . things and people. We think this is the correct interpretation because Engels's next sentence is:

> The social organization under which the people of a particular historical epoch and a particular country live is determined *by both kinds of production*: by the stage of development of labor on the one hand and of the family on the other. (pp. 71–2 our stress)

This means the production of things and the production of people need to be looked at in their historical and situational specificity; but they are both forms of work – equally important, equally social and equally complex. However, time and again the first two sentences are taken as making an antithesis between the production (of things) and the reproduction (of people), the latter being reduced to procreation and child-rearing via a play on words.

We shall need to spend the next three chapters (4–6) looking at some of the uses, and the political significance, of the term 'production'. But 'reproduction' too is a complex and loaded term. As Felicity Edholm, Olivia Harris and Kate Young demonstrated in an excellent article published in 1977, it subsumes (at least):

- biological or human reproduction;
- social reproduction, that is, the reproduction of structures within societies (including particularly the reproduction of social classes and succession) and the reproduction of new generations of individuals socialized to fill positions within these social structures; and

• the reproduction of the labour force required by the dominant mode of production (and in marxist writing specifically the reproduction of labour power required by capital).

Edholm and her colleagues show the problems of confusing these three uses of 'reproduction' by disentangling them in the work of Claude Meillassoux on the oppression of women in preindustrial African societies (Meillassoux 1975). Meillassoux starts with the assertion that in such societies reproduction is more important than production because the supply of labour is crucial. At this technological level, labour is the main factor in production. He then jumps from this to the conclusion that the need to control the supply of labour involves controlling not only the labourers but also the people who give birth to them – women. In his account women are seemingly the only people who have anything to do with biological reproduction and childcare, but equally they are somehow not so integrated into society as to share 'its' concerns for the supply of labour. He thus assumes women will not procreate 'according to the interests of the society' unless they are coerced. Therefore, he says, primitive societies are especially concerned with controlling women.

Meillassoux sees women as reproductive objects rather than social actors and he confuses control of women's gestatory power with (or rather he deems it to be the same thing as) control over the differential allocation of labour power. His work is typical in seeming to tackle issues while actually incorporating the very gender hierarchy he says he is questioning.

Edholm, Harris and Young say that while the reproduction of the class structure over time is often confused with the everyday reproduction of labour power, the confusion Meillassoux makes between human reproduction and social reproduction is especially common. Although social class is seen as a social phenomenon (by most people and obviously particularly by social scientists), its transmission is often naturalized. People use 'reproduction' as a way of clearing away the problem of how classes are composed and how heredity is socially structured: as a way of bracketing off all the rules and mechanisms whereby social positions are, or are not, hereditary. They seem to assume that the working class which is 'reproduced' consists simply of the babies of the working class of the previous generation. Miners' sons, it seems, are born wearing hats with lamps, or at least blue collars! However, although our societies are certainly hereditary, and although social positions are related to what is deemed 'biological' sex and 'biological' parenthood – there is much more to it than this.

It should, therefore, never be said, even as a shorthand, that the working class family exists 'because capitalism needs it to reproduce the proletariat'. On the one hand something other than working class families could do the job, and on the other, families do not do it on their own. Anyone can be turned into a proletarian. Indeed everyone who is one has had to be turned into one, even if he or she was born into a working class family. To be a proletarian is to occupy a social class position, and the constitution and reconstitution of classes is social, not biological. It involves the full complexity of not only the family (household and lineage), which is a social not a biological system anyway, but also the education system, the media, the medical system, and processes internal to the labour process itself – in brief the whole society. To forget this even for a minute by eliding 'the family' and 'reproduction' is to confuse biological reproduction with

- first, the social institution within which most new individuals are physically produced and initially socialized, and where individuals' ability to work on a daily basis is maintained, and
- secondly, the continuation (with changes) of different social positions; and the allocation of people within these in any society over time.

When we review the actual usage of 'reproduction' in the last two decades of feminist writing, however, we find the various meanings of reproduction (not to say the various means of production) constantly (if varyingly) conflated.

In the 1970s an antithesis was frequently drawn between capitalism (as the producer of commodities using labour power) and the family (as the reproducer of labour power to sell to capital). There was therefore no allowance that there might be any 'production' in the family, and 'reproduction' was used to cover biological procreation, generational relations, and day-to-day care.

Shulamith Firestone, for instance, put forward the outrageously biologistic thesis (in 1970) that the whole oppression of women is determined by our role in reproduction: by the 'natural handicap' of pregnancy. And Roberta Hamilton has as the guiding framework of her book (1978) a division between 'marxism' and 'feminism' whereby she claims 'feminism' is concerned with combating patriarchal ideology which is predicated on biological differences between the sexes. Both suggest that since 'feminism' can show that biological differences can now be overcome, we are no longer the victims of our biology and equality between men and women is attainable.

Barbara Ehrenreich and Deidre English's influential book (1979) is not as biological reductionist, but they nevertheless see the key to understanding women's present situation as industrial capitalism's having moved 'production' out of the home, leaving the household concerned only with 'the most personal biological activities – eating, sleeping, the care of small children, and . . . birth and dying and the care of the sick and aged' (p. 9).

Gayle Rubin, in her very widely used attempt to combine Marx, Freud and Levi-Strauss (Rubin 1975), started off on the right foot in asserting all systems are productive *and* reproductive, but she then went on to use 'the sex / gender system' as relating only to the (biological and psychological) reproduction of people. And in her later work (1984), she has moved to equating 'gender' with sexuality.

Mary O'Brien developed a lengthy critique of western political philosophy's concentration on production and its lack of concern for reproduction / birth (1983). In this work she plays on the word 'labour' (saying motherhood = productive labour and giving birth = reproductive labour). She argues that men are 'alienated' from reproduction in our society and that they resent this and are jealous of women. They therefore oppress women to 'appropriate' the children which (O'Brien says) belong naturally to women. She calls for a reintegration of women into production and men into reproduction – but she does not explain why the exclusion of women from production should make them subordinates whereas men's 'alienation' from reproduction has given them power.

Similar ideas, though using the concept of 'womb envy', have been put forward before (for example, by Margaret Mead (1950), Ashley Montague (1952) and Annie Leclerc (1974)). Where O'Brien is original is in constructing these into a critique of Hegel.

But all such analyses worry us because of their use of the familiar, and dubious, opposition between men = culture and woman = nature, and because they employ an eternal transhistorical male who worries about whether a child is or is not 'his'. That is to say, because they take over *western* cultural presuppositions – that maternity is obvious but paternity is problematic; that social inheritance must involve a relationship between one man and one woman and each child; and that it is our link to an individual child (and not to future generations of our society) which gives us a future, a sense of continuity (that is, that historical continuity is the same as genetic continuity) – and then construct these into universal truths. But anthropologists have shown repeatedly than many cultures do not think in these ways. That these are not 'obvious and inevitable human ways of thinking'.[16] Feminists should be questioning such ideologies, not confirming them by reworking them.

In the mid 1980s the production / reproduction dichotomy was again in vogue, this time combined with analyses of the welfare state.[17] Patriarchy and reproduction were here no longer distinct from capitalism but rather part of the overall capitalist society. 'The reproductive sector' was the annexe to the production system. It was the realm which was the condition for the production system, the part which, while not itself capitalist or economic, reproduced the social structure necessary for the capitalist / economic sphere. It was 'all those parts of the society which ensure workers turn up at the factory gates' (daily and from generation to generation) to have surplus value extracted from them. It was outside the production system (the labour process proper) but it included all those areas of society which concern caring for (work done to) the people who comprise the present, future and past labour force. It therefore included kitchens, nurseries, old people's day centres and hospitals, and other parts of the welfare state – that is, all those areas in which women's work predominates. In this way the dichotomy became just a way of linking together structurally and theoretically unrelated things (having babies, taking sole responsibility for nursing the sick, doing the housework, and society continuing from one generation to the next) which happen, empirically, all to be consigned to women. This is analogous and empiricist, not explicative thinking. It is a way of continuing to say there is a man's sphere and a woman's sphere in society, and the latter is to do with procreation and childcare and continuity – and is less social and more natural than the former – but with this statement wrapped up in (what is currently) more acceptable language.

Why the antithesis between production (of things) and reproduction (of people) continues to be so popular is probably because it resonates with a series of other dichotomous presumptions, all of which are forms of gender ideology (of a patriarchal world-view). For instance:

Housework is never-ending   Saying domestic work is 'reproductive' feels right because it fits with saying there is no end to it and that it never gets anywhere: it has no product to show for itself. No sooner are floors cleaned than they are dirtied again, meals cooked than they are eaten, etc. It is trivial, women's work.

But in fact there is no more 'no end' to baking than to car-making or governing the country. The assembly line never stops either. Industrial production in the main replaces things used up – otherwise why should we calculate 'industrial growth' (that is, what is over and beyond replacement)? And only 2–3 per cent of industrial production is 'growth', whereas the rest – 98 per cent of all 'productive' production – serves only to replace what has been consumed or destroyed during a year. That *this* is not seen as trivial work has more to do with who does it and who profits, than with the work having an end product.[18]

Women are the child-bearers and rearers – the people who are responsible for procreation   Saying domestic work is reproductive also feels comfortable because it fits with the common view that women reproduce human beings. It links the sexual division of labour, and gender as a whole, to the physical differences of the sexes in procreation. And then it links procreation itself to women alone. We have a sneaking suspicion men have something to do with procreation too, but, as we have already noted, patriarchal thought sees women as the detached reproductive organs of, and the child-rearers for, men. Some feminists do not quarrel with this because they want to hold on to motherhood, and some seem even to believe in parthenogenesis.[19]

Women provide continuity and stability in society and support life values and important links to nature   Lacking a theory of social inheritance, many writers (including marxists) tie continuity of the social structure to procreation/reproduction. But since they see contradictions within capitalism as the motor of history, the home and reproduction is cast by them as the source of stability, stasis – even inertia. It is production which requires time and energy, learned skills and social relations. Reproduction is natural, instinctual, biologically given, etc., etc.

The present situation regarding the concept of reproduction is thus that the term is used in a thoroughly sloppy way, and at the limit is merely another way of distinguishing women's (supposedly caring) work from men's (supposedly instrumental) work; and / or the rest of society from the capitalist mode of production. In sum, it is a way of continuing to distinguish 'sexual divisions' from 'economic divisions'[20] – suggesting the former are not economic but naturally based and / or 'just' ideological, and presuming the protagonists within the capitalist mode of production are men. Sexual divisions therefore continue to be of secondary importance, and a patriarchal division rests at the very centre of the theories supposedly attacking it.

Dual systems

There are, however, occasional exceptional marxist feminists whose work atones for other marxists' sins by producing a materialist feminist analysis – albeit they did so rather late in the day. The best known is Heidi Hartmann in the US, whose two famous essays 'Capitalism, patriarchy and job segregation by sex' (1976) and 'The unhappy marriage of marxism and feminism: towards a more progressive union' (1979), agree with radical feminists like ourselves that patriarchy is distinct from capitalism and that it involves a system of labour relations. Hartmann defines patriarchy as:

> a set of social relations which has a material base and in which there are hierarchical relations between men and solidarity among them which enable them in turn to dominate women. The material base of patriarchy is men's control over women's labor power. That control is maintained by excluding women from access to necessary economically productive resources and by restricting women's sexuality. Men exercise their control in receiving personal service work from women, in not having to do housework or rear children, in having access to women's bodies for sex, and in feeling powerful and being powerful. The crucial elements of patriarchy as we *currently* experience them are: heterosexual marriage (and consequent homophobia), female childrearing and housework, women's economic dependence on men (enforced by arrangements in the labor market), the state, and numerous institutions based on social relations among men – clubs, sports, unions, professions, universities, churches, corporations and armies. All of these elements need to be examined if we are to understand patriarchal capitalism. (Hartmann 1979 reprinted in Sargent 1981: 18–19 Hartmann's italics)

In these two articles, Hartmann provides a largely historical account of a (supposedly universal) sexual division of labour which became hierarchized within the preindustrial 'nuclear, patriarchal, peasant family' in Europe. Here men controlled the labour of women and children. Then, with the development of capitalism and industrialization, a gendered wage labour market developed which supported the existing (adult) male-dominated domestic structure. She argues that in the nineteenth century, working class men reached an accommodation with capitalists which restricted the entry of women and children into the workforce and crowded them into specific occupations. Women's exclusion from well-paid employment ensured they needed to continue to have access to men's wages, and hence ensured men continued to have unpaid domestic labour provided for them by wives.

Hartmann considers that capitalism is now the dominant system, and she believes that it is job segregation by sex which has become 'the primary mechanism in capitalist society that maintains the superiority of men over women, because it enforces lower wages for women in the labor market'. But she also insists patriarchy continues independently to have effects on capitalism.

> Low wages keep women dependent on men because they encourage women to marry. Married women must perform domestic chores for their husbands. Men benefit, then, from both higher wages and the domestic division of labor. This domestic division of labor, in turn, acts to weaken women's position in the labor market. Thus the hierarchical domestic division of labor is perpetuated in the labor market, and vice versa. This process is the present outcome of the continuing interaction of two interlocking systems, capitalism and patriarchy. Patriarchy far from being vanquished by capitalism is still very virile; it shapes the form modern capitalism takes, just as the development of capitalism has transformed patriarchal institutions. The resulting mutual accommodation between patriarchy and capitalism has created a vicious circle for women. (Hartmann 1976 reprinted in Eisenstein 1979: 208)

Hartmann thus inverts the causal link which is usually assumed to exist between marriage and the labour market. She sees not only the family situation of women influencing their capacity to work outside the home, but also the situation of women in the labour market constituting an objective incentive for them to marry. Marriage plays a part in the exploitation of women's paid work, but the labour market itself plays a part in the exploitation of their domestic work.

In these articles, and in a third one on 'The family as the locus of gender, class and political struggle: the example of housework' (1981), she is firm that women's work in the family is really labour performed for men as husbands and fathers, that men benefit from women's labour because they receive individual, sexual and child-rearing services at home, and that this fact is crucial to the maintenance of patriarchy. She accepts that women's domestic labour clearly reproduces capitalism as well, and that the content and the amount of the work women do varies by class and ethnic or racial group. But this does not detract from the fact that men of all classes and ethnic groups still control women's labour inside as well as outside the family, even when women also have paid employment, and that men benefit from women's labour by having 'higher standards of living than women in terms of luxury consumption, leisure time and personalized services' (Hartmann 1981: 9).

Her work does not, however, actually explore relations inside the family. She simply provides a theoretical outline of the relationship between men's control of women's labour inside and outside the domestic situation, prior to concentrating on the labour market. (This holds even more true of Sylvia Walby's *Patriarchy at Work* (1986) which uses both Hartmann and our own earlier publications to ground a study of changes in the labour market in Britain.) Hartmann does not try to describe, analyse and establish a domestic mode of production. She merely argues (1) for the existence of patriarchy and its independence from capitalism, and (2) that patriarchy has a material base. Indeed it may well be precisely the fact that she does not explore men's domestic exploitation of women, together with her calling herself a socialist feminist, which account for the relative acceptability of her ideas to marxists.

Not that her ideas were not controversial, at least initially. The paper on the unhappy marriage of marxism and feminism, which was first published in 1979, was reprinted in 1981 as the lead article to a collection of papers commenting critically upon it (Sargent 1981).

Many of these commentary papers were supposedly refutations of her dual systems theory – but consisted simply of a priori dismissals rather than reasoned critiques. They were purely formal arguments, saying not that Hartmann was wrong substantively, but rather that her analysis was 'awkward' or that it is 'inelegant' or 'analytically difficult' to have two systems. Such arguments are in our view ridiculous and not to be taken seriously. We may discover there are 3, or n, systems of hierarchy which interact with each other, and we have to accept this. (There certainly are three at least, since the neo-imperialist/racist system needs to be taken into account too.) 'Theoretical elegance' or 'ease of handling data' has nothing to do with it.

These rejections of dual systems theory came from a kind of formalism arising from intellectual laziness or conservatism which can make scientists refuse findings which do not fit with the dominant paradigm; and also from a confusion between the unity of society which we experience as we live in it – the empirical system – and the analytical level. In real life there are no time or space discontinuities between patriarchy and capitalism. We do not see signs saying 'at this point you are leaving the capitalist zone and entering the patriarchal zone.' Even if there were, they would be misleading because the two systems are always present at all times. But this does not mean that when we seek to understand the system we cannot and should not make distinctions.

With the failure of attempts to integrate housework with capitalism theoretically by fiat (as discussed in chapter 2) or via the labour theory of value (in the domestic labour debate), there were several other attempts to use marxist concepts to establish a version of a unitary system of patriarchy and capitalism. Some writers tried to employ the concept of 'the division of labour' or 'alienation', while others re-emphasized the indissociability of 'capitalist patriarchy' or 'patriarchal capitalism'.[21] But these proposals generally involved substantial moves away from marxist methodology.

Subsequently, however, although a few socialist feminists have continued to argue against there being a *system* of women's oppression at all,[22] most now accept some sort of dual system of capitalism and patriarchy, though with varying degrees of interconnection and autonomy. Some combine a standard materialist analysis of capitalism with an analysis of patriarchy in terms of psychic and cultural structures, or patriarchy as a hybrid of material and psychic structures.[23] Others settle for the 'patriarchy as the reproducer of capitalism' approach described above. But a few, like Hartmann, provide accounts which see both capitalism and patriarchy as operating at the same level of the social formation, and as both concerned with the appropriation of labour. They suggest the two systems articulate with and often reinforce each other – though they may sometimes be in competition. But they see neither as reducible to the other.[24]

Thus the idea of two interacting material systems, which was dismissed at first, has slowly but steadily gained acceptance; and current divergences are around a central consensus: an acceptance that patriarchy is a separate system. It is now agreed women are subordinated; and it is generally agreed that the exploitation of women's work is of paramount importance in this subordination, and that patriarchy constitutes a material as well as an ideological system.

But most work by marxist feminists has focused on the labour market. It has not developed Hartmann's sketch of materialist relations in domestic work. Instead a few have taken up Hartmann's suggestion that a direct personal system of individual men's appropriation of individual women's labour in marriage has become supplemented by an indirect, impersonal system of control, mediated by society-wide institutions – notably the labour market but also including the state. They argue (as did Carol Brown in her original paper responding to Hartmann in 1981) that there has been a move from 'private' to 'public' patriarchy. Consequently there is (once again) no pressing need to study the family.

Authors differ somewhat in their use of these new terms,[25] but the gist of their argument is that women are no longer segregated in their homes as they were in the nineteenth century, physically confined and economically restricted by the ideology of separate spheres for men and women, under the tight legal control of their husbands or fathers, with their sexuality and their children alienated from them. Women have (re)entered the public domain: they usually now have paid employment;

they interact directly with the state as enfranchised citizens; they can obtain a divorce and move from one husband to another or live independently; their sexuality is controlled by cultural institutions such as pornography rather than directly by individual men; and their child-bearing and child-rearing labour is used by society as a whole rather than by individual men, since men's reasons for having children have changed.

That is to say, the issues are presented as being, first, the extent to which the oppression of women is still operated by individual men in the domestic arena, or whether our oppression is not now more a product of impersonal forces, benefiting men in general and capitalism in spheres outside the family. And secondly, whether the new forms of women's oppression are more or less onerous, more or less extensive, more or less difficult to combat, than those which operated 50–150 years ago.

Such discussions have been useful in drawing attention to historical changes in the form and locus of men's expropriation of women's labour. But they have been much less helpful when they have been used to suggest, explicitly or implicitly, that marriage and the appropriation of domestic labour are no longer important elements in the oppression of women (and that individual feminists can go on living with men and getting married because this is not the main arena of women's oppression any more). In addition, as it is currently being developed, this approach is in definite danger of following the dominant ideology in splitting life into private and (what it calls indiscriminately) public or 'social' spheres. It is precisely such ideas that it should be subjecting to critical analysis (not to mention the idea that the private sphere is not social).

Hartmann herself specifically contests the view that capitalism has eliminated patriarchy in the family. However, she does see a shift from family-based to industrially-based maintenance of patriarchy, and also (1981: 25–6) a shift away from the 'family wage' to 'wage differentials' as the mechanism necessitating women's continued dependence on men. In addition, while she stresses that women still do much more housework than men even when they have paid employment, she suggests the increase in married women's employment has produced more benefits for capital than for men. Women still work very long hours and nowadays are under even greater pressure, but, Hartmann believes, it is capitalism which is mainly benefiting from this increase in their hours of work, via labour power. For husbands it is something of a zero-sum situation: they do not have to provide as big a share of the cash as they used to, but on the other hand perhaps they also do not get as high a standard of servicing.

We think these are interesting hypotheses, but the evidence is against them. Domestic patriarchy is more self-sustaining, less dependent on capitalism, than Hartmann suggests; and the dynamics of change and recent cost–benefit variations between men, women and capital are also different from those she proposes. This only becomes clear, however, when a much fuller picture of domestic labour relations than she presents is developed – as we intend to show in this book.

Conclusion

Feminism has certainly produced major changes in marxist theorizing, but the main advances have been in ideas about working class women's super-exploitation and in theories of the constitution and functioning of the labour market. Progress towards materialist understandings of other areas of women's oppression has been much slower. Thanks to challenges from the women's movement, few on the Left would now put forward the 1950s misogynistic thesis that women are responsible for undermining the revolutionary potential of the proletariat because they demand 'their' men's primary allegiance, rear individualistic or submissive children, and dampen down the effects of alienated labour by providing comfort and release for the proletariat. Feminism's stress on the variety of forms and the importance of the oppression of women, and on women as social actors in their own right, has made it hard any longer to see women as the allies (or even the dupes) of capitalism.

But feminism has still only undermined *some* of the central tenets of earlier (supposedly) marxist accounts which *did* recognize women were oppressed. These accounts said that working class women's experience is different from working class men's for biology-related reasons. Working class women do different work inside and outside the home from working class men. They more than share such men's low standard of living and they also experience some oppression which is specific to them as women. But, according to these accounts, working class women's experience and oppression exists only as a secondary effect of an oppression aimed primarily at 'the workers': that is, at working class men.

Socialist feminists have fought the premise that the proletariat is composed of adult married men; and even more the premise that it would actually be better off without women. They have made considerable progress in developing labour market theories to include recognition of women wage workers and to contest the idea that skills, etc., are biologically based. Thus as far as paid employment is concerned, socialist feminists recognize women can do useful work which is worth exploiting. But their accounts of the family have, to be blunt, been mystifying and protective of patriarchy. They still hold firmly to the world-view that capitalism is *the* system to which all else has to be related. It may be (as Hartmann says) a very flexible system, but it is still seen to dominate everything in the society.

Those who see patriarchy as inextricably bound and subject to capitalism can still end up seeing the true victims, the real subjects of women's oppression, as working class men. They can still see not only women's social presence but also their very oppression as mediated through the men to whom they are 'attached'. Such accounts not only adhere to the premises of patriarchal ideology (and indeed have these premises as their foundation and motor), they also contribute their own stone towards

building the ideology itself. For such 'feminist' accounts apply patriarchal thinking to a new philosophical field – to neo-marxism – thus
extending it and contributing to patriarchal ideology's renewal and
reproduction.

The worst of it is that this concern and haste to show the functions of
the family for capitalism and to 'articulate' the oppression of women with
that of the proletariat has come from a good political intent. (Or rather
marxist feminists' concern to attach the oppression of women to the
oppression of the proletariat is well intentioned since there is no shadow
of symmetry in their formulation of what has functions for what, or what
articulates with what.) It has derived from a concern to establish the
reality of women's oppression, to make it visible, to get it taken seriously
(that is, politically), to make it seem important and part of a system (that
is, to give it theoretical status). Feminists in universities, in grass roots
struggles, and in left-wing political groups have been endlessly tempted
to seek legitimacy for the women's movement and to gain acceptance for
their special interest in women by showing that the oppression of women
really matters. They think they can best do this by showing that women's
oppression is also caused by *the* important agency, the one everyone
opposes. It therefore does not really divide women from men. Some hope
to convince their male colleagues or partners to care about sexual divisions
because of this, and because this 'new' oppression can be accounted for
in (slightly modified) existing terms and concepts. They seem to find it
hard to accept that women's oppression is important if it is specific to
women and that it may well divide men and women.

The concern to focus on the benefits to capitalism has meant that marxist
feminists have looked almost exclusively at the exploitation of women
who either have working class jobs or who are married to members of the
proletariat – that is, to focus on the oppression of 'working class women'
(since writers do not always distinguish the two categories, and anyway
many women are in both). Despite the fact that many marxist feminist
writers are themselves in middle class jobs and / or married to middle class
men, and know themselves to be oppressed as women, they have largely
ignored the oppression of middle class women. They have stressed the
divisions between women on the lines of class. The differences between
the wives (or cohabitees or daughters) of middle class men and the wives
(cohabitees and daughters) of working class men is based, however, on
the 'class' relationship they have in common: their relationship with a
husband / father. They are all defined by the men to whom they are related.

We have looked elsewhere at the guilty conscience which leads middle
class women always to be fighting battles for people other than themselves.[26] Those who are socialists feel especially guilty at having any
class privileges at all. Being women, they do not feel they have the right
to even the derived or lesser privileges they do have. However, it is
unfortunate (to say the least) that this socialist feminist guilt has been
expressed not by looking at the actual articulation of class and gender

struggles, but by concentrating only on the group oppressed by both patriarchy and capitalism; and by a willingness to attack 'bourgeois women' and radical feminism.

We may be able to empathize with feminine self-flagellation – though it hurts to be personally attacked; but there is no disguising the fact that marxist feminists' analyses of the family have been disastrous. They have hardly ever engaged with middle class family relations – or with the families of any men other than proletarians. And they have been loath to criticize working class men's patriarchal powers, which is a real selling out of working class wives and daughters.

In addition, many marxist feminists (now more often calling themselves socialist feminists) have recently completely abandoned the analysis of any possible material advantages even for capitalism of domestic labour, and have headed off to look instead at the 'discourses' which maintain the power imbalances between men and women in the family and elsewhere. They now use psychoanalytic and post-modernist arguments rather than marxism in their search for an understanding of gender. They study the 'constitution of gendered subjectivities', the genesis and expression of sexual desire, and cultural representations of familial relations, not what actually goes on in households.[27] They have thus shifted such limited attention as they once gave to housework and domestic relations, including domestic violence, to look instead at 'familial ideologies' (rather than actual family relationships). They do not try to uncover the origins of these ideologies, however, other than by looking at how they have changed historically; and the power dimension within them has been flattened or lost sight of entirely.

By initially eliding 'economic' and 'class', and skipping over the possibility of patriarchal economics completely, most socialist / marxist feminists have thus ended up seeking explanations for most aspects of women's oppression back where patriarchal ideology itself always located them: in anatomical differences, in motherhood, in sexuality, in childhood experiences, in the structure of the unconscious mind – and in ideologies and discourses. Anywhere but in men's material advantages. For them the world stays in ever more interpreted states, rather than their having to seek collectively to change material relations.

Notes

1   This was argued by radicals from Germany in the 1930s and 1940s, e.g. Wilhelm Reich (1969) and the Frankfurt school (especially Max Horkheimer (1936), see Benjamin (1978)). A version appeared in the 1970s in Louis Althusser's work in France, when he included the family as one of the ideological apparatuses of the state which support capitalism (Althusser 1971). It is nowadays generally presented in a marxist-psychoanalytic variant, e.g. the work of Mark Poster (1978).

2   See the summary of the New Left's theoretical interest in the family in Middleton (1974).
3   E.g. Zaretsky (1976) and Shorter (1975).
4   E.g. Galbraith (1973; 1974), Weinbaum and Bridges (1976), Game and Pringle (1984)
5   E.g. on the first point, Bruegel (1979) and on the second, Beechey (1977).
6   E.g. Harrison (1973), Gardiner (1976) and other protagonists in the domestic labour debate (see below). On the wider point that capitalists facilitate continuing self-subsistence activities by workers to enable the payment of lower wages, see Corrigan (1990)
7   E.g. Humphries (1977), Foreman (1977), McIntosh (1978), Barrett and McIntosh (1980). A variant of this argument says that a family wage is paid to men to support wives because family care for children, the sick, etc., saves the state money, see Gardiner (1976), Wilson (1977).
8   The original papers in the DLD included: Dalla Costa (1972), Dalla Costa and James (1972; 1975), Gerstein (1973), Vogel (1973), Harrison (1973), D. Smith (1973), Seccombe (1974), Coulson, Magas and Wainwright (1975), Gardiner (1975; 1976), Gardiner, Himmelweit and Mackintosh (1975; 1976), Adamson et al. (1976), Himmelweit and Mohun (1977), P. Smith (1978), Mackintosh (1979).

    For overviews of and reflections on the DLD, see Rushton (1979), Molyneux (1979), Malos (1980) Kaluzynska (1980) and Beer (1984).
9   I.e. Benston (1969 reprinted 1970), Olah (1970), Delphy (1970), Morton (1970), Larguia (1970) and Larguia and Dumolin (n.d. c.1973). On an earlier article by Mitchell (1966), see chapter 4 n. 3.
10 See chapter 4 pp. 80–2 n. 15.
11 Specifically Harrison (1973), Seccombe (1974), Gardiner (1975; 1976) and Himmelweit and Mohun (1977).
12 See Delphy (1977).
13 See for example, articles in Fox (1980) and Dickinson and Russell (1986).
14 This point has been made by, for instance, Maureen Mackintosh (1979); and the phrase 'gender-blind' is used by Hartmann (1979). But we think their critiques do not go far enough. They need to go further back and to recognize the extent to which marxist theory is not so much 'gender-blind' as premised upon a sexually structured base (see Friedman (1982), Delphy (1980; 1989b)).
15 Ros Coward (1983) among others has also pointed to the vagueness of the distinction and the way it slides back into biology and essentialism.
16 See Edholm (1982), Delphy (1989a).
17 E.g. Bourgeois et al. (1978), Stacey (1981), Chabaud and Fougeyrollas (1984).
18 For a much fuller development of similar ideas see Waring (1989).
19 See Delphy (1989a).
20 A contrast between 'sexual' (family) and 'economic' (workplace) exploitation is actually used as the basis for some analyses, see for instance McDonough and Harrison (1978).
21 For an analysis using the concept of 'the division of labour' see Young (1981) and for one using 'alienation' see Jaggar (1983). On the indissociability

of 'capitalist patriarchy' see Z. R. Eisenstein (1979) and on 'patriarchal capitalism' see Mies (1986).

22 E.g. Rowbotham (1981) and various moves into post-structuralism, see n. 27.

23 For a materialist analysis of capitalism combined with an analysis of patriarchy in terms of psychic structures, see Mitchell (1975); cultural structures, see Barrett (1980); and 'the sexual / affective sphere', see Ferguson (1989).

24 French language work has developed from Delphy's earlier articles, e.g. Dhavernas (1985) and Lagrave (1987a) using her concept of the domestic mode of production, and Barthez (1982; 1983). Fougeyrollas says she was 'inspired' by it. Leonard (1980), Finch (1983) and Walby (1986) also draw on her substantially.

25 Compare, for example, Brown (1981), Ferguson (1989) and Walby (1990).

26 See Delphy (1977).

27 See, for example, Mitchell (1975), Barrett and McIntosh (1979; 1982), Barrett (1980), E. Wilson (1985), Beechey (1985), Sayers (1986), Smart (1989), Feminist Review Collective (1987), *Feminist Review* no. 34 (1990). See also comments in Delphy (1980; 1989a).

PART II
A NEW THEORETICAL APPROACH
TO THE WESTERN FAMILY

4

HOUSEWORK, HOUSEHOLD WORK
AND FAMILY WORK

Because even the most obviously materially productive tasks done by women have been so neglected, it was, as we said in chapter 1, a major step forward for feminist analysis when the newly emerging women's movement of the late 1960s and 1970s started to recognize the activities women perform in the home as work. Feminists stressed that women at home do not 'do nothing'. Housework and childcare, never mind affective and sexual work, take up hours and hours of each woman's day. Even in so-called egalitarian relationships, men do not do very much, and sons do nearly nothing. This has all sorts of direct and indirect advantages for men. Part of this new recognition of housework – or as we now know, *renewed* recognition of housework[1] – and its interaction with other forms of women's work, meant it became established as a new object of knowledge to be taken seriously by historians, economists and sociologists, whereas for the greater part of the twentieth century it had been not merely ignored, but treated with contempt.

From 1920 to 1970 virtually the only major sustained research on household activities were time-budget studies. In the main these sought simply to describe and quantify, but despite many methodological difficulties they did emphasize the enormous numbers of hours of housework which were still being done, mainly by married women.[2] They showed, for example, that:

1   The number of hours women work has not declined during the course of this century. The working week of a full-time housewife with children is still 60–80 hours in both rural and urban areas (although the working week for full-time male workers in industry has declined by about 10 hours, to 40 hours plus overtime).

2   The proportion of housework done by wives (as against other women in households) has actually increased this century. Domestic servants have departed and daughters do less. In addition, the development of household technology has allowed higher standards to be established (for example, several changes of clean clothes each week). It is wives who have taken on the extra tasks which have arisen with mechanization. (For example, men may help with the washing-up, but if the

household gets a dishwasher, the wife is likely to take on all the loading and unloading of it.)
3   Men never do much housework – whether they live in France, Britain, the USA, Russia or Sweden. And married men do less than half as much as bachelors, whereas married women do twice as much as single women. What married men do is seen as 'helping' their wives.
4   Although husbands of employed wives do a larger *proportion* of the housework than those married to non-employed wives, this is over-whelmingly due to the smaller amount of time women devote to house-work when they also have paid work, not because such men actually do more housework.
5   Finally, women work a longer weekday and more hours at the week-ends than men, especially if there are small children in the household or the woman has paid employment.

Although time-budget studies are undoubtedly interesting and impor-tant in establishing that the much heralded 'leisure society' is still a long way away and that there has not yet been a redistribution or sharing of housework between husbands and wives, more important questions about the theoretical status of housework only began to be asked with the be-ginning of the second wave of the women's movement, around 1970.[3] Subsequently, and after a predictable time-lag, even such experts as J. K. Galbraith (1973) have come to recognize the importance of domestic labour and to use concepts forged for the most part outside the academic world.
    The literature on housework has subsequently grown year by year and reached the point of schools starting to form. There is still consensus, however, as to its essential economic characteristics:

• it is work (which is indeed the main reason why it is studied);
• it is unpaid (which is why recognizing it as work was not automatic in a society such as ours, but rather constituted a scientific discovery);
• and it is done mainly by women.

Beyond this point, however, differences of opinion start to appear.

1   Some studies have focused on the usefulness of housework for capit-alism – as we saw in chapter 3.[4]
2   There has been a debate about whether or not housework is 'pro-ductive', and about whether or not the fact that it is unpaid is because of the specific nature of the work (because it is only for use and not for exchange). We shall show the various misunderstandings and errors underlying this debate in this chapter.[5]
3   There have also been various attempts to assess the monetary value of housework, either to the family (in terms of how much compensation

should be paid in legal cases or for insurance purposes), or in order for it to be included in the assessment of the gross national product. We shall look at some of the problems with this work too in this chapter.[6]

4 Some authors have stressed the aspect of 'work' in the sense of 'tasks,' looking at changes in the nature and the component parts of housework (the decline of brewing and weaving and the rise of cleaning and child care) and the history of domestic technology.[7]

5 Others have looked at how the time spent on housework and the type of commercially produced product bought-in as substitutes varies with whether or not wives have paid employment, and at changes over the life-course.[8]

6 Yet others have looked primarily at how the work is experienced by those doing it.[9]

7 Finally, some interesting work has been done on ideologies of men's and women's separate 'spheres', tracing the changing representations of 'the private sphere' of the home and 'the public world' outside it in the nineteenth and twentieth centuries: how the spheres were differentiated and the attempts made to hold them apart – or to reintegrate them.[10]

These topics are all obviously interconnected and particular studies have often covered a number of them. Our focus is on the 'unpaid' aspect of housework, that is, on the form of relationship within which a (changing) variety of tasks are performed, and spreads out from this. We consider this to be crucial because, in spite of the current interest in housework and the number of books and articles devoted to it, one thing remains hazy, though it is quite fundamental. This is the definition of housework – what it is these scholars are actually studying. This is exacerbated by the words 'housework' and 'domestic work' being used interchangeably.

This is not because the meaning of 'housework' is the subject of an unresolved debate. Quite the contrary. It is because there is a tacit consensus. No one thinks it necessary to define housework because what it means seems to go without saying. Authors generally adopt uncritically (or with just a few initial comments) the current, everyday definition that 'housework is the work done within the home by the wife.' Strictly speaking this should then require them to define 'home' (since housework includes for example shopping, which takes place outside the house) and to say more about the situations and conditions within which the work is done. But in fact they move straight on to a commonsense list of tasks – cooking, washing, cleaning, etc. – generally adding as somewhat separate categories, childcare and the care of the sick and elderly.

We do not think an empiricist definition – a list of tasks, however minutely specified it might be[11] – is satisfactory. Nor are we clear how this list relates to the generally agreed characteristics of housework (that is, that it is unpaid work done by women) which we identified in the literature. Obviously, what is in practice included in 'housework' depends on how the subject is interpreted theoretically, and we believe that many of the impasses which have been encountered in discussions of housework could be avoided if there was agreement (or at least clear disagreement) as to its principle features. We need a formal and not an empirical definition of what it is we are studying.

As a move towards this, we propose to begin by taking just the generally agreed characteristics of housework – that is, work which is unpaid and done by women in or related to the household.[12]

Faced with these characteristics, we want at once to ask two questions.

1 Do the defining characteristics cover all the work done in the home? (a) Is all such work done by women? and (b) is it all unpaid?
2 And conversely, does the empirical definition of housework (do the tasks listed) cover all the work women do unpaid?

The answers seem to be clearly that:

1 (a) *Not all work done within households is done by women. Men and children (and sometimes servants) do some too.* Although there is variation from country to country, by class, and from one household to another, in general in the West, women do almost all the laundry, ironing and sewing, most of the childcare and care of the sick and elderly, most of the work concerned with helping children's education, and most cooking, washing-up and shopping. Men and children do, however, do odd jobs like taking out the rubbish and some tidying and washing-up. Men also routinely do home maintenance and most car maintenance, and care for the garden and animals. And at certain phases in the life-cycle in middle class households, full-time, part-time or casual domestic helpers are employed. But many authors ignore this in both their theoretical analyses and their empirical studies. (For instance, we know of no time-budget studies which include work done by children.)

1 (b) *Not all work done within the home should be considered 'unpaid' because some of it would seem to carry its own reward.* Men mending their cars, for example, are recompensed for their work by saving themselves money. We therefore need to sort out further what we mean by 'unpaid' and to look at who if anyone does unpaid work.

2 *The defining characteristics of housework – unpaid work done by women – mean the term should cover much more than the classic list of cooking, cleaning and shopping, etc.* The 'unpaid work done by women' also includes things which are not, as it were, narrowly to do with the house or 'materially' productive, namely, a whole series of other tasks wives and mothers do for their husbands and families – such as booking holidays, visiting sick relatives in hospital, working in the family shop, helping neighbours, giving moral support, taking children to play with

other children, sending birthday and Christmas cards, etc. Such work varies between households, depending on the particular needs of the members and the occupation, wealth and preferences of the household head. Such work has been even more ignored than housework and one of our central concerns is to make it more visible.

We therefore think it important to clarify terminology. **We propose to use the term household work to cover all the work done within or related to domestic locations by any person (man, woman or child)**. This includes a very wide variety of tasks. Since we want to consider the work of wives within the context of work done within family relationships as a whole, **we shall use the term family work to cover all work done by subordinates / dependants for the household head**, noting that most of the dependants who do such work nowadays are women as wives or cohabitees.

To explain why we have reached these conclusions, we shall first present some of the problems which economists and sociologists have come up against when trying to use the empirical definition of housework. We hope thereby to clear up a variety of confusions, including what is actually meant by 'housework', as well as to make our own position clear.

Is housework unpaid because there is something special about it?

Much of the 1970s literature on housework suggested that the reason why the housework done by women is unpaid is due to the goods and services produced within households being in some way different from goods and services produced either within a family business (petty commodity production) or in other sectors of the economy. This, it was said, accounted for the assumption that the work, and hence the people who do it, are of little or no value in a money-dominated economy.

We would not disagree with these authors (mainly marxist) if it were simply clarified that what they are saying is that (most) housework is different from waged work, and the reason it is not paid is because it is not done within the capitalist mode of production.

Where we part company with most of them is that we do not use this assertion as a prelude to just outlining the ways in which housework is not like waged work – and then ignoring housework, or presuming we know what it actually is. As we said at the start of chapter 1, our particular concern is precisely to explore the work women do for the households in which they live, and the mode of production within which they do it.

However, we also part company with even the minority of authors who *have* attempted to say what is special or specific about housework (and what accounts for its being unpaid) because we do not agree with their analyses. They have argued that housework is special:

- either because it is not productive,
- or because it is for consumption rather than production,
- or because it is for use and not exchange.

We do not accept any of these hypotheses, as we shall show.

Is housework special because it is not productive?

Two recurrent themes in work on the family are the idea that the productive family is a thing of the past; and an idealization of relationships, and particularly the status of women, within so-called productive families of the past. Consider, for example, the following typical passage:

> If women were then [in the sixteenth century] subjected – as they often still are – to the caprice and demands of their husbands, there was one crucial difference. Before the industrial revolution women were one half of an economic unit, that of the husband and wife. The division of labour in the home as it was created and perpetuated by capitalism, was then unknown. Home and work were inextricably linked. Often men and women worked at home, so the home was the productive unit. 'The home and the outside world were one; real life was *domestic*. It was concerned with survival in a hostile environment and depended on the skill and effort of every member of the community, regardless of sex or age.'
>
> To describe housework up until the middle of the seventeenth century is to describe the whole spectrum of woman's life: it was neither compartmentalized, isolated or solitary. 'Their labour was visible and was seen by all as a necessary (though perhaps inferior) complement to the labour of the husband father.' Women's work in a rural family was gruelling and virtually unending, but it was also creative, productive and responsible. (Mackie and Pattullo 1977: 10, which includes quotations from Comer 1974 and Gardiner 1975, stress in original)

This quotation reveals a set of ideas which can be summarized as follows.

1 The family was 'once' (in the sixteenth, seventeenth or eighteenth century, depending on the author) a productive unit.
2 But it is no longer productive.
3 The former productive family was egalitarian (or relatively egalitarian) *because* it was productive and because the family members worked alongside each other and could therefore see and recognize the importance of one another's work. Alice Clark, for instance, in her classic work on women in seventeenth-century England, talks of there being a 'rough justice' between men and women when 'close to the land'. The family was transformed when its resources became individuals' wages as opposed to produce from the family's farm or workshop.
4 Industrial capitalism caused the family to lose its productivity. It moved

production outside the home into factories and hence caused inequality to appear (or greatly to increase) within the family.

5   When women remained at home, they lost the status (social recognition) that was attached to having a productive function.

6   To this can be added another common idea: that the family is now being reunited around consumption in its leisure time.[13]

These ideas are shared by a host of authors. They are internally coherent, but wrong.

The idea (nos 2 and 4) that capitalism destroyed the productive function of the family household is factually incorrect. What it did was provide many *other* sites / units of production in the society, so households as locations were no longer the main units of production. Concomitant industrialization meant that many of the goods and services which were once produced in households with family labour were produced (in addition or almost exclusively) within factories by waged labourers. But this does not mean that family households no longer produce anything.

Rather, most now produce a range of things which is more restricted than it used to be, but these things are produced to a higher standard, for example, clean, warm and tidy rooms with attention to comfort and decor, and more complex meals with a variety of forms of cooking and courses. Family households also provide a wide range of personal services, with the purchase and presentation of domestic commodities itself an important medium for the expression of love (for example, one shows one loves one's children by buying and using brands of kitchen floor cleaners with germicide). Also households have not simply lost productive functions, because they now do things they did not do in the past (for example, providing pre-school reading tuition for children), and some production which at one time moved out of households and into factories has now been reintroduced into the household (for example, laundry for economy and convenience, and food preservation by freezing and bread and cake making for the superior quality of the product). Nor should we forget that many families are still (or again) units producing products and services which are sold on the market (see chapter 5).

The idea (no. 5) that it was women's losing their productive role – including the growth of a nineteenth-century ideology which required ladies to be at home and idle – that caused women to lose status, overlooks the fact that gentlemen of the period were also not supposed to work. A gentleman in the nineteenth century gained status through not being gainfully employed but rather living off rents from his land or investments and spending his time in voluntary activities (for example, doing natural history). This idea also ignores the evidence that nineteenth-century ladies were far from idle when at home: they worked hard at feminine tasks which included managing servants, maintaining and improving the family's status through various social activities, and pleasing men.[14]

The idea (no. 4) that it is because the family household lost its productive function that it became inegalitarian and oppressive for its dependent members, or that this is why subordinates lost status, shows great ignorance of the family (and other productive units) both now and in the past. Are peasant farms not patriarchal? Are factories, which are productive, not hierarchical? And family businesses? Popular historians would do well to pay more attention to the functioning of contemporary petty commodity producing families which may well provide insights into earlier periods. In such families today (for example, market gardeners, corner shop keepers, small hoteliers) women still work to produce goods and services which are sold on the market – but their status is no higher (that is, it is no different) from the status of wives in other families. A publican's wife who prepares food for sale at the bar has no greater 'dignity in . . . domestic life' thanks to 'women's distinctive skills' (Ehrenreich and English 1979: 12) than the wife of such a man who focuses exclusively on caring for children and keeping the flat above the pub clean.

On the contrary, **the family household was (and is) hierarchical precisely because it is a unit of production:** because it consists of relationships which enable one person to use the products or services of another person's (or persons') labour.

The attribution of equality, or high status, to wives in the pre-capitalist family, stems not from looking at the evidence, the contemporary and historical record, but rather from a concern to make industrial capitalism responsible for (all) the present-day evils of housework / women's oppression. And it is this same concern which underlies the first factual error (ideas 1 and 2). The first three assertions all imply a very classical definition of production, effectively limiting it to what is currently so labelled by both bourgeois and marxist economists.[15] This definition of production boils down to saying that,

productive = for exchange on the market, or
productive = produced by waged labour, hence a source of
surplus value = productive for capitalism.

These assertions are substantialist, ahistorical and ethnocentric.

They are substantialist because they imply, among other things, that the productiveness or unproductiveness of goods is inherent in the nature of the goods – that it derives from their physical being, from the fact they are a particular sort of service or tangible object / substance (hence the name), and not from the social relations within which the services or goods are set (that is, produced and transmitted).

Substantialism itself derives from ahistoricism and ethnocentrism: from not taking into account social relations and how these vary over time and from one society to another. But it also *causes* ahistoricism and ethnocentrism, since by asserting that 'productive' goods are productive by nature, it projects back into other historical periods and onto other contemporary cultures a catalogue of goods which are described as being productive then or there because they are so described here and now.

Thus, as a typical example, writers who make such assertions consider that when in the past women spun wool to make yarn and cloth for the family's clothes or for their husbands to sell to middlemen, this was *then* considered and valued as 'productive' work because spinning and weaving are considered productive today.

What they do not recognize is that, on the contrary, it is spinning and weaving which have become (seen as) productive because spinning and weaving have changed their mode of production. Spinning and weaving in contemporary western societies are carried out almost exclusively within a particular set of social relations of production – those of wage labour for capital. This is what makes them 'productive'. The writers ignore the possibility that this and other tasks done within the family by women, which would now be considered productive and valued, could then have been considered to be unproductive and little valued; just as, and for the same reason as, housework is nowadays generally considered unproductive and little valued.

To understand the position of women we must take a wider definition of production (see chapter 1) – one which includes all work 'producing or increasing wealth and value' (*Shorter Oxford Dictionary*) and all 'goods and services that are socially useful' (Gardiner 1976: 111).

It may be that the growth of capitalism and the hegemony of its values (notably only valuing, or even only recognizing the existence of waged work) resulted in a worsening of the position of women / family dependents. But this seems to us to be an empirical question which has yet to be answered satisfactorily – largely because it has rarely been asked properly. It has been taken as read. It certainly seems likely that women were badly affected by the changed significance (and increased stringency) of their exclusion from the market as this area of the economy expanded (see Hartmann in chapter 3). But was this due to developing capitalism or retrenching patriarchy? In any case it is at least arguable that men today value their wives' / dependents' work (even when it is done largely out of their sight) just as highly (or poorly) as did the weaver sitting at his loom surrounded by a 'working' wife and children.

If there has been a changed evaluation of wives' work (and we have yet to be convinced of this), it is certainly not due to their now doing different tasks, nor to their work having become unproductive. For when operations which were previously part of housework (for example, baking bread), or which are still carried out in the home (for example, making clothes, cooking meals, or caring for the sick) are done outside the home or for people other than family members, they are considered productive. Bakers, tailors, dress shops, restaurants, nurseries and hospitals sell work which was done unpaid in the home – and which is still done there, unpaid, today. This manufacturing and paid servicing is considered part of the overall national production (it is included in the gross national product) and the individuals who do the work are considered producers. This was not (and is not) the case when the goods and services were (or are) produced with family labour.

The unpaidness of housework does not therefore depend on the special nature of the tasks, since all the goods and services produced at home can also be bought on the market (that is, they exist also in paid form). Nor does it depend on the actual human being doing it, since when an individual does the same work outside the family (for example, nursing) as they do within it, she or he is paid for it. **The unpaidness, the specific character of housework, depends rather on the fact that the tasks which comprise it are performed within a particular relationship, one where the people who usually do the work do not own the products of their practical, emotional, sexual and reproductive labour.** Or to put it more formally, it depends upon their being done within particular relations of production. Mostly nowadays they are done by women in marriage. It is this relationship which makes the tasks (and the performer) appear 'unproductive', not their (or her) nature. If a man marries his housekeeper or a prostitute, the same work and the same woman suddenly become unpaid and 'unproductive'.

Is housework special because it is done for consumption rather than production?

A second variant of the mystifying arguments current in the literature about housework suggests that the unpaidness of housework has to do with its being concerned with consumption rather than production. In many cases it is simply baldly stated that families have shifted from production to consumption, and no more seems to need to be said because anything to do with consumption is seen as automatically unpaid. But more sophisticated writers in this vein raise valuable points about the ways in which advanced capitalism and the welfare state have changed (and often increased) the work done by housewives. They stress that when women today go to supermarkets or to hospital out-patient departments with family members, they are doing work ('consumption work') which (for the middle class at least) used to be provided by family grocers taking orders, boxing them up and delivering them, and by family doctors making home visits.[16]

Unfortunately, however, such accounts continue to obscure relationships within the family by dichotomizing

- paid work = labour = production (the accumulation process in the market), and
- women's-work-outside-the-paid-labour-force = consumption = reproduction (the meeting of people's needs for food, rest, shelter and so on in the home).

To untangle this confusion, we need briefly to show the dubious nature of the line usually drawn between production and consumption. This can best be done by looking first at contemporary examples of families which *are* recognized as producing for their own consumption, such as small farms, and then broadening the argument to the rest of the population.

On many small farms and market gardens in Europe today, family members produce quite a lot of the goods and services they consume; that is, the family directly absorbs much of its own production. What it produces is, however, marketable: things produced could be taken to the market and sold instead of the family using them itself. This is why produce from farms consumed on farms is considered part of their income by the people involved, and part of overall national production by the economists who compile the national accounts (this is why they include it in their estimate of the GNP).

In such circumstances, when the producer and consumer are one and the same, it is obvious that there is a continuum between production and consumption. Such families sow wheat in order to grow corn, they mill what they harvest because they cannot eat grains, and they cook flour because it tastes better and is more digestible. None of these operations is useful without the other, because their objective is the final consumption, the eating of bread. It would be absurd to stop half-way.

Stopping half-way is, however, precisely what both experts and lay people do in their accounting, for they consider only part of the process as production. They count up to and including the milling of flour as 'productive', but the rest of the process (cooking bread or pies) is described as 'unproductive' or 'housework' or 'for consumption'.

But surely, either all the work which people do in making something to eat is productive, or none of it is? The latter alternative is clearly absurd, since the wheat which the farm family grows, processes and eats *could* be sold (though it would then have to be replaced by equivalent food bought on the market) – and production for the market is unequivocally 'production'.

When farmers start to specialize and produce only one or two crops, or raise only one sort of animal, they obviously sell almost all their produce and buy in a variety of other vegetables and meat because a diet of exclusively peaches or chickens would be monotonous to say the least. This is even more obviously true when a family enterprise produces goods, such as decorative garden plants or animal fodder, which its members cannot consume at all; and it also holds when we move from farming to family production of other goods and services (for example, artisans and small shopkeepers) and to families which sell not goods and services at all, but the labour of certain of their members.

In such moves, from family households which are to a considerable extent self-sufficient to those selling specialized goods and services or labour, the fact that the objective of all production is consumption tends to get hidden because products have to be exchanged twice before they can be consumed. People have to sell either their products or their labour power, and then they have to purchase goods to consume – either directly or, more commonly, after further work has been applied to them. What breaks the continuum between production and consumption is not the fact that some of the activities needed for the final goal of consumption are not productive, but that when production is specialized, consumption is mediated by exchange.

Most households in the West today produce very little of their own raw food material, though those with gardens or allotments produce a not inconsiderable amount.[17] They are therefore faced with a choice, not between selling or eating particular products, but rather between buying food in a raw state and applying work to it to make it consumable, or buying it ready prepared and paying for the extra (market) work (that is, the value) added by the manufacturer or caterer and his or her staff. In general they choose to do the former.

> One could say that the household itself produces its final consumption goods, just as a firm produces its final goods. To do this, the household uses essentially work (housework), machines (durable goods), and raw materials (intermediary products, bought directly from producing firms) which are transformed by the household itself using a certain amount of work and capital. Viewed in this way, the household differs from a business only in so far as it adds to the production (which is the sole function of the firm) the activity of consumption. (Wolfelsperger 1970: 20 our translation)

Thus whilst expenditure on prepared food and eating out has increased very considerably this century (in the USA one meal in four is now eaten outside the home),[18] most of a French household's spending on food still goes on basic raw materials. These constitute the main item of the family budget, taking between 50–80 per cent of the net income.

The reason why 'the household' chooses to use its income in this way is because it rarely has enough money to achieve its desired level of consumption otherwise. Most households prefer to buy raw food and transform it at home, leaving more income free for other purchases, because housework costs nothing; and men prefer it because almost all housework is done by women. It may of course mean forgoing possible female wages, and where there is suitable work for women available which does not prevent them from still doing a lot of housework, things may be changing: households (household heads) may accept rather poorer quality and more expensive bought food some of the time, in return for significant additions to their overall income.

But even if a few people are rich enough to eat out all the time and to live in hotels and have their laundry done and their clothes laid out and their packages carried home from the shops, most are not. And even those who could afford to live like this would, on the whole, not want to anyway, since purchased goods and services are not personalized – they are not always exactly what the consumer wants, nor delivered at precisely the time and place he (or she) wants.

For the vast majority of people, therefore, consumption is (still) reached in two stages: first the purchase of more or less raw materials using the monetary income from the sale of goods or labour power; and then the transformation of these raw materials into a directly consumable product via household work, sometimes performed by paid servants, but more commonly nowadays by unpaid family labour.

This is quite the opposite of the crude ideology embedded in accounts of the economy which suggest that the wage of the husband, on its own, pays for the entire consumption of the household, and hence that the housewife is 'supported' and does not earn her own living. In fact a lot of value is added to purchased goods prior to their being consumed, and most of this is contributed by women. This constitutes a very substantial part of the household's standard of living – perhaps equal to the amount coming from the husband's wage.[19]

Is housework special because it is only for use and not for exchange?

A third major failing of the literature, especially, in this case, the more theoretical literature on housework, is closely tied to the same general faulty approach that underlies the confusion around its 'non-productivity' or its 'being only for consumption'. It is a peculiar and unacceptable use of the notion of 'use-value'.

There are plenty of quotations available which would illustrate this, but we shall use just one example from a pioneering paper of the late 1960s. In this, Margaret Benston (1969) recognizes that housework is productive, socially necessary, and of far from marginal importance to the overall economy of our society; but she explains its unpaidness, its exclusion from the realm of exchange, and its 'non-value' as deriving from the nature of the work. This rests on, and is expressed in, two suppositions:

1 'Women [are that] group of people who are responsible for the production of simple use-values in those activities associated with the home and family ... They have no structural responsibility in [the] area [of wage work] and such participation [as they have] is ordinarily regarded as transient. Men, on the other hand, are responsible for commodity production; they are not, in principle, given any role in household labor ... The work women do is *different* from the work that men do ... [it is] private production for use, not for exchange' (Benston in Tanner 1970: 281–3 stress in original).
2 Women are largely excluded from production for exchange, that is, from industrialized, large-scale, rationalized, efficient, public production which is part of an integrated social network (whether for private profit: capitalized; or for human welfare: socialized) (Benston in Tanner 1970: 283–4).

In other words, women

1   produce objects with 'use-value' not 'exchange-value', and
2   are restricted to working in an arena where no surplus is produced.

However, far from it being the tasks which women perform (the things that they make and do) which explain their social situation, it is their social situation in the family which explains why they do what they do and why their work has no exchange value. Family workers as economic agents are excluded from exchanging what they produce on the market. Wives may work at rearing children, or rearing pigs, or servicing their husbands, or working in his business (or any combination of these and other tasks), but the children take the husband's name, it is the husbands who put the pigs on the market, or who sell labour power (as their own) or who own the business which the wives have helped to build up.

Women may work outside marriage and the family, as nurses or teachers or farm-hands or housekeepers or office workers – and receive wages. That is, they can do the same tasks as they do unpaid in marriage, but in exchange for money. It is the fact of doing certain tasks within the family, that is, within a particular social relationship, which makes the work lack exchange-value, not the nature of the tasks themselves. It is not in this sense 'the sort of work involved'.

What we are faced with in articles such as Benston's is a reification of the notion of value. She treats 'value' as if it were an actual, material thing. But it is not, nor does it exist apart from society. It is created by and exists because of a particular *social relationship* – that of exchange. (In a monetary economy, money-value and exchange-value are effectively synonymous.) Because of this reification, Benston talks of use-value as if it were a characteristic of certain products, and she suggests in addition that this distinguishes them from other things as physical objects. However, not only are use-value and exchange-value not physical properties of things, they are not mutually exclusive. They are two aspects of the same goods and services, not qualities of different goods and services. This was demonstrated very clearly by Marx in his theory of *Capital* and is one of the basic premises of his work.

Exchange-value (which is really just 'value') is not the opposite of, and is certainly not exclusive of, use-value (which is better called usefulness or utility). On the contrary, value presupposes usefulness. If people are going to want to exchange something for something, or to buy something, the thing they are after is something useful to them, in the broad sense. (That is, it may be something they can eat or drink or use to keep warm, or it may be symbolic or for ideologically complex use, for example, a painting.)

The reverse is, of course, not necessarily true, or at least not always true. Something can be useful to one person but not to another, or not to anyone else at all – though in fact, it is likely that if something is useful to one person it will be useful to others. That is to say, it is likely it could be exchanged or sold. There is therefore a strong presumption that if something has use-value in a culture, it also has exchange-value. This certainly seems to be the case with housework.

Marx also showed the error of the other idea which is implicit in much of the literature we have been considering (as well as in everyday ideas about all types of work, and especially domestic work), namely that whoever produces things necessarily owns them and receives whatever value they may have. But it is absolutely not true that things necessarily belong to the person who produced them (see chapter 2 pp. 37–44). They can be 'stolen' from him or her, and the producer may receive little or none of the value the thing he or she produces has within the society. Marx demonstrated this predominantly in regard to the exploitation of those in waged employment. He showed that the workers do not own the goods they produce; but rather the goods belong to the owner of the factory or mine or farm (that is, to the owner of the productive property / the means of production). Marx himself gave little attention to domestic work, but we believe housework is further proof of the importance of his ideas in understanding the nature of forms of exploitation – in this case, the exploitation of women. Family relationships cannot be understood until it is recognized that wives (and other dependants) do not own what they produce within the family, but rather these products belong to their husband / the head of the household.

To summarize what has emerged from this consideration of the errors embedded in the existing literature on what is supposedly special about housework:

- Within the family-based household, women, men and children produce economic resources.
- These goods and services are useful (they have use-value) and are part of a continuous process of creating and transforming raw materials into consumable forms, and of personally and emotionally servicing people.
- They are also potentially exchangeable (they have exchange-value).
- The desired form of consumption and the desired quantity of cash, together with prevailing market circumstances, determine what is put on the market and what is done within the household itself. Overall nowadays, however, women do much more of the work which does not pass through the market, or whose products do not pass through the market, than do men.
- This production of resources within the household is not a question of specific tasks being performed or specific goods and services being produced in all households. Rather it is a question of instances of a common social institution, family households, maximizing resources and satisfying their own perceived needs. There is in fact a lot of variation from one household to another, especially as between town and country and by class and occupation (see chapters 7, 8 and 9).

Which work for self-consumption in households is considered productive (and which non-productive)?

If we leave theoretical work which sees housework as different and special, and look at the limited amount of empirical work which has been done on production for consumption within households, it becomes clear that past researchers have not been consistent in their approaches to it. They have neither considered all work for household consumption productive, nor all of it unproductive. Instead they have tried to take a curious middle line – which is illogical but, as it turns out, very revealing.

For instance, some economists are now prepared to accept in principle that housework should be included in estimates of the GNP, although, since they claim there are insuperable difficulties to assessing how much domestic production is done and what it is worth, most in practice still leave it out. But they do not leave all of it out. They include some and exclude most – but they give no rationale for their choices.

However, if we look at which goods and services they choose to include and which to exclude, and at the estimates they are prepared to make in some areas but not in others, we can get a clear insight into their implicit ideas about housework. We can also draw similarly on the working definitions used by sociologists when they try to differentiate between different types of work. Both help us to develop our own (formal) definition of housework.

What household work do economists consider productive (and hence what do they see as non-productive)?

As we said earlier, the main place where the national account feels it *has* to deal with the issue of products produced and self-consumed by families is with small farmers (though households in other sectors, for example, those of small shopkeepers, are also recognized to consume some of their stock rather than selling it). Since food produced and consumed on farms is non-market by definition (that is, it has not been the object of exchange), it has no agreed value. So if economists are to include it in the GNP, they have to attribute it a price.[20]

The very reasons why economists want to include this production within the GNP provides them with two, a priori equally legitimate, alternative estimates.

* They can assess what the family could have sold the produce for if they had not used it themselves (that is, they can estimate the selling price; the money forgone by the family business).
* Or they can assess what the family world have had to pay for the food, etc., if they had had to buy it (that is, they can estimate the retail price; the money saved by the family purse).

Either of these values is legitimate – but they are very different. The price a pig, for example, fetches at market is much less than the cost of a comparable quantity of pork, bacon and sausages in a butcher's shop. Britain chooses to calculate the loss of earnings to the farm by not selling the pig, while France since 1963 has chosen to calculate the saving on expenditure by not buying the meat (that is, the higher value). According to some, the latter solution has drawbacks because,

> it is the production price which represents the cost of the consumption in question . . . because commodities consumed on the farm do not carry the expense of transport, the profit margins of intermediaries and the taxes which are included in the retail price . . . Evaluation at the retail price therefore . . . includes the value of services which have not been produced . . . [though] it is true that [farms and their households] do fulfil for themselves some functions of transforming agricultural products. (Marczewski 1976)

We are relieved this expert chose to make some qualification to his statement in the last lines, because if he had stuck to his first position – that we should use the production price of goods because small farms perform no transformations on agricultural products – we would have had to assume that farm families consume the same products as they sell. That is to say, that they eat cabbages unwashed and uncooked and pigs that are still running around on all fours.

In France, therefore, at least some of the work needed to transform agricultural products into consumable food on farms is accounted. But only some. If the produce is valued at its retail price, it means that at least it is accepted that animals are killed, skinned and jointed, and meat stored till it is needed. But even the French accounting stops there, well before the food is edible. The final stages, the cooking, serving and clearing up, are excluded. So we must again assume such families have odd eating habits: they eat raw meat directly from the freezer. Similarly, government economists would have us believe urban households eat raw potatoes in greengrocers' shops, for they do not take account of shopping, storing, cooking, etc., in the GNP.

If we feel this does not fit with our everyday observations, then we have to accept it is economists who are somewhat arbitrary. They see some work and certain jobs as important contributions to the national wealth, which need to be included in national accounts, whilst other work apparently is not important and can be overlooked.

The question is surely why they stop where they do – at the point where households might (and frequently do) buy goods in the shops. Why not use the price charged for food in restaurants? It seems obvious the answer is because the work thus excluded – the transformations not counted in farming households, where production for self-consumption *is* recognized – is precisely the work which is not counted in any other household either. Virtually only farming households raise chickens and kill them, but all households cook them. *All* households perform the final productive activities needed for their own consumption; and the GNP *always* ignores this significant quantity of work.

Why they make this arbitrary omission can be gleaned by looking at how other studies approach a parallel problem: what work done by wives is, and what is not, 'housework'.

What work do sociologists separate out as 'housework'
(hence what do they see as non-housework)?

Time-budget studies of married women try to distinguish 'housework' from 'occupational work' even when wives work alongside their husbands in family enterprises. In other words, they follow the same categorizations as we noted in the previous section – though more explicitly than the economists since most sociologists actually note how difficult it is to make the distinction and they underline the way in which the two sets of work overlap in practice.[21]

But why should they want to make the distinction in the first place? What is the difference between 'housework' and 'occupational work' for such women? What criteria require or allow the work of, for example, a farmer's wife to be theoretically constructed as being of two different sorts? How are they separated out in actual sociological fieldwork practice (in the construction of questionnaires and when the interviewer fits the answers given into the boxes on the form)?

Tasks related to domestic, sexual, affectual and occupational work for husbands overlap concretely for wives. They may move from one to another within each and every hour and within the same geographical space. There is no difference of *work relationship* between 'housework' and all the other work wives do for their husbands which is specific to the particular relationship (that is, which varies with the husband's occupation and his individual needs). Nor, excepting sexual and reproductive work, is there a difference between the work done by wives and that done by other family members who work for their fathers or brothers (see later chapters).

The reason time-budget researchers want to make the distinction, and the distinguishing criteria they use, derive from a concern to distinguish between 'the farm holding' and 'the farm house'. That is, they see the opposition developed in the nineteenth century between the family business and the family household, or more generally between public and the private spheres, as being relevant to contemporary farms. (Or rather they try to apply the opposition to the farm enterprise as a whole.)

What is notable here is that these researchers construct as 'occupational' the same productive activities (for the market and for self-consumption) as are included in the GNP by economists. They account and call 'occupational' or 'farming-related' all the production by family members which takes place in the fields and barns and in the house – except what is called 'housework'. Housework itself is therefore only defined implicitly and in opposition to (or rather by subtraction from) occupational work. Housework is 'that which is not occupational work'. The reasoning is remarkably circular, and not surprisingly produces a theoretical impasse.

Occupational work and housework are certainly related to each other, but in the absence of definitions, they are related as empirical objects (as different lists of tasks), not as concepts. If they are opposed (that is, if they are mutually exclusive as currently empirically defined), it is not in the economic logic from which they are supposed to derive, but in an implicit logic which we still need to unearth.

To do this we need to look again at the empirical situation and practice. We then see that researchers call certain operations 'housework' which on the official (economic) level are no different from other operations performed by the wives of small businessmen or farmers which the same researchers label 'occupational'. The only thing distinguishing the first from the second is that the former are also performed in families without businesses and in non-farming families. All wives clean the sitting room, balance the weekly budget and may feed domestic animals. Only the wife of a baker cleans the shop; only the wife of a farmer does a farm's accounts and feeds farm animals. In other words, the operations called 'housework' are those which are not specific to agriculture or family businesses in general. They are done elsewhere as well. And they are usually done by women. Thus housework is what is not specific to family enterprises' production for consumption. **Housework is what is common to all households' production for self-consumption; and it is nowadays nearly always done by a particular female member of the family.**

This gives us the key to the mystery of why economists take account of some production and not other. The real definition of the 'production for self-consumption' which is included in the French GNP, the one which underlies and is implicit in its reasoning, is '*all* self-consumed agricultural production *less* the self-consumed production common to all households, rural and urban'. Or alternatively, '*all* production *over and above* the production for self-consumption common to all households'.

It might of course be argued that this definitional problem of what is housework and what occupational work, and the related arbitrary cut-off between work for consumption and production, merely shows that researchers are improperly applying urban (or industrial or capitalist) criteria to farming households. That is to say, that in towns, or in predominantly industrial or capitalist societies, or indeed in non-subsistence farming, production is what is done outside the family and household, and that everything done inside the home is for consumption (and therefore is not productive and not for exchange), but that is cannot be extended to (subsistence) farming because here the division is arbitrary and invalid.

However, the problem is in fact far greater than simply one of making urban industrial accounting categories adequate for subsistence farming, for these categories are no more valid in the urban industrial situation than they are in our rural examples. For as we have shown, although the prototypical urban household, with a male industrial wage earner and a dependent wife, is deemed to be unproductive, in fact such households are just as productive as farming households. Both supply (even on present inadequate measurements) hours and hours of productive activity each week towards the final goal of consumption. (Recall that more time is devoted to unpaid materially productive work than to paid work each year.)

In other words, the reason why housework is treated as a specific entity in everyday thinking, why statisticians try to separate it out from other work, and why it is not included in the GNP, cannot be explained by the economic theory which is overtly referred to. We need to go on looking for the theory which underlies the categorizations which are actually practised. This theory is equally economic, but refers not to the distinction between production and consumption, or between housework and occupational work, but rather to who does the work, for whom, and under what circumstances, that is, it concerns relations of production.

The only economic characteristics which distinguish housework from occupational work are that the former is done in all households by women and characteristically without payment. It is only exchanged in the 'usual manner of work' – that is, for wages – when it is done for someone who is not a relative.

This does not mean that occupational work is always paid. On the contrary, as we shall stress in chapters 8 and 9, if family members do farm work, or work in a family business of whatever kind, they generally do it (and wives always do it) in the same conditions of non-remuneration as housework – unless of course they are formally paid or given an official job category such as that of company secretary so as to claim money from the government or for tax purposes.[22]

It means, rather, that government economists and others

1   take it as a basic postulate that housework (a set of tasks done in the home by women) is unpaid; and
2   use (implicitly) as a criterion of distinction the generality of this unpaidness.

That is to say, they assume that a certain minimum of tasks will be performed unpaid within *all* family households, and they take these for granted. Other goods and services produced (unpaid) for self-consumption in only *some* households may, however, actually be seen, and accounted. Who does the work, and within what sort of relationship, is the clue to its visibility.

Before finally tying together the points we have been outlining, we need to consider further what we mean by 'unpaid'. We must answer our earlier question as to whether all work done within the home, and specifically whether all housework, is 'unpaid'.

Is all work done within the home 'unpaid'?

If we hold that the main characteristic of housework is its unpaidness, it might be objected that this is not specific to the work done within the home by wives, but applies equally to all work which individuals do for their families or for their own consumption. A husband doing the gardening or mending the car, a wife washing-up or putting a child to bed, a widow cleaning her windows, and a bachelor sewing on his shirt buttons, might all seem to have something in common. This has certainly led some people to conclude that all housework is unpaid, and, further, that it is improper that it should not be paid. The campaigners around Wages for Housework in particular have been vociferous in claiming that since housework is productive labour and necessary to the continuation of society as we know it / to capitalism, it should be paid for by the state.

We think that stressing the commonality of such situations, and the demand for wages for housework, all involve a fundamental mistake in defining housework as a set of particular tasks. As a result they include within their definition of 'unpaid housework' services which people do for themselves; whereas we stress that the only work which is 'unpaid' is work done within particular social relations. **We restrict the term 'unpaid work' to work which not only receives no payment, but also is done for someone else. Far from being a set of tasks, unpaid work is any work done within a particular set of social relations.**

To illustrate this, let us suppose that certain individuals (men or women) living on their own bake their own bread. If they do not eat a particular batch of loaves, they can sell them; and if they do not bake on a particular week, they will have to buy bread. To suggest that they should be paid for baking their own bread (that is, that it should be called unpaid labour if they are not paid for doing it) is obviously silly. They clearly remunerate themselves. If they did not bake their own bread, the baking would certainly have to be paid for – but it would be the individuals concerned who would have to pay, and a baker who would be paid. If they make their own, they have already collected the price of the baking by their industry.

The value of such home baking could legitimately be added to the GNP if its incidence was assessed. (Loaves are actually baked, and the fact that the producers consume them almost immediately does not detract from the fact that the value of x loaves of bread has been added to the overall national wealth.) Nor is there any reason not to add the value of the bread to the assessment of the overall income of the individuals, since they have profited from it. (Whether they eat it or sell it, they are richer by a loaf – though of course there are problems in assessing the value of the loaves, as we said above.)

It is therefore a mistake to suggest that because an individual is not paid in money, he or she has done unpaid work. In our example, people are remunerated for their bread-making by saving the cost of the baker or by consuming an extra loaf. They may be seen as well or as badly remunerated if we choose to calculate the monetary saving they have made against the time they spend. And we would not want to restrict the argument merely to money anyway, but also take into account such things as the quality of the bread, the satisfaction (or tedium) felt in making one's own bread, home baking as a source of status (or sign of poverty), etc. But in any case it would be absurd to pay people from an outside source for doing work for themselves. The work would then be remunerated twice over.

This argument applies to all the goods and services people produce for themselves. The work involved is productive and should be recognized as such, but since they then consume the product, often in the very act of producing it (for example, in the care they provide for their own bodies), the individuals concerned are remunerated. To argue otherwise implies starting to pay people for cleaning their own teeth. The only work we would want to call 'unpaid' is work which receives no money and no remuneration either, because someone else appropriates the labour. By appropriation we mean that the labour is owned by / belongs to someone other than the worker, that someone else has a monopoly on it. Hence the worker is not free to decide what shall be done with it, nor to sell it to whomever she / he wishes.[23]

We can now start to be more specific about what is involved in describing housework as 'unpaid'. We see cooking or cleaning done by single people for themselves, or by heads of households for their own dependants, as carrying its own remuneration; but we see work done within the family by those other than the head of the household as done for him and therefore as strictly 'unpaid'. As wives, women work 'for the family' from a different position from husbands. Men who are heads of households work for their families. Women (as wives or daughters or sisters) work as members of their husbands' (or fathers' or brothers') households. (We will discuss the position of women who are heads of their own households in the next chapter.)

Women who live with men thus not only do more work in the home than men, their work is also qualitatively different from men's. Men work on their cars and houses and gardens, or in their family businesses and have rights over profits. Wives work for the household / family of which their husband is head. In short, for him. A wife shops 'for the household / family' (*his* household / family) and cooks for everyone he 'maintains' (that is, he gives her money and she buys, carries, processes and serves the food they all eat). But it is he who is 'the breadwinner', he who is responsible for supporting them all. They are his dependants. She cares for 'their' children, who take his name – as generally does she.

Thus if full-time employed men and women want to get domestic work done for them, they typically get it done under quite different sets of social relations. Employed men get it done as unpaid family labour by a wife. Women get it as paid labour by a servant (though people fight shy of the word today and prefer the more specialized 'nanny' or 'childminder' or 'cleaner'). Men's need to support a wife is a culturally acceptable reason for seeking high pay and being ambitious; women's need (even single mothers' need) for nannies is not. And if men and women actually buy child-minding or domestic work, they buy it in very different capacities. Those men who do buy it, buy it for themselves (because they have no woman to do it for them unpaid). Whereas most women who buy it do so either as their husband's delegate and domestic manager (if he covers the costs), or to replace the work they themselves are supposed to do (if they buy it out of their earnings).

Putting this stress on the differential structural position of heads of households and dependants (generally husbands and wives, though it can equally apply to daughters housekeeping for their fathers, or a sister for a brother, etc.) is, we know, quite a departure from the way middle class radicals like to look at family relationships and household structures. People, even feminists, are often uncomfortable with it and seek to deny it,[24] claiming that whatever it may have been like in the past, things have changed. They want to see marriage (or at least contemporary western middle class marriage) and cohabitation, and especially their own marriages (or living situations or heterosexual relations), as voluntary agreements arrived at between equal and complementary partners. Or alternatively they avoid facing unpalatable facts by attributing the family division of labour entirely to external factors, arguing, for instance, that although they accept that in the end it is generally women who stay at home to look after children, this is because men can earn more, so it is a rational choice (that is, not the couple's personal choice) to follow the traditional masculine / feminine divide.

A focus on choice and community is, as we noted in chapter 1, part of the ideology which sustains and reproduces marriage and family relations, and it leads many to overlook the regularities of the sexual division of labour and power relations within (even middle class radical) households. The 'naturalness' of the heterosexuality which leads to it being always 'one man and one woman' who 'voluntarily' form couples, and why it should be that the labour market continues to pay men so much more than women, is either not questioned or seen as inevitable. Many people also do not recognize the speciousness of the argument that it is 'generally' women who care for children. It is virtually always women who do the major part of household work in heterosexual couples. An Australian study found, for example, that only 3 per cent of fathers took on even an equal share of childcare with mothers; and almost no 'role swap' couples have ever been located in sociological studies, despite vigorous hunts for them.[25]

But even if some people overtly deny our analysis, at another level most in fact recognize the truth of what we are saying. For although they may argue that men do not have that much power over their wives and children, the very form of denial recognizes that they do have *some*. And even if writers start by speaking of spouses as equal partners, two or three pages further on they will be found referring to men 'heading their families'. Or they may contrast (and thereby implicitly also compare) family workers to wage workers, and in so doing show that they intuitively see heads of households as at least petty capitalists, and dependants as experiencing something approaching proletarian exploitation. Also the fact that they do not compare housewives to self-employed workers shows that they take for granted that family workers do not own the houses or businesses they work in or the tools they use or the products they make or the bodies or the labour of the people they service.

Protest as intellectuals may, and for whatever reason, the fact remains (as we said in chapter 1) that the great majority of domestic groups consist of people recruited by kinship or marriage to the man who is its head; and kinship and marital relationships are gendered and / or generational, and hierarchical. The law may have been changed so that ex-spouses have, formally, equal responsibility to maintain each other after divorce; and the government census may no longer insist that a husband / father if present is automatically taken to be the head of the household. Indeed it may be so liberal as actually to allow a woman, or more than one person, to be recorded as the head of household if respondents insist.[26] But these changes have not actually affected most people's practice. Most households have one head, properly and usually a man, and he maintains its members. His dependants work for the general good of the group under his (hopefully benevolent) direction, and owe him love, respect, obedience – and various kinds of labour.

Conclusion

Housework is performed in all households. Most households are family based. Most housework is performed within families, unpaid, by women, for their household head (their husband, or sometimes their father or brother). This is obvious, but it still gets forgotten. Consequently when people started to look at housework in the early 1970s, they tried, unfortunately, to use technical aspects of the tasks to explain social relations, rather than starting with the social relations as the basis for explaining what is done, where and by whom.

It is of course legitimate and interesting to study certain tasks (for example, brewing or laundry or childcare) which are, or were, done within the home, so as to compare domestic and industrial techniques or changes over time, and to look at how technological developments and social relations have interacted. It is also important to collect information to contrast the practices and the perceived needs of family members in various social classes. But if we want to discuss the characteristics of housework, we need a formal definition. To talk of the 'structural characteristics' or the 'political economy' of housework while continuing to define it as a list of tasks, is a contradiction in terms. The inadequate definition of housework (or rather the constant confusion between its common definition and the more formal study of the relations of production within which these tasks are typically done) has greatly hindered our understanding of house*wives*.

In this chapter we have looked at various attempts to define what it is that is special about housework and about women's work. Although we have suggested flaws and problems with all these attempts, including the way they elide housework and women's work, they have helped to make a number of points clear.

First they have shown that if we want to explain, or at least to begin to understand, the unpaid nature of the work done within the home by women, then all unpaid work must be taken into account and not just housework; and we must define what we mean by 'unpaid'.

Work can be classified as follows:

- exchangeable and paid (for example, a baker baking bread),
- exchangeable but unpaid, though with a return (for example, baking bread for oneself),
- exchangeable but unpaid and unremunerated, that is, strictly 'unpaid' (for example, a family dependant working for the head of the family in the family bakery),

Our concern is with all family production, all 'strictly unpaid' work, not just the unpaid work for consumption done by women which is recognized as common to all families / households (that is, not just housework).

Secondly, the problems encountered in previous discussions of housework show the importance of distinguishing work done by various family members in terms of the status they have within the family. That is to say, the work done *by* the head of household must be distinguished from the work (all the work) done *for* him (or occasionally for her) by others.

With this clarification the boundaries of what we are studying can be theoretically delimited. Otherwise they are set empirically and so follow the 'obvious' (mystifying) divisions of the culture.

Since the relations of production characteristic of housework (that is, unpaid work, done in the home, by women) are not in fact restricted to the commonly agreed list of tasks of housework (cooking, cleaning, etc.), but also characterize other tasks and work done by dependants (whether it be caring for poultry, giving parties, taking children to sports or clinics, or having to spend inordinate amounts of time sitting and listening to the things the head of household wants to grumble about over and over again), we need some new terminology.

We propose using the term **housework for just the composite of regular day-to-day tasks which are judged necessary to maintain a home in contemporary western society** and which are nowadays done mainly by women as wives – though some are done by male or child members of the household or by servants. We propose to use in addition the term **household work to cover all the work done within family household units. This includes, but is certainly not restricted to, housework alone.** It also covers emotional and sexual servicing, procreative work, and frequently the production of goods and services which are not for self-consumption but rather for exchange on the market.

In addition we separate out and distinguish as **family work, all the unpaid work done by dependants, to emphasize that the relations within which the work is done are those of dependency and that people are recruited (obliged) to do this work by kinship and marital relationships.**[27] Household work is 'unpaid' when done by family dependants, but carries its own remuneration when done by a head of household or a single person for themselves.

Since our concern in this book is the situation of women, our focus is principally on the appropriation of the work of daughters, wives and mothers within family relations of production, though we also look briefly at the appropriation of various male dependants' labour. In the next chapter we shall lay out the formulation of family economics which we find best explains contemporary western domestic life. (We hope it may be helpful in understanding domestic relations elsewhere in the world – but do not feel qualified to judge this.) We focus on family work relations and recognize adult male dominance in domestic and lineal family relations – as we must if we are to understand the nature of gender and generational relations in our society.

Of course, we also recognize that adult men's power and responsibility within the family is not unlimited. They have duties to their dependants which they may experience as onerous, and women (and children) resist men's domination and make the best of their situation in various ways. Men (sometimes) have to struggle to maintain their position, but that is not to say that a patriarchal hierarchy does not exist and is not being continued.

Notes

1   For reviews of first wave feminists' concern with housework, see particularly Davidoff (1976), Hayden (1981) and Dyhouse (1989).

   Important work on housework published earlier this century by feminists includes Perkins Gilman (1903; 1966), C. Hamilton (1912), Bernard (1949), Komarovsky (1962) and Michel (1959; 1960). See the review article by Glazer-Malbin (1976).

2   The main time-budget studies were those funded in the USA by the Federal Government in the 1920s, 1930s, 1950s, 1960s and 1970s; and in France and Scandinavia in the late 1940s and 1950s and now ten-yearly. A big cross-national survey in the 1960s was co-ordinated by Szalai (1972). For recent work in France see Grimler and Roy (1987).

Useful reviews and contributions to such work are to be found in Vanek (1974), Walker (1978), Michel (1978), Oakley (1974b) and Robinson (1977).

British studies, which are not strictly comparable, are those of Moser (1950), Mass Observation (1957), Young and Willmott (1973) and Oakley (1974a). Young and Willmott's book contains an appendix on the methodological problems of time-budgets by Mills.

3   An earlier work by Juliet Mitchell, 'Women: the longest revolution' (1966), which was widely read in the women's movement, is notable for how little attention it gives to housework, as other authors have pointed out. It is not one of the four structures (reproduction, production (within capitalist relations of production), sexuality and socialization) on which she focuses (see Glazer-Malbin 1976: 916); nor does she give much emphasis to economic factors overall. Instead Mitchell moves swiftly to 'superstructural' features to explain women's oppression (see Benston 1970: 282).

4   Examples of work which focus on the 'use of housework to capitalism' include Galbraith (1974), Gardiner et al. (1976), Weinbaum and Bridges (1976), Gardiner (1976), Hartmann (1979; 1981), Barrett and McIntosh (1980), Chabaud and Fougeyrollas (1984) and many of the articles in Kuhn and Wolpe (1978), Malos (1980) and Sargent (1981).

5   Examples of work suggesting housework is unproductive and unpaid because it is only for use, include Benston (1969), Larguia (1970), Coulson, Wainwright and Magas (1975), Gardiner et al. (1975) and Adamson et al. (1976).

6   Examples of attempts to assess the monetary value of housework are given in Glazer-Malbin (1976), and include Clark (1958), Walker and Gauger (1973) and Pyun (1972). See also Waerness (1978), Chadeau and Fouquet (1981) and Chadeau (1985). Examples of newspaper reports of legal cases in the USA include Van Gelder (1979) and Stephen (1980).

7   Examples of work on domestic technology and the changing components of housework include Oakley (1974a), Young and Willmott (1973), Hartmann (1974), Strasser (1982), Bose (1979 – which has a good bibliography), Kittler (1980), Schwartz Cowan (1983), Davidson (1982), R. Pahl (1984) and Freudenthal (1986).

8   Examples of studies of the influence of wives' employment on housework include Strober (1977) and Morris (1990); and examples of life-cycle changes in housework include Lopata (1971), Stafford, Backman and Dibona (1977), Pleck (1977), Robinson (1977), Berk and Berk (1979) and Berk (1980; 1985).

9   For instance what 'being a housewife' means for a woman's self-identity, what satisfactions and frustrations are to be found in domestic labour, and the effects of the domestic division of labour on differences in women's and men's social and class consciousness. See, for example, Lopata (1971), Oakley (1974b) and Porter (1978a; 1978b; 1983).

10 Examples of work on domestic ideology and the separation of the world and the home include Laslett (1973), Davidoff (1976; 1979), Davidoff, L'Esperance and Newby (1976), Hall (1979), Davidoff and Hall (1987) and Strasser (1982). On endeavours to reintegrate the spheres, see Hayden (1981) and Wynn Allen (1988). On the hegemony of patriarchal systems, see Coward (1983).

11 Glazer-Malbin has pointed out (1976) that the list of tasks is, in fact, not highly specified. She asks, for example, if 'shopping' for groceries is recognized to include a review of newspaper ads, making up a shopping list, purchasing the groceries, putting them away while removing uneatables from the refrigerator and empty packets from the cupboards. Ruth Schwartz Cowan found it important to stress also, via her concept of 'housework process', that 'housework is a series not simply of definable tasks but of definable tasks that are necessarily linked to each other. [Thus] when we try to discover whether industrialization has made housework easier [we] must ask not only whether one activity has been altered, but also whether the chain in which that activity is a link has been transformed' (1983: 12).

For critiques of what is included (and what excluded) from lists of 'housework' tasks see Gillespie (1972), Michel (1978) and Eichler (1981).

12 In setting out to produce such a formal definition we know we may be accused of constructing a circular argument, because in order to identify the major characteristics of housework we have to consider the object we are studying from the point of view of its structural and economic characteristics, and the characteristics we attribute it at the start could be the ones we want to emerge at the end as its essential features. The best way out seems to us to be to take as our starting point only those characteristics of housework which are very generally agreed.

13 This idea was put forward by E. P. Thompson (1963: 416) and popularized by Young and Willmott (1973).

14 See, for example, Branca (1975) and Davidoff (1973a).

15 Albeit the productive / non-productive divide is different in marxist and neo-classical economics.

For marxists the dichotomy between productive and unproductive labour concerns whether or not surplus value is produced. It was central to the 1950s polemic of workerism and arguments around who could and should comprise the vanguard of the working class movement because their labour produced surplus value for capital. It re-emerged in the 1970s, via the work of Poulantzas (1975). Its influence continues within socialist feminist writings in the (re)current division between 'production' and 'reproduction' discussed in chapter 3.

Neo-classical economics has no category of unproductive labour as such. But only some production – broadly speaking only those goods and services that actually enter the market, and government and non-profit services provided free – is included in national and international accounts of production and income. Domestic labour and illegal activities, for instance, are beyond the UN's 'production boundary'. See Waring (1989) and Boss (1990).

16 See, for example, Weinbaum and Bridges (1976) and Game and Pringle (1984).

17 See Pahl (1984) and Chadeau and Roy (1986).

18 Vaugh (1976) quoted in Bose (1979).

19 Burns (1975) estimated that in 1965 in the US $300 billion worth of goods and services came from unaccounted household production for self-

consumption. And *The Times* in 1987 calculated its value as £12,000 a year in the UK at a time when men's median earnings were £13,000.

20 Why then can they not do this with domestic work too? Perhaps because the figures they would come up with are huge and therefore unbelievable. Women cannot possibly be *that* useful!

Glazer-Malbin points out that economists do seem, however, to be able to estimate the monetary value of housework when *men* require it – e.g. when they want to use it in legal disputes over the value of services men lose when wives leave for other men, or to suggest men should insure their wives, or to estimate the costs of women forgoing employment (Glazer-Malbin 1976). In addition the ultra neo-classical Chicago school, in its evaluations of the rationality of 'household' decision-making, routinely attributes shadow prices to household production. See especially Becker (1976; 1981).

21 See Bastide and Girard (1959), Allauzen (1967) and Becouarn (1979).

22 An instance of it being presumed that wives will work unpaid for their husbands, but that when money is available for the tasks they perform a lobby gets mounted to justify their being paid (to their husbands' advantage), can be seen in a long-running battle between the state and doctors in Britain.

General practitioners used to be allowed to employ a maximum of two staff and to claim 70 per cent government reimbursement for their salaries – but only if the staff were not relatives of the doctors. The only concession was an allowance of £1,000 for rural GPs employing their wives. Despite campaigns supported by the British Medical Association and the House of Lords, successive governments refused to extend the reimbursement to all wives – for fear of the costs and false claims. When in 1980 it was extended to all GPs, it applied only when doctors' wives were qualified and worked as nurses.

Members of Parliament, on the other hand, have long been free to use the secretarial allowances paid to them to pay their wives – or their mistresses.

23 See next chapter for further discussion of the concept of appropriation.

24 See for example Olivia Harris's lengthy misrepresentation of Christine Delphy (1981, reprinted in Beechey and Donald 1985).

25 The figures from Australia are from Russell (1983).

'Role reversal' usually refers simply to the woman becoming the main earner in the household, and the use of the term is seldom dependent on the man taking on most of the domestic tasks. In none of the cases documented is it an equitable situation, nor is it an easy one to live with.

For example, a couple interviewed by Pauline Hunt had 'chosen to role swap'. The wife was the 'breadwinner', and there was a 'minimal gender division of labour' in the home. But the woman did as much in the home as the man, on top of doing her paid work. So 'instead of being mutually beneficial their overall arrangement seems to be somewhat weighted in [his] favour' (P. Hunt 1980: 181).

Lydia Morris, in her study of the families of unemployed steelworkers (see chapter 7), showed that even among couples who accepted 'the greatest degree of flexibility' in the division of labour and who *regarded themselves* as having 'role swapped' (albeit temporarily), the woman 'in effect continued to run the house'. In addition, couples felt such arrangements were always 'necessarily ... in some sense stressful for one or both partners' (Morris 1985b: 229–32).

26 Thus, for example the French census terminology has changed in the last ten years and instead of a 'head of household' it names a 'person of reference' who can, in theory, be of either sex (references to the family law having been dropped). However, as ever, the instructions given to the interviewers specify that if there is a man in the household, he should be the person of reference.

27 In an earlier paper (Delphy 1978) we called it *domestic work* to emphasize it is carried out within the *domus*, the home, in the broadest sense. But 'domestic work' is sometimes used simply as a synonym for housework, and anyway some of the work in question is carried out outside the house. We therefore now prefer to use the term 'family work' to emphasize the nature of the relationship within which it is performed.

5

THE FAMILY AS AN ECONOMIC
SYSTEM: INTRODUCTION AND
COMMON MISCONCEPTIONS

Our analysis of the western family focuses upon the social relationships associated with its economic structure: upon the hierarchy of production, distribution and consumption of resources within family-based households and on the hierarchy of transmission of wealth between kin. It is a formal, macro-sociological approach, looking at the rules of kinship and marriage and laying out a model of the economic relationships which exist between family members at particular points in time (synchronic) and over time (diachronic). It is therefore in marked contrast to most writing on the contemporary western family which is overwhelmingly concerned with either interpersonal interactions and individual attitudes and feelings, or ideologies of the family and control by external agencies (such as the law and social security systems, or doctors and psychologists, etc.).

We are convinced we need first and foremost to take an overview of the family and to analyse it as a social institution with its own indigenous rules of organization. Once familial structures are recognized, particularly hierarchical work relationships, we can more fully understand how and why individual meanings and actions are established and how these act to reproduce the institution, and how and why outside agencies may seek to intervene and control individual family members.

We therefore give little attention in this book to the processes of family life, to how and why people behave as they do in terms of their individual understandings and motivation, or to state agencies concerned with the family. This is obviously a deliberate choice deriving from theoretical priorities. It certainly does not mean we are not interested in, still less that we are indifferent to, the experiences of individuals and the activities of the state. It was in fact concern for, and anger at, women's experiences within the family which gave rise to our work.[1] We seek rather to understand women's subordination in order to change it – in order to improve women's experiences. And understanding has to start further back than individuals' experiences or regulation by laws and state agents: it starts with material and ideological structures.

The socio-economic aspects of family-based households which concern us involve both their functioning at particular points in time and their interrelations with lines of descent over time.

1   We are concerned with *the family as a unit of consumption*. This is the most generally recognized material aspect of the family household. Virtually every author who deals with the family at least mentions it, and many describe it as *the* principal economic function of the modern western family.

2   We are also concerned with *the family as a unit of production*. This, as we have said in earlier chapters, is much less generally recognized as a feature of the contemporary western family household. Discussions tend to say that the family used to be important as a unit of production, and still is in the Third World, but that this function has virtually disappeared in the West. This is to damn with faint praise, because it suggests that consumption (which is accorded less importance than production) is all that remains of the once glorious past of the family, and that it is the only economic reason for the family's continuation. All other aspects of household functions are thereby deemed non-economic.

As is clear, we do not accept that the family is no longer productive: (a) because production for the market is still carried out within many families even in present-day western societies; and (b) because the term 'production' should not be restricted to the making of goods which are actually sold on the market. Goods and services produced by members for their own consumption are an integral part of a society's production, and families are therefore 'units of production' not only when they produce for the market, but also when they produce for themselves – as they do in all advanced industrial societies.

3   We are also concerned with a third material aspect of the family: the family as a mode of *accumulation and circulation of property*. This is the least discussed socio-economic aspect of the family, but every year, indeed everyday, an important part of the wealth of the country changes hands through inheritance or gifts made from one family member to another. (Leonore Weitzman's work leads us to add here the importance of inter-family / household arrangements on divorce, which now exceed in value exchanges at death (Weitzman 1985: xvii).)

Related to these familial transfers of property, social class position too is transmitted through the family.

Although the family involves these three types of economic activity, they are seldom taken into account in official economic calculations or studied by economics as a scientific discipline.[2] This is not really surprising because historically economics and official accounting (the calculation of the GNP and the United Nations System of Accounting, etc.) have been concerned almost exclusively with the study of the market and, in turn, have taken the viewpoint of the market. What interests the market, and hence economics, is not so much how or why goods are actually produced or consumed, but rather how goods are treated on the market. Most economists therefore consider the things families produce only if and when these things appear on the market; and they consider the things families consume only at the point when the things leave the market. What happens before that arrival or after that departure, or in the case of family property transmission, aside from the market, does not often concern them as specialists. From the point of view of the market, family households, for many intents and purposes, are just single entities.

Further, since the market is not of course strictly a place where things appear, exchange themselves and disappear, but rather the place where the present and future owners of things (or their delegates) make transactions, it is also not surprising nor unreasonable for economists to treat family households as units. Goods produced or consumed by a family household are put on the market and purchased by single actors. Therefore, from the viewpoint of the market, the family can be taken as a unit of supply and demand and be presented as a single actor, whether bringing things (goods, services, labour power) to the market or taking things from it, and regardless of which member of the family actually does the exchanging. From the point of view of the market it is quite acceptable to use such phrases as 'the family wage' or 'the housewife (doing the shopping)', since from outside the household the project *is* unitary.

Since the study of the market is obviously valid and extremely important in and of itself, the restricted interests of most economists would not matter were it not for two facts. First, both specialists and public often fall into the error of seeing the market as the only economic realm there is, and into equating the market with the productive realm. So people forget that economic negotiations, bargains, discussions and divisions, and production and consumption also occur upstream and downstream from the point which commands economists' attention. And second, as Marilyn Waring has pointed out (1989), since public policy is made on the basis of national statistics (and UN and World Bank policy on the basis of global statistics), the absence of non-market transactions from national accounts has very profound effects on the consideration given to women and children in policy decisions.

But the fact that the family can be treated as a unit of production or consumption or of property-holding for certain purposes does not mean that the family (in the sense of all its members) produce and consume and hold property together as a block, nor that all have the same economic status and identical interests (see chapter 1). Much of the production and consumption of family members is carried out by them as separate individuals and occurs outside the home, and most property is individually owned. The family is thus often only one place of production, one place of consumption, and one source of property and status among others for each of its members.

This is perhaps fairly generally recognized in regard to production and property, but it is much less recognized as regards consumption. It is usually far from clear when authors speak of the family household as 'a unit of consumption' whether they are referring to the total consumption of all the members wherever it takes place (home, work, school, restaurants, etc.); or just to that part of their consumption which takes place within the home, whoever is present. (For this reason we prefer for the moment to think of the family as a place where consumption occurs, rather than a unit of consumption.)[3]

But even if we restrict 'family production' and 'family consumption' to what is done or used by family members actually within the home (that is, within the house, garden and maybe workshop), these processes are not unitary. Production or consumption may sometimes be simultaneous (for example, with all family members working together in the same place at the same time, or sitting round a table sharing a meal) – though often it is not. But even so the work done or the goods consumed by the various members are not of the same nature nor of the same value. Even simultaneous work or consumption is not necessarily identical work or consumption. Different people working round a table may be doing different things, and one may be doing (what is held to be) the more important work and directing the work of the others.[4] And when a family shares a meal, each member does not consume the same things, nor the same amounts, nor in the same way.

This last point, the difference in the quality of consumption of family members, is particularly important because it involves some of the most crucial differences between family labour relations and market labour relations. In the labour market, workers are paid a wage by their employer, but in the family-based household, members are maintained by its head. This means dependants have less choice as to what they get than if they were given money. What is provided for them is what is favoured (or at least agreed to) by the head. In addition, since much of what family members produce is consumed within the family, this in itself prevents goods and services consumed in the family being the same for all members. For example, when the husband and children consume meals served by the wife, she provides the services, so she cannot consume them in the same way as they do: as work done by someone else. She cannot both wait and be waited on. Hence there are real problems in treating the family as a 'unit of consumption' in any analysis.

Property 'belonging to the family' is also not held equally or similarly by all members of the family. The title to land, buildings, shares and goods, etc., is generally held by individuals, and even when it is held in some sort of trust, it is managed by individuals. When 'a family' owns a business or has a certain socio-economic / occupational status, 'the family' is not the association or the responsible body. One individual (or occasionally a partnership of father and son, or husband and wife – though then generally for tax purposes) represents and constitutes the firm in law and practice. He (or the formal partnership, which he manages) holds the lease on farmland or shop, or the licence to trade or manufacture; and he (or the legal entity) owns the products from the farm or firm, even if it is a 'family farm' or a 'family firm' and other family members work on / in it. (Their labour is assimilated, added, to that of the head so that it looks as if it is all his own.)

Even more unequivocally, 'the family wage' earned by the breadwinner is his and his alone. He is the sole owner of his labour power and the money he earns from its sale, even if other family members contribute towards his maintenance and well-being (that is, to his ability to have labour to sell). This does not apply to wages earned by young adult members of a family household, nor to money earned by wives. Dependants' rights to 'their money' are much more contingent, as we shall show. In addition, different members of a family have different amounts of 'family capital' invested in them, particularly through their education, which means they have different skills and experiences which they sell on the labour market – as individuals.

Holding property, or having income-earning skills, gives power and advantages – even when the holder is bound (by law or custom) to give certain things to certain people at certain times (for example, to maintain children or to pass property down the line when s/he dies). In any case, law and custom in our cultures actually allow property holders considerable latitude concerning whom they give what to and when, so property holders / owners are in fact not actually particularly constrained.

When 'family property' (held by one person) is transmitted to another individual, this transfer is not treated by the everyday culture as an 'economic' transaction, but rather as falling squarely within the realm of family law: of prescription or choice, not contract. This makes its economic aspect disappear, because the ways in which goods are attributed in the family mode of circulation are seen to derive exclusively from 'personal relationships' and these are posited as different in kind from, and independent of, 'economic' (read: impersonal, contractual, exchange) relationships. Thus the way in which inheritance is conceived serves, like the concept of the family as a unit, not only to mask economic relations within the family, but to deny the very possibility of the existence of such relations.

In a similar way sociologists who study the family have also de-economized it by treating relations of production, consumption and transmission as just elements integrated into and determined by a form of interaction between people which is essentially non-economic in character. Housework, for example, is seen as a vocation, a proof of love, a character trait, or even as a hobby – any and everything except production. For such sociologists (mainly American-inspired), the concept of 'role' plays much the same part as the concept of 'unit' plays for economics. It masks not only material relations within the family, but also the very possibility of the existence of such relations. It makes the roles of husband and wife seem complementary or entirely emotional, and never opposed and economic, with one exploiting the other. It makes one's role, one's given place in a family household, seem like fate: beyond politics or judgement.

This overlooking of economic activities within the family by various sorts of officials and intellectuals doubtless has its origins in, and is perpetuated by, the resistance of the culture as a whole to seeing family relationships as in any way calculative, unfeeling or structurally ordered (these being regarded as the characteristics of 'economic' or 'work' relations). As we said in chapter 1, to discuss the economics of the family – the work, consumption or property holding therein – is viewed by many as undesirable, as bringing to light things which merely invite discord because they show oppositions of interest between individuals – between calculative family members. This is seen as harmful in itself and also incorrect because it misses the whole point of the family.

We clearly do not accept most of this criticism. As we have now argued from various angles, to understand and change the disadvantaged position of women we must look at the different interests, in particular the different material interests (that is, those related to work and the distribution of wealth and management of resources), of different members of the family.

But there would be a certain amount of truth in the comment about missing the whole point of the family if what we were doing was suggesting that the family unit reproduced within itself merely the same sort of (impersonal, calculative) transactions as are effected in the market sector of society, though on a smaller scale: that is, if our critique consisted in bringing to light just another level of (instrumental, exchange) relationships. However, the opposite is the case. As we said in chapter 1, we want to emphasize that although the market system and the family system are both economic, they are different, though both are gendered. There are structural characteristics which we believe to be common to family production, consumption, and transmission of property and status which unite them, and which make them very different from production, consumption and transmission in the labour and commodity markets.

We suspect, however, that the sub-text of many of those who say that the family is quite different from the market or that to look at the economics of the family is to miss its whole point, is that the family is the opposite of the market in the sense of being a haven of free choice, equality and selflessness: that relationships within it are not structured and exploitative. Here we definitely part company with other authors, for we believe **family relationships are essentially hierarchical and comprise an exploitative system** – but a system with a structure and a process very different from that of the (also but differently exploitative) market system. Women are oppressed and exploited in both – but differently, and the two forms of inequality interact. What is novel about our approach is that we do not say just what family relationships are *not* like: how they are different from (rotten old) wage labour. We also explore the real nature of family relationships – and some of this is less palatable, since the other novel aspect of our approach is its recognition of hierarchy and exploitation *inside* the family (that family life is perhaps no better than rotten old capitalism – even if it is different from it).

In the next section we shall summarize the structural characteristics of the family as an economic system, and then develop this outline by discussing some misinterpretations of these ideas. We shall go on to develop a fuller account of the family system in chapter 6.

The characteristics of the family as an economic system

The points we have been developing in previous chapters show the chief economic characteristics of the family to be as follows:

1   Each family-based household typically consists of a head and his dependants / helpers. The latter are limited in number and who they are is regulated by kinship and marriage. Or, putting it the other way round, kinship and marriage are the idiom within which family (household) work relationships are located.

2   Within such households, subordinate members work unpaid for the head, and should receive maintenance from him during his lifetime and a specific share of the family property when he dies. (That is, a family consists of gendered and generational labour relationships.)

3   The obligation to do work within family households is prescribed, especially by sex and marital status. That is, family dependants, and especially female dependants, must do unpaid family work; and wives must also do sexual and reproductive work.
   The actual tasks done and the rewards received vary greatly, however, from one family to another. Jobs and inheritance are attributed on the basis of the dependants' status within the family, and they also depend on how wealthy the head is and on his personal choice. They do not depend on the ability or needs of the dependants (again particularly in relation to women).

4   Dependants' maintenance (and inheritance) is not handed out in exchange for the work they do – as a wage to which their work entitles them. It is rather a duty of their family head. He is obliged to provide for their basic needs. But he may give them a good deal more than this if he

is able to and if he chooses to. On the other hand, he is obliged to support them even if they are sick or disabled and unable to work, or if they refuse to work.

The level of maintenance dependants receive is, in turn, also independent of the work they do. They must work for their household head and respect him whether he is generous or mean and whether he earns a huge salary or a pittance. Thus, for instance, a wife looking after a home and three children receives a much higher standard of living if she is married to a mine owner than if she is married to a miner. And the family of a miner who is 'home-centred' has a better time than the family of one who keeps a lot of pocket money for himself to spend on his hobbies or beer or gambling or a mistress. But whatever the maintenance provided, wives are always obliged to do family work.

5   Since the characteristic feature of familial production is that subordinates owe work to their head and he owes them maintenance (including education and training), we cannot study the relations of production within the family, the way in which work is extracted and rewarded, without at the same time studying relations of consumption and transmission of wealth. The specificity of the family mode lies precisely in the form of remuneration for work: the fact that the workers are not paid in money but rewarded in kind.

6   There is no formal exchange and usually no bargaining between head and dependants. (Payment is contractual, reward is discretionary.) Since it is a relationship of personal dependence, dependants must be careful to keep on good terms with their head. Wives and children have to study their husbands and fathers closely and handle them carefully so as to keep them sweet. Conversely, of course, husbands – like other managers – experience various difficulties in managing and motivating their workers / dependants, who often resist and manoeuvre in variety of ways. Husbands may well get the best out of their dependants if they manage 'loosely' and foster their subordinates' feelings of affection for them.

7   The head of the family may have a near monopoly over, and he always has greater access to and control of, the family's property and external relations, particularly the transactions which take place on the market. These invest him with authority over the (monetary) resources of the family, and hence over its ongoing economic life.

8   Even when dependants have access to employment and could be seen as providing for their own upkeep, they (especially wives) are still obliged

to perform unpaid family work to the extent that it is needed. They must either do family work on top of their job, or replace their family services from their earnings. Their conditions of employment outside are therefore conditioned by their family obligations, and family obligations are used as a pretext by employers to exploit those with the status of family dependant.

9   Although the head of a family should be an adult man, it is possible for women to attain this status under certain circumstances. That is to say, it is a gendered not a gender-specific position. But so tight is the fit between gender and household status that in many languages the word for husband and man, and wife and woman, are the same, for example, *femme* in French and *mann* and *frau* in German. The social role (with specific rights and duties attached to it) is so widely associated with a biological sex (and vice versa) that they are synonymous.

The circumstances under which women can become household heads have varied with time, place and social class. Though single women and widows in the West have sometimes headed households (composed of other women, or women and children, or even including male lodgers and servants), if a male relative has been present, he has usually taken over as head of the household. Where a woman's husband has been present, even if the woman herself owns the house or is the major breadwinner, she is at least semi-subordinate, owing her husband respect and obedience and having responsibility for domestic (and sexual and emotional) labour. This is not to say that the position of a woman with property or a high earning capacity is not stronger than that of a woman who is totally economically dependent on her husband, but rather that there is variation within a common structural location.

Common confusions and clarifications

Even these basic characteristics of the material relations between family members have often been misunderstood, however. So before we go into further details we need to sort out some of the common arguments with which writers have sought to refute them.

Can we really say households should have, or typically do have male heads when nowadays so many are headed by women (especially in urban areas and in Black communities)?

While there is regrettably little historical information about the occasions when women have managed to head households in western societies in the past, their numbers have never been large and their social status has almost invariably been low (which is in part why they have been ignored).

Today there is certainly an increasing number of households headed by single mothers (and a tradition of such households among those of African Caribbean origin now resident in Europe); and an even more rapidly increasing number of elderly women, generally widowed, who could be said to head households because they live alone. It is also now possible, to a much greater extent than in the past, for employed, middle class, adult women to establish an independent household if they want to do so, since by law they no longer suffer disabilities in acquiring a mortgage or establishing any other sort of contract, and there is much less social stigma attached to their leaving their parents' household.

However, the total proportion of women who are heads of households is still small – only about one in ten in the active population (that is, aged between 16 and 60). Only one woman in twenty-five in this age group heads a household containing other adults (that is, children over 16 or other relatives or non-relatives). Even among African Caribbean women in Britain, less than half head households; and among Asian women in Britain there is a notably lower-than-average rate of woman-headed, single-parent and lone adult households; and conversely, quite a high rate of male-headed, patrilineal, extended family households.[5]

But women who *are* heads of households do have some patriarchal authority in their own right, though it is limited by the fact that they cannot have wives and rarely have other dependants who work for them. This authority is, however, generally achieved at the expense of a low (sometimes a very low) standard of living and long hours of work. Economic survival may be possible in a single adult or woman-headed household today, but a comfortable existence depends on having a particular size and structure of household – generally at least one 'male' wage, and preferably two incomes.

In addition, in many cases such women household heads' autonomy is actually limited, or illusory, since many non-married women (single, separated, divorced or widowed) are merely detached from, but still have labour appropriated by (male) beneficiaries who live elsewhere. These men may, but often do not, contribute to the women's upkeep. For example, sisters or sisters-in-law caring for elderly relatives on their own absolve their brothers or brothers-in-law of vast amounts of unremitting, unglamorous and unrecognized toil. While after divorce, or the ending of a relationship, the labour of ex-wives or former girlfriends often continues to be appropriated by their ex-husbands or lovers for childcare even when the marriage / relationship proper has been dissolved. Women (possibly helped by female relatives and friends) do unpaid work from which such men benefit if they choose to continue to have a relationship with their children. This happens even when the man does not maintain the woman and pays just a small sum for child support – confirming our point that the obligation to work and the obligation to maintain are independent and not exchanged.[6]

Is it fair to say that the obligation to do household work is prescribed on the basis of sex when men feel obliged to do it too?

We would be the first to agree (see chapter 4 p. 78) that most men do some household work. Our argument is, however, that very few men are obliged to do what we have specified is unpaid household work (that is, family work).

Housework, as we have suggested, is a particular set of tasks: the basic day-to-day work done in all households in western societies. These tasks are usually done by family dependants, mostly by women, and nowadays generally by a woman related to the head of the household by marriage (that is, his wife), but a female neighbour may exchange help for a short time (for example, if a wife is in hospital), or a daughter or sister or elderly aunt may take on housekeeping for a male relative / household head who is not married (and he may then in turn support her). Failing all of these, a male household head will either hire a 'daily woman' to do the housework, or simply do it himself.

There is, however, a clear order of responsibility to care for children, the sick and elderly which extends out to women in various degrees of relationship if there is no closely related woman conveniently available. It is only if there are no women at all available that such work gets undertaken by closely related men. The exception seems to be if a wife becomes disabled, when her husband commonly takes over caring for her, including doing the housework, especially if they have no daughters.[7]

That is to say, household tasks are gendered (that is, seen as more suitable for, more the responsibility of, and more likely to be done by women than by men – or vice versa) rather than their being rigorously divided into 'men's work' and 'women's work'. And what individual family members do always depends on what other family members there are who might also do the work.

But our point is rather that although men may do housework, or care for their wives, they do not do these things within the same relations of production as their wives (or other female kin) do them. Men remain the heads of households – so the work they do is not unpaid. In such instances they directly contribute work towards the maintenance of their dependant(s), instead of (as more usually happens) maintaining another family member or paying a servant who does it. In any case, if there is likely to be a lot of work involved, for example, if a man has small children, another female relative or a female employee – or maybe a new wife – is generally recruited. What is very rare indeed is for a male relative, for example, a brother, to do such work in return for upkeep, that is, to do unpaid domestic work: to do family work.

The obligation on women to do unpaid household work, to do particular tasks within a particular relationship, is created by kinship or marriage. It exists, but much less markedly, when men and women just share a household (for example, men and women students flat-sharing). It is strengthened by cohabitation (that is, where there is a non-marital but sexual relationship), and develops with marriage, and more fully still once the woman has had children.[8]

As servants have departed, preferring other forms of paid employment to household work, male heads of households have come under pressure to do *some* housework: to 'help' their wives at certain periods of the life-cycle when women have enormous work-loads. Some men agree to do this, particularly to take on certain aspects of childcare (see chapters 8 and 9), since the reasons for having children have shifted from producing heirs, who could be physically cared for by more or less anyone (wet-nurse, nanny, general servant or mother), to producing psychic extensions of oneself in time, whose psychological / personality growth requires interpersonal interaction with specific others. Many men therefore now feel they need to spend time with their offspring. But what they do with their children is only what they choose to do. And whatever tasks they perform are not undertaken by them as subordinate family members. Equally, men may agree to help their wives because they prefer their wives to have paid employment (because their wives are happier, or for the money, or for the status) and the working day defined by employers does not allow wives to do all the housework a couple feels needs to be done. But again men choose to undertake such tasks and do them as household heads and not dependants.

Most women nowadays are not full-time housewives. They too have paid employment, and some of them have employment which is as well paid as that of their husbands. So can we still say they are dependants maintained by their husbands? They support themselves and so are able to be partners, not subordinates.

Although our analysis focuses on the work done within the family household, we obviously recognize that many wives have full-time or part-time employment outside it for much of their married lives – the incidence and pattern of full-time or part-time paid work varying with class, ethnic group and region of the country, and from one western country to another. But this does not mean that women's duties as wives or cohabitees have become limited to the reduced number of hours of housework they actually perform, nor that the money they earn directly supports them as if they were single. Rather it means that, given today's need for a greater monetary income into households and the lesser possibility of domestic production for exchange, paid employment is what 'households' (that is, heads) have decided some of their wives' time shall be used for (even if is often seen as wives themselves persuading their husbands to let them do it).

One of the main effects of industrialization was to make production for the market impracticable within the family in many sectors (although, as we have said, it continues in others). As a result, the number of independent workers who could use the unpaid labour of their wives and children for exchange diminished, while the number of wage earners who could not exchange this labour increased. Whether this process is still continuing, or whether it has bottomed out and perhaps started to move in the opposite direction (that is, whether household production has started to increase, and husbands' ability to use dependants' labour has increased) is a matter of current debate – though not phrased in quite these terms.[9]

In sectors of the economy where all production intended for exchange is now performed by paid labour, the unpaid labour of a wife can only be applied to production which is not intended for exchange. Or, to be more precise, the unpaid labour of wives (and other family members) can no longer be exploited in production intended for exchange and is (seen as) limited to housework. To put it even more sharply, what we call housework is the set of tasks to which the unpaid labour of the housewife is now (seen as) limited. (We think wives do a lot of other, unrecognized work, see chapter 9, which is why we put 'seen as' in brackets.)

Thus in contrast to the way the question is phrased above, the fact that many married women today have paid employment actually proves rather than disproves our case. **Our analysis reveals clearly that wives' labour power is appropriated, for even when women have well-paid full-time employment they still do the bulk of the childcare and domestic work.** (Or else they are responsible for finding a paid nurse or cleaner and paying her out of their salary.) In such circumstances their provision of domestic work can no longer be justified by the economic exchange to which the servitude of the housewife is often attributed. That is to say, it can no longer be claimed a wife performs domestic labour in return for her keep, and that this upkeep is the equivalent of a wage, and that therefore her family work is rewarded. Women who go out to work may earn enough to keep themselves, some may even earn as much as their husbands, though they are a small minority,[10] but wives and cohabitees are still responsible for most of the domestic work. The domestic work is therefore clearly done for nothing. **At the same time, wives do not have the same rights to control the money they earn as their husbands or boyfriends have to the money they earn.**

It might seem that women's employment outside the home shows that the total appropriation of their labour power which was characteristic of 'traditional' marriage has now been transformed into a partial appropriation. That is, wives no longer owe *all* their time to their husbands, but only specific tasks, which once they are done leave women at liberty to earn 'their own' money, possibly even freeing themselves of certain of their domestic obligations by paying for substitutes. This would parallel the changes which took place from the Roman Empire to the late Middle Ages, when the master's appropriation of slaves' total labour power became the partial appropriation (three days a week) of serfs' labour; which still later became the obligation to do a specific task (the corvée) or to make a monetary payment.[11] But we think wives do not in fact actually recover either time or value by outside employment, though they do partially escape a relationship of production characterized by dependency.

The marital obligations of wives do not involve a discrete workload (that is, particular responsibilities which are limited in nature and in the time taken to do them), which when they are completed leave women free to work elsewhere. Rather, wives' familial duties involve an obligation to devote whatever of their time and energy is needed to whatever their husbands require. It is still quite possible for wifely obligations to be so extensive that the possibility of a woman's working outside the home is excluded, for instance, when there are young children, or when a husband's job demands his wife's help, or when she must conform to his 'not holding with women working' and wanting her to be at home. On the other hand, some wives are required to have full-time employment all their lives to provide a stable income for the household if their husbands have insecure employment, for example, because of their class or race or because of his disability. (Annie Phizacklea (1982) reported this to be true of one in four of the West Indian women she interviewed.) Married women pay for the 'freedom' to work outside the home and to have 'an independent income' (that is, one over which they have some limited rights and which could support them should the marriage break down) with a double day's work.

Our analysis sees wives' work as appropriated, by which we mean that wives (and daughters and occasionally male kin too) are not free to sell their labour to a third party without their household head authorizing it.

They do not own their own labour power. Hence they cannot sell it to their husbands even in the presence of a monetary economy, and if they sell it to anyone else they do so under limiting conditions. It is not just the tasks which women have to do for the household, or the difficulties of finding quality childcare, that restrict women's access to the labour market and so restricts their earning capacity – which means they need to marry to have a decent standard of living. It is marriage itself which confines them.

This is the point Carole Pateman also makes when she talks of marriage and heterosexual cohabitation as key elements in *The Sexual Contract*: the general power that men legitimately exercise over women. She suggests that the marriage contract, like other contracts women enter into with men (including 'the prostitution contract' and 'the surrogacy contract') is claimed to be the product of free social choices, but like other contracts about property in the person, it in fact 'generates a political right in the form of relations of domination and subordination' (Pateman 1988: 8). The rights husbands are given through the marriage contract, though no longer as extensive as in the mid nineteenth century when wives had the legal standing of property, still include husbands' rights to their wives' work and unlimited sexual access to their bodies.

Heidi Hartmann's work (see chapter 3) points out how wives' (and other family dependants') access to the market, which had been regulated since markets first developed in Europe, was further restricted following the industrial revolution. Existing regulations on women and children selling goods and labour were tightened up in the late eighteenth and early nineteenth centuries, establishing firmer patriarchal control and avoiding much potential conflict for their labour. For instance, 'couverture' (the civil incapacity of married women to make contracts) was strengthened and extended into new areas (including the exclusion of married women from the exercise of various rights including those to property), the division between married and unmarried women was formalized, and the Napoleonic Code decreed that if women wished to sell their *biens propres* (their own unalienable property, including things they inherited) they required their husband's authorization to do so. Hartmann also stresses how the thoroughly sex-discriminatory labour market which developed during this period when inequalities in family law were firmly in place, also acted to exclude women from the market or to give them low wages, so they continued to need to marry to gain a share in a man's wages in order to survive.[12]

But it is not women's exclusion from (or restriction within) the labour market which caused the non-exchange typical of marriage, since this exclusion and restriction itself presupposed and still presupposes they do not own their own labour power. To explain their exclusion and restriction, and to bring it to bear on the argument, we have first to postulate that wives' labour is appropriated. This appropriation then accounts for the unpaidness of family work (because there is no need to pay for what is already owned: wives cannot sell their husbands their labour because they already owe it to him) without there being any need to invoke external constraints. Moreover, the concept of appropriation accounts not only for the position of wives in the labour market, but also for the diversity of forms taken by family labour. (This is one of the main features of family labour and is the topic we explore in chapters 7–9.)

But despite patriarchy's tight grip, competition for women and children's labour has existed between it and capitalism; and over time, in various ways, and at differing speeds in different places, capitalism does seem to have undermined and to still be undermining patriarchy. Some historical information is now available, but the questions we want answered – how and why and to what extent did various family members escape the obligation to do family work and gain the right to work for wages as freely contracting agents – have not yet been asked sharply or often enough.

We know for instance that daughters from peasant and working class homes were sent out to work by their parents in mid-nineteenth-century Europe and their wages were paid directly to their parents; but the girls started to receive spending money of their own at the end of the century; and after the First World War they started to keep more and more of their wages. Or again, we know that middle class families in England stopped keeping one daughter unmarried to care for parents in their old age around the turn of the century.[13] But on the other hand, sons only began to escape the obligation to do family labour on small farms in France in the 1950s.

To what extent has this also happened to married women? Too often it has been assumed (by women who wish to believe they are free agents and by men who want to continue to have heterosexual relationships but do not want to see themselves as exploiters) that we already know the answer and that women have already become full and equal citizens and full and equal partners in marriage. But the question actually needs to be approached more open-mindedly, as a real question, to be answered by looking at women in different situations (by class, husbands' occupation, race, age, region, etc.), and cross-nationally. Has married women's access to the market so ceased to be regulated that it has now reached a threshold where there is real conflict between patriarchy and capitalism for women's labour? If so, are dependants consciously or unconsciously using this tension in any way? Is change occurring evenly across all classes and ethnic and racial groups? And how far are men also escaping family obligations – in their case their obligation to maintain?[14]

We think family patriarchy *is* being undermined by capitalism, but as a system it is resisting and changing, not simply disappearing; and the capitalist labour process is itself also gendered and exploitative, so for women to 'escape' into this is not an unmixed blessing. In any case, women's obligations to do family work are still strong and have not in fact changed all that much. Nor have external exclusions and restrictions: try sending a married woman to open a bank account, or let her fill in a census form or an income tax return as head of household, or apply for a job (especially a well-paid, 'man's' job), or try to join the Rotary Club or other informal business association, and note the questions she gets asked (and the questions that get asked about her behind her back) and the progress she makes.

Rules determine who can make what contracts and exchanges in our societies, and while some of these are formal written rules, most are informal unwritten rules, 'custom and practice', or sets of ideas about what is appropriate and who is 'the right man for the job' – and these are changing slowly if at all. Some of these rules relate to the market and exclude women from certain occupations or levels in hierarchies or insist on giving them special 'protection', etc. Others come from common law or the *Droit commun*. But most are embodied in and camouflaged by civil law / the *Code civil*, which regulates the status of individuals, and particularly family law. Even though some written laws have recently been changed – and we are talking about changes within the last 50 years, well within our mothers' and even our own lifetimes – custom and practice has been little affected. And it is only a few laws that have been changed – and legal actions for redress have notoriously low success rates.[15]

So the conflict for women's labour is still often avoided and is generally more apparent than real. To the extent that it exists it may well (as Hartmann suggests) be being resolved by women working longer hours: working for both capital and their husbands. Thus family patriarchy is still firmly in place, despite women's increasing presence in the labour market, and women's (and children's) labour is (still) routinely appropriated.

Can the work women do within the family really be said to be 'unpaid' (unremunerated) when they also benefit from the housework they do?

If a wife redecorates the house and saves money from the housekeeping to buy a carpet, she shares in the household's enjoyment of a pleasant room. If she entertains her husband's boss and helps to get her husband promotion, she may enjoy a higher standard of living. If she helps in the family shop, she may increase the overall income and get more money to spend. And this does not look very different from a husband putting up curtain rails to make a more pleasant room or going out to work to support the family.

But it *is* different, because his work and hers are done within structurally different locations. He is working to support *his dependants*. She is working *for him*, doing work for him which has been delegated to her by him as household head; and then, since her maintenance is his responsibility, in turn benefiting from this work – as his dependant. In addition the operative word in the above sentences is 'may'. A wife only *may* get to share in these things. She is not assured of getting them. Her husband can hold on to any extra pay he gets or property he accumulates, using it for himself alone and not spending it on the family. He may help her out with her domestic work. But he may not. It is his choice. She has to try to persuade him to do as she wishes.

Can we really describe wives' and other dependants' work as 'unpaid and unremunerated' when they get something in exchange: when they are maintained during their husband's lifetime and inherit when he dies?

While there are certainly mutual obligations between heads and dependants, we have stressed that family labour relations are typified by the work dependants do not being a repayment or return for the maintenance they receive. The work they do and the maintenance their head provides for them are *not exchanged*. Neither is evaluated. There is no attempt to establish an *equivalence* between them, nor is there any direct *counterpart*.

- Equivalence implies that the goods and services must be more or less evaluated.
- Counterpart or reciprocity implies that there is a link, a one-to-oneness, between the goods and services and between the actors (whether individuals or groups). The counterpart is always directed to the original good and the original actor.

This absence of exchange is one of the features of family transactions which makes them specific and different. But it does not mean that family transactions are not highly regulated and obligatory. Like other non-market transactions, such as the exchange of gifts by people on various occasions, family transactions are reasoned and ordered. One is obliged to give gifts, and when one receives them one is obliged to give something back. Heads of households are obliged to maintain, and dependants are obliged to work for them, and each side has to accept what the other provides.

Where gifts and family transactions differ is that gift-giving is a form of exchange (in many ways like the market, as Marcel Mauss (1954) showed) because it involves notions of counterpart and equivalence. Gifts are always evaluated, even if (indeed precisely if) the counter-gift is to be more magnificent than the original. Overbidding – always offering a bit more – as in the competitive gift displays described in various societies by anthropologists or in our own giving of Christmas presents, is not possible unless there is first at least an approximate determination of the value (according to the criteria of the culture) of the gifts given.

But both counterpart and equivalent are (supposedly) absent from family transactions. Things passed between family members should not be evaluated, and counter-transactions are not necessarily directed to the original giver. The right to maintenance from the head of one's family, and the obligation to work for him, exist independently of one another. A head of household must support his dependants whether or not they work for him: whether they are sick, or disabled, or lazy, and whether or not there is family work for them to do. Similarly, dependants have a duty to work for and to love, honour and obey their head of household however well or badly they are maintained: whether he keeps them in the lap of luxury or is cruel, miserly and defrauds them of their inheritance. Thus family relations involve distinct obligations, not equivalent obligations – not repayment, recompense or return, and certainly not exchange.

It is worth noting, however, that within the culture the upkeep dependants receive tends to be seen as a gift from their head. That is, upkeep is not (always) seen as the right of family members, nor (often) as a return for work they have already done. Rather, the work they do is seen as their counter-gift to an original gift from their head. Consequently, those who do family work are seen as eternally in debt to the head of family who maintains them. Their work is thus doubly annexed. The products of their work do not belong to them but to their head; and their work itself does not belong to them since they are seen as owing it to the head in return for maintenance they have already received. Because their upkeep is seen as a gift from the head, married women in employment generally feel they must earn enough to cover the costs of replacing their personal labour before they can keep any income of their own. And since husbands are also said to 'give' their wives orgasms and to 'give' them babies, their appropriation of their wives' sexual and reproductive work is also seen as simply a just return for what the women have been 'given'.[16]

This double mediation, or double appropriation of the various types of labour, is procured precisely through the family model and institutions. The head of the family appears institutionally to cut the worker off from the value of her production, and from the production itself. On the one hand, the family work done by the dependant does not produce goods or services which she can exchange herself. (Her production is alienated.) Rather her work is considered to be owed as a personal service to the head of the family – an obligation unrelated to and unequated with her upkeep. On the other hand, what the work actually produces (including children and her husband's labour power) is owned and used or exchanged by him. A sale gives him an income over which members of the family have no rights. (It is alienated from them.) Rather they are owed rights by the head of the family.

It might be argued, however, that even if being maintained is not an exchange for dependants' work, because it does not involve evaluation and equivalence, we ought at least to recognize it as a form of payment, of *remuneration*, because it does involve reciprocity. 'To live (and work) one must eat', so eating must be some sort of a return for working.

But in saying to work one must eat, the 'must' can simply cover the interests of the person who benefits from the work – and this is not necessarily the worker. Even a slave owner cannot expect to benefit for long from a labour force unless he allows it to reproduce itself. If we are to consider the mere maintenance of workers as a form of payment or remuneration, then with the exception of death camps, one would have to say there has never been any 'unpaid' labour. Even in systems of forced labour, the workers are fed and housed, however badly. But this is not to say they are remunerated. Obviously in most such cases the labour force is reproduced at minimal cost and kept as close as possible to the lowest level needed to maintain life and strength, and this is different from most family situations. But some slaves have been (and are) kept at a good, even a luxurious standard relative to others in the society, especially domestic slaves who share the living quarters of their masters.[17]

It is therefore really not acceptable to regard being fed, or even being well fed and maintained, as the same as being paid. It is the provision of a standard of living, high or low, but not a remuneration. It is certainly very different from a worker's right to a wage in exchange for his work in the labour market.

The absence of payment, of exchange, within the family is also clearly revealed by the fact, already noted, that the maintenance and inheritance received by dependants varies not according to the work they do, but according to the socio-economic level and goodwill of their head. This means that a family worker can receive much more *or* much less than the money value she / he could get for the same work if sold on the market. For doing the same job (for example, taking care of the livestock) the son of a rich farmer can get a higher standard of living than he could afford to buy, and the son of a poor farmer a lower one. This has been called 'the paradox of housework': 'Men can receive from their wives a market value of housework that is greater than their own incomes, yet the housework is only a portion of what the wife contributes in order to have a partial claim on that income' (Curtis 1986: 179).

In the idealized model of the labour market, all workers get a more or less fixed wage depending on the services (hours and tasks) they perform. (By fixed we mean that they would get much the same from any employer.) In addition, they can always change their employer; and they can increase their income by increasing the hours they work or improving their performance by gaining extra skills through training. In reality, of course, the capitalist market operates rather differently from this. It is gendered and (racially and otherwise) segmented, and women are allowed to sell their labour only in certain sectors and under gender (and other) specific conditions. Wages for the same work can vary a lot. It is not particularly easy to change employer – especially when there is low demand for labour. The services (hours or tasks) workers provide are often not particularly determined; and they cannot always increase their income by working longer hours because these are not available or they already work long hours of overtime to get a living wage.

But, compared to family work, waged work returns are fixed, and extra hours and extra skills increase income. Whereas the wife of a business executive may receive 50 times the benefits provided for the wife of a carpenter, even though both keep house and the latter may have more skills and work harder than the former. In addition, compared to changing employers, changing husbands remains difficult, expensive and fraught. Hence it is very important to women to make 'a good marriage': to marry someone with the right earning capacity and the right temperament. And it is vital to children to be born to good parents.

Finally, are we suggesting that children exploit their mothers when their mothers brush their teeth?

Our interpretation does not say that it is the person on or for whom work is done (that is, the person who directly benefits from the work) who is necessarily the person who appropriates the labour. A small child or sick person who has their teeth brushed as a member of a family is not the appropriator of the work involved.[18] Rather it is the head of the family who appropriates the labour incorporated in the service. It is work for the maintenance of *his* household (or possibly *his* children if he has left their mother and lives elsewhere) and he would have to perform such work himself if his wife (or sister or daughter) did not do it. It is delegated work / care. Similarly the control a wife (or sister or daughter) exercises over junior members of the household is delegated patriarchal control.

And her use of her husband's wage to buy goods for all members is delegated purchasing. She manages the money under more or less close supervision.

This chapter has provided an initial statement of the characteristics of family labour as an economic system and sorted out some possible misunderstandings. In particular it has shown that maintenance within a household is specific in being a non-monetary and non-exchange transaction. It does not allow dependants to increase their standard of living directly by working harder, nor does it allow them choice in what they consume. In addition, family labour is a specific form of contract inasmuch as dependants' labour is unpaid because it is appropriated by, it belongs to, the household head.

We can now proceed to look in more detail at the formal structure of production, consumption and transmission within family relations.

Notes

1 See Delphy (1981).
2 Some exceptions to this generalization are Becker (1965; 1976; 1981) and his
   school (see Dex 1985: 73–6 for an overview and critique), Clark (1958),
   McKenzie and Tullock (1975), Bacharach (1976), Harbury (1962), Schutz
   (1974), A. B. Atkinson (1973), Atkinson and Harrison (1978), Brittain (1978),
   Sen (1982; 1983; 1984), Pollack (1985) and Lemennicier (1988).
        We are grateful to Charles Sutcliffe, Gail Wilson and Meghnad Desai for
   discussion on this point, and to Marilyn Waring for her book (1989).
3 See Delphy (1974).
4 This is clear in the descriptions provided in various recent empirical studies
   of, for example, homeworking and family businesses, and the distribution of
   resources within households, even though the authors do not always fully
   share our analytical model. See e.g. Scase and Goffee (1980a; 1980b),
   Bechhofer and Elliott (1981), Allen and Wolkowitz (1987), Westwood and
   Bhachu (1988) and Brannen and Wilson (1987). For references on the
   distribution of food and money, see chapter 6 n. 11.
5 In a large random sample of women aged 16–60 (i.e. excluding women over
   pensionable age) in Britain in 1980, only about 10 per cent were heads of
   household (Martin and Roberts 1984).

   73 per cent were married
   16 per cent single – living with parents
    2 per cent single – living with other adults
    4 per cent living alone
    4 per cent living with children under 16
    2 per cent living with children over 16

In a nationally representative sample of all ages interviewed for the Policy Studies Institute in 1982, 'a third of West Indian households [were] headed by women, compared with a quarter of white households and fewer than one in ten Asian households' (Brown 1984: 38).

See also A. Wilson (1974), Rex and Tomlinson (1979), Phizacklea (1982), Ballard (1982), Barrow (1982), Phoenix (1987) and *Social Trends 21* (1991).

6 See Delphy (1976a) on the situation post divorce.

While the Afro-Caribbean family system is often described as 'matrifocal' and very often deemed to be 'matriarchal', studies in the French Caribbean (Martinique and Guadeloupe) show marriage to be the goal of almost all women. One-parent families (women-headed households) are not the preferred social form even though they are statistically frequent. (See the special issue of *Nouvelles Questions Feministes*, nos 9–10, 1985, edited by Arlette Gautier, and particularly the article by Alibar and Lembeye-Boy.)

Afro-Caribbean women in Europe also do not usually choose to be alone with their children. Moreover in many women-headed households, men are only absent to the extent that they contribute no work towards the maintenance of the house and the children, and provide very little financial support. But they are physically present, having occasional or long-standing affairs with unmarried women (whose children are not born through parthenogenesis).

Women often get into these affairs because a lover gives some support and thus alleviates the poverty caused by their having an illegitimate child. But an affair only brings another birth – especially since having children, by as many women as possible, is a sign of virility for Caribbean men. Thus a vicious circle is created for women, who 'want a can of milk and get a baby'.

The situation of married women is not much better. Men demand the same services from their wives as they do from their mistresses: sexual access and unlimited domestic services, and they still do little work around the house. But married women do get access to a more regular and slightly larger allowance than mistresses, and their social status is higher. So it is better to be married – which is why it remains most women's ideal.

But on the whole this system is no less patriarchal than the European system, where women can expect (or could expect, since the incidence of divorce means patterns of expectation are changing) to be financially dependent on /supported by men most of their lives. On the contrary, the 'matrifocal' Caribbean family is the symptom of very harsh patriarchal conditions.

7 A study by Muriel Nissel and Lucy Bonnerjea (1982) found that all the men caring for an elderly handicapped person were married to the person, and that they were generally elderly (retired) at the time when they started this caring. However, overall they found many more women than men involved in caring work, and women were more likely to care for parents and parents-in-law than for their spouses. In addition, although some women started caring work when they were elderly, others started doing such work much earlier in their lives. See also Quershi and Walker (1989) and Finch (1989).

8   There is no study we know of which traces the progression through indi-
    vidual life-courses. But see Abrams and McCulloch (1976) on communes,
    and Stafford, Backman and Dibona (1977) on cohabitation and marriage.
        A parallel escalation as the woman's dependent status increases has, how-
    ever, been demonstrated for domestic violence. Violence by a man often
    starts when a couple become engaged, and increases in frequency and severity
    at marriage, and again when the woman first becomes pregnant. See Dobash
    and Dobash (1980).

9   See Pahl (1984), Morris (1990).

10 See chapter 9 n. 19.

11 See Bloch (1964), Mendras (1976).

12 See Hartmann (1976; 1979) and much recent work by many family and
    feminist historians, including Finer and McGregor (1974), Gillis (1985),
    Charles and Duffin (1985), Davidoff and Hall (1987) and Pahl (1988).

13 See for example, Millward (1968), Tilly and Scott (1978), Jalland (1986) and
    Davidoff and Hall (1987).

14 See Ehrenreich (1983) for a general discussion of men's eschewing family
    obligations among white, middle class Americans in the 1950s and 1960s;
    and Weitzman (1985), Eekelaar and Maclean (1986) and Maclean and
    Weitzman (1991) for accounts of men evading their obligations after divorce.

15 It was not until 1935 that an English married woman was legally capable of
    holding and acquiring and disposing of any property in every respect as if she
    were single; and only in 1946 that French women were no longer required to
    get their husband's written consent before taking employment. It was 1960
    before the latter had the right to work outside the family if he opposed it.
        The UK Sex Discrimination Act (1975) does not cover either government
    social policy provisions, e.g. taxes, pensions, income support schemes, etc.,
    nor family law. Actions taken under this act have only a 30 per cent success
    rate (cf. Snell 1979).
        The French law of 1983 forbidding sex discrimination in the workplace
    has more teeth than the 1972 act, and allows collective action – but only by
    trade unions. Feminist groups are barred. And no union to date has brought
    a case under the act.

16 See Bell and Newby (1976), Brannen (1987), Brannen and Moss (1990).

17 See Grace (1975).

18 Whether older children living at home, who are in waged employment, exploit
    mothers is a different issue (see Leonard 1980 chapter 3).

6

THE FAMILY AS AN ECONOMIC
SYSTEM: THEORETICAL OUTLINE

When we start to analyse the unpaid work done within households (and work exchanged between households whose members are related to each other) there are various ways in which to approach it. One is by looking at who the individuals are that do the work. Another is by looking at the work itself. We have already given some attention to both, but here we shall look at them more fully and then at the relationship between tasks and status, the management of family labour, and particular forms of work as rewards in themselves. Having established the characteristic features of family relationships in production, we can then show how these also apply to consumption and (briefly) to the transmission of property within families.

Production within family-based households

The individuals who do the work

If we look at family workers in terms of their gender, age and marital status, we see that all these social categorizations influence the type of work individuals do, though sex is the most influential division, and that the categories determine the very presence of individuals within the unit of production. Thus, for example, the younger brothers and sisters of the head of a household are part of the unit only while they are unmarried, while his children's spouses may join it, and any children his spouse may have from a previous marriage must join it (as stepchildren).

Tasks are generally allotted more or less fixedly by gender, but more flexibly by age – which is logical because age changes, and also because there are different ratios of people of different ages in each family household, whereas there is usually and should be a heterosexual couple (or a sister or daughter acting as a wife-substitute for a man). When men do family work (that is, when they work unpaid for a father or brother), it is generally a temporary situation and the older they get the more 'important' their tasks, prestigious tasks being seen as more 'complex'. But for women the obligation to do family work is usually lifelong and the tasks change less. Male unpaid workers are exploited not because they are men, but because they are young or old; whereas female unpaid workers (daughters, sisters, mothers and wives) are exploited because they are women. And among women, the particular category of wives have not only their productive and emotional labour but also their sexual labour appropriated.

Alternatively we can begin by categorizing family workers in terms of their relationship to the head of the family. In most contemporary households they are all linked to him by close kinship and marriage, and there are relatively few people in each household. However, more people, including more distant kin, unrelated apprentices and some servants used to work for their keep until the seventeenth or eighteenth century in Europe, and the unpaid labour of a variety of kin (that of younger unmarried brothers and sisters of the household head, of his wife, and of his children and their spouses) was taken for granted in the general economy of family households until industrialization. Thus, working unpaid for the head of one's own (or as a servant for some other) family was the rule for children, wives and younger siblings in all sectors of the economy until the late eighteenth century in England and early nineteenth century in France. It continued much later in certain sectors than in others (for example, until the Second World War in agriculture in France). It is still common in countries around the Mediterranean and among some of the groups who have migrated into Europe since the war.

Today, however, as we said in the last chapter, many northern European household heads cannot use much, if any, of their kin or children's labour directly because their households no longer produce goods or services for the market. Many husbands have become waged workers (though France still has a high proportion who are self-employed) and adolescents have been allowed to enter paid employment. These dependants are escaping the obligation to do family labour. They have managed to become free to sell their own labour power; wage labour is available to them outside the family; and most seek this form of employment. Indeed, nowadays, even in family businesses where their labour could be used, younger brothers and sisters of the head, and his children, especially his sons, often threaten to leave or actually do leave if their labour is not paid for. The extent to which they do this varies with the sector of the economy, but such labour is not paid by law in France while the individual is under 18; and it is generally unpaid or very lowly paid while the person is living in the family. (Such workers may, however, receive some recompense when their parents die, see chapter 7.)

The unpaid labour of a woman can still be used full-time or part-time in a household, however, and it is still taken for granted. Such women (more than 80 per cent of women at any point in time) may be struggling to establish a more egalitarian relationship with their husbands or cohabitees, and they may threaten or initiate divorce if they think they are getting a bad deal in a particular marriage, but while they remain married there is no talk of payment rather than maintenance.

Women are now legally free to work outside the home, though as we said in the last chapter this is only a recent legal freedom (dating from 1965 in France); and we are formally not supposed to experience any discrimination related to sex or marital status in the labour market (since 1975 in Britain and 1972 and 1983 in France). Of course we continue to experience both direct and indirect discrimination, and we are also often in practice not free to undertake employment at all, since our labour power is still appropriated. It is used in part or in full, as and where necessary, for wives remain both the best 'emergency service' and the best long-term care providers available, and they still fulfil all their domestic responsibilities to their head of household. The work of single women (with or without dependants) is also appropriated because they may do work for other kin, as well as their own domestic work. **Not only has going out to work not freed women from family work, it has hardly interfered with it at all.**

What wives are now free to do (subject to their husbands' approval) is have a double workload in return for different working conditions – outside the four walls of their home, where they can meet a wider range of people and have the social status of having a job. They also have a degree of financial independence because their earnings no longer legally belong to their husbands (since 1907 in France and 1870 in England), though in practice in most marriages almost all the wife's income goes into the communal budget over which the husband has overall control, whereas the husband has personal spending money (see chapters 7 and 9). Non-married women are free to have the same (or a slightly reduced) domestic workload and more financial autonomy, but their standard of living is lower and they are socially less acceptable – and sometimes downright stigmatized (that is, they are ideologically positioned and oppressed).

The work which is done

We can also analyse the work which goes on inside a family according to whether it is production for a household's own consumption (or for related families in separate households, for example, daughters-in-law caring for an elderly parent in the old person's own home) or for exchange with other households or on the market. In the West, as we have said, all families produce for their own consumption, and most also exchange at least some goods and services with other households in their community. Some also produce goods and services which are regularly put on the market (for example, in farming, the retail trades, some artisans and many professions).

- When families produce exchangeable goods and services some or all of which are put on the market, men restrict themselves to production for the market, while women do almost all the work which is not put on the market as well as contributing to some production for the market (and/or selling some of their labour power).

- When family production is almost entirely for family consumption, the head of the family, most grown children, and at various times also the wife, sell most of their labour power on the market. The wife does most of the material and affective work for the family's consumption (as well, of course, as reproductive work and sexual work for her husband), but the head himself may also contribute to household work.

In the next chapter we shall look empirically at examples of families at the two ends of the continuum of family production.

- On the one hand we shall look at family units where a range of kin of both sexes work for the head of the family producing goods and services for their own consumption and for the market (the families of peasant farmers in France);
- And on the other, at families where the only family production is of domestic and sexual services, child-bearing and rearing, and the care of the sick and elderly, and it is virtually all performed by the wife (the families of men who work in factories in Britain).

The latter type of family is held to be typical of contemporary industrial capitalist societies, since (as we said in chapter 4) it is conventional wisdom that industrialization 'stripped the family of its function as a unit of production'. The spread of the factory system and wage labour supposedly led to a population composed overwhelmingly of the families of male wage earners. Such men sell their labour power, not family-labour-produced products.

We believe, however, that in many more cases than is generally recognized, and in an increasing number of cases with the crisis in western economies, heads of families still put on the market goods and (especially) services produced by their families. That is, most families are intermediate in form rather than being at the supposedly typical end of the continuum.

This is the central theme of Ray Pahl's book (1984) in which he argues that the high tide of waged employment in the 1950s and 1960s, from which there has since been a sharp decline, was an atypical, extreme situation rather than the norm of postindustrial society. Towns where households living on housing estates became entirely dependent for income on regular wage labour in a few factory-based industries, with minimal opportunities for by-employments (which Pahl calls 'occupational easements') or informal service work, were the unfortunate exceptions rather than the rule.[1]

> In retrospect, the years when it was said that [men and women] never had it so good . . . were the years of incapacitation. The messy back streets with their potential premises for small workshops were knocked down as part of slum clearance . . . It was held to be a victory when overtime was 'won' . . . Households with a limited and narrow view of work as factory employment were exactly as employers in the 1950s and 1960s wanted them to be. Completely socialized to the time and work disciplines of industrial capitalism, they had, perhaps for the first time in English history,

lost the means of getting by with a household work strategy. (Pahl 1984: 56–7)

Janet Finch (1983) also argues against the supposed typicality of post-industrial households where the husband sells merely his own labour and none of his wife's production. She holds that in the majority of the various different occupations entered into by husbands, the husband's employer benefits from unpaid work done by wives (that is, husbands directly or indirectly sell family labour as well as their own). We shall develop this further in chapter 9.

But Pahl does not recognize the gender hierarchy in the households whose changing work strategies he studies; and Finch looks only at the work done by wives which benefits their husbands' bosses. So while one recognizes all the work done in households which is for self-consumption, and also that wives work even harder when men are unemployed or self-employed than when they are waged or salaried; and the other recognizes differences of interest between husbands and wives, their work needs to be combined and developed if we are to get the full picture of family work.

This we shall do, for (as we stressed in chapter 4) in order to set up the structural characteristics of the family it is important to cover the whole range of family work. We shall therefore look at a number of different types of family, and particularly at those at the end of the continuum where a range of kin work for the household head producing goods and services for their own consumption and for the market. This type of family is especially interesting and helpful in developing our analysis of the family for two reasons.

First, because it includes providers of work other than wives. This allows us to get out of the context of the couple and marriage (and our ideological unquestioning acceptance of many aspects of this relationship) and to compare relationships based on marriage with other family relations. It is taken for granted that wives will not be paid for doing housework and childcare, but no such presumptions are made (any longer) about brothers working on a family market garden or daughters in a family shop.

Secondly, since this type of family produces goods and services for the market, we can easily compare it with other units (for example, factories and businesses) which also produce for the market, making differences and similarities clear.

For the moment, however, we shall continue to consider formally how the categories to which individuals belong influence the work they do as members of a family household, postponing looking in detail at the content of what they do, as the details vary.

Tasks and status

When looking at the division of labour within a co-resident family, we might seem free to broach the question from a number of angles:

- how tasks are assigned;
- who does the prestigious tasks; and
- who gets what benefit from doing various things.

But in fact these are part and parcel of one another. A whole variety of tasks are done by the different members of families, and

- these carry different amounts of prestige, from breadwinning to cleaning toilets, and can be roughly ranked on a scale;
- they are distributed among individuals according to the status of the individuals; and
- the value given to a task depends on the status of the person who normally does it.

In general in family households (as also in the labour market) prestigious tasks are reserved for adult men and, conversely, any task done by men is more prestigious than tasks done only or mainly by women or by children.

So which came first, the prestige or the task being done by men / adults? If at first sight the criterion by which job division occurs seems simple (intrinsically prestigious jobs go to men), it is complicated by the fact that the prestige may well derive not from objective features of the work but from the person to whom the task is assigned. The same task can be high prestige in one culture or region, or at one point in time, when done by adult men; and low prestige in another culture or region with an essentially similar economy, or at another time, when done by women or minors.

What is certain is that it is neither a simple question of certain tasks being functionally more necessary to the family (and therefore intrinsically of higher prestige) nor a question of the division of labour being technical, that is, based on the different capacities and / or abilities of the individuals concerned – though both these explanations are frequently put forward. For instance, it is argued that some work (done by men) is more important to the family and that it therefore carries greater prestige and rewards. Or that men or adults do certain jobs – heavy, outdoor, dirty, complex or stressful tasks – because they are better fitted for them. However, what is seen as 'essential' and what is 'heavy' work varies with the status of the type of person who typically does the job.

Whatever men do in a particular region or at a particular point in time is 'more important' and 'heavier'. If men farm smallholdings and their wives do wage work, farming is what is important. But if men earn wages and their wives tend smallholdings, then earning wages is what counts. And of course Black women in the West, and working class women in the eastern bloc and elsewhere, do heavy, outdoor and dirty tasks but this depresses rather than raises their status. Women's 'light' household work includes lifting children and carrying buckets of water or baskets of shopping; their 'clean' household work includes changing nappies, mopping up vomit and cleaning ovens; and their 'simple', 'unstressful' household work includes looking after the sick and senile. So the terms are clearly mystifying rather than objectively based.

But while there is no simple correlation between the objective importance of a task and its prestige, there does seem to be some inverse correlation between the arduousness and unpleasantness of a task and its prestige. Prestigious work is generally less boring and tiring than low status work, but this is of course quite the opposite of what is popularly believed. Work that is skilled or difficult or heavy or arduous is supposedly recognized and valued and a person who does it is supposedly rewarded. But in fact work done by women or younger siblings in the family, or by women or youths in the labour market, is little valued however arduous or skilled it may be. Its importance, its very existence, may not even be recognized. There is, in other words, no automatic compensation (high valuation or material rewards) for hard work. On the contrary, certain tasks are given to those of low status because this low status itself allows those of higher status to unload unpleasant activities onto them. (An example of the material effects of ideological causes.) Prestigious work on the other hand generally allows more autonomy, freedom and decision-making: the autonomy which is part of the status of the individual is extended to the tasks he does. Conversely, arduous tasks may be devalued because they are done by people of low status; and doing such lowly tasks without material compensation or prestige in turn confirms the low value of the people who do them.

Hierarchy and valuation are not set up after and independently of the division of labour, but in and by the very process of attributing lots: by the social, not technical, division of labour. It is not the intrinsic utility of a task (its importance to the family / household unit), or its nature, or its interest, or its skill, which determines the authority which is commanded (and the prestige which is received) by its performer. On the contrary, it is the authority which the performer commands which determines society's appreciation of the usefulness / nature / interest / skill of the task. As soon as wives do things (that is, as soon as it is customary for a task to be done within a relationship of subordination), they are little valued.

It would be a mistake, however, to suggest that the division of labour by gender and age within the family is a question of a rigid division of tasks (any more than it is in the labour market). It is not a question of women in our society cooking and cleaning and caring for children while men never do such things. Such tasks are 'women's work' and not highly valued, but men do do them from time to time within family households – though it should be noted that they generally do the more prestigious and interesting varieties of them: for example, cooking for guests or taking children for walks. Rather, domestic work is women's work in the sense that the status, the conditions of doing it, the relations of production of this work, are specific to family subordinates. It is not that the technical operations which comprise household work at the instrumental level – washing, ironing, cooking, etc. – are only ever done by women. Male laundry workers, washers-up and chefs do more or less the same technical operations. What makes domestic work women's work is not each particular operation, nor even their sum total; it is their particular organization and location, which is itself due to the relations of production in which each person doing them finds herself.[2]

What we have within the family is not a division of tasks, but a division of jobs – by age, gender and relationship. 'Jobs' comprise typical tasks plus their conditions of performance and remuneration and status (in the case of family work, the obligation to do it within the home, unpaid, invisibly, and poorly valued). This is why debates about whether or not, say, cooking is 'really interesting' or 'really important' can remain endlessly unresolved. Some say it is, some say it is not, some men say they enjoy it. But people are usually talking about tasks extracted from the relations of production within which they are typically done. (Men virtually never do cooking in the same conditions as women, that is, routinely, for household consumption, as economically dependent housewives.)

People often ask why housework is poorly valued, but they should first ask why it is assigned to women. It is not household tasks but the job which is not valued; and this is because it is work done in a subordinate position by people who have the general status of subordinates in society. Likewise, people sometimes discuss the possibilities of socializing housework, for example, having communal kitchens, or neighbourhood restaurants, or socializing childcare in nurseries, without seeming to realize that the place where household tasks are performed is not just a technical feature. The privatized nature of home cooking and childcare is directly derived from the relations of production within which they are done. The fact that housework and childcare are done at home flows from it being done for the household head without payment and precisely as and when he wants it done.

The management of family labour

Choices about what is to be done, and the attribution of who is to do what within a family are regulated by tradition, the circumstances a household or descent group finds itself in, and the head of the family.

The head of a household, as the name implies, is the overall manager and decision-maker. He decides what needs doing and what should be done in the given situation, and he either assigns the tasks he wants done to individuals or he delegates responsibility for particular areas to another family member. This does not make a household head a despot,[3] but rather a patriarch, possibly a very benevolent patriarch, but the 'chief', 'head' and 'ruler of a family', the respected 'founder' of an 'institution', none the less (*Shorter Oxford English Dictionary*). It is also not to say that household heads do not depend on and feel affection towards their wives and other dependants. Like all power relations, family relations are reciprocal and 'however wide the asymmetrical distribution of resources involved [they] . . . manifest autonomy and dependence in both directions' (Giddens 1979: 149). But the dependency between husbands and wives is not symmetrical: they are not different but equal, but rather different because unequal.

At times the head's control is not apparent because custom appears to prescribe who does what, or circumstances seem to constrain choices so much that the head has little if any leeway. Alternatively, only the responsibility and not its delegated nature (for example, the wife's control of the kitchen) is noted. But there is always *some* room for decision-making. There are always some matters of choice and judgement – and whatever the actual limits within which decisions can be exercised, the choices are made by the head of the family, even if his choice is simply to follow tradition and continue as before or to allow the decision to be made by someone else in the household. We think that many of the areas controlled by men have, in any case, been left out of past studies of marital decision-making precisely because the wife and other family members have had no say in them whatsoever.

Like all exercise of power, decision-making and direction by heads of families may bring forth resistance from dependants. Husband / fathers have to persuade their dependants at least to acquiesce in, and ideally to work with wholehearted enthusiasm for, the way they want things to be run. Wives and other kin must be motivated, which may often involve discussing decisions with them and taking note of their views, and there are limits – laws and customs and community controls – on what a head can expect or demand from, or do to, them: 'While men have to control their wives' behaviour, if they behave too badly the wives will retaliate . . . At best men must be torn between the wish to establish a satisfactory marital link, and the desire . . . to appear the boss' (Whitehead 1976: 195 and 199).

Dependants are not passive recipients and executors of instructions, and although they hold fewer resources than adult men and have greater social and economic need for relationships with men than men have for relationships with them, they may resist and / or try to manipulate their situation in various ways and with varying degrees of success. They often seek to influence the decisions their head of family makes by appealing to him, or arguing with him, or insisting they be consulted. And they may even manage to change his mind. But the mind to be changed is his.

This power of husband / fathers in western family households, though historically changing and varying somewhat with social class and life-cycle stage, is none the less very stable. It has proved 'an extraordinarily resilient form of social relationship' (Bell and Newby 1976: 166). Various attempts have been made to explain this stability: to look at the processes which reproduce men's power in the home. Many have drawn on other studies of hierarchical relations and stressed the importance of such relationships being seen as 'legitimate'.[4] Those concerned accept the givenness and morality of marriage and family relationships because they are seen as social institutions which are natural, moral and justified because they have been handed down from generation to generation.

Relationships which are not accepted as legitimate, but are based instead on the continuous use of coercion, are generally unstable. Colin Bell and Howard Newby have suggested marriage itself is so stable because although coercion, 'the naked power of the hand and the purse', remains close to the surface, it is not generally resorted to.

This assertion needs to be accepted with definite reservation, since physical and economic violence are both prevalent and socially tolerated in family relationships. Men's physical coercion of women and adults' coercion of children, and men's sexual abuse of women and children, is endemic in western society. It is not restricted to individual men who batter their wives, nor parents who assault their children, nor fathers and stepfathers who rape their daughters and sons. The application of physical force to compel obedience from subordinates, intertwined with obtaining pleasure from aggression in sexual relationships, is so pervasive and prevalent in the dominant western patriarchal heterosexual culture that we cannot treat physical and sexual abusers as a small problem group of men / parents / fathers. Nor can we overlook the blatant use of economic coercion to control wives and 'bribe' children. Such action is within the mainstream of normal male / adult behaviour, albeit exaggerated. It is extreme not aberrant behaviour. Men who beat up their wives can get away with it (indeed it may get them public sympathy if they do not actually kill their victims); and they do it because it gets them what they want and / or because it makes them feel good (at least at the time).[5]

In general, however, we take Bell and Newby's point that family relations in general and marriage in particular are not stabilized by the use of overt violence. Rather most are stable because they are almost ideal-typical examples of traditional authority: of a hierarchy accepted because it has been handed down from the past. So men rarely need to use force because their authority is accepted.

Both men and women (but especially men) often object to direct state-ments that men possess greater power, and that a husband should be the head of a couple. There is in fact widespread support for an abstract ideal of equality between husbands and wives, and men's attitudes to this are often even more favourable than women's (especially among educated, city dwelling, Black and younger men). But the practice is different. Men (and women) resist large alterations to marital and employment roles – roles which cumulatively afford men large advantages. They want men to take charge in many situations. They believe that what women do should be more determined by men than vice versa, that men should be given more attention, and that the things men do are actually more important than the things women do. Even women and men who are influenced by feminism and who feel that it is neither natural nor desirable for men in general to lead women in general in society, often actively seek for themselves a partnership where it is 'appropriate' that the man takes the lead and the woman defers to and supports him.

There are tall, mature, educated, high-income, high-status women in this society. Conventionally they ally themselves with taller, older, more educated, wealthier, higher-status men. Thus, what may be absolute excellence is regularly experienced by these women as relatively ordinary. In what is presumably their most absorbing and significant social interaction – that involving their husbands – our society's superior women find themselves in second place. (Steihm 1976: 15)

Men and women (but especially men) attribute the exploitation of women to men outside their family, and husbands/fathers usually get very angry and protective if they think their women are being threatened by violence or experiencing discrimination elsewhere. They want their wives, daughters and sisters to be happy and successful, and they get very upset if the women concerned express feminist anger towards them and their advantaged position (see Goode 1981).

Leonore Davidoff suggested in 1975 that patriarchal relationships are also stable because, as in other legitimate power relations, the two sides are seen to have complementary 'needs' and 'natural skills' relevant to the division of labour which exists between them. Thus just as masters and mistresses 'need' fine china and linen and 'cannot' do things for themselves, while servants have lower sensibilities and derive pleasure from being of service; and officers have an inborn ability to command while ordinary soldiers prefer to let other people make decisions; so men are naturally assertive and ambitious but emotionally reticent, while women are compliant and nurturant. Of course men may also be (stereotypically) feckless womanizing charmers, or reliable workers and trade union comrades, and women can be sassy independent economic supporters of their children or salt-of-the-earth homemakers – depending on their race and class subculture. (White middle class values too often obscure the existence of other sets of norms.) But what is noteworthy is that the particular forms of masculinity and femininity of each class, race, ethnic, regional or national group always complement each other. They go two by two like the creatures entering Noah's Ark (itself a celebration of heterosexual coupling).

The gender stratification system affords men status and attendant powers of control and provokes the appropriate behaviour from subordinates. That is to say, it is not women's (wives') behaviour which produces the system, but the system which produces women's behaviour. Women are not responsible for their subordination. The behaviour required of wives – deference – is also characteristic of other highly stratified face-to-face social relations and involves two opposing elements: differentiation and identification.[6] Men and women are constituted as different from each other, and their difference is constantly emphasized. This is essential in any hierarchical relationship, but differentiation is also potentially disruptive because it sets up antagonisms. What makes marriage so stable is that this is crosscut not just by the interdependence to be found in all hierarchies (that is, the real similarity of interests in the well-being of their households which husbands and wives have in many situations), but also the positive, affective identification and eroticism (in a word, love) which is encouraged between the two individuals.

The marital relationship is perceived as being an organic, natural partnership, a co-operative enterprise between two people who are emotionally attached to each other and who complete each other sexually. Each couple sees itself as organizing to suit itself and to maximize its own resources, with each partner caring for the other. Romance disguises the power imbalance – even though the sexual act is interpreted as the man entering and possessing the woman, and even though the protection he offers her against other men and the vagaries of the labour market are such as to maintain her dependence and continue her exploitation. A wife defers not to some abstract ethic of traditionalism or masculinity, but to the embodiment of that ethic in a particular person, whom she loves.

Marriage is also a particularly stable hierarchy because it provides a total environment. It encompasses the whole of the subordinate's life and may cut her off from most contacts with the outside world. It also involves lots of personal, face-to-face contact with the individual who is the superior, and often his interpretation of situations is the only one available to her.[7]

> Because deference to traditional authority is most easily stabilized in relatively small, face-to-face social structures, the corollary of this is an emphasis on a correspondingly small unity of territoriality – the home . . . [Ideally behind hedges, fences and walls and within a garden, ensuring privacy.] The encouragement of ideologies of the home and home-centredness enables the identification of the wife with her husband's super-ordinate position to increase by emphasizing a common adherence to territory, a solidarity of place. A woman's place is in the home, partly because to seek fulfilment outside the home could threaten to break down the ideological control which confinement within it promotes. The ideology of the home . . . is therefore a social control mechanism in the sense that escape from the home threatens access to alternative definitions of the female role . . . It allows the wife to obtain 'ideas above her station' . . . which identification with the home will prevent. (Davidoff, L'Esperance and Newby 1976: 160)

Although this physical confinement and ideological control of a wife is less marked at some stages of life than others, and in some social classes and subcultures than in others, it can be extremely tight. As Davidoff and colleagues point out, in the nineteenth century, respectable wives, servants and children were never to leave the precincts of the 'domestic domain' except under the closest scrutiny and control. There were no alternative living places for women (except nunneries and homes of relatives) and no other external relationships were sanctioned for family inmates. No followers were allowed for servants and no close intimates outside of kin for women and daughters. This enabled men to be tyrants over dependants, and masters and mistresses to be tyrants over children and servants (Davidoff, L'Esperance and Newby 1976: 153 and 163). Today most girls and women are expected to stay at home only at certain phases of their lives, but they are always more geographically confined than boys and men. Certain parts of towns and cities – and indeed the countryside – are 'off limits' for them if they are on their own. Their proper place is within homes and gardens in suburbia. They have less access to personal transport, so they cannot travel easily; and they have to take local jobs. And the media, which might present them with alternative ways of seeing things, in fact present them with a notably more conventional picture of 'women's role' than the actuality of their lives.

Nevertheless, husbands do sometimes face problems of containing, controlling and dissipating threats to their wives' identification with them. Research has shown instances of husbands preventing their wives getting an education, or developing a feminist consciousness, or seeing certain friends, or gaining access to money by going out to work.[8] Keeping her 'barefoot, pregnant and in the kitchen' may seem to be overdoing it, but installing (isolating) her on a nice housing estate, being prepared to 'talk through' (convince her of the rectitude of your view of) crises, and 'showing you care' will do as well. Paternalism deflects dissatisfaction. It takes the edge off the harsh realities of economic dependence and 24-hour work commitment. How can a wife complain when her husband is such a personally kind and considerate individual who recognizes his responsibilities and has problems of his own at work? When he is tolerant and does not care when she does her work so long as it gets done and so long as she takes good care of the children and the costly house and equipment? What does she have to reproach him for when he is home-centred and wants her loyalty and companionship for shared activities, not her disciplined obedience; and when he will share *his* problems at work if only she will listen?

Another danger for a husband, the other side of the coin, is that his wife comes to identify with him too closely. Familiarity can either breed contempt or lead a wife to think she actually *is* her husband and can act like him. Bell and Newby suggest this is routinely managed by everyday interactions and differentiation. They suggest gifts are particularly important in ritually transforming the things men do into 'services' done for their families. To give is to show superiority. To accept a gift without returning it is to become a client who must feel grateful and faithful. Hence the significance of husbands being seen to 'give' their wives their wages, and their 'taking them out' and buying them a drink. Similarly husbands 'help' in the house, thereby ritually confirming the work should actually be done by the wife. These acts are asymmetrical: the wife may make a gift in return – indeed some wives say one of their reasons for taking on paid work is in order to be able to 'buy their husbands something sometimes' to overcome this constant indebtedness. But what they give back is usually of a lesser value and they can never catch up. Nor can they match the ways in which (the demeanours with which) men give things and treat women: opening doors and offering chairs 'to ladies', and 'protecting' their dependants from insult and physical harm.

A final reason for the stability of deferential patriarchal systems such as marriage is that wives (like servants and farm workers) are not *seen* to be exploited. This is not because their subordination is not sometimes at least acknowledged, but because this subordination apparently does not matter when set against the charms of the job and the place in which they work: against the domestic (or rural) idyll. The aesthetic, particularly the physical environment becomes blurred with the social relationship. Because a home can be physically and aesthetically pleasing, with warm tidy rooms, good food, and an affectionate family, it is assumed it contains equally highly valued social relations, from which everybody benefits. The feelings of security consequent on decision-making being taken over by social superiors, and the psychological stability of knowing one's place and having no doubts as to the nature of one's place, get stressed – without regard for the negative aspects: of being at the bottom of the social hierarchy, doing socially invisible work, and without control of one's own body.

Once we recognize family hierarchy, however, the decisions which lie within the overall control of the head of the family become clearer. They can then be seen to involve both the distribution of work within the family and commercial choices: what to put on the market, and when, where and to whom to sell (including which family members shall sell labour power and under what conditions). The head controls who does what within the home: he regulates the responsibilities of members and their hours of work (and at what times they have to return to the home from outside) according to custom, according to family and external circumstance, and according to the prestige he wants to bestow on different members. He decides what human resources to put into the particular tasks he thinks need doing, and he allots different tasks to different people – including sometimes requiring wives and children to do no 'work' but rather to be conspicuously leisured: to play, or to engage in philanthropy. He has to negotiate these decisions with his dependants, but providing he makes decisions which are overall to the family's good, he will get their support, because the well-being of the household is the best guarantee of each member's individual well-being.

Household commercial decisions are in fact usually much more extensive than is imagined and, as we have noted, they exist even if the decision is not to make any changes and to continue as before. Until recently, however, household economic decisions were considered almost entirely in terms of how much control men have over the hours they themselves work in the labour market and whether or not their wives should also seek employment. But even in more thorough, recent studies, authors always assume either that 'households' distribute resources within themselves in such a way as to maximize members' joint satisfactions, or, if they do recognize gender inequalities, they do not recognize the systematic nature of family hierarchy.[9] **They do not see gender inequality as reproduced within the family: as being part of the structure of the family.** They see inequalities only as the product of the sexist attitudes of some husbands and fathers, or as the result of families having to accommodate to sex inequalities in institutions outside the household (particularly the labour market). That family-based households have internal structures, that members are differentiated by gender and generation, and that their heads routinely determine overall what members do and how much members shall consume (how much will be saved and invested and in what, and how much will be spent) seems to have escaped them.

Wives and other family members who work unpaid within the household are usually granted some autonomy in deciding what needs doing and some control over resources to effect this. But these are always within limits set by the head (even if some heads have to struggle to maintain this against their wives' and other dependants' resistance). Wives do not control the cash their husbands bring into the home because this income is not theirs. Rather they (the house, its keeper and the children) are some of the *uses* for their husband's money. To be able to distribute money, or to have a say in the distribution of money, requires that one own the money; and whether work done in the home produces goods which are sold on the market or reproduces the labour power of the household head, it is the husband who sells the goods or his labour power, he who collects the money, and he who decides what it is to be used for. Dependants decide how to use money only within areas where responsibility has been delegated to them by the head.

The head also controls dependants' access to waged employment. He may require a son or daughter to cease formal education and to work for the family, or he may allow or require him or her to continue training so as to be fitted for a particular occupation (and to acquire a particular status) in the future. It is he who has the final say on whether he will 'let his wife work'. He may prefer her making things at home to using delicatessens, frozen food and cleaning agencies, and he may want his wife's personal care for himself or his children rather than have the care provided by servants and nurseries. But equally he may prefer (or she may persuade him to accept) extra income, since two incomes are generally now needed to maintain a household at the same relative standard of living as was provided by one 20 years ago.[10] If his wife has a prestigious job (for example, as an actress) or a worthy feminine one (such as nursing), a husband may wish her to work to give the family extra status and / or extra income. If a husband is in business and his wife works with him, he may rely heavily on her work and her judgement and share information and decision-making with her. She may even be able to demand autonomy in a sphere (if she is lucky and he can cope with this sort of behaviour from women without feeling threatened). But all these decisions ultimately rest with him. In the end a wife has either to accept her husband's decisions – or leave.

Dependants who are themselves in paid employment, or who produce articles within the household which are sold on the market (butter and eggs on farms, child-minding or home working in towns), have their own limited access to cash. But this money is not fully theirs even though they have earned it. The head budgets for this income, which he can generally estimate in advance, and he stipulates openly or *de facto* what it is to be used for: for example, the purchase of certain commodities, reducing the amount he needs to pay for the upkeep of the household, or as the dependant's 'spending money' (for example, to cover the cost of her own clothes). Dependants do not have access to cash on the same scale or with the same freedom of ownership as the head, nor do they have 'money of their own' in the same sense as he does. But earning an income, especially a high income, does substantially improve a wife's (or an adolescent's) bargaining power within the family.

If a wife is employed, however, the cost of any bought-in childcare and household work and any additional taxes are paid for from her income. (That is, the husband takes both tax allowances against his income and then considers her income to be taxed at the higher rate.) The fact that expenses are not taken from the couple's income as a whole shows:

1   that it is believed these services should be provided free, unlike, for example, housing or transport which are considered normal expenses to be taken from the household income as a whole; and
2   that the wife alone is exclusively responsible for providing these services, since it is deemed that the part of her wage which goes towards paying for them is cancelled out, as though she had never earned the money in the first place.

As a result of these calculations it is often discovered that a wife 'earns almost nothing' and that economically it is not worth her having a job. The fact that she may still want to have one shows that it is very worthwhile to her in some other way. But the fact that it brings in so little net extra cash to the household means her husband has a strong argument against her taking one, so women have doubly to carry the costs of paid employment if they 'choose' to go out to work.

Particular forms of work as rewards in themselves

Before leaving the division of labour within the family household to look at consumption (a term we use very broadly, to cover the various standards of living of family members), we want to make explicit something which was implicit in earlier sections. This is that there is in fact no gap between the division of labour in the family and the benefits received. There is not on the one side a division of labour with a series of jobs on a scale of prestige, and on the other side various standards of living. For the division of labour carries its own rewards. It is a system of rewards in itself.

Since some jobs are deemed important and prestigious, having these as your allotted tasks is a benefit. Conversely, being assigned 'unimportant', 'simple', 'light' work – especially when such work is actually arduous and time-consuming – is a deprivation. In particular, earning the 'family wage' in a monetary economy can be considered a form of differential and superior consumption even if the work you have to do to get it is unpleasant. Having decision-making power and the right to manage the household, that is, to tell others what to do and to determine what you will do yourself, especially if the work you decide to do is interesting and less tiring, and being seen as the essential family member on whom all others depend, in itself constitutes a benefit. Conversely, being seen as a dependant, being told what to do, caring for and serving others, and having little room for self-determination and regulation, constitutes a deprivation.

This is then linked to another system of rewards, the consumption system proper. Here again the head of the household gets the dominant share. He controls the overall quantity and quality of goods and services coming into / produced within the family household, and how these are distributed. For example, the food bought is the sort *he* likes, and he gets more of it and the best bits. This is 'justified' by his performing the work of breadwinning / management. Likewise, women and children's lower share in consumption, which is popularly held to be due to the subordinate, 'minor' character of their work, constitutes, and is in itself the sign of, an inferior status.

In other words, there is no break between the benefits in the division of labour and the benefits derived from this in the distribution of resources.

1   Freedom to decide what one does (that is, self-determination in one's work) and control over others, gives
2   prestige. This self-determination and prestige are the source of
3   other benefits: differential consumption (using consumption in the widest sense). Finally, by a process of feedback, the fact that a function / role / task is the source of material benefits,
4   adds to its prestige.

The division of labour is itself a source of differential benefits in the form of jobs which are more pleasant, more prestigious and chosen; and this in turn explains the differential distribution of other resources: the consumption of family members. The beneficiaries in the division of labour are also the beneficiaries in the distribution of resources. There is no hiatus between these two orders and neither one causes the other. One factor alone, upstream of both, that is, status in the family, determines both an individual's role in the family division of labour and his (or her) share in family consumption.

Consumption within family-based households

Turning to consider differential consumption within families, we at once come up against the paradox that although virtually every economist and sociologist at least mentions the importance of the family household as a unit of consumption, there is a striking dearth of systematic studies of the ways in which it fulfils this function. There are very few studies which take as their topic what goes on inside households: how goods and services are actually distributed and used by individual members.[11]

National surveys, such as the Family Expenditure Survey in Britain, measure what is purchased by the household on the market, and they assume for statistical purposes that everything is divided up equally among all the members. They are concerned with the relative consumption of different households (that is, with differences between what households purchase or with differences between households in per capita consumption), not with what different individuals actually consume. They do not compare consumption by different family members, which includes what is consumed at home plus everything that all members consume outside, wherever the consumption takes place and whatever its form and modalities. They see the household as 'the unit of consumption', rather than as one distribution point among others for individual consumption.

Everyday experience tells us, however, that there are disparities of consumption between family members, and indeed that these differences are constitutive of family structure. **Differences in consumption are due to the existence of differential family status and are part of the way in which actors perceive and realize their own and other people's relative statuses.** We believe the overall resources of a given family (including the goods and services produced in the family for its own consumption) are distributed between the members according to the same principles as govern the division of labour. That is to say,

- resources carry differential valuation within the culture and can be ranked on a scale of prestige;
- they are distributed to individuals not according to rational or technical criteria of need or the amount of work people do, but according to their status as persons (according to their relationship to the head of the family and their sex, age and marital status); and
- the value attached to a resource is not itself independent of the status of the person who enjoys it. The head of the family, then any other men and eldest sons, have a consumption which is superior in quantity and quality to that of younger sons, women and girl children, and old

people (and, where present, distant kin or servants). What men consume carries prestige, and what carries prestige is consumed mainly or solely by men.

It is usually suggested that there is a relationship between the characteristics of individuals and what they need to consume – for example, between body size, energy expended and food requirements; or between the activities people perform and their needs – for example, men as breadwinners need pocket money (or regular sexual intercourse, or time to socialize outside the house, or whatever) to motivate them. These are even embodied in 'scientific' tables (for example, of calorific requirements or leisure spending needs – though not, so far as we know, of sexual needs). It is striking, though, how closely 'scientific' evaluations of 'needs' vary with the allocation of goods considered 'normal' for particular individuals in particular societies at particular times! The figures produced even by the UN Food and Agriculture Organization and the World Health Organization are as much reflections of *social* needs (that is, reflections of what is regarded as necessary for proper to each category) as everyday assumptions are.[12]

Part of the reason why actual differences in consumption are ignored by social surveys is because it goes against the somewhat socialist grain of many social scientists to admit that in conditions of scarcity or among members of the working class there is not equality of misfortune. It seems iniquitous that when there is barely enough to go round, some still take the lion's share and leave others seriously deprived. Being painful and morally unthinkable, this proposition has remained largely unthought by researchers. Yet in poor families in the West today even food, the most basic element of consumption and the most obviously familial, is not equally distributed; and the same applies to other essentials such as medical care, leisure time, education, money of one's own to allow modest self-indulgence outside the home, and access to sexual activity. Certainly historians have shown all these to have been very differentially distributed between family members in Europe in the past.[13]

The other side of this moralistic attitude is seen in the fact that social scientists do not seem to think differences between family members within rich families matter very much, even though in such families whole new areas of differential consumption are opened up – access to travel and transport (holidays and cars), leisure activities and hobbies, and clothes, food and drink of high quality or symbolic value. Sociologists certainly have not studied them. But we think the differences matter. After all, the fact that the rich have a lot more than the poor has not stopped sociologists looking at differences *between* rich and poor families, so why not also look *within* both? Especially as one of the differences between rich and poor families may be that there is more room for differential consumption between family members among the rich. Our colleagues may have little sympathy with 'bourgeois women' – for reasons we suspect have more to do with misogyny than with socialism – but that does not mean to say such women are not very differently placed from bourgeois men.

Differential consumption within the family cannot in any case be reduced simply to quantitative differences in access to particular goods. How you consume is at least as important as what and how much; and while it is difficult to identify a form of consumption which distinguishes the dominant from the dominated in the capitalist mode, since consumption is mediated by money, things are very different in the domestic mode. Here consumption is of primary importance and does discriminate, since one of the essential differences between the modes lies in the fact that those exploited by the domestic mode are not paid but maintained. In the domestic mode consumption is not separate from production, and the unequal sharing of goods is not mediated by money.

A woman who receives a coat does not receive the value of a coat. She receives a coat – which her husband may accompany her to buy and then pay for, or which he may leave her to pick out on her own. She 'just' has to tell him how much it cost. To say she receives its value abolishes the distinction between maintenance and free consumption, which is inependent of the value of the goods consumed. Anyone who thinks this a trivial distinction has forgotten their childhood and never lived as a 'kept' adult. It is one of the things married women find most unpleasant about their situation. A child being taken on an outing does not consume the family car in the same way as its father who has decided where to go and is the one who owns and drives this status symbol. We doubt they can really be said to consume the same trip.

Up till now, however, mainstream studies of consumption have been preoccupied exclusively with volumes and varieties – the very existence of different modes of consumption has not even been hinted at. Because of this, and in addition to it (one error leads into and adds onto the other), studies of consumption have also virtually ignored the distribution of everything produced within households for their own consumption. In research on family budgets (for example, the studies of farm production discussed in chapter 4) we are left to think that families eat raw food in shops – because the fact that goods are purchased, carried home, stored, cooked, served, and cleared away is ignored. But people consume not only primary materials, but also their preparation. Family members at home consume all the housework done by the 'mistress of the house', of which cooking is just a part. This includes some highly personalized services, for example, knowing the exact hour to serve meals, or how hot and how sweet particular people like to have their tea, or which clean shirt they are likely to want to wear for a meeting on Monday. Wives do such things for other people. They almost never have them done for them by others.

How differences in family consumption are maintained

In some cultures with a sexual division of labour, differentiation by gender is maintained by physical segregation and / or by work done and goods
consumed by men and women being quite separate in kind or timing. For
example, in Tunisia men and women eat different things at different times
(Ferchiou 1968). In European societies, however, although certain tasks
are exclusive to adults or to men or to women (that is, many work situations
are age and gender specific) and certain things are only or mainly consumed
by adult men (for example, all manner of sexual services, the facilities of
many clubs, sport, hobbies, cars and alcohol), generally the household's
rooms and food are 'shared'. Women and children get subordinate
consumption not because (or not only because) they eat separately from
men, but because when they do eat together food is chosen to suit the
household head's tastes, and because they get smaller portions of food of
more mediocre quality (fish fingers against cod fillets) while sitting at the
same table. Also, as far as women are concerned, they get a qualitatively
different meal from their husbands because they are in charge of the day-
to-day processes of purchase, preparation and clearing up.

This unequal distribution of 'family' goods and services is usually so
commonplace as to escape recognition. It is not something endlessly
renegotiated. In a particular social situation, in a given family, and at a
given standard of living, the content is not flexible. For example, the
same dishes appear regularly on the table and it is not necessary to work
out a new menu or a new distribution each time. The shares are fixed. If
father likes chicken but not curry or quiche, then the family will not have
curry or quiche; and on each chicken there will be 'his piece' (for example,
a drumstick and a lot of breast). But under new situations or in new
places, or in families other than our own, we may notice the general
principles of attribution in play since the specific content varies from the
one we are familiar with. That is, we may see that children are being
coerced and that women are self-sacrificing.

The physical infirmity of babies and young children and of the elderly
may make coercing them so easy it is all but invisible; but coercion is
necessary and visible when children are of an age to be 'thieves' – that
is, when they can move about freely but do not accept their restricted
access to certain desirable goods (that is, when they have not internalized
prohibitions). The goods then have to be stored on top shelves or in
rooms away from the kitchen and living room. Children are warned not
to touch them, and this injunction is backed up with threats of punishment
and proverbs, sayings, beliefs, and folk tales which justify controlling
their consumption.[14]

But it would be inconvenient if women were forbidden to touch certain
things, or if prized objects had to be physically protected from them,
since they manage the house and prepare the food. So women usually

have access to everything – even things they do not use or eat. They are controlled instead by honour and shame and fear of gossip. They are not in the house by themselves all that often, which means they can keep little of what they do secret, and if they do illicitly 'treat themselves' when on their own or 'steal' a drink from the cooking sherry, they are seen as greedy and sinful. They have to hide their 'misdemeanour' if anyone catches them in the act. However, women mostly impose restrictions on themselves and leave the best of everything for others as part of the wider repressive ideology of the good, self-sacrificing wife and mother. Women have latitude – great flexibility as to the details – in the form of the restrictions they put on their own consumption, provided they follow the simple general principle of always preserving the privileges of the husband and father and 'sacrificing' themselves. They thus 'choose' what to do in any new situation for which there are no existing instructions (and as managers of the home they, like all overseers, confront such situations constantly). They feel they have 'chosen' to do certain things from personal preference when in fact these are precisely the inferior things to which they are entitled. By and large, however, they are not aware of 'choosing', since self-sacrifice becomes second nature. The mistress of the house takes the smallest chop without thinking, and if there are not enough for everyone, she will not have one at all. She will say she is not hungry, and no one is surprised, least of all herself, that it is always the same person who 'doesn't want any' and 'doesn't mind'.

The flexibility of consumption – the fact that what is defined is not a specific content but rather a general principle of attribution – allows for discretion when, for whatever reason, a household's scale of relative values changes. For instance, if we look from rural to urban households, or between low and high income sectors, we find an overall increase in the food consumed, and we might therefore expect differential consumption to become less marked in this area at least. But in fact it still continues. A particular delicacy, or something in short supply, is still purchased and reserved for the head of the household. Thus even in wealthy families food can still provide a symbolic marking of privileged access.

But in addition, in wealthier families with their higher standard of living, differentiation of family membership via consumption is also possible in a whole series of other areas. For example, the acquisition of a car by a household in which previously everybody travelled by public transport introduces differentiation into an area – transport – which up till then was undifferentiated, and considerably increases the overall difference in consumption (variance in the standard of living) between the user(s) of the car and other family members. When there is only one car for a household the husband / father usually takes it to work leaving his wife carless, even though women make as many trips as their husbands (shopping and taking children to school or clinics or parks or libraries) and even though the design of housing estates assumes everyone has a car.

This is especially likely in households using company cars (one in ten of total UK cars). Of those provided with a company car in 1986, 85 per cent were men and 15 per cent women . . . Furthermore, even if the household buys its own car, there is a marked tendency for the car to be seen as 'his' and this is demonstrated by the preponderance of male drivers and women passengers. A recent survey of couples arriving in cars to visit the Thames Barrier found that even when both had a driving licence, 97 per cent of drivers were male. (Beuret 1991: 63)

Women are therefore faced with unreliable, expensive public transport, with routes which do not always go where they want them to, while coping with children and carrying shopping. Men also use cars for their leisure trips (to pubs, clubs, etc.) while women's social trips are mainly by foot (visiting). This is not simply because women cannot drive, because significantly more women in France and the UK have held driving licences since the mid 1970s, but because few women (and particularly few among the poorer groups of women) have real access to a car.[15] There is, of course, in any case a vicious circle between not having access to a car and not learning to drive.

The purchase of a second or third car can introduce further, symbolic differentiation: a BMW saloon for the household head, a Peugeot hatchback for his wife, and a Mini for the daughter.

The unequal distribution of resources within a family is therefore added to the inequalities of the division of labour. One inequality leads into another, rather than being compensated for. Those who do the most valued tasks and who are considered functionally the most important are also those who benefit from the highest and best consumption. Men are better treated because it is customary, and also because heads of families (and men generally) are seen as doing more important work so it is 'only fair' that what they get reflects their contribution. Men need to be spoiled in the home otherwise they might go away and the family would lose its breadwinner.

Transmission in the family

The family involves not only production and consumption, which are our main concerns in this book, but also, like all economic modes, circulation and reproduction: the passing of property and status from one individual to another over time and the re-constitution of new groups and the overall system. This includes:

- the transmission of property at death or on marriage (inheritance and dowry) and as gifts in the form of land and buildings, tangibles such as livestock, furniture, equipment and other stock, and intangibles such as financial assets, jewellery and cash;

- the transmission of office / position / rank (succession); and
- membership of a kin / social group (descent / affiliation).

In dealing with transmission we are concerned not with the family in space (the household) but with the family in time (the line). The line includes certain individuals in the group constituted by a current household, but it is not restricted to them. Within the household the line is principally represented by individuals who are members of different generations (grandparents, parents and children), though it also includes individuals of the same generation (brothers and sisters) in so far as they are descended from the same ancestors. It is this common descent which is the foundation of the line, and it is along this that family property (patrimony) is passed.

Western Europe has what is technically termed a bilateral descent system with a patrifilial bias. That is, descent is traced and property and status are devolved through both mother and father. We do not distinguish between relatives on our father's and our mother's side (for example, we use the same names – uncle and aunt – for the siblings of both parents and do not stress the ties with any particular set of grandparents); but the father–son line is prioritized. Our system is also (and has long been) characterized by a strong focus on the nuclear family group and the marital relationship, with links to the wider kin group being of increasingly less significance.[16] Women can inherit, own, use, manage and testate (will to other people) most forms of property and we can succeed to most statuses (ranks and positions) – but we usually only do so in the absence of a suitable male heir and / or under certain limiting conditions.

In western culture the transmission of property and the generational recruitment which is required by human mortality is implicitly and self-evidently hereditary. The passing on of wealth and status and the replacement of the holders of certain positions other than by descent and affinity is often simply not envisaged. Other forms of recruitment certainly exist – people can join groups by election or adoption or co-option or the drawing of straws, and positions can be attained by achievement – but the terms 'transmission' and 'inheritance' connote *family* transfers and are reserved for this sort of devolution. They are used, moreover, whatever the things transferred may be – property, status, customs, habits or physical traits.

Provided transmission takes place within the nuclear group, therefore, both individuals and the state take the devolution of goods to descendants for granted, and conversely the designation of other beneficiaries is regarded with suspicion and accepted only when strongly justified. (The fact that inheritance by anyone other than the spouse or children must be justified, and formally recorded in a will, shows that inheritance by children itself requires no justification.) Passing a major share of things on to anyone other than members of one's close family is regarded as 'wronging the children', confirming they are the 'normal', 'proper' heirs; and indeed despite almost complete freedom to leave their property to whoever they wish, 90 per cent of testators in the US, for instance, limit substantial bequests to just spouses, sons and daughters.[17]

As with consumption, the only aspect of patrimonial transmission which has really been studied to date has been the way in which inheritance creates divisions *between* households, or between male (actual or future) heads of households. The action of heredity is assumed to produce similarity between parents and children – or rather between a father and all his male children. Thus when a father and son are in the same socio-economic group, that is, when there is supposedly 'stability', it is attributed to heredity; but when they are in different socio-economic groups, the difference is seen as needing to be explained – and an explanation is sought outside of the family. Social mobility is, for example, attributed to a rise or fall based on ability, or to changes in the overall class structuring of society.

But transmission is part of the institution of the family, and like other aspects of the family it is hierarchical. Although studies of inheritance, social mobility and cultural transmission may treat all the children of a family as if they are equal to one another, as if all are equally 'heirs', this is in fact not the case. The fact of being born into a family does not guarantee you will be an heir, still less that you will succeed to your father's position or status. With transmission too there is differentiation between family members, and the same general principles as we have described in relation to production and consumption apply again. The number and nature of inheritors or successors is restricted and regulated by rules of kinship and marriage; inheritance and succession is prescribed; and property and positions are distributed on the basis of status, not on skill or need, especially as regards gender.

- The resources which are devolved carry differential valuation.
- The value of a resource is not independent of the person who transmits and the person who receives it. The head of the family, then other men and elder sons, inherit, own and transmit more (in quantity and quality) than younger sons, women and children.
- Resources are distributed to individuals not according to need or work done, but according to their status as persons (according to their relationship to the head of the family and their age, sex and marital status). Land, commercial property (including shares in private companies) and trade and professional skills seldom pass to women, except when there is no male child. Daughters tend to inherit cash or valuables or houses rather than firms or businesses; and the professional classes invest more in the education of sons than of daughters, thereby passing on to males middle class occupational positions and earning capacity. Widows may inherit, but they hold mainly deposits in building societies, cash, and stock market securities (which are often managed for them by male members of the family).[18]

- Although overall there are rules and norms governing inheritance, the head of household has considerable discretion regarding to whom he gives what and when.

Transmission of goods in the family is clearly very different from the circulation of goods in the market. In the market, goods are exchanged either directly or via money, by and between actors who are (typically) free to choose a favourable occasion, who their protagonist shall be, and the amount to ask for what they exchange. Whereas in the family, goods are passed without equivalence or counterpart by actors who (often) do not choose either the time or the beneficiaries (the latter being determined by legal rules concerning obligations to persons of a certain status relative to the benefactor), or the nature and amount of what they transmit. That is to say, the same principle, the absence of exchange, which we encountered in relation to production and consumption again characterizes family transactions.

There is a bewildering variety of detail in the laws (and customs) governing transmission within the various jurisdictions of western countries, and patterns of transmission have changed over time with changes in the forms of property, taxation (for example, inheritance tax), social insurance (for example, pensions) and demography (the average number of children per family and individuals' life expectancy).[19] But it is still possible to see some general patterns.

Transmission of position or rank (succession) is still regarded as obvious and legitimate when access to a position requires the transmission of goods. For example, to become a farmer or a shopkeeper it is necessary to acquire a farm or shop, and this generally involves inheritance of the land or the premises. Given private ownership of land and buildings, the handing on of land or buildings from father to son is taken as quasi-natural, so the transmission of status is an almost fortuitous consequence. But transmission of status is less licit for the majority of the contemporary population who operate in those areas where access to positions is supposed to be by merit – that is, where access is determined by a proven capacity to fill an office, as shown by, for example, having done an apprenticeship or passing exams or holding certificates.

This is of course a relatively new innovation in western society. Until quite recently many positions which are today (formally) acquired on merit, for example, being a professor, a manager, a Member of Parliament, a judge or solicitor, or a surgeon, were directly inherited or purchased with inherited money. And many positions which are supposedly merito-cratic today involve both qualifications and wealth and kin connections – not to mention being of the right sex (for example, becoming a docker or a railwayman or a barrister or an officer in the Guards).

But the continuing growth of positions access to which is governed by formal channels (courses, examinations and formal training) has meant succession as classically tied to material inheritance has been displaced by (or complemented by) transmission of status via the transmission of cultures and techniques which help to ensure success in courses and examinations. Middle class children acquire a culture which enables them to do well in the education system, and their parents know how to handle this system to best advantage. So today it is not so much a question of the transmission of a father's actual position or even his occupation to his sons (that is, it is not a question of the sons of farmers becoming the owners of particular farms, or the sons of doctors becoming doctors), but rather a transmission to (male) children of a socio-economic or class position similar to that of their (male) parent via the provision of an education which ensures entry to an occupation equivalent to his.[20]

What has so far escaped attention, but is intrinsic to transmission as part of the family system, is that overall, whatever the details of the laws and customs and the changes over time, **each system of inheritance and transmission is based on advantage / disadvantage and inequality.** In some cases girls and younger sons have been absolutely disadvantaged: they have not been able to hold or earn or inherit any property whatsoever (and therefore *a fortiori* have not succeeded to their father's position when property is needed for this). But in general girls and younger sons have been relatively disadvantaged: they have inherited less or different things than boys and eldest siblings.

For example, although the laws and customs of our societies today allow daughters and younger sons to have the same education and training as older brothers, they often do not actually have the same cultural capital invested in them. We believe this produces much of the difference between boys and girls and by birth order which has been recognized in research on schooling and by psychologists – though to date these differences have always been treated as attributable to general social processes, for example, to sex role socialization or experiences in school, rather than to the logic of family hierarchy.

Inequalities in inheritance and succession are especially clear when there are a large number of children in the family and relatively limited resources, or non-partible inheritance (so only one child, or at most two children, can be placed in the father's position). Inequalities are also clear when the father chooses to display marked favouritism and refuses to give help to particular children. But even when the system and the individual head is 'egalitarian', when property is divisible, and when there are few offspring, children are not treated totally equally.

Property and goods can be divided so they have equal face value but not equal functional value, and of course notions of what equals what are flexible. For example, a professional father is more likely to invest in the education of his son than his daughter, by supporting the son in going to university and the daughter in training as a nurse, though he could spend an equal sum on the daughter by sending her to a finishing school in Switzerland. Either way the son and the daughter end up in very different market situations. A father who is a garage owner may give one son the business and another (what he has decided is) the equivalent value in cash. The latter may soon be dissipated, and in any event is unlikely to yield an income at the same rate unless the second son is lucky enough to buy another good business with his money. Or a father may help his daughter's husband to set up in business, or give his daughter gifts (for example, help buying a house or with school fees) which essentially go to her husband or children.

What the non-heirs actually get under any one system is obviously of enormous importance to the younger brothers and all the daughters concerned, but it has virtually never been studied. Studies of inheritance have focused on the small minority of families with wealth or property (especially those with land) and the rather larger minority of people who leave wills. Or else they have been concerned with changes in the law itself (which is a bit of a contradiction because by writing a will you can largely ignore the descent and distribution patterns established by the state). Studies of social mobility, on the other hand, have been obsessed with looking to see how many people (men) rise up the social ladder, and they have simply assumed parity between siblings (or rather between brothers). No one has seen that some family members may go down as a condition of others going up. That is to say, that resources may be put into one child at the expense of the others. However, the fact is that some sons have to struggle to acquire what is bestowed upon their brothers. The non-succession of the majority of children may be the price of the succession of one of them to the entire estate of the father.

Inheritance and mobility studies also typically do not consider gender differences, or indeed women at all. Women, however, rarely own and control productive property, nor do they acquire the skills which are highly valued within a sex-discriminatory labour market. In the nineteenth century unmarried girls and women routinely worked unpaid for their fathers and inheriting brothers, or they were conspicuously leisured and supported by their male kin. Nowadays they usually have (quite lowly) paid employment until they marry, and then work unpaid for an 'inheritor' from another family (that is, for a husband).[21]

Transmission thus produces both similarity and difference: between fathers and sons, between brothers, and between sons and daughters. It is both a stabilizing factor and a system producing mobility. It can define that some are downwardly mobile – not to any old where but to a particular lower position (dependent on the forms of property, the degree of primogeniture and the numbers of children of different sexes). It distributes people into classes and subclasses, and creates individuals without a class position of their own (for example, girls and sometimes younger sons). It therefore acts directly on the very constitution of each class.

The structure of family transmission means that certain people born into a social class are not still in it. Some have been helped to rise at the price of some others having to fall. It also means that certain people born into a social class are in it in a different way from others born into it.

Certain people fill the positions which define the class (for example, they are farmers, or have working class or middle class jobs), while other individuals are also part of the class but specifically do not hold these positions, that is, they are the dependants of the position holders.[22] These 'non-holders' are now principally wives, though other dependent family members – unmarried brothers and sisters and grown children of the household head – still exist in Europe, especially in the south. They have a particular situation within a social class. Their status is that of not holding a class position.

Transmission therefore produces not only effects across time (it creates non-inheritors and non-successors as a condition of producing inheritors and successors), it also produces effects at particular points in time (it creates family roles) because the non-inheritors / non-successors fill particular positions. The patriarchal system rests not only on customs and laws governing the relations of generations and of spouses, it is also reinforced at another level, one which does not seem directly to concern gender divisions and the position of women – namely, inheritance and succession.

Depriving women of the means of production by patrimonial transmission is not, however, the only way in which they are dispossessed of direct access to their means of subsistence, if only because many families precisely do not have any family property not to transmit to them. The same effect is produced by the systematic discrimination which women face in the wage-labour market. This also pushes women to enter domestic relations of production (mainly by getting married or cohabiting with a man, though some may act as housekeepers for kin). That is, the labour market itself plays a role in the exploitation of women's domestic work – and this has become increasingly important as inheritance has become of more restricted importance.

Patrimony is 'the property of the family', but it is held at any one time by particular individuals, and it is passed by them (usually men but sometimes women) to other individuals. Patrimony is not in our systems of law the property of the family as a group. All goods are private property: they belong to specific individuals at any given time – except for the special case of family trusts which are set up specifically to ensure one particular individual does not misappropriate property intended to go down the family line.

Holding family property as an individual gives the person concerned power and advantages, for although he (or less often she) may be bound by law and custom to give certain things to certain people at certain times, he still has a lot of latitude. A husband / father can dispose of the property he holds entirely, alienating it from his dependants venally (that is, he can sell all he holds and squander the proceeds); or he can give much of it away during his lifetime; or bequeath it to whoever he wants in his will (though if he leaves it till his death his descendants may be legally entitled to a significant share).

Equally the income coming into a home, even if it is a so-called family wage or money from the sale of goods and services produced by the family, or even if it is a married couple's pension or unemployment benefit, is under the authority of one individual. This gives him certain power and advantages. He may choose to pass his whole wage-packet over to his wife to handle (see chapter 7), especially if there is not very much money coming in and struggling to make it cover the family's needs is a chore. Or he can use some of it for household expenses and some for his personal consumption – and then save the rest and use it to establish or increase or improve existing property and capital held in his name. His wife and perhaps children continue to work for him unpaid whatever he decides to give them, so their labour may serve (if he so chooses) to increase the property he holds as the head of the family.

Conclusion

We have constantly stressed that it is not possible to treat the family as an economic unit except from the viewpoint of the market, because it is not a company of equals. On the contrary, the family is a unit with a hierarchy. Its members are not all of the same status doing the same sort of work and getting the same sort of rewards. Rather the family in space (the household) and in time (the line) are sets of gendered and generational statuses regarding both the division of labour and the distribution of re-sources. And families are in turn located within wider societies in which there are other age and gender inequalities, and the various sets of in-equalities feed into one another.

Other units of production, for example, factories, are also sets of statuses relating to the division of labour and the distribution of resources, but family households cannot be likened to a business or company, with the head of the family equal to the head of the firm – except again from the point of view of the market. The head of a family enterprise certainly has in common with the head of a firm that he owns property and the products produced by his subordinates, and that he is consequently the one able to exchange them. But the subordinates in a non-family business are wage earners. They sell their work to the head of the firm. Their exploitation is based on the extortion of surplus value. The work they do and the rewards they get are subject to the laws of the market. A wage implies exchange and notions of counterpart and equivalence (which is not, of course, the same thing as equity). Furthermore, the existence of generalized exchange – of a labour *market* – leads to the development of a generalized and more or less universal wage scale.

Neither payment nor exchange exists in the family, and there is no universal scale for what might be considered to replace the wage: maintenance. So,

- in two different families the work of persons of similar status (for example, that of wife) can be 'rewarded' by very different standards of living; and
- dependants within one family doing the same work can get different rewards depending on their status (for example, children and apprentices did the same work in the past but got treated differently, as do and are eldest and youngest children today).

The specific exploitation of family workers is not based on the extortion of surplus value but rather on the fact that their labour is not 'free'. This does not mean they are not exploited, whatever crude marxists may say. It means rather that 'exploitation', like 'class', has become used too narrowly: as only occurring within the capitalist mode of production (see chapter 2). Family subordinates do not own their labour power in the same way as heads of households, and so cannot sell it, or can sell only some of it – and then they do not fully own the money received. The specificity of family work is that the worker's whole work capacity is appropriated; that it is appropriated by a particular individual from whom it is difficult or impossible to separate; and that the worker is not paid but maintained.

In comparing family workers to wage workers, as people constantly do, they presume an individual can be equally one or the other. But this is in fact the case for only the more privileged family members. That is to say, the very possibility of not being a family worker is a privilege.

The differences stressed here do not exhaust all the ways in which the family economy and the market economy differ from each other. They are rather the major oppositions on which are based the theoretical and empirical differences we shall be examining in the rest of the book. However, in so far as this chapter has established that the domestic (family) economy has different relations from, and does not obey, the laws of the market (that is, exchange), we shall from here on consider it to be a separate form, or mode of production.

The structure and action of the domestic mode of production outlined here provides a basis for greatly enhancing our understanding of the 'articulation' of gender and class which is so important to materialist feminism. We have shown how gender is created and socio-economic differences reproduced by the family: that is, how actors are differentiated (by gender, age, and their possession of various forms of property) by the family mode of production (through the processes of production, consumption and transmission). Individuals learn different skills in family households, some own but others do not own what they produce in the family, some have only limited access to the labour market, and different individuals are provided with different inheritances and different investments in their education and training. These differentiated actors therefore become differentially located protagonists in the labour and other markets; and we know from other studies (though we have not explored this here) that gender (and age and socio-economic) differentiation is also independently created within the market systems themselves.

In other words, we are moving towards an understanding of the gender constitution of classes and the class constitution of gender, recognizing that within both the domestic and the capitalist modes of production, men and women constitute opposed classes or class factions, in that men (as fathers and husbands, and employers and privileged wage workers) directly benefit from the oppression / exploitation of women's work.

Notes

1   Where, for example, the only public land consists of parks or areas around high-rise flats, with no chickens or goats allowed and no allotments; where most of the houses are rented so there is little scope for home improvement or working from home; where one cannot even keep rabbits in a hutch or mend cars in the road if one wants good relations with neighbours; where washing is done in launderettes not by local laundresses; and where there is negligible scope for living off rents or subletting accommodation (see R. Pahl 1984).
2   See Delphy (1976b).
3   I.e. a person 'who takes all decisions and others just obey . . . with complete command over all economic actions of everyone in the family'. This is, however, how some have chosen to characterize all models of the family household which recognize that such groups do have heads. See for instance Harris (1981) and Sen (1984).
4   The concept of legitimate authority relations uses the ideas of Max Weber (trans. 1947). Using his models of ideal types of authority relationships, the relations between husbands and wives have been compared with the relations between masters and servants (Davidoff 1973b) and slave owners and slaves (Genovese 1972, used by Anyon 1983), as well as with a variety of other relations also characterized by deferential behaviour (see Newby 1972, used in Bell and Newby 1976).
5   Jalna Hanmer has noted, however, that men's reasons for using violence in domestic situations is often unclear. Inflicting violence is certainly not a good way to get housework or childcare or even straightforward sexual servicing done effectively, since the woman is often so injured (physically or psychically) as to be incapacitated for family work for short or long periods. See Hanmer (1978) and also Dobash and Dobash (1980).
6   See Newby (1972) and Bell and Newby (1976).
7   Davidoff, L'Esperance and Newby (1976) note interesting parallels with the use of the rural community as a means to keep the rural working class subordinate. They stress the zealousness of the Regency and Victorian upper and middle classes in re-creating conditions favourable to stable deference to traditional authority so as to keep people in their place. The gentry and

bourgeoisie restricted working class geographical mobility and stressed the virtues of stable, rural, village communities and the local leadership of a squire who took care of and protected his dependants, making decisions on their behalf. Davidoff, L'Esperance and Newby also note the hostility of the upper classes to both unrestrained market determinism (market values entering into relations between farmers and farm workers, and between the gentry and the local poor) and to ideas of egalitarianism and socialism.

8   E.g. Pauline Kirk (1980) found that when married women Open University students took time to pursue their own interests and to do a course, their husbands (or elderly parents or in-laws) might prevent it by playing up / not supporting it / criticizing her housewifery / creating tension / or downgrading the importance of the qualification. Kirk concluded that wives were not supposed to spend time on their own longer-term interests and development, e.g. attending courses and conferences, and certainly not on any women's organizations (neither those for the advancement of individual women nor those for the advancement of women as a group).

9   See particularly Becker's work (1981) on household time allocation, Sen's work (1983; 1984) on family economies as a 'bargaining problem' with 'co-operative conflicts', and R. Pahl's (1984) concept of 'household strategies'.
   Becker has applied human capital models to the distribution of members' time in multi-person households. Sen has sought to qualify traditional price theory, market allocation, and welfare analysis by recognizing that families have internal structures and that all family members may benefit from co-operating but that different members have 'strictly conflicting interests in the choice among the set of efficient co-operative arrangements' (1984; 357). Pahl has considered how, within the constraints of local conditions and possibilities, households determine their cash income and what in general (or in every last particular) it is used for.

10 See Hamill (1979).

11 Cf., however, recent work on differential consumption of food: Delphy (1974), Murcott (1982), Kerr and Charles (1986), Charles and Kerr (1987; 1988) and Charles (1990). On the handling and distribution of money, see Whitehead (1981), Edwards (1981), J. Pahl (1983; 1990), Morris and Ruane (1989) and Wilson (1987). On the distribution of other resources in households, see p. 126 n. 4.

12 See Den Hartog (1973), FAO / WHO (1973) and Delphy (1974).

> There are by now a great many doubts about the whole basis of nutritional requirement calculations. There seems to be a substantial amount of interpersonal variability, and even for a given person much variation over time. Also possibilities of 'multiple equilibria' of energy intake and use – at various levels of consumption – seem to exist. Furthermore, there are good reasons to dispute the assumptions about the energy use of activities performed by women, which are not as 'sedentary' as calorie calculations tend to assume. Also the extra nutrition requirements of pregnant women and lactating mothers require fuller acknowledgement.

Finally, there is a great danger of circular reasoning in linking calorie 'requirements' to physical characteristics, since energy 'requirements' are calculated by multiplying the body weight by 'energy requirements per kg body weight', related to the activity level, while the person's body weight as well as his or her activity level does depend crucially on the energy intake of the person. Calorie deficiency can, up to a point, justify itself! (Sen 1984: 351)

13   See for example, Young (1952), Oren (1974) and Davidoff, L'Esperance and Newby (1976: 156).

14   This argument is developed and examples given in Delphy (1974).

15   Only 27 per cent of women in London drive a car at least once a week – but among Afro-Caribbean women and disabled women the proportion is even lower (10 per cent of Afro-Caribbean women, 14 per cent of women with a disability aged under 60, and a miniscule 4 per cent of disabled women aged over 60). See the GLC Women and Transport Surveys (Greater London Council 1984; 1987) quoted in Beuret (1991: 62).

16   For further discussion of past changes in what is characteristic of western inheritance, see Goody (1976; 1983).

17   See Shammas, Salmon and Dahlin (1987: 207).

18   See Bourdieu (1972), Marceau (1976), Harbury and Hitchens (1979: 86) and Shammas, Salmon and Dahlin (1987).

19   Research on the history of inheritance is mostly centred on the period before the nineteenth century and is principally concerned with the inheritance of land. See Goody (1976; 1983) and Goody, Thirsk and Thompson (1976). We still lack information on the relationship between inheritance laws and marital property legislation, and also on the relationship between inheritance and demographic patterns. On recent changes in inheritance related to changes in forms of property see Glendon (1981) and Shammas, Salmon and Dahlin (1987).

20   See especially the work of Bourdieu and Passeron (1964; 1970), though this topic has been one of the major foci of the whole of the sociology of education.

21   The sexual division of labour means that there is a heterosexual couple at the heart of each household. This allows the continuation of the family in time by biological reproduction rather than by, say, adoption or co-option.

22   I.e. it produces members of a class in the strict sense of the word, and members of a class in a wider, group sense (see Delphy and Leonard 1986.)

PART III
EMPIRICAL STUDIES

7

FACTORY WORKERS' FAMILIES
IN BRITAIN

In this chapter and the next we shall describe and discuss families which are at the two ends of the continuum of family production outlined in chapter 6. That is to say,

- families where production in the household is almost entirely for members' own consumption, and it is done mainly by wives;
- and units where a range of kin of both sexes work for the head of the household, producing goods and services for their own consumption and for the market.

In both cases, but particularly in the former, part of the wife's time may also be devoted to paid employment at stages in the family cycle when she is not needed full time for family work.

As examples we have taken factory workers' families in Britain and farming families in France. In chapter 9 we shall look at the families of men in other occupations, arguing that although the factory worker's family is taken to be the typical household form of industrial capitalism, in fact in far more cases than is generally realized, the head of a family not only uses the labour of family members (and some of his own) for 'self-provisioning', he also still sells goods and services produced in his family household on the (formal or informal) market.

Farm families in France are well suited to our purpose since because of their national importance (and a nostalgia for rural life) they have been quite extensively studied by economists, sociologists and historians, and the work of farmers' wives and other dependants has been studied directly. More information is available about them as economic units than about virtually any other sort of family.

Factory workers' families present us with more problems, however, because despite their significance in the evolution of industrial capitalism, we actually know little about the family lives of male factory workers as such. We know about the men's work lives in factories, but researchers have tended either not to be interested in such men's domestic lives or to presume they know what they are like. They have therefore generally not bothered to ask men about their households, let alone to take on the time-consuming exercise of locating and talking to such men's dependants.[1]

Fortunately, however, there are a few studies which provide good information, and we shall discuss in this chapter an influential sociological study of workers in car assembly, ball-bearing machining and the process production of chemicals in Luton, a town just north of London, in the mid 1960s; a study of 25 couples where the husbands were production foreman, shop stewards and rank and file production workers in a firm making cardboard packing cases in Bristol, a city in southwest England, in the early 1970s; and a study of steel workers in Port Talbot in South Wales who were all made redundant in the early 1980s.[2]

These case studies tell us more about the division of labour than they do about decision-making and consumption within households, and they tell us very little indeed about sexuality, family planning or the transmission of property. But since their material was not gathered to support our analysis of the family, the fact that it does support it so well, shows the usefulness of our approach.[3]

These three studies looked at different parts of southern Britain and were done over a period of 20 years. We are not seeking to suggest they cover either the whole range of marital roles to be found among male factory workers, nor that they show general changes over time – though it is worth noting that the earliest study shows what is often presented as the 'modern' working class pattern and the mid 1980s one a more 'traditional' role division. Rather we are simply taking instances where there is good information available on the domestic lives of male industrial wage earners to develop our model of the family and to show some of the variability associated with even one particular type of male occupation.

The researchers deliberately selected married men as their respondents, so none of the studies tells us anything about the domestic lives of single men or widowers in such occupations[4] (and they obviously tell us nothing about the divorced, widowed or single women who were or had been associated with such men). The researchers were also exclusively concerned with married men in the age groups likely to have dependent children, not youths or men close to retirement. In addition, they do not tell us whether there were any ethnic differences within their samples, or whether or not there were any adults other than the spouses in the households studied (for example, grown children, elderly relatives or lodgers), and if so what their contribution to household economics might have been.[5] We therefore do not know the extent to which women were caring for sick or elderly relatives, or how much domestic work was done by or for teenage and young adult offspring, nor how much income was contributed by wage-earning sons and daughters, and to whom.

The Luton study interviewed 219 blue-collar married men between the ages of 21 and 45 in 1962, seeing each of them for about an hour in their factories and again at home for up to three hours with their wives. They also observed life in the factories but not in the homes and local communities. Since men, unlike women, bring little of their home lives to shop-floor culture, the description of factory life is rich and detailed but the account of domestic life is thin. Indeed their selection of material for analysis from what was covered in the questionnaire on areas relating to family and community seems noticeably patchy. The team did not ask what women's jobs were when they had them, though many wives in Luton did have paid employment, nor do they distinguish their findings on the division of domestic labour by whether the wife is employed or not, or by the hours she works, or by whether or not there are children and of what age. We are told information was gathered on these factors, but it has not been written up.[6] But whatever its shortcomings, this study was a great improvement (for our purposes) on other studies of similar male workers at the time.

These particular workers were selected because they were 'affluent' and supposedly far removed from the 'traditional' working class. The researchers wanted to see if, as was claimed, such well-paid manual workers were becoming 'embourgeoised' (that is, if they had attitudes to work and domestic life-styles and political orientations which were becoming more and more like those of the middle class). So questions were focused on the ways in which the working class and the middle class were seen to differ – not on areas where the researchers assumed the 'traditional' and 'new' working classes and the middle classes were already alike, for example, as regards the basic structure of marriage.[7]

The men were all employed in 'fairly conventional mass production'. What made them notable was that many (60 per cent) of them had been prepared to move from other parts of the country to Luton, an area of existing high immigration, and to shift their occupation from work they found more satisfying, in order to get the higher wages, better housing and secure employment to be found in the southeast of England.

The Bristol study set off from a concern to know how husbands' industrial experience and views on trade unionism get mediated to their wives, and how wives' experience of their own work, both paid and unpaid, was mediated to their husbands. It ended up comparing differences in the class consciousness and class ideology of husbands and wives. The factory chosen 'lacked any extreme features' (the work was not dangerous; the factory was medium sized – 500 employees, mainly men; and there was no history of major strikes). Bristol is a prosperous city, but these men had a basic wage about one-third below the national (male) average and even those who worked a lot of overtime were unlikely to get much over the average.

Men who saw themselves as fulfilling the criteria of being married with dependent children (under 16) and whose wives were 'principally occupied at home' were asked to volunteer to be interviewed. Not surprisingly, therefore, the sample is made up of conventional couples: self-defined 'family men' in their mid-thirties with long marriages (and only one second marriage), mostly born and bred in the city, with wives who were not employed full-time. The researcher made first contact with the men at work in the firm's time, but then saw them at home and she maintained contact over the course of a year. Half the sample lived on a large barren postwar housing estate four miles south of the city; the rest closer in, in more traditional prewar working class areas near the factory.

In Port Talbot in the 1950s and 1960s the vast majority of the male inhabitants worked for the British Steel Corporation. Jobs with BSC were well paid and sought after, but de-manning began in the late 1960s, and in the summer of 1980 the workforce was suddenly cut in half (from 12,000 to 5,000). A team at Swansea University studied the town two years later to see which men had found what kinds of employment and what had happened to domestic life. From a sample of 750 redundant workers, Lydia Morris took a sub-sample of 40 married men aged 20-55, and interviewed the couple jointly and then each spouse independently and separately, about their employment, leisure, division of domestic work and financial management.

Production by family members

Men's work outside and inside the home

The 'affluent workers' of Luton are described as working long and hard at boring jobs for high pay in pursuit of a continuing rise in living standards. Despite 'progressive management', their work was unrewarding and stressful: tasks were monotonous, the pace was too fast, and the men disliked the rules which restricted their freedom of action and lead to (what they saw as) an unfair allocation of work and levels of pay. 'On the line' they 'blanked out their minds' or 'thought about crossword puzzles' or 'about the kids and the next premium being paid'.

Many of the ball-bearing machinists and car assemblers had previously had more skilled and interesting but less well-paid and secure work with other firms and in other towns. In Luton they worked long hours round the clock on conveyor belts or beating the clock on piece-work, under close supervision. Even those employed as craftsmen were put to very specialized, regulated work. The chemical process work was not so physically hard or unpleasant, nor so closely supervised, but here too overtime was routine. The average week was nearer 50 than 40 hours, and there was regular night work and a double day shift system. This gave some daytime leisure, but even so it could have adverse social, psychological or physical effects. Men with heavy domestic responsibilities were particularly likely to take on even more overtime. Thus paradoxically men who were home-centred, who spent a lot of money on home comforts and family needs, and whose wives might be particularly busy with home-building or small children, tended to work very long hours away from home.

Most men interviewed had no commitment to the job or the company they worked for, just an overriding concern with economic rewards to enable them to enjoy their time off the job, which was largely spent at home and centred on their wives and children. They worried about redundancy and short-time working because of their mortgage and HP commitments and they wanted a car to drive to work and 'to take out the wife and kids'. They did not want to take on supervisory jobs because they felt they would not then be able to slough off work worries at the end of the day: they distinguished very clearly between work and out-of-work life. Many did not use their firm's quite extensive social facilities because they wanted nothing to do with the company after working hours; and they rarely carried ties with workmates into friendships outside the plant.

Work in the cardboard factory in Bristol was also heavy and noisy and the atmosphere was always unpleasantly hot and dusty. The men there operated case-making, stapling and printing machines, or moved materials around sometimes using fork-lift trucks. The work was all semi-skilled: 'No jobs on the factory floor took more than a fortnight to learn.' But although it was monotonous and a lot of it physically exhausting, the men had more control over it than assembly-line workers and they were not as alienated from their company and workmates. The workforce was very stable with low turnover. As in Luton, the men were ambivalent about getting promoted to foreman, but in Bristol it was because although it would give more money it would lose them friends.

The men were quite sure that their motivation for taking on such work was to fulfil their responsibilities as breadwinners. They answered questions about why they had gone to this firm in the first place and why they stuck with the particular job in terms of family priorities: it paid better money than where they were before and they needed that with a family even if the work was less interesting; and they stayed because the work was secure, steady and reliable, and near home, and because they could earn extra for shifts and overtime when the family needed it. At least half did regular overtime, up to 20 hours a week. Some were on three shifts and were paid extra for night work, though most were on two.

All the men in the sample were in a trade union, and half were shop stewards. One of the unions in the factory had been on strike for a month before the fieldwork and this had been a busy, exciting and worrying time for everyone, especially the shop stewards in the union involved. Union work always took up a lot of time – on Sunday mornings and when meetings overlapped into the evening; but during the strike there were also frequent telephone calls to the men at home and they had spent long extra hours in meetings.

In South Wales, work in the steel mills had been seen as skilled and secure: a job for life and an enviable one, which men sought hard to get, using contacts through relatives or friends already working there. After redundancy, the men had experiences varying

> from long term unemployment . . . to immediate or eventual success in acquiring a relatively secure job . . . whilst between these two extremes

[there were] complex patterns resulting from different combinations of short term employment [under poor working conditions], retraining, unemployment, and 'unofficial' employment in the informal sector of the economy. (Morris 1984c: 6)

The short-term work was with contractors (often working for BSC itself) and the 'unofficial' work was for neighbours (for example, help with building work and odd jobbing). Both of these were generally acquired 'by virtue of membership of a well-developed network of social contacts' (Morris 1984c: 7) often based around a pub, sports club or social club. This ensured secrecy, which was essential as such work was generally not declared to tax or social security officials.

The Luton men, in their time outside of work, were either constantly 'on the go', or collapsed with tiredness.[8] The overtime and shift system sapped their 'social vitality'. They commented to the interviewers that the researchers probably thought their lives were very dull, consisting as they did of work, 'odd jobs and chores round the house', and passive relaxation – taking it easy. They spent very little time on leisure pursuits with mates outside the home (Goldthorpe et al. 1971: 105).

In the house they did 'men's work', including repairs to their cars, building garages, fitting cupboards and shelves, and gardening. Some helped with the washing-up (about 4 in 10) or the main shopping (1 in 5), though very few (3–5 per cent) took on 'main responsibility' for such areas of 'women's work'. But they did engage with their children quite a lot: many 'shared responsibility' for taking out younger children and babies, and for reading to children and putting them to bed.[9] They obviously liked spending time with members of their families: three-quarters of all the men reported they carried out all off-the-job activities in their wife's company or together with other members of the household.

The researchers were clearly struck by this pattern, especially that working class men were giving so much help with the housework (which may tell us as much about academics' own domestic life in the 1960s as anything else!). But part of the men's involvement is probably explained by their being on shiftwork and their wives having jobs with more regular hours. The men did tasks round the house such as cooking (which can mean just putting a pre-prepared casserole in the oven) simply because they were often at home alone – and because they were keen to have their wives earning a second income.

In Bristol the self-selected group of men said they spent quite a lot of out-of-work time at home and sometimes helped with tasks, but both they and their wives agreed housework was women's zone of responsibility. The men

expected to do some of the household chores [case studies show this to include shopping, washing-up and 'even' cooking supper], and at least half had taken full charge for short periods [for example, when the wife was in hospital having a baby]. Virtually all expected to look after the children in some way when they were at home. Sometimes it amounted to 'playing' with them while the wife got the supper . . . [but] sometimes it was the husband who 'went up' to the school to sort out problems or even took 'time off' work to take the children to medical appointments . . . A few couples used the shift system to enable both of them to work. (Porter 1983: 119)

In Port Talbot, however, most men were unwilling to give much help with the housework even before they were made redundant – and they resisted it fiercely afterwards as a threat to a masculinity already undermined by unemployment. This was especially true of those men who had a highly developed network of male friends with a sense of group identity. These men often left the house each day to work on allotments or in workshops, or to spend time in social clubs, rather than be at home during the day. When they *were* at home, they spent a lot of time on house maintenance and domestic and car repairs. Many spent most of their redundancy money on home extensions and improvements.

Lydia Morris distinguishes four patterns of men's involvement in housework, the first two being markedly more common.

traditional rigid (35 per cent) – where the man showed no evidence of flexibility before or after redundancy, nor was there any actual blurring of boundaries between male and female spheres.

traditional (40 per cent) – where men gave 'occasional help' in the woman's sphere: 'reasonably frequent assistance which, though not in any way regularized, is neither so rare as to be insignificant':

This kind of help is most commonly proffered [in the areas of] preparation of food, transport for shopping, help with the dishes, minding and playing with children [for short periods] . . . [However] there were twenty men who identified areas of domestic labour in which they refused to participate. Among them, these twenty men made thirty objections related to the washing and ironing of clothes, and ten objections to tasks which were specifically seen as highly visible [for example, cleaning windows at the front of the house].[10] (Morris 1985b: 233)

traditional flexible (15 per cent) – where men showed a significant degree of adaptability as some point after their redundancy, but in which domestic organization was nevertheless based on the traditional pattern.

renegotiated (10 per cent) – where the man assumed responsibility for a substantial number of traditionally 'female' tasks, though one could still identify a remnant of the traditional division of labour.

In other words, some men were willing to increase their contribution to housework slightly when they became unemployed if their wife had some sort of a job. It was one way to deal with their initial boredom and disorientation. But some then gave it up because it was monotonous or because their wives criticized their efforts. In no case did a man take on anything like full responsibility for housework when he became unemployed, whether or not his wife was working; and whatever help men gave was clearly viewed as temporary. If a wife also lost her job, her husband's contribution usually decreased even when he was unemployed. And in this community at least 'both before and after the redundancies the participation of men in child-care in order to free their wives to take up paid employment was minimal' (Morris 1985b: 228).

Women's work

All the women in these studies saw their primary focus, their real work, as the home: 'only when that was satisfactorily disposed of ... could [they] turn their attention to the world outside' (Porter 1982: 118). According to men and women in Bristol,

> 'Women's work' fell into three main areas. The first was housework proper. The women all had husbands in regular employment so they were not 'poor', but they had to manage on average or below-average money (depending on the size of the family). All had children [an average of three]. The houses or flats they lived in were adequate but not spacious. Merely to contain the detritus of living was hard work. They had the bare necessities for keeping the place clean, e.g. running water and electricity, but by no means all had vacuum cleaners or washing machines. [Only two had a telephone.]
>
> A second area of responsibility was feeding the family: shopping and cooking. Most of them, especially the ones who lived [on the estate], were badly off for shopping facilities. Few had access to a car. They also had to cope with the complication of timing meals to suit the different schedules of children and husband, i.e. school times and shift times. Some tried to set a common meal; others just kept a running cafeteria. The day-to-day budgeting and shopping were the most direct connection with the capitalist cycle, via prices at the point of consumption.
>
> The other main area of 'women's work' was the more diffuse but no less onerous one of psychologically and materially sustaining the children and, to a lesser extent, their husband. It encompassed a wide range of responsibilities: keeping the household running through the daily round of unfixed but inexorable chores, looking after babies and pre-school children all day (and all night), 'being home with their tea ready' when they were older, and for the husband after his shift, holding at least acquiescent views on the husbands' industrial action ... All these things meant

subordinating their own needs and identity to those of other members of the family. (Porter 1983: 112–113)

This was the order of priorities given by the women when they were interviewed, and in informal discussions too it was always housework which came up first as the reason why they could not go back to work, and as the work which was really hard and undervalued. The wives had a sense that childcare was also somehow 'the most important' thing they did – but childcare certainly showed greater variation between them in what they felt needed to be done to do it 'properly'. Some women felt they could care for children and have a part-time job; others were adamant they would not get a job while their children were small. Quite a high proportion of children were in playgroups and nurseries during the day, but some couples refused ever to leave their children with anyone outside the immediate family, and 'a majority of the couples refused to allow anyone outside the immediate family to baby-sit in the evening. Usually this was restricted to one or other of the partners' "mum". Sometimes younger sisters were deemed suitable. Others would not even allow their mothers to stand in for them' (Porter 1982: 120). However, whatever the pattern, it was women's responsibility to organize whatever childcare was used.[11]

In Luton, blue-collar men's wives were expected to do much the same things, though here there was more stress on wives being their husbands' leisure-time companions. Luton wives had, however, even bigger problems coping with their husbands' complex shift system: a continuous working week, with a rota over 44 weeks, making men's working at weekends the rule rather than the exception, and with their time off falling on a different day each week. This must have meant not only the problems with cooking mentioned in relation to the Bristol studies (extra meals and at odd hours – a Saturday night meal at 10.30 p.m., and men not present to share family meals); but also with washing (two washdays a week – one for the normal wash and one for the husband's dirty clothes at the end of each shift cycle); and the problems (as well as the pleasures) of having husbands at home during the day. There was also extra work for wives nurturing men who were constantly tired and sexually drained. People are extra irritable and in need of especially careful handling when on night shifts.[12]

In Port Talbot local gender roles also emphasized women's domestic obligations, but here the stress was especially on the rearing of young children, and most men did not expect or want their wives to share much of their leisure. When husbands became unemployed it did not reduce wives' work substantially because, although some men might take on doing more general tidying around the house and looking after children for short periods, women continued to organize and be primarily responsible for domestic affairs and childcare. They planned family meals and did the weekly shopping, and in all cases the washing and ironing of clothes, even when they had full-time jobs.[13]

Men's 'help' was not always an unmixed blessing for their wives anyway. The women often felt men did not do the housework properly, or that they were unreliable, and trying to organize a man was more effort than it was worth.

> He doesn't like housework anyway. I suppose he thinks it not manly. He'd dust and tidy downstairs but he won't do upstairs because no-one sees it, and he won't clean the front windows in case the neighbours see him. I don't mind housework myself as long as I've got time to do it [she had two part-time jobs], but I get irritable at the weekend when there's a backlog of things to do and he won't help. He just tells me to leave it. He doesn't understand that it's got to be done sometime.

> It wouldn't work . . . there'd be more quarrels than it's worth. I'd rather do the work myself . . . I couldn't stand the strain. He'd be out with the horses most days (his friend runs a stable) and I'd get home at tea time to find nothing done. (Morris 1985b: 230–2)

In fact men's unemployment generally *increased* the stress on women. Wives were concerned to help maintain their husband's happiness and self-respect, knowing his ego was already deflated and that he was 'worried sick' that 'he wasn't playing his part in things', namely, keeping the family. They felt it 'wasn't fair' to further threaten his sense of worth by getting him to do women's (that is, low status) work; and they had also to put in extra caring work to boost his morale.[14] Wives might keep on outside employment to improve domestic relations: to prevent them and their husbands being 'on top of each other all day'. But this meant they not only had to do two jobs, but also had to sort out their husband's irritation or unhappiness when he saw her getting up and going out to work. However, stress certainly increased if a wife was at home during the day and her husband 'had difficulty filling his day', because she could feel her freedom constrained by his presence:

> I like to do the housework myself really, because I need something to do, and don't want to be bored. If he does something I just do it again, but I still get cross to see him sitting about doing nothing and getting in the way . . . It disturbs my routine, and my friends don't like to pop in any more with him here. (Morris 1985b: 236)

Wives could also come under strain from the psychological pressure of being constantly responsible for decisions about the allocation of finance, and, where the man did not have a set amount for his personal spending, because she had to try to get him to control his social contacts and hence financial outgoings.

The study of Port Talbot was done only two years after the closure of the steelworks and the men were at that time still receiving special payments or using up severance lump sums. In the future, the burden of housework itself might increase for these women if they tried to maintain the same standard of living on a lower income by increased home production, for example, by making and repairing clothes or home preserving of food from allotments. At the time they were interviewed, however, women were simply delaying buying some items and cooking cheaper cuts of meat, rather than doing more basic work and buying less processed food.[15]

Although the Bristol wives' 'real work' was their responsibility for the home, their husbands' low wages 'created a constant pressure on them to earn some more money in order to make their task *in the home* easier' (stress in original, Porter 1982: 118). All of the women had worked full-time before they were married and most had worked up to the birth of their first child. A few had been clerks or typists or shop assistants, but most were unskilled workers in tobacco and fibreboard factories, in a wine shippers, or in other small works – that is, in traditionally women's jobs and sex-segregated occupations. When they were interviewed, more than half (14 out of 25) were doing some part-time work and most of them were looking to increase their hours. Of the remaining 11, at least half were actively thinking about doing some paid work in the future. Their paid employment as wives was mainly cleaning, catering and shop work – all traditionally low-paid, sometimes shockingly badly paid, forms of 'women's work'. Marilyn Porter's informants earned only half the national average female wage and brought in less than a quarter of what their husbands earned. They 'chose' such jobs because they were 'handy' (nearby) and had convenient hours – or just because they were not factory work, which carried a social stigma.

Factory workers' wives in Luton left employment early in married life to 'start families' (over 90 per cent had children), sometimes even before the couple had established a home. They had more children on average than white-collar workers in the same firms (2.02 as against 1.35) and 'lengthy periods of active motherhood during which full-time work was difficult'. The researchers observed that since the husbands' income was not going to rise and indeed might decline with age, it was therefore rational not to delay the period when women needed to be at home full-time for childcare.

Almost all wives in Luton who did not have small children were employed, as indeed were some who did have such responsibilities. Overall a third of wives worked, and half of these worked full-time. Their husbands' shift-working must have made this difficult, and it is unlikely that many, if any, worked much overtime – in contrast to their husbands.[16] In addition, if their husbands were trade union activists their opportunities for paid work might possibly be reduced still further, not only because there were extra hours when he was out of the house, but also because, according to Huw Beynon in *Working for Ford*, shop stewards were often careful their wives did not 'work' so as to avoid antagonisms. One told Beynon:

During a strike a man whose Judy is working is obviously better off than the man with a wife and three kids about the house. So you're bound to get some backbiting – 'Oh it's alright for him his missis is keeping him in ale and ciggies.' A steward just can't afford to be mixed up in that sort of thing, especially a senior steward who may have to recommend to the men that they stay out. (Beynon 1973: 123)

South Wales, by contrast, used to have the lowest rate of women's participation in the labour force in Britain, but by the end of the 1970s it was not far below the UK average,[17] and prior to the closure of the BSC steelworks, 12 of the wives of the men made redundant were employed full-time and 5 part-time, with 23 not in paid work. As in other parts of the country, women did not simply take on jobs to provide an alternative source of income when their husbands became unemployed. On the contrary; their employment rate *fell* when their husbands lost their jobs. (Nationally the wife of a man in employment is almost twice as likely to be herself in employment as the wife of an unemployed man.) In Port Talbot, the decline was especially marked in women's full-time employment (from 12 to 7 women); and although more women worked part-time after the men's redundancies (an increase from 5 to 8 women), they worked shorter hours. One or two entered into joint ventures (self-employment) with their husbands.

'Suitable' work for married women was that which used their skills and experience (or lack of skills and experience in anything other than domestic work) – for example waitressing, cleaning or sewing machining; which was 'off the cards'; and which either fitted around work at home (that is, had suitable hours of work) or allowed the woman to find childcare. Some women earned a little money by selling from home in some form or another. This required them to see their customers regularly to collect the payments and to have a widely dispersed set of social contacts.

The only women employed full-time in Port Talbot (before or after their husband's redundancy) were those who had no children or only adult children. Women with small children did not have paid employment: no woman with children aged under nine was employed even part-time. Those with older children and part-time jobs worked hours which fitted around childcare (for example, as school dinner ladies), or they took the children with them to their jobs, or they depended on female kin and friends for childcare (sometimes exchanging it – each caring for the others' children at particular times each week). Only one, whose husband had left her, paid for a babysitter.

The few women with full-time jobs and school-age children used friends or sisters or mothers for supervision in the school holidays or to cover the brief period after school. An occasional husband would relieve his wife's mother of a child on his return from work; or an unemployed man might cook for himself and his school-age children whilst awaiting his wife's return from work, but unlike what we are told happened in Luton, in South Wales 'this was by no means a regular or even a predictable occurrence' (Morris 1985b: 228). In three cases where women took on short-term temporary work after their husband's redundancy, one used her mother and mother-in-law for childcare, and two used their unemployed husbands – though 'one of [these] simply took the child to his mother.'

Most of the wives whose views are recorded had mixed feelings about their paid employment. Those in Bristol supported equal pay formally and in principle, but none of them thought they personally should get it as they did not do a man's job – as an example of which they typically instanced coal mining. That is to say, they did not compare their work to that of their husbands, but rather to what is seen as the most macho, dangerous and unpleasant 'men's' work. All the wives who were not solely occupied with domestic responsibilities regarded themselves as deviant, and Marilyn Porter suggests one reason they made so little fuss over their low pay was because they felt 'guilty' about 'working'.

Most were not in a trade union – 'unions, strikes and even meetings were a distraction from the simple business of going out, doing a job and getting money as painlessly and quickly as possible' (Porter 1982: 125), a view these women held not only while they were wives but also when they were employed full-time before marriage. But they did consider certain community issues – for example, rising prices, schools, clinics, parks, playgrounds and leisure facilities, bus routes, and pedestrian crossings – to be women's domain. It was 'up to women to get things done' about them, by, for example, writing repeated letters to councillors, arranging meetings and petitions and 'all the time-consuming detail of democratic protest'. But the women who did try to act, did so individually, not as part of groups or political parties, and they became frustrated and gave up because of their lack of impact.

In the Luton study we are told quite a lot (in a concern characteristic of 1960s sociology) about wives visiting neighbours and kin. Unfortunately we are merely told the frequency with which they saw each other and whether or not they were emotionally close, not what they did together or whether or not the visits were in connection with domestic work (for example, nursing or shopping for kin, sharing baby-sitting, picking up children from school in an emergency, keeping an eye on elderly neighbours, feeding someone's cats when they are away on holiday, or taking in parcels as part of reciprocal exchanges with the people next door). It seems clear, however, that unlike wives in more established, homogeneous, 'traditional', close-knit working class communities, women in Luton did not help raise a family's status by joining clubs and undertaking voluntary work in the neighbourhood or by maintaining a high standard of housewifery for display to visitors.[18] They were expected to stay at home, or go out, with their husbands.

The management of family labour

Decision-making

The Luton researchers analysed their data on marital relations in terms of how 'joint' or 'segregated' the domestic lives of husbands and wives were.[19] Couples were said to have joint roles when

• a (domestic) activity was done by husband and wife together,
• or by either equally,
• or where an activity which would conventionally be regarded as women's work was done by a husband 'when both were at home'.

Goldthorpe and his colleagues saw 'joint' marital roles as more middle class and more modern than traditional / working class / 'segregated' roles and concluded that blue-collar workers in Luton had adapted 'traditional working class' family patterns to a new, but still working class, form. Their informants did not have nor did they aspire to such elements of 'middle class' life-style as entertaining at home, joining local societies and clubs, or looking to friends rather than relatives for support and companionship. That is to say, in this respect at least they had not become 'embourgeoised'.

In trying to establish the pattern of 'marital roles' in Luton, the researchers asked questions about the numbers of couples who (said they) shared responsibility for putting children to bed (48 per cent), for the washing-up (41 per cent), and who decided jointly 'what to do for holidays' (84 per cent), 'whether to buy something new' (71 per cent) and 'what colour paint to have' (41 per cent).[20] But it is hard to interpret any of this information because, firstly, husbands and wives were interviewed together, and if they had been seen separately they might not have agreed on their answers, and secondly, when the authors refer to 'our respondents' they sometimes mean the husbands *and* their wives, and sometimes just the men. It is therefore far from clear who exactly decided what – if indeed either spouse fully decided anything. Decisions are often made over a long period of time and involve lots of 'bits' of decisions: whether to buy a car or not, what make to get, what to pay, what colour to get, what dealer to get it from, etc. But more importantly, deciding things jointly, 'sharing' the domestic work, and doing things together in your free time are not the same thing as equality in marriage – though they are often taken (by this and many other studies) to each be measures of the other. A couple can discuss where to go on holiday and then the wife can go round all the travel agents, taking her husband back with her to just the one which is cheapest for him to pay, or they can shop around together. But in either case it will be the head who pays and his views which are given most weight. In addition, some of the most important domestic decisions are made with no discussion at all, or with the wife used just as a sounding board by the husband.

Issues surrounding employment

Like many other marital decision-making studies, the Affluent Worker research does not even consider some really big 'decisions' – like those relating to family planning and the making of the key choice of moving to Luton, away from old ties of kinship and neighbourhoods, where the men would take on alienating but well-paid jobs. Some of the men moved when single, but others were already married. What their wives felt about such changes is not clear.

The Bristol study, by contrast, tells us specifically that wives were little involved in decisions about their husbands' employment. 'Wives rarely [took] it upon themselves deliberately to influence their husband's choice of a job' (Porter 1983: 88). A man might discuss decisions with his wife, but they were clearly his decisions. Likewise, whether or not a husband accepted promotion was, in the end, his decision alone. This was said by the couples to be because 'after all he has to do the work' – but the relative level of wages, which was the chief reason given for taking the job, affected the wife's life enormously, so she certainly had a vested interest. But in the end this did not count.

When talking about men's work, women always entered the caveat that they 'did not know much about it'. They did not identify with their husband's position as a worker, and few men told their wives much about what they did – either because they felt it was not their wives' business, or to protect them, or because they knew their wives were not interested. Wives' only recognized interest in their husband's work was with his wage-packet. They were therefore generally not sympathetic to his union involvement, because of the extra unpaid work involved, and particularly not to his going on strike, because it reduced the money coming into the home. This applied even to wives who held quite radical views generally.

On the other hand, as Porter's research makes clear, there was 'considerable explicit disagreement' (even between these self-selected and otherwise non-conflictual husbands and wives) about *wives'* employment. Men, with few exceptions, did not like their wives to have jobs, and/or to have particular types of jobs. For example, she says of one husband: 'Alan's deeply ambivalent views conceded far more than most men in the study did to women's rights and abilities – but he still wouldn't like to see his wife [work in a factory].' (Porter 1983: 70). She reports men as being generally unaware their wives wanted to get jobs, or that those who had jobs wanted to do more hours. Nor did men recognize the strength of women's feelings about having 'money of their own'. This issue was resolved not by these differences being 'talked through', but by 'external circumstances'. Both husbands and wives took the view that a wife should not *need* to take a job; and men were concerned that the housework and childcare would not get done if women 'worked'. But both have to agree that in practice they could do with the money, so in the end most men grudgingly accepted their wives' insistence that they be allowed to submit themselves to further exploitation, to the couple's mutual benefit.

Even male redundancy did not produce a reversal of familial responsibilities for income earning and domestic labour. In Port Talbot women became the main earner in only two households: 'In one case all the children had grown up and moved away, and the woman (aged 53) holds a well-paid and responsible position . . . In the other case the couple have no children and the woman (aged 27) works as an insurance bank clerk . . . [both] having held the job for some time prior to [their husbands'] redundancy' (Morris 1985b: 225). In neither case did the men take over the housework.

As already noted, overall, women's employment declined after their husbands were made redundant. Other writers have suggested that this pattern is due to couples finding themselves in an 'earnings trap' whereby any money wives earn gets deducted from men's state benefits, and / or to unemployed men wanting their wives at home for extra domestic services – to be a companion, to boost his morale and to cook a hot lunch.[21] Morris says, however, that the Port Talbot studies found that it was not a conscious decision made by the couple, related to the husband's employment status, but rather it was the result of women's jobs also being affected by recession, or, in a couple of cases, of their getting pregnant. Conversely, most women who started work did so because they found a job, not through a conscious, deliberate decision to seek employment to improve the family's financial position, followed by a job search, but informally and fortuitously, often through information conveyed by friends.

The domestic division of labour

As with the overall issue of men's breadwinning / employment, women's overall responsibility for domestic work was not a topic which was open for discussion among the couples interviewed. The decisions made were restricted to the specifics of how much help men were willing to give, and in the interviews they speculated on what they might do if circumstances changed drastically.

Luton husbands helped their wives a lot, especially with childcare, because they wanted the extra income coming from women's jobs and because they spent a lot of time with their wives and children. They had cut many ties with the places where they had lived previously and with all but close kin, and they had few workplace friends. Instead they maintained a close-knit nuclear family household and enjoyed playing with their children and taking joint family outings.

In Port Talbot, by contrast, men made employment very difficult for their wives, and few wanted their wives as their main leisure-time companions. In the 10 per cent of cases where there was 'renegotiation' of tasks after redundancy, this occurred because the man remained unemployed and his wife was either in poor health or in full-time employment. In most cases, however, husbands of women who were in full-time employment were actually more often 'rigid' or occasionally 'traditional' about housework and childcare even when unemployed. In the few instances where men showed very considerable flexibility, the men had just a few friends they met individually for a drink a few times a month (that is, they did not belong to a large male friendship group) and their interests were generally centred on their homes, and they had no children – and these men *still* did not take on *full* responsibility. They might hoover, dust and make beds during the week and cook meals prepared by the wife the night before; but the wife cleaned the house at weekends, did the budgeting and planning, and all the washing-up, washing and ironing.

Employment was easier for a wife if her husband would help with 'her' work; but women did not get help from husbands *because* they were in paid work. Whether they got help or not depended on their husband's willingness to be 'flexible'. Some women got it even if they did not have jobs. But conversely, women with full-time employment might get no help at all.

If women wanted jobs they looked instead to a network of women outside the household (female friends, relatives and acquaintances) who not only relayed the information which enabled women to identify and gain access to 'suitable' employment, but also provided the childcare and other domestic services which made employment possible – before and after the husband's redundancy. Morris suggests that in the latter case the network could be seen as helping to preserve the low level of the husband / father's participation in domestic work. Our interpretation would be rather that husbands' and wives' obligations remain the same before and after redundancy. Since maintenance and unpaid labour are not 'exchanged', the husband's no longer being the breadwinner does not absolve the wife from her obligation to provide any and all necessary household work (either herself directly or using help from other sources).

The handling of money

Bristol men's ambivalence about their wives' employment was part of their general anxiety to justify their domestic arrangements in terms of what they saw as agreed norms, and to explain why they deviated from these (as most of them did). This was particularly marked in relation to patterns of money handling. Porter gives an extended comparison of two couples, and in both cases the wives handled the household finances. She stresses both husbands were 'kind, considerate and anxious to avoid conflict if they could, and devoted to their . . . energetic, vivacious and independent-minded' wives (Porter 1983: 55). But although 'both men felt strongly that it would have been wrong to keep their wives short, or for them not to know how much they earned', they still expressed 'residual disquiet' that anyone should know that they did not control the financial affairs of their households (p. 63). Other husbands were equally defensive when it was revealed that their wives had no say at all in the apportioning of their wage-packet.

The fact that either way men can feel they are not fulfilling a norm is due to the handling of finances in households not being a frequent topic of conversation. British people are secretive about their money – and about their sexual practices. They may be aware there are different ways of doing things, but they are not really sure what these are. It is only recently that sociologists have started to look systematically at what happens to the money entering households in the form of men's wages, state payments, wives' wages, casual earnings, gifts, and interest on savings. (And they still have not looked at marital sexual practices.) Such information is complex and needs to be collected specifically, so only the most recent study – Lydia Morris's – gives good information on this. She says, however, that 'one of the most significant and straightforward findings in [the area of household financial management] is that although women are more likely to have management or budgeting responsibility, control commonly rests with the husband' (Morris and Ruane 1989: 11).[22]

Another significant and straightforward finding is the critical nature of personal spending money. In most systems of financial management, women do not have any money designated for their personal spending. However, even when a man is unemployed, his personal spending money tends to be the most protected area of household expenditure.

1   In Port Talbot, when men were employed the most common system of financial management was an *allowance system*. The male principal earner would give his wife a set sum of money each week for the house-keeping. In such cases a wife might never see the whole wage-packet and she therefore did not necessarily know what her husband earned.

If a man is paid by the hour or on piece-work, then the less he gives his wife in regular allowance, the greater his choice about how many hours to work in a given week. This freedom to take time off can be important in heavy manual work, and may be supported by a strong peer culture and a 'them and us' attitude towards both bosses and wives. Wives may worry if husbands miss work, but a wife will almost certainly not tell her husband he ought to go to work. Providing he gives her 'her' allowance, she has no grounds to comment. However, if wives know their husbands are working and making a lot of extra money and not spending any of it on collective needs, they may argue with them.

Men generally avoid any contention about how much they keep for their personal spending, however, by taking on responsibility for certain collective expenses as their income increases, so their dependants also benefit, at least in part. Their families therefore get more consumer durables and holidays than do families with heads on the same wage but practising other financial management systems.[23]

An allowance system means men keep control of their family's collective expenditure and also hold the means of working towards a specific collective goal if the circumstance arises and they agree something is needed. Wives have to call on their husbands to pay for everything over and above the regular weekly standard. It also means that 'a large amount of a man's good wages can be frittered away on his amusements, and the wife has little say in saving' (Morris and Ruane 1989). With this system, earnings from informal work (that is, whatever a man may get apart from his regular wage or unemployment benefit) are usually kept by him – for personal spending, occasionally for collective expenditure, and sometimes for a 'treat for the wife'.[24]

2   Among unemployed steelworkers in Port Talbot, a *whole wage system* became common. Men handed over all their benefit payment (or new, smaller wage-packet) to their wives, and the women gave them back personal spending money.

This is a common pattern when a household's income is low, and when the income comes from some kind of state benefit (for example, unemployment benefit, sick pay or a pension).[25] (Of course, dependence on state benefits and low income tend to go hand in hand in any case.) It delegates the chore of managing a low income to wives, and it is also used because men are not seen to unequivocally own state benefits in the same way as they are seen to own their wages. Hard work is needed to spread the available cash to cover even essentials, and it helps to have just one responsible person holding the purse strings and working out who shall get what. This person bears the brunt of everyone's complaints and she can help things along by cutting back hardest on her own consumption.

When wives 'worked' part-time in Port Talbot their household tended to have a whole wage or allowance system – and their wages were used simply to augment domestic income (that is, they were added to the money available for spending on collective needs – on food, fuel and accommodation, etc.). This did not mean wives had a substantially greater influence on the financial system as a whole. It merely reduced calls on their husbands' wages. That is, wives' income increased the family's overall standard of living, but it did not give the women money to spend freely on themselves.

Child benefit also went into the general housekeeping. However, women saw themselves as having a right to control *this* money, not only because it was paid in cash directly into their hands at the post office each week, but also because men were not seen to own state benefits. At the time of the Bristol study, child benefit payments were under threat – it was being proposed that larger child tax allowances should be given (to men) instead – and the women interviewed were vociferous in support of its continuation.[26]

3   Only those households where male earners had previously been in higher occupational grades with higher disposable earnings, and some couples where the wife was in full-time employment and / or where there were no children, used a *joint management system*, in which both partners had access to all household income and were jointly responsible for management of, and expenditure from, a common pool. Personal spending money was taken from the pool as needed, or was covered by separate retentions or allowances.

Such a system looks as if it requires more overt trust and agreement on spending priorities between the couple than the other systems. It means each has to ask the other if it is all right to take and spend money, and so norms of men's and women's needs and of collective needs are especially important. But access to similar amounts of money is not equal access. The money women take is spent on domestic needs, and they feel guilty about spending on themselves. Indeed the system actually makes them *more* accountable – even though at this income level the odd pound here or there is less significant. Women who have no income can have absolutely no secrets from their husbands under this financial management system – even the birthday presents they buy them have to be paid for from the joint account.[27] On the other hand, with this system, various sources of income and savings accounts are often not declared to the other spouse – and are only revealed (if at all) on divorce.

A joint system is hard to resist and difficult to pin down. A discourse of egalitarianism disguises the power relations.

> For a long time I made the mistake of assuming . . . that when people asserted that in their marriage there was no distinction between his money and 'our' money, that this was true for all couples who subscribed to the ideal. It was only when I thought back over my own experience of such a situation and when I questioned more deeply that the politics of financial dependence became apparent. Loyalty and self negation are powerful agents of economic oppression. If any sociologist or interested person had inquired into the financial arrangements in my marriage I would have lain my hand on my heart and sworn that we shared money equally. And, in theory, I would have been telling the truth. In fact, it would no more have occurred to me to spend money on anything but housekeeping as it would for him not to. (Comer 1974: 124)

Consumption by family members

None of these studies gives much information on the distribution of re-sources other than money between family members. They tell us little, for instance, about who gets what food, or shares in the space in the house, or access to transport, or health provision, or care in old age, or who visits clubs and cinemas and sports events or takes trips and holidays outside the town – all of which have been shown by recent studies to be sys-tematically inequitably shared. They do not even tell us the relative hours the husbands and the wives work each week. All we know about in any detail are some leisure activities and associated spending, and husbands' and wives' patterns of friendship.

The 'affluent workers' of Luton and their dependants had a higher standard of domestic comfort than many other manual workers of the period. The reward for the men's hard and stressful factory work was being able to afford nice homes (mostly new houses, often owner-occupied, on private estates), good food and such things as refrigerators and cars. The men also had subsidized canteens at work, pensions, sick pay schemes and medical facilities, plus a wide provision of social and recreational facilities through a works club.

But out-of-work they were often tired, and their leisure and holidays had to be taken at odd set times. They are described as going for walks or trips in their cars in the country and visiting kin, accompanied by their wives and children, watching TV or playing the guitar at home with a son, reading the newspaper, and drinking with a friend or a brother-in-law in the local pub. The men's social life was centred on, and largely restricted to, the home and conjugal family. At first, after their move to the town, this was perhaps by necessity, but later it was certainly by choice. Many men had local friends with whom they associated independently of their wives, though half the men mentioned no friend not shared with their wife. They rarely joined clubs or local associations.

Women are described by Goldthorpe and colleagues as doing things with their husbands, or knitting, writing letters to relatives 'at home', and going to church on their own. They had important sets of women friends based on family and neighbourhood (defined as within ten minutes' walk), and they saw these women independently of their husbands. Half had no more than a casual acquaintance with (that is, they would not drop in on) their neighbours. They expressed little interest in specifically neigh-bourhood life and did not join leisure or political clubs or other groups. They rarely did much entertaining at home other than having relatives or one other (unrelated) couple round to play cards or listen to records and tapes.

Parents, brothers and sisters and in-laws played an important part in the Luton families' lives. Even when such kin lived out of Luton, they still comprised nearly a quarter of the respondents' most frequent associates and more than half of those who visited them at home. These households almost always kept in contact with both the husband's and the wife's parents even when they lived in another place, but they were more selective about which brothers and sisters they maintained contact with.

Although the researchers were struck by the companionship of husbands and wives, we wonder if they do not overstate their case, given the problems of continuous shiftwork. This would have affected not only outings, but also togetherness at home – especially when the children were in school and the wife had a full-time job with different hours. To an extent, the families in Luton may have 'organized away' contact between husband and wife. Their jobs ensured they spent no more time together than working class couples with segregated roles. A man's weekday time off cannot always have been treated as the equivalent of a weekend because meals had to be made for children in school, friends could not be visited (because they were at work), and public entertainments and social activities (sporting fixtures, Saturday night at the pub, political, religious and social groups, and community events) were not available. On the other hand, couples would sometimes have had a day together without the children, and time out when the shops, etc. were not crowded, and on such occasions they do seem to have had a different, more egalitarian, interaction than segregated role couples.

The people interviewed in Bristol did not have the material benefits of those in Luton and the men's jobs do not seem to have had as many perks attached to them but, on the other hand, what facilities there were, were more likely to be used, at least by the men (notably the skittle club). Husbands here too were home-centred, but less markedly, and Marilyn Porter suggests this was often because they lacked spending money rather than from a definite choice.

Few couples went out socially more than once a month. Nor did they join clubs, or take part in organized activities: there was one active churchgoer, one active Labour Party member, and one Buffalo. None of the couples interviewed felt part of a local community, especially those living on the council estates. The women in particular joined nothing and claimed 'to have no leisure anyway'. Television was one woman's only pleasure because 'she didn't go out' (Porter 1983: 71). In part this had to do with childcare and problems with husbands working shifts, but it was also because wives felt they had no money of their own and were not free to spend what they saw as family money on their own pleasures.

Most men and women relied on 'a few relations and fewer friends for their contacts outside work'. Women tended to have one or two close friends (who might be relatives) living nearby. Men less frequently made comparable friendships at work or among neighbours, though they are reported as often going out two or three nights a week for a drink with friends, or drinking with workmates after work. More often they formed a foursome for social events with other couples bound together either by their wives' association or by some previous bond.

Contact with parents and at least some siblings should have been easy, but even if relatives live only three or four miles away it may not be easy to see much of them if you are hampered by inadequate bus services and the needs of small children. These difficulties were felt most acutely by the young wives [on the estate], who expected to be in daily contact with their mothers [living nearer the city centre]. Men who worked in [the town] often found it easier to 'pop in' regularly to see their parents – and it was resented if they did not do so. (Porter 1983: 19)

South Wales, by contrast, is characterized by a tradition of independent male social activity, much of which revolves around pubs and social clubs and (men only) sports clubs. More than half the men Lydia Morris interviewed had what she calls a *collective* pattern, for example,

> Mr Philips, aged 31, who goes to the local rugby club for training sessions 2–3 times a week and meets the boys at the club for a drink on two additional evenings. 'Its the same crowd in the same place. Year after year it's been.' Three of the 25 men are particular friends, but he doesn't make any independent arrangement to meet up with them outside the club. (Morris 1985a: 331–2)

A further quarter had a *dispersed* pattern – they saw one set of friends in a club once a week and had other acquaintances they had known for years whom they encountered when, for example, out fishing, passing in the street, or doing occasional work in perhaps a garage. An equal number had an *individualistic pattern*, with a couple of separate friends each of whom they meet three times a month or fortnightly by arrangement for a drink. Only two of the couples she interviewed (5 per cent) *shared* the majority of their social activities (the Luton pattern).

These patterns of activity had important financial consequences because most men went out frequently and there were substantial numbers of them involved, all of whom had to be bought a drink by an individual man when it was his round. Women accepted men needed money for their leisure – 'If he couldn't go out he just wouldn't see anyone' – and when a wife was in charge of the household income she usually made great efforts to ensure there was a little free to give her husband 'for a drink'. But social spending was certainly one of the areas where cuts had been made following redundancy. Some unemployed men took on 'unofficial' work specifically to get such money; and when men got financial help from their fathers, it was usually small amounts for such personal spending.

Some men, Morris says, accepted their wives' decisions about how much could be afforded for their 'pocket money' and took pride in limiting their spending; but others brought pressure to bear in a number of ways. Those men who were home-centred clearly asked for least, and the personal spending of those whose pattern was individualistic was generally fairly restricted anyway: it was planned in advance and predictable. Men who had a regular collective pattern of activity needed more money but the amount could be budgeted for and their spending controlled. The real difficulty came with husbands whose friends were dispersed. Their spending was unpredictable – the result of chance meetings or mood and (especially once they were unemployed and had more free time) potentially extensive. Such men might allow their wives financial control and accept an allowance, but if they insisted on access to the domestic income for their spending, or took over financial control and gave their wives too little for the housekeeping (as happened, though we are not told how often), the family might get into severe financial difficulties, and the marital relationship would come under strain.

Women in Port Talbot did not see themselves as needing money for leisure, and any help they were given by their mothers – gifts of food or money for clothes for the children – went towards the housekeeping. They had their own networks of contact with kin and / or friends, but these were focused more on the home (and hence their sociability would be curtailed by their husband's presence if he stayed at home all day when unemployed). Those who had a 'collective' pattern (about a third of the sample) were less collective than the men. Some women, for example, met as a group in a pub, but only once a fortnight for a 'hen party'; and they also went out as the same group with their husbands (some of whom knew each other independently from a rugby club) every Sunday night. Just under half had several friends, neighbours, mother, sisters and other kin they saw regularly but unpredictably; the rest had little social life apart from parents and one or two friends.

Women's friendships were often tied in with the exchange of practical help, for example, childcare and doing each other favours. The same was true for men, and to an extent, therefore, men's spending might be economically justified (and in fact self-sustaining) since their social contacts provided access to opportunities for informal economic activity – and hence to independent income, which was used for social spending (in contrast to women's independent income, which was used for domestic expenditure).

Transmission in the family

These particular studies were concerned with family households at particular points in time, not with their reproduction over time. They therefore tell us nothing about (what were for those concerned) major transfers of property – about what individuals might have been given by their parents or have given to their children (for example, on marriage), nor about what informants had inherited or if they themselves had made wills and who they had left things to. Nor do they tell us about the socio-economic class position of their informants in relation to their parents, and in relation to their brothers and sisters – whether they had gone up or down in the world.

Morris's work does, however, tell us about some of the short-term gifts of money and practical help made between relatives and friends when sons and daughters or brothers and sisters had a period of economic misfortune. For instance, she mentions help in finding employment (either initially at BSC, or 'suitable' work for women, or casual work for unemployed men), practical help with childcare, and financial help from mothers to daughters with the housekeeping and fathers to sons with spending money.

The researchers clearly recognized that the major form of 'property' held by their informants were skills which could be sold on the labour market. So the Luton researchers, with their concern with changing social class divisions and patterns of mobility, gave some attention to parents' concerns for their children's education and occupational aspirations. They asked detailed questions about what help informants thought they as parents could give with their children's education, and they noted that among their informants an above average proportion (for manual workers) wanted their children, particularly their sons, to go to selective secondary schools. (Nearly 70 per cent wanted their sons to go to grammar schools, though much more varied responses were given for daughters.)[28]

The Luton respondents were also asked what sorts of jobs they would like their sons or daughters to get; or, when the children were already older, what jobs they had got. And again, an above average proportion wanted their children to 'get on' and go beyond a working class job ('a trade' or 'a steady job') to white-collar work with possibilities for continuous advancement. (Unfortunately it is not clear if this was the fathers' or mothers' or a joint view – though information given elsewhere suggests less than half the couples discuss their children's schooling.) Parents said they would be happy for a child to do as they had done and move away from the town if this were necessary to get a good job.[29]

What parents stressed, according to the authors, is that a particular child should have work which was as rewarding as possible to him (Goldthorpe et al.'s pronoun), whether economically or otherwise. They were not concerned with children getting the *status* of middle class jobs. For boys the jobs most often singled out were not clerical and administrative work but such things as electronics engineer, industrial designer or draughtsman; and for girls (we are told in a footnote) nursing or (chiefly junior school) teaching. The researchers made no comment on (that is, they took as unproblematic) the very different occupations, and hence socio-economic positions, desired by their respondents for sons and for daughters (Goldthorpe et al. 1971: 133). Within a sex-segregated labour market this would mean that Luton daughters would not earn enough to support themselves even at the standard of living they had enjoyed in their father's household unless they married (which is anyway undoubtedly what their parents wanted them to do).

Goldthorpe and colleagues do say, however, that the grown-up children of their informants had in fact strikingly *not* achieved the schooling or

occupations desired for them: 'What was chiefly missing . . . was neither
seriousness of intention in their parental aspirations nor willingness to
support their children's efforts, but rather certain dispositions and capacities
necessary to make such support really effective' (Goldthorpe et al. 1971:
137). These parents could not provide the necessary help with school
work, nor the right conditions for study, nor the fostering of appropriate
attitudes towards knowledge, nor the consultation with teachers and
understanding of how the educational system works, that middle class
parents can provide.

What is remarkable is that the authors' overriding concern with boys
seems to have prevented them noticing that twice as many of the
respondents' daughters (13 per cent) as sons (6 per cent) actually went to
selective secondary schools, and that those girls who had already entered
employment had in fact broadly attained the (lower) socio-economic
categories their parents aspired to for them (58 per cent of girls but only
18 per cent of boys had jobs in the Registrar General's socio-economic
category 2). Most sons (57 per cent) had gone into skilled manual work
(Goldthorpe et al. 1971: 135).

Conclusion

We shall make most of our general comments on these factory workers'
families at the end of the next chapter, where we can also refer to farmers'
families. Here we want just to raise and combine some insights from
Marilyn Porter and Lydia Morris's work.

Morris has made important critiques of the recently developed notion
of 'household strategies' by showing that previous writers have been over-
optimistic about the 'creative variations' which it is possible for households
to make in response to economic restructuring in the wider society. She
stresses both the way in which Britain is increasingly divided into
'employed' and 'unemployed' households and how the latter are trapped
in a downward spiral, and the constraints within which household strategies
get constructed. Her book, *The Workings of the Household* (1990), looks
at the internal dynamics of households and how these relate to the
employment position, work prospects and state entitlements of the various
members, and to other networks of contacts which may extend well beyond
household boundaries. She suggests the concept of 'household strategies'
suffers from the same shortcomings as many theories of the labour market.
It assumes too much rationality and interchangeability between people in
their efforts to 'maximize resources'. Such theories do not adequately
allow for the constraints of a gendered division of labour, for patterns of
handling finances, and for gendered support networks and state structures.

At times, however, such a stress on structures and constraints can lose
sight of power, male supremacy, and agency – which remain more clearly
visible in Porter's work. Men and women are not only constrained and

shaped by economic circumstances; they also make choices and men act in ways which (by and large) maintain their privileged positions.

Men's gender 'identity', as well as their superior social position, is tied up with being the breadwinner: with 'keeping' their families. Their labour market situation is not always great – but at least it is almost invariably better than women's. As Porter comments, women sell their labour in a clearly differentiated market at lower rates and in poorer conditions (1983: 126) and it is regarded by men and women as secondary and quite different from 'men's work'. Men in Bristol made a clear distinction between full-time and part-time employment (which women did not) and they valued women's labour less than men's.

Women notice the bad aspects of domestic work more than men. In Bristol, we are told,

> both men and women saw child-care as generally rewarding, but women were much less positive about housework, speaking particularly against its physical toughness, boredom, loneliness, repetition and lack of social recognition; and against the difficulty of providing meals at the right times and making ends meet. [The fieldwork was done in a period of particularly rapidly rising prices.] Wives were vocal about being deprived of an economic identity because their work at home was unpaid (though they did not think this should or could be changed). Men however scarcely noticed their wives' economic dependence. (Porter 1978b)

Porter also noted that wives, who sometimes thought of the wage-packet as 'theirs', had suddenly been made to realize how distant they were from it and how little control they had over it, by the recent strike (Porter 1978a: 267).

Morris tends, by contrast, to see men's actions as almost entirely the products of constraining circumstances. For example, she sees the friendship groups men are involved in as the reason they have so little flexibility in changing their domestic arrangements (see Morris 1985a: 326–37). We might simply turn the argument around and ask whether it could be men's marital roles which prevent them from altering their patterns of sociability. But in fact we think that while leisure patterns and domestic patterns certainly correlate – the one goes with the other – neither *causes* the other. Rather they are both due to, and are the mark of, and a means to continue, men's power in the home and outside.

The South Wales study shows men as having a choice between four different patterns of sociability and four different patterns of domestic life. Even if they are under heavy peer group or marital pressure, and economically constrained, the fact that certain men can go right against the herd and spend most of their time with their wives, shows that it can be done, that it is a cultural possibility, that choice exists, and men exercise these choices. Men's position in the family hierarchy (and in the world outside) allows them to make decisions which influence the lives of the rest of their families. And the ability to make such choices and to have such an influence is a reward in itself, an entitlement not accorded to women, and a marker of family status.

Family households are gendered hierarchies, and men play an active role in reproducing the situation, for example, by the hours they choose to work (even when unemployed), the form of financial management they agree to use, how much spending money they take, how much time they want to spend at home with their wives and children as against going out with male friends, and whether or not they delegate responsibility to their wives for choosing and purchasing things. To these individual choices within couples are added collective male actions in the public sphere – in the labour market, in trade unions, in men's clubs, and in male networks.

Obviously women also make choices – and their individual and collective co-operation and resistance needs more attention. But they make their choices from a subordinate position. Again Porter's work is helpful in showing wives talking back and arguing, soothing and persuading men round, and scheming – and she also shows the humour and good nature with which they handle most interactions.

The accounts of factory workers' families used in this chapter obviously support our analysis of the family as an economic system, even though the authors are not all feminists. (Indeed Goldthorpe and Lockwood have shown in later publications that they are markedly anti-feminist.) But the next chapter shows that much stronger supporting data can been gathered if the right questions are asked, for it draws on research on French farm families which specifically used Delphy's (1970) theoretical framework.

Notes

1   It is often a problem in any case to speak to wives if a researcher makes the initial approach to husbands at their place of work (see Banks 1956). Some men refuse a request to speak to their wives; the places where they live are scattered over a wide area; and not all wives can be seen on the first visit, so interviewers may need to make several follow-up attempts which requires a lot of travelling time.

2   On Luton see the *Affluent Worker* series: Goldthorpe, Lockwood, Bechhofer and Platt (1968a; 1968b; 1971). Also Platt (1969). This study included a comparative sample of white-collar workers which will not concern us here. This research has been subject to sustained critiques and numerous other research projects have developed from it (see Platt 1984), but few of the critiques or the new developments have given as much attention to family life as it does.

On Bristol, see Porter (1978a; 1978b; 1982; 1983). On Port Talbot, see Harris and Morris (1986), C. C. Harris et al. (1987) and L. Morris (1984a; 1984b; 1984c; 1984d; 1985a; 1985b; 1990).

3 We try always to make clear where our interpretations differ from those of the original authors.
4 A rare exception is Zweig (1961). Although he asked for the proportion of single men among his *The Worker in an Affluent Society* sample to be kept low, he does devote a section (pp. 155–66) to them. The material he collected relates mainly to the men's emotions, possessions and hobbies, however, not to the domestic work they did or the sexual relations they had, if any.
5 Porter does note that two of her couples (8 per cent) had relatives living with them: one had an orphaned nephew and the other lived with the mother of one partner. But there is no further information on these domestic arrangements.
6 Partly because it was realized that not enough information had been collected on wives' employment (personal communication).
7 Not everyone presumes this. Engels for instance argued there was a major difference between bourgeois and proletarian marriage (Engels 1884).
8 We will never know whether the indexer had a sense of humour or not, but the main entry under 'relationship with wife' in the index of Huw Beynon's book on *Working for Ford* leads to:

> It's hard enough now but in those days it was terrible . . . I was working in the headlinings and I never thought I'd survive. I used to come home from work and fall straight asleep. My legs and arms used to be burning. And I knew hard work. I'd been on the buildings but this place was a bastard then. I didn't have any relations with my wife for months. Now that's not right is it? No work should be that hard! (Beynon 1973: 75)

9 See Goldthorpe, Lockwood, Bechhofer and Platt (1971: 105 table 11).
10 Morris notes, however, that

> Normative statements from respondents do not necessarily offer a clear guide to their behaviour. Indeed, the men who most readily identified areas of domestic labour to which they would not contribute were in fact those who in general proved to be most flexible. Those men whose behaviour was most rigid in refusing to contribute to domestic labour often denied that there was any particular task in which they would not participate. (Morris 1985a: 232–3)

11 Porter (1982:119–20; 1983).
12 These examples are taken from Banks (1956). See also Zweig (1961) and Beynon (1973). The *Affluent Worker* series, like most other studies of shiftwork, looked at the effects of such patterns of work on men as employees, not at the effects on their spouses or children.
13 Most other studies also show the same division of labour continuing after men become unemployed (e.g. Marsden and Duff 1975; McKee and Bell 1985). Those which suggest 'most men *are* willing to share domestic labour' (Wheelock 1990, cover blurb) have taken biased samples in that they select couples where husbands are unemployed or non-employed (e.g. sick or students) while their wives work full-time – which is not typical of unemployed men's households.

14 A few recent studies have looked at the effects of unemployment on men, including its effects on their health. Fagin and Little's case studies (1984) show how women bear the brunt of men's depression, frustration and anger at unemployment. There has not been comparable research on women's unemployment / redundancy and its effect on their husbands and children.

15 Morris points out that this is contrary to what is suggested in some domestic labour debate writings (see chapter 3).

16 Peter Moss looked at mothers' involvement in overtime working and found that less than 5 per cent of employed married women work more than six hours paid overtime a week (Moss and Fonda 1980).

17 41 per cent against a national average of 46.6 per cent.

18 Cf. Littlejohn (1963), Davidoff (1976), Frankenberg (1976).

19 This uses the work of Elizabeth Bott (1957) which looked at how relations between husbands and wives vary with the networks of support available to them outside the family household. Bott found a general dimension of jointness versus segregation in conjugal roles associated with being middle as against working class, and with having separate, close-knit male and female as opposed to shared mixed-sex, loose-knit external friendship and kin networks.

Platt in her article (1969) says that in fact the Luton team found it impossible to classify couples as having overall 'joint' or 'segregated' marital roles. It was too simplistic. Different areas of household work varied independently of each other in the extent of sharing between individual husbands and wives. She also notes they asked no questions relating to whether the few household tasks generally considered to be men's work were ever 'joint'.

20 See Platt (1969: 289).

21 See Denis Marsden who suggests wives give up work to look after husbands when the latter are at home all day (Marsden and Duff 1975).

22 This uses Jan Pahl's distinction (1983) between:
control – the way money is allocated, that is, how decisions are made about the distribution of income and responsibilities for different areas of expenditure;
management – how control decisions are actually put into operation, usually via management of designated areas of expenditure; and
budgeting – the process of spending within particular expenditure categories.

23 Dennis, Henriques and Slaughter (1969) suggest that among miners the allowance system provides protection for basic family expenditure against fluctuating earnings. But Morris and Ruane point out (1989) it can equally defend men's additional earnings from collective demands.

Work by Grey in Edinburgh (1979) showed that when a husband kept a large retention (as was frequent among skilled workers and those who were owner-occupiers of houses) the families were in fact better off materially than where the man handed over his whole wage-packet after having taken out his personal spending money. When he kept a large retention, the proportion of the wage going to personal spending money was actually less, and husbands also worked longer hours, because they saw the extra money they earned as going to meet household needs. Such husbands were more home-orientated, more flexible over-housekeeping, more likely to share over-time earnings, they owned more consumer durables, and were generally more sharing of responsibilities.

24 See J. Pahl (1983; 1990), Morris (1984b; 1985a), Morris and Ruane (1989).
25 See J. Pahl (1983; 1990) and Morris and Ruane (1989).
26 See Porter (1983; 121–2) on the campaign to retain family allowances. Also Land (1977).
27 See G. Wilson (1987).
28 See Goldthorpe, Lockwood, Bechhofer and Platt (1971: 131).
29 This is of course a study based on attitudes expressed to interviewers. Parents may *say* they are willing, but reveal different values in other ways. See Leonard (1980) on the ways in which parents may try to keep their adult children living close to and in contact with them.

8

FARM FAMILIES IN FRANCE

There is a curious tendency to suggest that small farms using mainly
family labour, which are called peasant farms in France,[1] represent just a
small backward minority of the population. Because of this, the fact that
we use them to show general principles of family organization is said to
be unjustified: it shows simply that the family structure we describe is out
of date.[2] In fact, however, although only a small proportion of the population is employed in agriculture in northern Europe and North America
(42 per cent of the active population of France in 1911, falling to 20 per
cent in 1960 and under 10 per cent in the early 1980s),[3] family farms are
the rule rather than the exception in this sector of the economy in western
societies, and of course world-wide an estimated 80 per cent of women
work in agriculture. In addition, the fact that an ever smaller proportion
of the population of Europe works in agriculture does not make agriculture a backwater. Quite the contrary. The numbers are declining because
of increased mechanization and improved crops and general agricultural
efficiency.

People keep confidently predicting the decline of family farms, and
some experts say that agriculture will (or should) see more and more farm
amalgamations to provide economies of scale, increased mechanization
of work, and an agricultural labour force which is more and more like the
industrial waged labour force. But in France today still fewer than 10 per
cent of those who work on farms are waged, and 80 per cent of farms
have mainly (or only) family workers. In England, where the cereal farms
of the south and east used to hire perhaps a dozen male farm workers, the
numbers of full-time, male, waged workers have sharply declined; and
with recession, the number of farms relying mainly or solely on family
labour seems actually to be increasing.[4] Though 'swimming against the
economic tide', 'their tenacity in the face of . . . unfavourable circumstances
is remarkable.' They are 'an exceptionally stable element in the agricultural
labour force' (Newby, Rose, Saunders and Bell 1981: 46).

Family farms are now generally specialized producers of livestock
(including dairy produce, sheep, and factory production of pigs and poultry)
or horticultural produce (vineyards, glasshouse crops, soft fruit or market
gardening and plant nurseries). There is less mixed farming than before

the war. But even peasant farms in France, which were less commercially orientated in the nineteenth century than farms of the same period in England, have long been less self-sufficient than was generally presumed. (The agricultural sector in France retained only 25 per cent of its gross product in the 1960s.)[5] In addition, since the 1950s there have been major changes in agricultural techniques and an increase in the production of commodities for the national market. A distinctly commercial approach has spread.

Peasant farm families are therefore not as different from urban / industrial households, nor as independent of the market, as is commonly assumed (especially since, as we have stressed, urban / industrial households do so much more production for self-consumption than is estimated). Farm families are fully integrated into industrial society, even if the unpaid work of family members is not always recognized and even if it does not fit easily into the classical categories used to analyse work – which is of course partly why this sector interests us. (The other reason is because one of us has done research in rural areas.)

As we said at the start of chapter 7, family production and transmission in agriculture has been the subject of a well-developed rural sociology in Europe.[6] Consequently, better information is available on family economics, and especially on women's work in farming than in any other sector, albeit in the case of consumption it is far from perfect. For feminists seeking to understand the situation of women, peasant farms constitute a natural test case because the work farm wives do is so clearly 'productive'. They so visibly help produce goods for exchange on the market (and not services or goods just for family use) that they, of all wives, should be equals with their husbands. But as we shall see, they are no more their husbands' equals than city women.[7]

Production on farms

There is no such thing as a typical farm or a typical farming region. Some family farms are in areas comprised predominantly of small farms while others are scattered in among larger capitalist farms; there are differences between lowland and upland areas; and according to which agricultural products are produced. Farms also vary with wider economic circumstances, technological changes and social relations (including the sort of land tenure and taxation systems which exist and the extent of state support for farm prices).

The work done by men and women on farms is also very varied – over time and from place to place. But producing for the market in agriculture in France has always been and remains a family activity, recently renamed a *métier de couple*, a job for a couple, to take into account the generational changes, namely, that children are more and more loath to stay on the farm, and especially to work there without a wage or a status. However, this couple, as one French politician remarked in 1980, is ruled by 'a peculiar arithmetic where one plus one equals . . . one!'

Within the group working on a farm there is always a clear hierarchy: there is a (nine times out of ten male) *chef d'entreprise* (farmer), and various (female and male) *aides familiaux* (family helpers), as well as (male and female, full-time and part-time) waged workers.[8]

Farmers work almost exclusively 'on the land' in small farms, spending most of their time performing manual work alongside their (few) employees and other family members to produce goods for the market. Only on larger, mainly arable, farms do farm owners become primarily managers. In neither case do male farmers do any household work.

Wives help their husbands with some of the farm work, as well as doing almost all the work to produce goods and services for the farm household's own consumption (including gardening), running small enterprises on the farm (for example, keeping goats and making and selling cheese, or taking in paying guests) or sometimes selling some of their labour (if they are not needed on the farm).

Work on the farm holding

The relative prestige and responsibility of farm tasks in France is well known and documented.[9] Who does which tasks, and how specific tasks are valued, has varied over time and between regions, but there has always been a clear division of responsibilities by sex (though which tasks were done by which sex has varied with time and place). Men do what is considered the 'heavy' and more important work which is central to the well-being of the farm, while women do 'light' work on the farm, sometimes seasonally, as well as regular domestic work and by-employments. Men and boy family members and waged workers work with the farmer, and women and girls with his wife.

The division into heavy and light work is obviously a social and not a physical classification, since work can be 'heavy' in one region when done by men and 'light' in another when done by women (for example, earthing up potatoes or driving draught animals) and can change over time. For example, milking was done by women before it was mechanized, but is now done by men, yet hand-milking was one of the most exhausting jobs on the farm and also one of the most constraining in terms of timetable because it has to be done at the beginning and end of each and every day. (Women marrying farmers in France used to try to have it written into their marriage contracts that they should be exempt from hand-milking.)

The arbitrariness of the classification is also clear because 'light work' includes lifting equally heavy loads – but of water rather than manure – or even heavier loads; for example, in the past gathering and binding sheaves of corn rather than scything, or today hauling bales (weighing 50 lb.) with a pitchfork onto a trailer rather than driving the tractor – even though a tractor driven at its lowest speed is so easy to manoeuvre that one regularly sees young *male* children, sometimes no older than ten, guiding them round and round the fields while the adults lift the heavy bales.

One couple we know, a brother and sister, stick to the conventional division of labour despite the woman having a heart condition. When asked why, the sister replied she would not know how to turn the tractor round (at two miles an hour! and she drives a car) and furthermore that driving the tractor is heavier work than it looks. 'You should see their blood after they do it. It's all cooked. My doctor told me it turns into blood sausage!' In other words, when questioned, men's doing the lighter work gets rationalized – in this instance by a truly mind-blowing irrationality, where blood manages to cook inside living men's bodies and those same bodies still continue to function!

Although there is some variation in women's work on smallholdings from one part of the country to another, they are nearly always assigned the preparation of animal foodstuffs for whatever livestock is kept, the raising of young animals, cleaning out and milking of cows and goats (where it is not done by machine) and the care of pigs and poultry. They may have sole charge of egg production (collection, grading and marketing). But they are much less likely than men to work with any machinery. On very small marginal holdings they may well have outside paid employment to contribute to the overall family income. On larger holdings, especially on large arable farms where the husband plays a managerial role with waged employees, they are less likely to do manual work and more likely to do office work (including doing the farm accounts and making up wages, seeing callers and answering the telephone, running errands, and sometimes deputizing for their husband when he is off the farm – making decisions and issuing orders to employees). Or they may have a largely domestic role. But almost no wives of farmers 'never ever' help on the farm.

On some larger farms, if wives are keen on farming they may be delegated charge of a particular farm enterprise which contributes to the overall business (for example, growing fruit and vegetables for market or managing a rabbit breeding unit). More and more women nowadays, especially younger ones, are seeking to establish their professional capacity as farmers and to contribute to the farm income on a semi-independent and therefore visible basis. They want to escape as far as they can the role of jack-of-all-trades, of helper, and so they set up their own workshops on the family farm (sometimes called *ateliers hors-sol* because they do not require land or produce from the farm land). These involve raising animals, for instance pigs, on a contractual basis for the manufacturers of specialist foodstuffs (agro-industry), or, as in Lower Normandy, fattening calves. But since these workshops are created to increase the farm income without involving any capital investment, 'a woman sees . . . her work undervalued and has to put up with bad conditions . . . She may consider getting better organized . . . and she knows how hard the work is [but] she believes any improvement [in her conditions of work] would be costly and so she prefers to keep quiet' (Lajus 1969 our translation).

On the majority of farms in France, which are medium-sized holdings where the husband himself works long hours on the land, wives work as many hours a week on the farm as they spend on domestic duties. They can be asked to do anything: to fetch and carry, or just to stand by and hold things or to pick up a spade and be a navvy. They perform tasks regularly under supervision, and help with other tasks occasionally and in emergencies. Many of these are the most dirty, arduous and non-mechanized tasks. For example, they go round each day and check on cows and sheep in the fields and poultry in the yard or sheds. They move animals from one place to another. They will turn out to catch stray animals in the rain in the middle of the night and do the milking in an emergency. They help at lambing and harvest and fetch spare parts for machines as and when required. They will get professional advice when it is needed. But their contribution is little valued despite this – or rather it is little valued because of this. The work is demeaned because it is done by low status people, and low status people are confirmed in their subordinate position by the work they do – which is decreed unimportant, facile, worthless, easy, etc.

The division of tasks on farms by age has always been more flexible even within a given region, but the older the children grow, the more important and complex the tasks they are given – according to the local evaluation. For instance, using the tractor is usually a task and a privilege reserved for the future heir, though it is hard to see how it is technically more complex or functionally more necessary for the farm than looking after the herd of cattle, which is done by a younger brother. Unfortunately, there is no systematic study of the customary distribution of tasks on family farms according to family status (age, sex and kinship link with the head), and no studies which attempt to link the prestige of tasks and their technical complexity, or which look at how the attribution of *tâches de confiance* (tasks requiring trust) ties in with the handing over of power.

By the last we mean that there seems to be a connection between the gradual handing over of power (of authority in the decision-making area) and being given 'complex' tasks. Thus when the eldest son starts to drive the tractor it seems to be an indicator that he is getting more important, and that he is being given more voice in the management of the farm.

What adult men do is always seen as the 'more important' work. It therefore carries more prestige and rewards, although again which tasks are seen as 'important' and 'essential' varies from time to time and place to place and it is difficult to see particular jobs as actually objectively more important to the overall farm economy or the process of production than others. In fact for 'difficult' read 'impossible', since the sexual division of labour is such that if we follow a given product through from its inception to its being ready to be sold, it is clear, especially given the long cycle of agricultural production (sometimes more than a year), that men and women take turns in the necessary series of operations. Each operation would be useless if the one prior to or after it were not done. So technically no one can be deemed more important than the others.

Related to men's work being seen as more important is the suggestion that women's work is now 'marginal' in agriculture. This is, however, far from true. In 1968 the wife of a small farmer in France devoted an average of 4 hours a day (according to Bastide 1969) or more (50 hours a week according to Allauzen 1967) to farm work – as well of course as doing most of the work associated with children, home and garden. The so-called countryside crisis – the French rural crisis – has been due largely to young women no longer wanting to marry farmers. The work is too hard. But by common consensus a farm cannot be run without a woman. Michelet said that when a farmer could not afford to hire a domestic servant, he took a wife, and this still holds true. As a neighbour said only recently in southwest France, 'Michel needs someone to help him and nowadays he can't get a servant. If only he could get married.'

So whatever women may do on small farms, and however it may be downgraded, their contribution is absolutely necessary. A man on his own cannot run a farm without having a double workload. He has to do the 'woman's work' as well as the 'man's', for both are essential. At the limit, a man on his own cannot run a farm, full stop, even if he has no small children. All the studies made of peasant farms in France show that those run by bachelors lag behind 'normal' ones in economic and technical matters, that is, behind those run by men with wives (or sisters or mothers). The unpaid labour of a woman – generally a wife – is thus presumed in the general economy of a small farm.

This used also to apply, and still does though less and less, to the unpaid labour of the head's children and his non-inheriting brothers and sisters. But as capital is substituted for labour in modern agriculture, not only are there fewer and fewer wage workers and more and more farms which emply no hired labour, but even the son who is to inherit may have to work off the land while awaiting his inheritance, since the farm does not require two men to run it. Indeed in marginal situations farmers themselves may sometimes seek alternative sources of income for part of the year (for example, running a haulage business). In many cases today, therefore, the adult children of farmers leave his farm. His sons and his younger brothers will certainly leave farm work if he does not pay them a wage.

Work in the farm house

While many farmers' wives find satisfaction in their work and in living on the farm, their domestic as well as their occupational role is heavier than that of many urban housewives. They have to cope with the problems of rural isolation and bad weather (being snowed in in winter and mud being brought into the house); with a fluctuating income; and with a business which is run from home. There are peaks of labour demand and farm crises which make a husband work long and unpredictable hours and he may constantly have the weight of the world on his shoulders as he worries about bad weather and crop failure. Their husbands' work means farmers' wives have few family outings and holidays – so their work may include comforting disappointed children. Many say one of the worst things about their lives is feeling tied to the farm and they stress their low incomes more than their husbands do.

If the household is large, farmers' wives may have some help in the house, but rarely full-time domestic help (even when there is full-time waged labour on the farm). This despite the extra work they have washing dirty clothes, providing food (growing fruit and vegetables, preserving garden produce, shopping in bulk from distant shops, and sometimes making cheese and baking bread or cakes), looking after farm dogs and cats and other pets, and having to transport children to school and to out-of-school activities. In addition some wives paint and decorate the farm house or let cottages or provide bed and breakfast for paying guests. If they spend a lot of time on the farm with their husband, however, they may do a minimum of household chores and fairly perfunctory child-rearing.

Farmers' wives are often the mainstay of rural communities. Their family status may require them to perform such neighbourly acts as nursing, running voluntary activities for children and the elderly, and organizing fund-raising events and fêtes for women's organizations attached to the church or in the general community, and for the societies and sports which their husbands support.

While we have here distinguished farmers' wives' 'household' and 'farm' activities, it is important to remember (see chapter 4 pp. 92–3) that wives themselves only make this distinction with difficulty, and only try to make it at all (at least until recently) when requested to do so by sociologists. For them, there is no difference of work relationship between 'housework' and all the other work they do: work which is specific to the particular husband to whom they are married. (It is all 'the work of a farmer's wife'.) It is also virtually impossible to separate out the two, anyway, since the tasks of 'housework' and 'occupational work' which time-budgeters want to distinguish, in practice overlap. For instance, a wife may be waiting to take a delivery of tractor parts while making the breakfast and comforting a child, or decorating a room a corner of which is used as the farm office. It is small wonder, therefore, that time-budget studies come up with widely varying figures for the number of hours farmers' wives spend on 'farm work'. They are trying to measure things to one side of a line, when where the line is drawn is highly subjective and variable.

A recent study has again confirmed that farm wives themselves do not use such categories as 'occupational' and 'domestic'.

Even if some activities have a resolutely occupational quality (e.g. *elevage hors-sol* and work in the fields) [farm wives] hesitate to confer such a quality onto accounting or bookkeeping or tending the kitchen garden or the poultry and the pig, etc. For with these activities there is no barrier between what will be sold and what will be consumed by the household. On the other hand, they do draw a distinction between the 'inside' (of the house) and the 'outside'; but this line does not coincide with the separation between housework and occupational work. (Filippi and Nicourt 1987 our translation)

Following first Christine Delphy's and later Alice Barthez's questioning of the categories classically used to describe women's work on farms, Filippi and Nicourt used an ergonomic perspective and continuously observed the work of 37 women. Their study led them to question the validity of time-budget methods whose 'imprecision conceals the continuous incursion of one activity into another'. Instead they found women's work on farms to be typified by:

- an absence of continuity in the completion of any task;
- short work-sequences; and
- there being few benchmarks during the day.

The benchmarks which do exist are: morning and evening care of indoor animals; getting children up; preparing meals at noon and in the evening; and children coming home after school. Other activities get fitted in around these times, and are in competition with each other. One of the main elements in this competition is the wife's liability to be interrupted by her husband wanting help. This leads to a great deal of stress as well as physical exhaustion: 'women almost never sit down.'

The women they interviewed echoed the saying that 'Our work does not show. It shows only when it is not done.' This feeling seems to stem from the kind of tasks allotted to women, but in fact it derives from the way others look at the work which women do (which becomes 'women's work'), and therefore from their relations of production. 'Doing lots of little things *for my husband* isn't work' (our stress).

Decision-making

In small farming in Europe until the 1950s or 1960s many might have argued that it was hard to see the head of the family enterprise as having much leeway for decision-making and management. The tasks which had to be done seemed as 'old as the hills' and who should do them seemed equally firmly regulated by custom. There were also the constraints of circumstances – the need to maximize resources to scrape a precarious living. Historians may have shown that the tasks and the people who did them varied from time to time and region to region, but there seemed no choice at any given time or within any one region.[10] 'Custom' and 'necessity' apparently, and not the head of the family, decided that herds should be tended by children in this region and women in that; maize harvested by women here, men there, and both in a third place; and that women would have considerable autonomy in fishing–crofting where the men were often away, but less in hill sheep-farming where they were needed as assistants by the men.

But even within the rigid customary framework of rural farming society, there was some room for the exercise of decision. As regards production on the farm, the timing of agricultural work, the choice of which crops and which varieties to grow and their rotation, what to grow on which parcels of land, when to harvest, the balance to be struck between the production of animals and vegetables, the size of the herd, and which animals to keep (sheep, cows, chickens, rabbits, etc.), were all matters involving choice and judgement. Even where custom played a great role, it played it less and less, so the space for decision-making got bigger and bigger – and more and more complex as the market was increasingly set by the government after negotiations with the farmers' organizations. But even in times and places where circumstances were most constraining, where the crops, their rotation and their balance was customary and the land most marginally fertile, there were still decisions to be made; and whatever the limits within which decisions could be exercised, this margin was used, well or badly, by the head of the family, the farmer. The wife would usually give her opinion, but whatever course was followed was credited to her husband.

To these decisions about production were added commercial decisions: what products to put on the market, when, where and to whom to sell (which were affected by the nature of the product, where and when it was produced, how perishable it was, and whether or not it needed processing). These sorts of decisions were not seen as 'marital' at all, so they never formed part of rural 'marital decision-making' studies. When they *were* studied they were seen as 'political science'. It was men who were and are active in local politics and national associations, and who were and are involved in, for example, trying to keep out competitors, opposing industrial development and regulating the local labour market.

Within the lifetime of today's farmers, however, 'agricultural production has been revolutionized and any sense of continuity has been shattered' (Newby 1985: 77).

> Farmers need no longer spread the risk of farming across a variety of commodities to the extent that was once considered advisable. A degree of risk – associated with the weather and the market – inevitably remains, but it has been reduced by new technological developments and particularly by the intervention of the state in the determination of prices and guarantees. (Newby 1985: 83)

There have been major scientific and technological innovations in pursuit of profit – new machines, genetic improvement of crops, chemical fertilizers and insecticides, and improved animal husbandry; and 30 years of secure prices and support from successive (national and EEC) governments.

The fact that decisions continue to be made, as also the scale of the margin of decisions, is clear, however, in what has been called the 'conflict of generations' within small farming in France. In rural areas there have long been disputes between those (generally the young people) who want to use the margin for innovation, and those (generally their elders) who want to go on much as before. The elders have the power to decide and usually decide to carry on the same routine. But the fact that conflict exists shows that decisions are being made which could be different.

The head not only makes decisions about what to produce, and how and when to sell, he also makes decisions (within the limits set by custom and his particular circumstances) about who is to do which jobs, or which parts of a particular job. He makes his decisions according to custom, the availability of individuals, and also according to the prestige he (or occasionally she) wants to accord a particular family member. That is to say, the head decides what human resources to allocate to the tasks he has decided need doing; and which tasks to give to individuals, given that the tasks themselves carry differential status. Thus although a farmer might not be able to decide that sons should look after the chickens (poultry being a woman's job), or to send a daughter to market to buy a cow (it being a man's job), he can show favour to a particular son by delegating him, rather than his brothers, to sell cattle or to drive the tractor; or favour a particular daughter by excusing her (in the past) from doing the milking or (today) from doing any manual farm work at all.

When women work on the farm holding on production for the market they are usually subordinates – just as when they work in the garden or house on production for the family's own consumption. If they work alongside their husbands on a common task, they do so not as equal participants, but as assistants. They have to be around when their husbands need help and they do what their husbands tell them. They have little if any autonomy in their work and they get landed with the arduous, least-valued tasks. They take little part in making decisions about the farm – either about the day-to-day matters of what is to be done and who is to do it, or about the overall management of the enterprise. In particular it is the husband who decides what to sell, he collects the money received, and he decides where it is to go. This is generally the case even when the wife is formally the owner or part-owner of the farm (see below).

Wives may be well aware of what is going on, and be asked for advice, and they may even expect to be consulted on major policy decisions, but they are not responsible for making decisions on their own. They may answer the phone and see callers, but they do not *deal* with callers; they may make up the wages but they do not decide what level the wage should be, and they often do not pay bills even when they do most of the office work and have had experience in their employment before marriage in banks as bookkeepers. If their husband discusses what he is planning to do, it is recognized that this is because it helps him to make up his mind to have someone to tell what he intends to do (Gasson 1981: 31–2). Most women are happy with this situation and say they would not like to be responsible for more than they are. Some are less content. But what irritates wives is 'not so much their husbands always having the last word in farming matters . . . but rather . . . men's unquestioning belief that this is their right' (Gasson 1981: 50).

The house is the only domain where farmers' wives have any autonomy and any control over the distribution of resources. Like all housewives, they are free to do what they want within the limits set by their husbands. But also, like all housewives, they do not control the income into the house; and like many urban housewives, farmers' wives rarely handle any money which has not gone through their husband's hands.

This, as we said earlier, is one reason why we consider farmers' wives a test case for feminist theories of the family. Farmers' wives produce goods which reach the market, but they themselves are not 'producers' (that is, they are not exchangers, they do not own the goods). When some writers on the family suggest that because women produce goods for the market, they receive value, or that they own the money received when these products are sold, they ignore this distinction. But this is not a small fact they are overlooking. It is not any old distinction. **The distinction between the person who directly produces goods and the person who owns these goods is the very basis of exploitation according to materialist theory.**

What wives contribute to production jointly with husbands is his. In the case of wives working alongside their husbands on the farm this is unequivocal and very evident. In cases where the wife is given control of an enterprise within the overall farm business, for example, running a dairy and poultry yard and selling butter and eggs in a farm shop, the money she makes is pre-budgeted for by the farmer and is only contingently 'hers'. Although the wife gets satisfaction from the work and from her contribution to the household, the money goes towards the maintenance of the family for which *he* is responsible; it reduces the amount the farmer has to make from the rest of the holding, or alternatively it allows him to retain more from the profit he makes on other areas for whatever purposes he decides. Wives have only delegated control, which motivates them to continue and to make a good profit so they can have some say in the spending of some money. But this is just good management practice.

A second reason why we consider farm families to be interesting test cases of the nature of the family system is that the rapid changes which farming has been undergoing keep throwing into relief the patriarchal nature of the family. Particular features are illuminated as women struggle to improve their situation alongside the modernization of agriculture.

In some cases, as farms have become bigger and / or more prosperous, women have stopped working on the land and they have been returned to – or rather set to – making a home. This term only has a meaning in a situation where 'family' and 'work' are separated; and the distinction did not previously exist on French farms. Now, however, farmers' wives are being put in charge of creating homes and gardens and 17 per cent of farmers' wives in the mid 1980s declared themselves to be *sans profession* (without occupation), which could be translated as 'housewife' even though they do some work on the farm.[11] This is reflected in much of the farming press and in pronouncements from the political parties.

Women are setting about the task by establishing the category of housework and making it cover in practice as much as possible of what is included in such work in the urban situation, thereby creating a higher standard of living in the farm household. Family members now eat more elaborate food, relax in stylish interiors with modern conveniences, and the children have more time and attention devoted to their upbringing. The (male) farm dweller has thus attained parity with men in towns – and the woman on the farm parity with the work of her town (or rural but non-farm) sister. Like certain French working class women, some farmers' wives are pleased to be relieved of 'occupational' work, even if their work is increased by previously unknown housework.[12] The work they did on the farm never brought them status or autonomy anyway. They now supposedly work less hard (though this is debatable) and their status has not changed.

Some women on farms, however, have rejected this development and are claiming their right to return to, or to continue, working on the land – but under different terms and conditions. They want to be *agricultrices*, farm women, not farmers' wives. They enjoy farming not housework; but they do not like being subordinate and economically dependent. They want to have a say in management decisions on the farm and to have the social status of a farmer.

Until recently, to get an income 'of their own', the wives of most small farmers had to seek employment off the farm. (The holdings were too small, or external circumstances did not allow wives to develop independent enterprises within them.) Employment away from the farm was likely to be (to put it mildly) badly received by both their husbands and the local community. Farmers married in order to have (amongst other things) help on the farm. Only women who had a non-farming occupation before marriage, and who lived on a farm which badly needed some extra cash income, could hope to continue it afterwards (and it would of course have to be done in addition to whatever 'housework' there might be). But nowadays, more and more French farm women / wives are claiming access to 'the dignity of work' and to financial 'autonomy'. Some 12 per cent in the mid 1980s had employment off the farm and considered this other job their main activity. But many others want to exercise what they say is their chosen occupation – farming.

The impasses they encounter make clear the nature of the service contract of married life, for when trying to gain status, that is, when trying to get one part of their work valued and recognized, they are forced to devalue the other. They have to use the distinction between housework and occupational work used by economists and time-budget studies (see chapter 4). This distinction, as we have shown, is quite arbitrary and used to be foreign to farm thinking. But in order to claim that some of their work should be paid, farm women are having to reaffirm that some of it should not be. They hope that if they concede that doing the washing-up is unproductive, it will be accepted that caring for poultry is productive. To get it accepted that they work part-time (instead of having no occupation at all), they have to agree to regard doing the washing-up, waiting for the once daily bus to the town to do the shopping, the care of the elderly, taking children to school, and writing letters to their husband's family, to be non-work: that is, to be leisure and pleasure.

This dual status of women's work is formalized in the newly formed farming co-operatives (Groupement Agricole d'Exploitation Collective, GAECs). The co-ops allow the existence of associations between participants of different statuses and there is no head of the overall estate. Since the status of associate in a GAEC can derive from contributing either property or work, it should have been easy for women to become associates and to acquire an equal right to a say in the management of a farmstead and over the income this gives. The two situations which exist in practice are, however:

1 where the wife is not an associate, when she either works on the farm for free (her work is assimilated with the rest of her domestic work), or part of her work – that having to do with 'the occupation' – is counted with her husband's contribution to the co-op and paid to him (so as to avoid having to pay wages and therefore social security to her); or
2 where the wife is an associate (in which case there has always to be a third person in the association), when her contribution is usually counted as part-time because it is deemed she cannot contribute more since she has to do domestic work.

In a sense the last situation epitomizes the situation of working women: not only do they work more hours per week than men because men do not do housework; but on top of this, the meaning of their work is reversed. They cannot spend as long in the paid-market arena *because* they perform unpaid domestic work. But their exploitation in one sector – the non-market – is not compensated for in the market sector. On the contrary, it is redoubled since they get lower wages. They thus bring in less cash. But instead of this being seen as a reflection of the unpaid nature of domestic work, it is on the contrary seen as a reason to justify their doing the housework. They must make up in kind for what they do not bring in in cash. They are not once but twice penalized by the unpaidness of housework: once by having to do it; and a second time by not having enough time left to get a fair wage on the market.

This is an extremely clear example of one exploitation leading to another. Not only do women work longer hours (raising children and doing housework in addition to working on the farm), but instead of being recompensed for this, as the ideology suggests ('women may have a bad time in area x but they are compensated for it by having a better time in area y'), it in fact makes their situation worse. On the one hand housework is entirely unpaid in a co-op; and on the other it serves as a pretext for saying that since women bring less to the business, they should be paid less or not paid at all. When the accounts are drawn up it appears that women take little part in the farm business and contribute very little to the subsistence of the household, because a whole section of their work, on which the subsistence of the household also depends, is concealed. Only a money contribution counts – hence the husband's contribution seems most important – and the work in kind is ignored. In reality the wife does an enormous amount of work and it is this which prevents her earning as much as her husband.

This (false) representation of reality is of course paradigmatic. Women work longer hours than men on farms and contribute more to household consumption in general; but paradoxically it is they who are seen as 'supported' by their husbands. What the new developments in French agriculture do, is simply from time to time make women's oppression transparently obvious.

Consumption within farm families

No systematic data exist on differential consumption in farm families, but we can nevertheless draw together enough material to establish a good case for the hierarchical principle we set out in chapters 5 and 6.

There is, for instance, good information available on the distribution of food within farm households in the southwest of France in the postwar period.[13] Up until the 1950s this region contained families with some of the lowest incomes and standards of living in industrial societies (comparable to the present situation among farmers in eastern and southern Europe). We might expect, if we were optimistic, that the scant goods each family household had in this area at that time would have been evenly shared among its members. We might at least expect that enough food would have been provided for everyone, since these families not only produced food for their own consumption but also for sale. But in fact even this essential was consumed very differentially – according to the status of individuals within the family.

There was variation in both the quantity and the quality of food available to different people, and it distinguished primarily children from adults, and women from men, though among the adults the old ate less well than those of mature years, and junior but adult male members of the family ate less well than the head. The farmer always had the biggest and the best pieces. Children were fed exclusively on milk, flour and sugar until they were two or three years old; and the elderly, especially the infirm elderly, were returned to a similar regime based on cereals and milk, bread soups (*panade*) and broths. Meat was rarely served, and even more rarely served to everyone. When it did appear on the table, it was often only consumed by the head of the family, especially if it was butcher's meat. Less expensive meat – chickens reared on the farm and bacon made at home – were not subject to such exclusive privilege. However, women and children never got the choice piece, which was reserved for their father, or on social occasions for distinguished guests. For example, the prime piece of ham, a prime food in itself, was given to the future son-in-law. Alcohol and tobacco were also strongly differentiated – they were for adult men, not women and children.

The absence of protein from the diet of infants and the elderly led to food deficiencies which had serious repercussions for the development of the former and the health of the latter – and the life expectancy of everyone. The relative absence of protein in the diet of women had consequences for their general state of health, the effects of which were doubled by the physiological burden of pregnancy (as was seen in the very high rates of maternal and infant mortality in all rural areas). None the less, it was believed that babies and children did not need meat and that women needed it less than men. Vegetables, which according to local belief 'go straight through you' and do not 'build up a man', apparently nourish women and children.

The locals also believed that the quantity of food needed by an individual related to their body size and constitution (in a very similar way to 'scientific' tables of consumption), but it is obvious that this was a rationalization and not a principle underlying actual distribution because of the number of exceptions to it which existed. Someone who was a husband, a master, a father or an eldest son, however small and puny he might be, would never give up his privileged share to a wife, a worker, a child or a younger sibling, however tall or heavily built.

Local theory also used an argument based on differential expenditure of energy (again like the one used in 'scientific' tables) depending on whether the individual did 'heavy' or 'light' work. But again, whether an activity was classified as light or heavy depended on the status of the people who did it. In any case, when women did what was generally held to be heavy work, either exceptionally (at certain times of year) or ordinarily alongside men, the evaluation of the energy they were deemed to expend, and the food they were therefore held to need, was not adjusted. For instance, in Brittany and the Alps women did all the agricultural work – but they did not get more food in these regions. Anyway, a simple counting of the number of hours of physical activity per day, more than a third higher on average for women than for men on farms, would have led one to expect that women's expenditure of, and hence need for, energy was greater than men's, in this sector of society at least.

Rural evaluation of need for food certainly did not take into account the subjective desires of those concerned. The feeling of hunger and need for food experienced by children and adolescents in the countryside was legendary, but it did not lead to the conclusion that they needed more food. On the contrary, if they asked for food, they were given the set response – 'you don't need it.' A state of hunger was considered normal among the young in poor rural areas. Or rather, satiation, the pleasure of eating one's fill as and when one wants, was not recognized as one of their needs. 'Being hungry' as a characteristic, not of specific cases but of a whole category of individuals, 'the young', was considered not as due to their social condition, but as an unalterable physiological fact.

Although differential distribution of food does still continue in the countryside, it is of course not the only area of differential consumption, and more are emerging with increasing prosperity. Newby and colleagues' work in southeast England (1978) shows richer farmers spending considerable sums on their own cars, and more modest sums on their wives' transport; paying to go for days of hunting and shooting; having expensive hobbies (they found many farmers were collectors of paintings and watercolours, horse brasses, old farm machinery, silver and china, exotic wildfowl or dogs); drinking and eating pub lunches with fellow farmers and sales representatives of agricultural manufacturers; and spending a lot of money on trips to agricultural shows. Their wives spent quite a lot on clothes and their appearance (the men were 'not dressers'), but otherwise the wives' main consumption was of expensive renovations to 'their' houses. Two or three times a year the husbands treated them to a trip to London for a meal, a visit to the theatre and a night in an expensive hotel.

Also at issue in France is the difference between maintenance or 'given' consumption, and chosen consumption (that is, differences in the mode of consumption). The problems which are currently being put forcefully in rural areas where two adult generations live together, reveal that the conflicts experienced are not between 'the generations', but rather arise because the adult children, who live with and are described as 'guests' (*invités*) of their parents, are now claiming the right to free consumption, rather than the maintenance imposed / given by their parents/'hosts'.

Transmission in farm families

The great majority of small farmers get to be farmers not by having formal agricultural training or demonstrating farming ability, but by inheritance – by being transmitted patrimonial property or quasi-property. Land or tenancies are handed over between relatives, generally from father to son but sometimes from an uncle to a nephew, etc. Which person gets what depends on their relationship to (that is, their personal association with) an existing holder. He has the personal capacity to dispose of 'his' property – he can give it to someone during his lifetime, or leave it to someone in his will, or let the rules of intestate succession and inheritance tax take their course.[14]

At succession all the land and buildings of a farm usually have to be kept as a unit if it is to remain technically and commercially viable. Splitting it into several bits would arguably seriously prejudice its perpetuation down the family line. However, in France, according to the Napoleonic Code, there is formally egalitarian inheritance. Goods and property are supposed to be divided equally among all the children of a family, including the daughters. But in practice in farm families throughout the country the father's position, which is defined by the status of occupying a farm, is transmitted integrally to just one of his sons. What happens to the rest of his children varies in different regions. In parts of Normandy, for instance, where those who farm are tenants, although one son alone gets the father's lease on the farm, the other goods and property are divided up. In the province of Béarn, however, all daughters and the younger sons are disinherited – the oldest boy gets everything.[15] What both these systems have in common is that sons and daughters have quite different fates.

Farmers' sons who do not succeed their father (that is, who do not acquire his position) but who stay in the community and continue in agriculture, have a strikingly inferior status to that of their brother who does succeed – and obviously to that of their father. Just how much inferior depends on whether or not they are also excluded from inheritance.

In Normandy sons who do not succeed their father do usually nevertheless manage to become nominally farmers. The modalities of succession, the equality of inheritance, and the structure of the family property allow more than one son to be installed on his own account. Non-successors slowly and painfully acquire what was given to their brother from the start. Their careers are long and difficult. They put in twice as much time to establish themselves as their brother, and even then they cultivate land which is only half as good. In addition these non-successors become 'farmers' not only by the strength of their own arms, but also thanks to the help of their fathers. They are thus disadvantaged by the Normandy inheritance system, but not absolutely disadvantaged. They are disadvantaged within certain limits and to a precise extent.

In Béarn, by contrast, non-successor brothers have no possibility of setting up on their own, and they can stay in agriculture only by becoming cadets on the estate which has gone to their 'elder brother'. (It is generally the eldest brother, but the head can in fact choose another son if he wishes or thinks it advisable.) They are family helpers, without wages and compulsorily unmarried. Their status is the same as that of other dependants of the head of the family – except they get state insurance for accidents at work and other dependants do not.

These *cadets* in Béarn do not have a personal position in the local class system. Their status is defined by their attachment to a farm household, hence to a head, and it is his status and class position which determines that of his household. Their status could thus be said to be defined or constituted by their lack of personal class position: to be, in brief, that of a person who does not have a position or status of their own (that is, who is a dependant).

In Normandy, inheritance puts certain sons into a different subclass from their father and succeeding brother. It produces downward mobility for elder sons (to being smaller farmers) as the price for unity of succession – for one son succeeding the father as a 'large' farmer. In Béarn, however, inheritance puts younger sons outside the class structure altogether, in the strict sense of 'holders of positions which define the class'. It puts them into the status of being the family dependants of the holders of class positions.

The other group who are without a class position in their own right, merely dependants of position holders, are of course the daughters of farmers – who typically become farmers' wives. While in Normandy and Béarn not all boys are successors, all successors should be boys. Girls are systematically excluded from succession when there are sons, even when they are not excluded from inheritance (as in Normandy). Girls get small plots of land or a monetary equivalent as their share.[16] This excludes them from being farmers in their own right and also means they usually get less overall than their brothers since the land or goods whose equivalent in money constitutes the daughters' share is commonly undervalued. At best a girl's money is used to buy land, or her small plot added to other land, which is farmed by her husband. 'The compensation paid to an heir excluded from patrimony is fixed as a function of the available financial means and not of the value of the heritage. To put it another way, it is never money which fixes the value of things, but the situation which fixes the value of money' (Mendras 1976: 45, quoted Barthez 1983: 29 our translation).

Women become heads of farms only by accident, for instance, if their husband dies while their sons are still young, or if they have no brothers or close male relatives that their father chooses to leave the farm to – and if they themselves remain unmarried.

But why should it be that, 20 years after the start of the second wave of feminism in France, it is still always the husband, if there is a husband, who is the head of a farm?[17] A farm is constituted either by a piece of property or a tenancy. When the land is owned, it is usually owned by a man since men inherit land more often than women. But for demographic reasons, one farm family in five has only daughters and so its land gets passed on to women; and in addition, although women more often inherit cash than land, they do inherit some land in some cases. So some properties are made up of land owned by the husband and land owned by the wife. Why then are not at least some wives farmers, or equal / joint farmers with their husbands? On this authors do not always agree, especially now, after important legislative changes in 1965, 1980 and 1985.

Most authors agree that one of agriculture's problems used to be that the law did not recognize occupational status in agriculture and that therefore recourse was made to family law in issues concerning the running of a farm. And in family law until 1965, the husband was the 'head' of the family and could do what he wanted with the *communauté* (the common property). (Although there were three alternative types of marital contract,[18] unless couples specified otherwise, they had a contract of *communauté*.) But even within this option each couple had three sorts of property:

1 the husband's own property (his *biens propres*), which he owned before he married or which he inherited during marriage;
2 the wife's own property, ditto; and
3 the *communauté*: everything acquired during the marriage by either of the spouses – their common property. In theory 1 and 2 could never become part of 3.

Until 1965 a husband almost owned the couple's 'common' property and he also managed his wife's own property. He could not sell her property without her consent, but he could lease it and collect the income from it, and since income in cash fell into the common property, hey presto, it was his. Thus, by law, he was the manager of all the real estate owned either personally or jointly by the couple – which made him automatically the 'head' of the farm, ruled as a patrimony, even when he was a landless son-in-law.

The same also applied to tenant farmers – farmers without land – since as sole owner of the tools, cash, etc. (everything except the wife's own real estate) owned by the couple, the husband was also the only individual in the couple who could be a legal partner in any business transaction.

In 1965, however, a new family law made each spouse entirely responsible for her or his own property. Husbands were no longer the managers of their wives' property. They stayed the *chefs de la communauté* (the managers of the common property) but their powers were somewhat controlled (for example, they needed their wife's signature for important buying and selling). So in theory women could have taken advantage of this to establish their own farms on their own land, if they had any. Why then did they not do so? It can no longer be solely for legal reasons, since one of the legal obstacles standing in their way has been removed.

In a second piece of legislation in 1980, the two Chambers of the French Parliament tackled the question of a 'status' for the 'spouses' in farming (in fact a status for the wives of farmers). After much heated debate, they came up with a proposal whose importance is still hotly contested. The wives of farmers could become (and in fact became without their knowing it) either 'collaborators' or 'co-farmers' with their husbands.

According to the lawyer Odile Dhavernas, the legislature wanted to favour the status of 'collaborator', hoping women would not choose the status of 'co-farmer'.[19] This at least is what appears from the preliminary debates. But sociologists such as Barthez and Lagrave who have studied the debates and papers prepared by the major agricultural union (the Fédération Nationale des Syndicats d'Exploitants Agricoles) think, on the other hand, that the trade union leaders were scared of the prospects opened up by the new marital regime. They believe the real issue was the possibility opened up by the 1965 law of wives splitting farms by managing their own part of the farm property separately.

The difference between the two statuses is that as a collaborator a wife is presumed to have been given a mandate to manage the farm by her husband; while as co-farmer, the mandate is presumed to be reciprocal, so that either spouse can act equally in relation to buyers, sellers and the banks, etc.

This may not seem like a big difference – but it is even less than it seems for two reasons. First, because in 1985 the system of marriage contracts was modified yet again, to get rid of what imbalance was left between the spouses. The husband is no longer the 'head' of the 'common property' nor of the 'family'. Paternal authority has been converted into 'parental rights', evenly exercised by both parents – and both spouses have equal powers over what they own in common (each being already sole manager of his or her own property since 1965).

This new law makes the status of collaborator in agriculture obsolete, since the wife no longer needs a 'presumption of mandate' from her husband to contract common goods or properties. The new marital law means every wife, or rather every spouse, is already a collaborator (in that sense) with the other spouse.

Secondly, the status of co-farmer has no advantages over the status of collaborator, since no welfare benefits (no rights to sickness, invalidity or retirement payments) are attached to it – even though this was why the issue of the status of farm spouses (in fact farm wives) was raised in the first place. But it was passed over by Parliament as well as by Senate, to such an extent that the *rapporteurs* of the 1980 Agricultural Law had to watch helplessly as they saw it emptied of any real meaning. They were desperate because, by refusing social security to 'spouses' (wives), Parliament emptied the status of co-farmer of any content, leaving just an empty shell – just a title. There are no *droits propres* for co-farmer wives: no possibility of their having a pension in their own right and their rights to social welfare benefits have not been increased one iota by the 1980 law. For a woman to have her own pension, the farm still has to pay a special contribution. This represents a drain on the resources of the business which most farming couples, like other self-employed workers, are unwilling to accept. They prefer a short-term increase in their living standards to a long-term possible impoverishment of the wife if (and for husbands it is always 'if' and never 'when') the husband dies and the widow is given only part of his pension. (Not to mention the case where they divorce and she gets nothing.)

According to Rose-Marie Lagrave (1987b), women are so aware of the emptiness of the new 'status' that they call themselves co-farmers only when they contribute to the pension plan on a personal basis. What they do not realize is that in the eyes of the law they are all co-farmers anyway – unless they declare they are not. But the banks are not unaware of the new status, for what the new 1980 law did was to remove the protection the previous law gave to women's own property. Now that the two spouses are jointly responsible for the debts incurred by the farm, liability extends to the wife's 'own' property. This tends to give credence to the interpretation that this status was actually favoured by the FNSEA over that of collaborator (which preserves the patrimonial assets of wives).

What the law also did was to put obstacles in the way of women who might want to be farmers on their own, while pretending to treat the two spouses on an equal footing. It specified that, in cases where the husband and the wife have two separate farms, they must:

1 prove their farms are separate,
2 in the case of wives, prove their professional capacity to be farmers, and
3 never receive more in grant aid than they would if they worked jointly on the same farm.

The grant in question is a sum (of about £10,000) given to young farmers who settle on a farm, provided they fulfil certain criteria. It is given to an individual, and is available to single women. But if a woman is married to a farmer, she will need to prove her farm is separate. Similar proof is not required of the husband's father, brother or friends – and even if she shows it is separate, the couple will receive only £15,000, not twice £10,000 – which is what they would get for being a co-farming couple anyway.

Dhavernas notes that the legislation not only establishes co-farming spouses as the norm and discourages separate farming, it also has an 'assimilationist' logic which extends its influence over the status of persons to the status of the properties themselves. Two farms are to be regarded as one 'for the sole reason that the people operating them happen to be married to one another'.

Meanwhile, what have wives gained in responsibility and consideration (especially given all the sickness and retirement benefits they have had to forgo)? According to Lagrave:

> Calling the husband a co-farmer does not neutralize the title and prerogatives attached to being the head of a farm. On the contrary, for wives the terms 'co-farmer' and 'collaborator' have no occupational meaning, for the titles give women neither payment for their work nor professional or social rights. They remain covered by their husband's social security unless they contribute individually. Behind the male co-farmer hides the head of the farm; behind the female co-farmer looms an occupational limbo. (Lagrave 1987a our translation)

Lagrave has also shown how Ministry of Agriculture statisticians classify men automatically as heads of farms. She gives striking examples of the recommendations made to field workers when conducting surveys. A man must be put down as the head even when he declares his main acitivity to be a job other than farming, and even when he is retired. But on the other hand, 'the wife of a farmer who has no other job and is neither unemployed nor retired, can be coded either "farmer" or "family helper". A woman who declares herself a farmer must be coded a "family helper" ' (Lagrave 1987b).

This sheds some light on the question of why men are always heads of farms when they are present. Unlike other trades and professions, there is no legal or professional definition of what constitutes a farmer. The only definitions are statistical, and they serve for legal purposes when the need arises.

On the other hand, the fact that men are considered to be heads for practical purposes (as well as by statisticians and judges) cannot be entirely explained by marital regulations, because these do not explain why men are heads of farms even when they do not own the land, since they no longer manage their wives' property. Ideology and custom still obviously play a part here. But men certainly *are* heads, even if there is no legal basis for this. And their being heads cannot legally be questioned either, since even though there are no clear rules constructing men as heads in all circumstances, jurisprudence (case law) has always operated as if they *were*, and should continue to be, heads. Judges and lawmakers have always followed the principle of avoiding any possibility of competition between spouses – not only in the case of farmers, but for all other couples too. **Commonality of interest is part of marriage and nothing must put that doctrine in question.**

This last point may be part of the reason why women are not taking full advantage of the legal possibilities of setting up their own separate farms.[20] Women balk at becoming their husbands' potential competitors – in the same trade, the same village, the same house. And they also do not want to have their professional success, or lack of it, compared. Most share the conviction that men are more business-minded and better fitted to handle all the 'family business'. In any case, whatever the changes in the laws concerning marriage and property ownership may be, there has been little change in the customs relating to their labour relationship.

These restrictions of custom and ideology, which are not dissimilar to other past and present restrictions on married persons' relationships to each other and to outsiders, reaffirm both the particular nature of marriage as a relationship and the fact that agriculture is organized around family production. For French women it means that, despite apparently egalitarian legislation, they can be involved in agriculture in marriage but not outside it. If they are not married they cannot manage a farm of any size because it requires 'a couple' to run it. If they are married their status as co-farmers is an expression in farming of their status as a wife in marriage. That is, on marriage a woman loses the possibility of acquiring an individual occupational identity in agriculture.

Family relationships thus restrict women's options, and if they want the emotional bonds and social acceptability of marriage they have to accept the economic relations of domination. A wife becomes the family helper type of 'partner' to her husband's family head / farmer type of 'partner'. One of the well-recognized ways in which women make their feelings about this clear is by seeking wage labour away from the farm, and by their refusal to marry farmers. In 1968 there were three times more bachelors aged 35+ among farmers than among other men in France. It was not the farming background that worried women (men from farming backgrounds who had left the land for jobs in town had no difficulty finding wives), but the occupation itself.[21]

The institutions of heredity and marriage complement each other. It is not just the quality of being a non-successor which makes girls into potential wives, since they share this quality with younger sons (who do not thereby become wives). Inheritance practices (which are but a part of the institution of the family) prevent daughters in Normandy acquiring an independent status, though they give this right even to non-succeeding boys. Girls cannot set up in their own right; they can only stay in farming as dependants. This they share with the non-inheriting Béarn boys.

But the similarity is limited by the custom and laws of marriage (another part of the institution of the family). A girl does not 'hold' anything; she is not given any goods of her own to control while she is single. But she can benefit from certain facilities if and when she marries, when she receives a dowry. However, when she marries, she 'carries' these things (lease, tenure, livestock, etc.) to her husband because, once married, she does not have a position of her own nor does she control even her own labour power. Thus a girl cannot *de facto* be a farmer; while a wife may have the material means to be one, but cannot be one *de jure*. A daughter may be given a farm in the division of property after her marriage, but this farm cannot be hers, precisely because she is married and thus not the head of a household / family / farm.

The only 'women farmers' are rare widows or single women who have inherited and who have managed to run a farm on their own, or (in Britain, according to Ruth Gasson) occasional women who inherit, who see their occupation as farming, who have husbands who do not want to farm (or not on their own account), and who agree to let their wives work as the head of a small (possibly not fully viable) holding.[22]

People often talk of the situation of father and mother, and husband and wife, as 'sex categories' or 'sex roles'. But they are in fact social class sub-categories – or categories within social classes. The institution of the family has a synchronic dimension (creating family roles) and a diachronic dimension (creating non-successors via inheritance). Inheritance feeds one of the family roles; and family roles in turn curb inheritance. Our whole discussion has been based on the hypothesis (and reality) that each married couple on a farm can transmit only one status – that of the farmer / father – and if only one position exists it is because wives hold no position and hence have none to transmit.

Kin of a farmer (brothers and sisters and sons and daughters) who stay on a farm work unpaid by law in France until they are 18; but after that they can (that is, they are legally allowed to) demand a postponed salary (*salaire différé*). That is to say, they do not actually receive any money until the family head dies, but if they are then still working on the farm, they are allotted a certain amount of either money or extra shares in the estate. This sum is called a *pécule*, the same name as is given to the lump-sum payment made to soldiers when they are demobbed from the army. How its value is calculated is revealing. Not only is a sum deducted to correspond to a generous estimate of the board and lodging they have received (as it is also from the wages of the very few agricultural workers who live in), but the wage they are estimated to be owed is not even equal to that of an agricultural worker, but only two-thirds of this.

When the relative is the future heir to the farm it might be argued that he recovers the loss of earnings when he actually inherits. But it is when the farm is transferred that this rule, which supposedly applies to all the kin / children, really shows its fundamentally inegalitarian character, for the heir then clearly benefits from the underpayment of his brothers and sisters. The *pécule* is thus part of the inegalitarian logic of inheritance, for instead of equalizing the position of all the children, it in fact accentuates the disparities between the heir and the non-heirs. The low level of the *pécule* of the non-inheritors is a form of exploitation by the heir.

Not surprisingly, therefore, now that an alternative way of gaining a living, waged labour, is available, an increasing number of children are leaving their families at an increasingly early age if they are not going to inherit, even among French peasants. The practice of children and younger siblings working unpaid continued longer in agriculture than in most other sectors of the economy, however – until the Second World War.

A further example showing that the unpaidness of women's labour on farms continues to be taken for granted, even though the unpaid labour of children or brothers is or has been called into question, can be seen in the conventions attached to exchanges between generations during the elder's lifetime.

In the case of two-generational farming families where a son continues to work with or for his father, when the son marries he is more and more likely to demand that he be paid for his work and not just maintained. (This applies if he is the one who is going to inherit in the future, but even more strongly if he is not.) However, although two people work for the father, the son and his wife, it is never suggested that the wife might also make the same demand: that the couple might receive two wages for two jobs. If an outsider were to try to propose it, the idea would be greeted with total incomprehension. While the unpaid work of men is being strongly attacked, the unpaid work of women / wives is being reinforced by the demand for one wage for the couple's work, paid to the son.

Another example of (and contribution towards confirming) the institutional unpaidness of women's work is the fact that a political party (the communist-controlled MODEF – Mouvement des Exploitations Familiales) has demanded that each farm worked by a husband and wife should be assured of an income 'equivalent to at least one [average male] wage'. This demand implies that the work of a wife, although incorporated in the production of a farm, does not merit a separate wage; or perhaps rather that since a wife's production is exchanged by her husband as if it were part of his own, the wife's work belongs to him. (Equally a farmer's son may argue for a higher wage for himself because his wife also works on the farm.)

Women in French farm families thus still work on the farm holding, and unlike men they are not starting to demand wages even if they are the head's sister or daughter, let alone his wife. Furthermore, they work unpaid throughout their lifetime, not as a temporary condition. They also of course work at least an equal number of hours in the house, reaching a working day of 12–16 hours (4 hours longer than their husbands). While work on the farm is done by both male and female members of the family, housework in farm families is performed exclusively by women. Both constitute contributions to increasing the standard of living and wealth of the *chef d'entreprise* – the farm head.

Conclusion

In the last two chapters we have drawn information from existing research on the families of men in particular occupations and re-presented it according to our own analysis of the family. We have tried to be faithful to the original accounts, even though some were not written from a feminist perspective. What we have been able to present has been somewhat uneven because what information the researchers chose to collect (and to report) varied between the different groups, but all show a clear, unequivocal, and by and large unquestioned differentiation between the lives of men and women (and children).

Some of the assumptions and silences in the texts are as, if not more, revealing than what is said; not least the failure to problematize the fact that divisions by sex and age in the family household are not just differences but inequalities. It is clear that men and women are differently valued – and not only by their local cultures but also by most researchers. For example, far more information was collected about men than about women in Luton and also in the larger research project on Port Talbot of which Lydia Morris's work was a sub-project. This also applies to most French and all the major British studies of farming. Men's work and leisure and attitudes are described in detail; women's work is taken for granted or only sketched in (and always described after men's). Life-course differences in family processes, which have a massive influence on the work women do, are not distinguished. Men are always interviewed separately but women are sometimes seen only as a couple with their husbands, so their voices are not clear.

In other words, it is taken as unproblematic that men's lives dictate women's, that men's jobs are more important than women's, that women and children fit around men, and that domestic work should be done unpaid. Researchers seem often to share the cultural assumption that the maintenance women receive is a gift and that men's earning capacity and wages belong to men themselves. The many things which are part of men's continuing control of their families are either not on the agenda for discussion, or are presented as the result of social constraints, or alterna-tively as mutual interpersonal choices by couples.

We chose to look systematically in each study at the tasks performed by and the conditions and relations of production of husbands (outside and inside the home) and of wives (inside and outside the home), noting the variation by husband's occupation and differences between com-munities (for example, between Luton and Port Talbot). Unfortunately there was too little information to say anything much on the variation between households within communities. There is limited discussion of what the authors see as 'the individual choices made by couples', which we see as issues involving the head's preferences and the wife's bargaining with him. However, Morris's work does give some information on what work women do in the home and how much they earn and the extent of their choice of occupation and conditions of employment (that is, about their positions as compared to their husbands' positions in the local labour market). But neither she nor any other of the authors make any mention of sexual or reproductive work.

Only in relation to farming was information available on whether or not there were people present in households other than members of the nuclear family, and when there were (for example, grown children, unmarried and elderly relatives), what (paid or unpaid) work they did, and their share in consumption. None of the studies told us about non-married (single, divorced or widowed) men and how they handled their domestic lives, nor if and when women could be heads of households. The studies of factory workers deliberately took samples which excluded such people, presumably because they deemed them atypical and less important, as well as numerically a minority. But community studies of rural areas often tell us next to nothing about them either – and thereby contribute their own stone towards building the wall of silence around homosexuality specifically, but also the variety of household structures generally.[23]

We also looked, in so far as it was possible, at the management of family labour – at the areas of decision-making open to men (and how they are constrained by, for example, commodity and labour markets,

custom and peer pressure); at what is delegated to a wife as her responsibility (always housework and childcare, but sometimes including also
the children's schooling, balancing the family budget and independent
income generation); and at what happens to any cash income the wife
may earn or property she may inherit. We noted – though the material
was even more limited – how subordinates resist and/or try to persuade
their household head to do things they want (and the community control
limiting both the head's power and the dependants' resistance) and the
extent to which women's work is given ideological recognition. None of
the studies mentioned domestic violence, and only Morris considered
the relative strengths of men's and women's support groups (friends,
neighbours and kin) and their solidary relations of support. Her account
shows women's groups are important but they in no way counterbalance
men's friendship and work groups.

Only a few studies gave any information on differential consumption,
and this is restricted to drinking, pocket money, food, social security
provision and leisure – and even then what is recorded is not really
adequate. They do, however, show food marking out privileged statuses,
and suggest differences in modes of consumption. To these can almost
certainly be added differential use of space in the house, of spending on
health, and of transport.

We saw how typically the daughters of farmers marry (become
dependants of) farmers, and how even if they do inherit a farm, they do
not run it. This also applies broadly to the daughters of factory workers.
They probably marry men from the same socio-economic background as
their fathers, and even if they do become teachers or nurses, they do not
enjoy the professional middle class lives of men in these occupations
(unless they marry doctors or educational administrators!).

We started this chapter by commenting on the way the countryside is
often seen as 'traditional' and backward, and in the previous chapter we
noted how 'the Luton pattern' of companionate marriage is seen as more
advanced than the 'segregated' pattern of South Wales (and of course
French farms). In part this is a middle class bias: Luton, with its style of
treating 'the wife' as a friend and companion, lesser task segregation,
home-centredness, emphasis on nuclear rather than extended family relations, and concern for children's education and mobility, is similar to
the (supposed) middle class behaviour of the researchers themselves. It is
therefore believed to be a natural, historical progression, followed when
it becomes possible: when there is relative freedom from economic
hardship.

But the move to companionate marriage and 'working' wives is not a
historical progression. That is, it is not new and not more 'modern'. The
Port Talbot study was after all carried out 20 years after the Luton one,
and French farmers' wives are only now moving to being 'non-working',
while wives of middle class professional men are seeking to get back into
the labour market. We doubt there has been the extensive overall change

in sex roles often assumed. There has certainly not been a linear development from segregated sex roles to the 'modern' symmetrical family. The same range of modalities of marital relations as exist now were present in 1900 and probably earlier. There was a deeply home-based culture in particular regions of western Europe in the early twentieth century, while segregated relations between husbands and wives with male community cultures continue in many other regions today.[24]

In any case, to see companionate marriage as progress seems to us to be not only class-biased but also male-biased. Is spending time with a husband in his leisure (in so far as Luton wives do, given the shiftwork situation) better than spending time with other women (kin or neighbours)? Ann Oakley has pointed out that where men are 'more involved' with their families, they take over only certain tasks – the more pleasurable, statusful ones – leaving their wives overall responsibility and the 'shit work' (Oakley 1972; 1974a; 1974b). And do women in companionate, 'Luton style' marriages actually have a more equal partnership than those in marriages where there is a clear separation of roles, as in South Wales, which after all eulogizes 'the mam', or than those who work alongside their husbands, as in the Dordogne or Normandy where it is recognized a couple is needed to run a farm? Are Luton car workers, or middle class men, nicer to women than steelworkers? Are they less exploitative? Togetherness does not equal equality. It depends who controls the interaction. It may merely extend the opportunities for the exercise of power by one party over the other.

Notes

1 We use the common distinction between European capitalist commercial farming, state collective farming and peasant farming even though

> 'Peasant' has an unfortunate pejorative connotation in English: ... we use the term quite technically when talking about a small agricultural-commodity producing unit, with a work-force linked primarily by kinship ties; in other words, a peasant farm, as a social organization, is one run solely or mainly by a resident domestic group or 'household'. (P. Hamilton 1985: 22)

The farms we discuss are small in terms of their size of business turnover, but not necessarily in terms of the size of their holding. (cf. Newby 1979: 96ff).

2 See, for example, Barrett and McIntosh (1979) who deny the conclusions we draw from the division of labour between farm family members can be extended to urban industrial waged labourers' families – though they are not specific as to why not.

In this their views as marxists seem to echo Marx's own prejudices about rural life (see P. Hamilton 1985: 31–3). Marx is not, however, a good mentor on agriculture. He predicted that the tripartite agricultural system which existed in England in his own time (landowners, capitalist tenant farmers and farm workers) would become the norm everywhere and that agriculture would parallel industry. He has been proved wrong. 'The English model' was long the odd one out in Europe, and recently 'British agriculture has become increasingly based on familial labour and, in that sense, approached ever more closely the typical forms of farming in continental Europe . . . [The trend is] towards a small number of primarily family-labour farm units, together with a smaller number of commercial capitalist farms' (P. Hamilton 1985: 29).

3   In Britain the proportion of the active population working in agriculture fell much earlier. It was below 40 per cent by the 1850s, under 10 per cent in 1900, and by the early 1980s under 3 per cent (as also in the USA). It remains high in parts of eastern and southern Europe, however: 45 per cent in Romania, 37 per cent in Yugloslavia and 13 per cent in Italy.

4   The proportion of small farms in the agricultural sector is likely to increase, not only because of such farmers' tenacity and adaptability but also because they have always presented an awkward dilemma for agricultural policy makers. Rationally, the numbers of small farmers should decline, but they are too significant a proportion of the electorate in rural constituencies for politicians to countenance this. They also make clear otherwise neglected paradoxes of postwar agricultural policy: namely, whether government should promote cheap food or seek to expand home production; the demand for increased efficiency and prosperous stable agriculture versus the problems of depopulated rural areas and a polarization of rural society; and the environmental effects of large-scale enterprises. See Newby (1979).

5   Milhau and Montagne (1968).

6   Though much that exists is folkloric (with the accent on curiosities) or ethnographic (with the accent on the particularities of this or that village, region or custom). For our purposes there is a lack of serious comparative work and accounts which look directly at the entire processes of production of specific products, or structurally at succession, rather than taking indigenous categories (see Delphy 1983).

    We use here Delphy's own research (see 1969; 1974; 1976c; 1978; 1983), also Barthez (1981; 1982; 1983; 1985), Segalen (1983) and articles in Lagrave (1987a).

7   The 'test case' argument is further developed in Delphy (1983).

8   After a decline of 50 per cent since 1955, there were 2,700,000 workers (*actifs*) in agriculture in France in the early 1980s:

•   1,250,000 *chefs d'exploitation* (farmers), of whom 90 per cent were male. The women farmers were widows and single women who farmed 'like men' (except that unlike men they do their own domestic work).
•   1,200,000 *aides familiaux* (helpers), of whom 337,000 were male and 777,000 female. *Aides* are family members and therefore unpaid.
•   250,000 (approx) waged workers (less than 10 per cent of the total).

According to Rattin (1987) using Ministry of Agriculture surveys, 2 out of 5 people working in French agriculture in 1987 were women. Of these, 67 per cent were wives and 15 per cent mothers or daughters of male farmers, and 15 per cent were heads of farms. Only half the female 'heads' were married, the rest were widows or spinsters.

9   See Moscovici (1960), Segalen (1983).
10 See Maspétiol (1946), Segalen (1983).
11 See Rattin (1987).
12 See the important study by Kergoat (1982).
13 See Cazaurang (1968), Delphy (1974).
14 This is of course a very simplified account of the transfer of land, which is a topic of abiding concern to historians and students of the farming sector. Transmission of farmland is also greatly influenced by the system of death duty and land taxation operating at any time. Our general assertions are, however, well established and accepted.
15 See a special number of *Ethnologie Française* on the Normandy village of Chardonneret which focused on transmission, which includes Delphy (1969). See also Delphy (1976c). On Béarn see Cazaurang (1968) and Bourdieu (1972).
16 In France three times more men than women have personal property in land. Women own only 26 per cent of the surface owned by men. See Barthelemy, Barthez and Labat (1984).
17 To attempt to answer the question world-wide would involve looking at the complexities of national law, social security systems, taxation and customs. We suspect, however, that something not dissimilar to the situation in France applies even to such nations as Canada and the USA where housewives have supposedly been given stronger claims to half the farm.
18 *communauté de biens* – the automatic form unless the couple choose otherwise, where the couple hold their property in common with the exception of inheritances given specifically to one or other partner;
communauté réduite aux acquêts – which gives each partner the right to keep at death or divorce any property he or she brought to the marriage; and
séparation des biens – where all property acquired both before and during the marriage remains that of the spouse concerned (which is important where there is a business to inherit, and limits responsibility in cases of bankruptcy). See Marceau (1976).
19 See Dhavernas (1985), a major work by a lawyer using Delphy's analysis of domestic work to look at the evolution of jurisprudence on this subject since the turn of the century.
20 Barthez, personal communication.
21 See Jégouzo (1972; 1977) quoted in Barthez (1983).
22 See Gasson (1981).
23 See Leonard (1990). Interestingly, Platt, who worked on the Luton study, elsewhere makes this part of her critique of the Institute of Community Studies (1971).
24 On earlier home-centred cultures see Lummis (1982), Roberts (1984) and Lewis (1986: 108). On contemporary segregated roles, see Dennis, Henriques and Slaughter (1969), Whitehead (1976), Edgell (1980) and Rogers (1988).

9

THE VARIETY OF WORK DONE
BY WIVES

The variation in the work women do as wives is rarely commented upon and yet it is one of its most distinctive features. Some of the historical changes in wives' work have been noted, especially those associated with the development of domestic and reproductive technologies; and life-cycle changes are also frequently commented upon – how the hours women work vary with whether or not they have children to care for and (related to this) whether or not they are in full-time or part-time employment. But these are seen as variations in women's roles as mothers and as waged workers, not in their role as wives. It seems to be assumed that women's lives as wives are pretty uniform. Each cares for her husband, maintains his household, and has sexual relations and children with him. But the extent to which their choice of husband leads to variation in married women's lives – in the hours they work, and in the productive, emotional, sexual and reproductive tasks they perform – is little recognized.

Commentary on the family, and in particular feminist writing on the family, has indeed so emphasized the labour women perform 'for children' that at times it has virtually excluded the work they do for other family members and specifically for male heads of household. This point has been made before, but it bears repeating. It reflects both the dominant ideology of the family in the West today, which is increasingly child-centred, the commonality of experiences and problems households share in providing good quality childcare, and the age group to which many feminists and other researchers belong, which makes them acutely conscious of childcare issues. It is also a middle class bias, for housework has been rendered invisible in the middle class home. It has gone underground, transmogrified into a 'leisure' activity, and 'positive learning experiences with the children' during the 'quality time' their mother spends with them. **The work which wives do for their husbands' occupations, for men's leisure activities, and for their emotional and sexual well-being, gets completely lost sight of because it is so, varied, so personalized and so intimate.**

We are therefore going to stress how women's work varies according to the men to whom they are married, and we shall only secondarily consider variations according to the dependants requiring care or 'the household's' need for the wife to earn money, since these are already stressed in the literature. The primacy of wives' work for husbands can, however, be seen from the way in which, during the Second World War, when the men were away in the armed services, children were happily put into nurseries, but the minute the men came home, despite postwar labour shortages, women were put back into the home to service the men. This was their primary role; and immigrant labour was sought to replace them in the labour market. Children were returned to the care of their mothers (or rather white indigenous children were placed full-time with their mothers – migrant women often had to leave their children with kin for many years before they could afford to have them join them) and the wartime nurseries were closed down.

The variation in wives' work according to their husbands' needs depends on both men's occupations and circumstances, and their personal interests and preferences. The occupational differences have to some extent been considered by Janet Finch in her book *Married to the Job* (1983), which uses Delphy's earlier work and collects together information on the effects of men's jobs on their wives in a number of specific occupational categories. That is to say, how men as doctors, dentists, academics, architects, creative writers, lawyers, diplomats, politicians, clergy, members of large corporations, managing directors, middle managers, young men in business administration and marketing, small businessmen and shopkeepers, policemen, army, navy, and prison officers, railway workers, miners, lorry drivers and deep sea fishermen use their wives' labour.

This is a very useful source, but it suffers from the same shortcoming as the literature in the domestic labour debate (see chapter 3). It is not concerned with all the work wives do for their husbands, but only with how husbands' employers benefit from their employees' wives' work. It therefore concentrates on only some wives, those with employed husbands, and describes the wives of small businessmen as 'quite untypical' (p. 104) because they work for a 'team' running a 'joint enterprise'. So the farmers' wives we discussed in the previous chapter fall outside Finch's remit, and so too do women married to men who are either employers themselves or the wives of retired or unemployed men (so wives like those in Port Talbot also get excluded). In addition, her approach deals only with the work wives do which passes via their husbands to the men's employers, so she does not consider the work done by the wives of employed men from which the husbands benefit personally. Thus her book does not discuss how a wife's life and work may vary according to, for example, her husband's leisure activities or personal needs and preferences.[1]

Finch thus extends the usual analysis of domestic work considerably, and she also notes the ways in which husbands' employers actively seek to maintain the many types of benefit they derive from employees' wives' work by supporting marriage or by discouraging wives' employment. But she gives no reason why we should not include as family work a wife preparing a formal tea for her husband's cricket team or for sale in a café which he owns, if we are to include her cooking dinner for people he needs to entertain for his job. Nor does she explain why a wife cooking her husband breakfast to set him up for work should be considered work, whereas a wife cooking her husband particular dishes at odd hours when he comes in from an all-male outing, should not. Nor indeed why a wife having to dress up and perform some of the sexual activities described in *Forum* magazine is not work – since it may also be part of her job as a wife. All these tasks are done under the same terms and conditions, whatever the final use the husband (and thence his boss) may have for a wife's products and services.

How wives contribute to their husbands' work and leisure

Wives commonly contribute to their husband's work by actually doing some of it for him or with him, as was the case with the farmers' wives in chapter 8. Wives also always help indirectly by doing most or all of the household work, which frees men not only for paid work but also for other activities, including voluntary work, sport, hobbies and socializing. Finally, wives give their husbands moral and psychological support which helps them cope not only with their paid employment but also with life in general.

Direct contributions

Husbands' direct use of their wives' work for occupational / direct exchange purposes is especially common and most obvious when the husband is self-employed and runs his own business. 'Many of those currently running their own small business would simply not have made it without their wives – and wives sacrifice as much as their husbands (though their sacrifice is less publicized)' (Scase and Goffee, 1980b).

Wives routinely work alongside their husbands and under their direction when men are artisans, such as plumbers, electricians and mechanics, who sell both goods and the services to install them. Such men cannot usually afford a secretary so their wives put in a full day's work when there is a shop of any kind, while the men go around to see the customers. When there is no shop, the wives work from home, sometimes in addition to having a waged job. They calculate, type and send out estimates and bills to clients. They order spare parts and other equipment from the warehouses, and they either do the books (which an accountant looks at each month) or all the accounts, including negotiating the tax return with the Inland Revenue each year. (The threat of prosecution by tax officials is one of the most stressful aspects of self-employment.)

When husbands are shopkeepers, wives may work from 8 a.m. to 8 p.m. six days a week at the cash desk, or they may actually run the shop if the man is a baker and produces the goods which are sold, or a greengrocer who has to go to market. They may serve in the family restaurant, work on the market garden, or be the junior partner in his law firm. They may help with office work – opening letters and filing, making appointments, and typing reports. Or they may work in their husband's stead: the wife of a driving instructor will sit in the shop waiting for customers and give instruction on the Highway Code (which is part of the lesson). The wife of a man who runs a health clinic can help not only by sorting out employees' problems and maintaining company morale, but also by giving aerobics classes.

Even when men are employed there are instances where wives do so much work that employers effectively get two employees for the price of one. This is sometimes so routinized and recognized that particular industries only employ married men, or they agree to pay the wife's expenses, though they do not give her any actual pay or insurance cover or a pension (other than the one normally provided for the dependant of an employee). Such jobs include work in the diplomatic service, the rural police force, and running a pub. The wife works because she is the incumbent's spouse. There is a particular role for a wife, an institutionalized consort position, and particular tasks suited to a (female) spouse, such as being a hostess or cooking meals or looking decorative behind a counter. In such cases, if the holder of the post does not have a wife he may have to provide a woman to fulfil that part of a wife's role or risk losing the job. Breweries in Britain, for example, only give tenancies of pubs to married couples and may take the pub away from a man if he divorces. The same applies to corner grocery shops which are parts of chains in France.

In addition to helping with the work men do to earn money, wives also often give direct help with their husbands' voluntary and leisure activities – which for women are not 'voluntary' and not 'leisure' because they do not choose them and because they have the knock-on effect of more work for them. Wives may be kept busy in summer getting grass stains out of white flannel cricket trousers and in winter cleaning football kits caked in mud; or collecting, preparing and boiling fruit for wine-making; or running fund-raising jumble sales for a Boy Scout troop. If a man wants to be elected to the local council, his wife and children will support him on the hustings and help deliver election leaflets. Particular duties can also fall to a wife because of her husband's voluntary activities, for example, if he is active in local politics and becomes mayor she will be expected to accompany him to formal dinners and to provide 'hospitality' for visitors to their home.

Even where a wife does not work full-time for her husband's occupation, she will often work for him occasionally, acting in his stead, as second best, in his absence, in a crisis or when he is busy. Politicians' wives take care of their husbands' constituencies while the men are away in the capital and they may write their speeches on local issues. Academics' wives often type up research reports, make indexes, proofread books and at a pinch mark students' essays. Diplomats' wives attend minor functions to save their husbands time. Doctors' wives may receive patients when their husbands are out and either give first aid advice or make the decision to refer things on to a hospital. Clergymen's wives give succour and spiritual advice as well as making appointments for weddings and funerals. And farmers' wives, as we saw, take on men's tasks and run the farm in their husbands' absence.

The ability of a wife to step in and act for her husband depends of course on her having certain competences, but men often have the sense to marry appropriate spouses (would-be politicians often marry women interested in politics, academics marry their research students, doctors marry nurses, farmers marry farmers' daughters who have had jobs giving them office skills, and clergy wives are expected to be committed Christians). Alternatively, if the spouse does not have the skills initially, she is expected to acquire them 'over the breakfast table'. In addition her husband (or his employer) may facilitate her doing the work by providing her with an office and/or a car – or even, at high levels, a social secretary.

How wives react to this varies. Some senior politicians' wives, for instance (about whom we know more than about most wives), love it. Others loathe it. Some do it well. Others are perceived as 'pushy' – doing it too publicly and inappropriately.[2]

Women get little personal recognition or reward for such work. Doing it well involves staying in the background and an individual must make it clear she is acting only in her capacity as a wife. In addition, even if the business depends upon the wife and / or (as far as the tax officials are concerned) she is paid a salary for working in it, or even if the husband's employer requires that she does the work, she will rarely be paid any money. If a wife is skilled and domestic circumstances permit her to run part of the business in a semi-autonomous fashion, her husband can still take the money she makes as part of the business's profits.

The most common work done by wives, whether or not they also do highly specialized work, for their husbands is as general backup workers. They answer the phone and take messages, or keep certain people away from their husbands, filtering serious from trivial enquiries. They may deal with visitors, clients and sales reps, take in deliveries, run errands, and tidy and clean an office. As Finch says, such work is 'central to the daily performance of a man's work but [it is] routine and non-specialized'. A wife may do it regularly, even on a 24-hour basis, or just occasionally (as in the case of the shop stewards' wives in Bristol who needed to do it only during a strike). In other words a wife is the much sought-after girl Friday: consistent, reliable and on the spot, who helps constantly or when the workload is heavy or at times of crisis. Her work in many ways parallels that of a personal assistant – as has been noted by writers on secretarial employment.[3]

Such wifely work is especially likely if the husband works at home, full-time or part-time. This includes many professional men, for example, freelance journalists and insurance salesmen, as well as locksmiths and window cleaners. It is also likely if the husband is actively involved in local associations, such as a neighbourhood sports club or a choir or a voluntary organization.

Wives also perform what Finch calls 'peripheral activities' for their husbands: 'things which are not central to day to day demands on the husband but which help the smooth conduct of his work and his ultimate success' (Finch 1983: 88). This includes knowing his clients / constituents / informants / patients; and entertaining, especially when living abroad or if the husband is self-employed. It can involve such simple entertaining as forever giving out cups of tea. Or simply being entertained: 'If a man wants you to go out to dinner and you haven't got your wife, he has to leave his wife out. If your wife is there, his wife can come too. Often wives get to know each other, and it's good for them *and* good for business' (managing director interviewed in Young and Willmott 1973, quoted Finch 1983: 91 stress in original).

A wife may find her husband customers, channel information from them to him, and be an advocate and representative for him to them. She can raise his social status by undertaking community activities or voluntary work, or acting out his ideals, or by becoming involved in his professional association. Thus Mary McCarthy in her novel *The Group* describes one character, Priss, who married an obstetrician, as having to have a baby and breast-feed it (which she loathed) to support her husband's ideas and professional standing.

Most of these activities can be done even if the wife herself has paid employment, providing it is not too demanding. Both she (indirectly) and her husband and / or his employer (if he has one) unquestionably benefit from the work she does.

But wives' 'up-front' involvement depends not only on their husbands having an appropriate job or leisure activity, but also upon his wanting her to do it. Thus a politician's wife may, or may not, be required / allowed to make speeches during her husband's election campaign. Patricia Jalland, drawing on personal papers from the families of British politicians between 1860 and 1914, summarizes the case histories she presents as follows:

> The individual talents, political knowledge and family background of the women themselves were naturally important [in determining the wives' public involvement] . . . But the extent to which the wife's talents could be exercised depended on her husband's political effectiveness . . . It was also determined by her husband's view of their marital relationship, and the degree of initiative allowed to the wife . . . [One] played a satisfying part in an unusually equal partnership [the husband was in his fifties when he married and the wife in her late thirties and they had no children]. By contrast . . . [two] were expected to acquiesce in the philosophy of 'separate

spheres' and their responses were quite different. [One] had expected the
subordinate and separate role and found contentment . . . [the other]
passionately desired active partnership but had to acquiesce in her
husband's traditional view of marriage. (Jalland 1986: 249)

We suspect very similar things happen today, but such private details are
not open to view in people's lifetimes. The details of the interchange
between the spouses, especially when they differ on the wife's proper
role, and if and how the husband's view eventually prevails, is therefore
less evident.

Giving moral support

While giving direct support to a husband in his occupation and other
activities can perhaps be seen as specific to certain men in certain
occupations (though in fact it covers a very large number of men in a
wide range of occupations and leisure pursuits), giving moral support and
caring for his well-being is more widespread. All wives do this and it
involves a lot of caring work. It is not just a case of feeling a general
affection towards one's husband, but rather active 'relationship work':
observing and moderating his emotions, arranging entertainment and
relaxation, and supplying his personal needs.

A good wife enables her husband to talk intimately and confidentially.
She is the person to whom he can unburden himself, who will share his
anxieties and siphon off his discontents. She is the sounding board against
which he can rehearse an argument or an important speech, who will
'reflect him at twice his natural size'. She will tell him not only how
clever he is but justify his ambition by saying how important it is that he
does well in his job and gets promotion and a higher salary because the
family depends on him. A middle class husband may have a personal
assistant or secretary who functions in some similar ways, but a wife is
a peer in the way a secretary is not, and her loyalty and identity of interests
is more guaranteed. It is certainly more guaranteed than that of a mere
friend. 'Arthur Koestler's wife, who committed suicide with him when he
was terminally ill, was described as his "lover, wife, nurse, housekeeper,
cook, mother, daughter and inseparable companion"' (Mikes 1983).[4]

Since men frequently unwind best post-coitally, wives also have an
important role as providers of trouble-free sex – which is why employers
may encourage men to take their wives with them on jobs abroad. (A
famous instance of employers being blamed for not sending wives with
husbands occurred in 1987, when US marines in Moscow were said to
have discussed secret information with their Russian girlfriends.) This is
certainly part of the reason why many men themselves (be they employed,
self-employed or retired) want their wives with them when they travel.

Clearly not all wives do *this* bit of their job all that enthusiastically all of the time. Shere Hite's research in the US suggests women resent the poor return they get from what they hoped would be an emotional and sexual 'exchange'.[5] Marriage manuals, gossip and feminist consciousness raising sessions suggest women often make excuses to get out of having sex, and they have to be persuaded, or are forced, and then retaliate by lying inert or (if their husbands want them to have orgasms) faking climax to get the process over quickly. But even if such things are common (and we do not know how common they are because there is very little research on marital sexuality anywhere and next to none in Britain and France), marital sex is a husband's right. If intercourse does not go well it is picked out as a sign the marriage as a whole is not going well – so the woman had better watch her step!

Wives 'make a house a home'. They manipulate the environment to make it comfortable, warm and undemanding. They do (should) not complain (for example, when a husband works late), or make a fuss (for example, when they have to move house), or engage in controversial activities which could embarrass their husband in the community. In other words, a wife should look after her husband's life so he is free to devote himself to living: to being an efficient worker or entrepreneur, and when he is not doing that, to enjoying his free time. This psychically stabilized, domestically serviced and economically motivated man is recognized as a reliable employee and sought by employers. But this aspect of a wife's work is probably even more important to the self-employed businessman who may need to cope with heavy stress and financial burdens, and to the unemployed or retired man who needs to overcome depression and a loss of sense of self.

Much of wives' servicing is thus emotional work – as is also, of course, much of women's paid employment. Women provide emotional care for others while controlling their own emotions. They defer to others and help establish and continue solidary bonds between groups of people. Sally Cline and Dale Spender (1988) describe how women 'feed' conversations with men to get them to 'open up', how we feign foolishness so men can expand and shine, how we smile and keep cheerful (because men are irritated with women if they are not happy in the men's presence), and how we thank men profusely when they behave well towards women. In other words, how women generally flatter, excuse, boost, sympathize and pay attention to men. This gives men a sense of belonging, of empowerment, and of general well-being.

Micaela di Leonardo's work develops this in one specific area: women's maintaining of kin contact between households, which is an important part of our cultural expectation of satisfying family life.

> Maintaining these contacts, this sense of family, takes time, intention and skill ... [it is] *work*; and, moreover, it is largely women's work. [It involves] the conception, maintenance, and ritual celebration of ... ties, including visits, letters, telephone calls, presents, and cards to kin; the

organization of holiday gatherings; the creation and maintenance of quasi-kin relations; decisions to neglect or to intensify particular ties; the mental reflection about all these activities; and the creation and communication of altering images of family and kin vis à vis the images of others. (Leonardo 1987: 442–3 stress in original)

If there is no adult woman in a household, such work is left undone, and single, widowed and divorced men say how much they miss it.

The creation of alternative images of family life is especially important, Leonardo argues, in ethnic minority cultures, such as the Italian American community in which her research was based. Women are charged with being the 'preservers of the culture' in this as in many other ethnic minority and religious groups. They have to observe the religion more orthodoxly and dress in more traditional clothes than men; they must be able and willing to cook traditional food and to keep festivals; they must generally behave modestly so as to maintain the family's honour; and must hold themselves and the children at a distance from the mainstream culture. In this way their work makes the home a *Walled Garden* (the title of Bermant's account of Jewish family life (1974)) in the face of alternative cultural values.

Domestic labour

The comfortable environment provided for a husband by a good wife is based on her taking on most of the household tasks. He is thereby fit for his occupational work and leisure and able to give them his undivided attention. 'A "normal" day's work is that of a person who does not have to do his own domestic work' (Delphy 1976a: 81).

Women's 'keeping the home fires burning' allows soldiers to wage wars, senior executives to work 12 hours a day and to fly off abroad at a day's notice, skilled manual workers to be called out to do overtime at short notice, (male) teachers to gain higher qualifications at evening and weekend courses, and trade union officials and local politicians to cope with emergency meetings. Wives' coverage of domestic work also, of course, enables husbands to devote themselves to leisure – it allows sportsmen to go away on rugby tours or to play golf on Sundays.

Women's coverage of domestic work also allows men to do nothing when they are unemployed or retired. French time-budgets in 1985 showed that in couples where both are employed, men did 2 hours 41 minutes of domestic work per day (20 minutes more than in 1965) and wives 4 hours 38 minutes, but the difference actually increased when men were retired. Women at 65 do three hours more domestic work a day than their husbands.[6]

The availability of utilities (running water, gas and electricity), domestic appliances (washing machines, vacuum cleaners, food processors) and industrially produced commodities (cook-chilled food, disposable nappies, ready-made easy-care clothes and spray furniture polishes) have not reduced the time spent on household work, although they have reduced some of the hard physical effort involved. Rather they have (1) enabled some tasks formerly contracted out to be taken back and done within the home (for example, laundry); (2) other tasks to be done to higher standards and more frequently (for example, cooking, cleaning, laundry and particularly childcare); and (3) middle class housekeeping standards to be maintained despite the departure of servants. Almost all the increased purchasing, transporting and domestic management has fallen to wives. They have taken on not only most of the work formerly done by servants in middle class households, but also, in all households, work formerly done by other members of the household, including husbands.[7]

Time-budget studies show not only that the amount of time women spend on domestic work has not declined this century and that they still do twice as much each day as men in all western and eastern bloc countries even when they have paid employment, but also that women do the more highly organized domestic work (for example, in the morning, from waking to 9 a.m., to get everyone off to work and school). When men spend time on housework, it does not involve the same kind of strain.[8]

The fact that husbands may now offer increased help in the home has thus very rarely affected their freedom to take any form of employment or to enjoy leisure outside the home. Men have a 'right' to time off, to some regular leisure time spent away from home and family each week; and they can also be absent from home for long periods, for days or weeks or even months to pursue a whole range of manual, managerial and professional occupations and / or a range of leisure activities.

But of course men do not necessarily have to be away from home for their wives to take charge of housework and childcare. On the contrary, as Janet Finch stresses, women's domestic work enables men to work at home while being assured of protection from disturbance – and in fact such men usually do less domestic work and childcare than those who work elsewhere (cf. the farmers in chapter 8). She argues that employers benefit from their (male) employees' wives' labour because they can assume that none of their workers has responsibility for the physical care of any dependants or needs to do much domestic work for themselves. But in fact it is men who are self-employed who most rely on their wives – who leave them to do the domestic work single-handedly. And it is not only men's occupational work at home which relies on women's domestic labour – so too does men's ability to spend undisturbed leisure time at home, whether playing with train sets in the attic or reading the paper in the sitting room, and their being able to find 'going out with the wife and kids' a pleasure.

When wives have servants, even part-time cleaners a few days a week, they may appear to do less domestic work, and they are certainly often reviled as lazy parasites when they rely on paid help with childcare and housework (even if they are in full-time employment). But women are actually only given servants or au pairs when their workload simply cannot be carried by one person (for example, when they have several small children and no kin living nearby) or when their husbands want their time to be shifted elsewhere. For instance, when their husbands prefer them to earn an extra (professional-level) income, and / or to undertake the extra work needed for a higher standard of living and more consumption: buying and maintaining more things (more houses, more rooms, more interior decorating, more suits of more elaborate clothes), more entertaining and more involvement in a particular cultural milieu. Husbands may want their wives to have time to organize frequent, elaborate kin reunions or weekends with friends in their country cottages. Or to do more good works for charity. Or to learn another foreign language, and to visit exhibitions and go to the opera and read the latest books so they can talk confidently to guests. Or to be conspicuously leisured – showing-off the men's wealth by demonstrating they do not need their wives to work and that they can afford for them to play bridge, or keep horses and go hunting, or to play tennis and ski, or to have beauty treatments and buy clothes, or to create an elaborate garden.

However, having servants in itself involves work for women. Servants have to be hired, trained and managed. (Management and training in industry are not usually seen as idleness!) They also require emotional work: helpers have to be listened to, praised, made to feel important, and to have their anxieties soothed, etc. This is especially true of au pairs, who are in many ways yet another member of the family whom the wife looks after, albeit they are family members who contribute labour.

In any case, most women do not have servants. Rather they are themselves, as J. K. Galbraith says (1973), 'crypto-servants'.

The extent to which husbands contribute to their wives' work and leisure

Janet Finch specifically considers the suggestion that marriage is an equal partnership and that what wives do for husbands, husbands also do for wives. She therefore reviews the limited research on husbands' contributions to their wives' occupations,[9] but she is forced to conclude the evidence does not support the hypothesis of equality. 'The implications . . . a man's paid work has for his wife are much more significant and far reaching than vice versa' (Finch 1983: 1).

Although marriage is a joint endeavour in the sense that both spouses benefit if their household prospers, and although most husbands do help their wives in various ways, husbands and wives do not get identical benefits if their household 'goes up in the world', nor do they do equal things for each other to achieve this end. Marriage is precisely a gendered and unequal division of labour, with most wives working more hours a day than their husbands in a subordinate role. Even when married women have full-time paid employment, they are still required to work for their husbands. They may even be required to provide a better service than if they were not employed, in order to justify having a job.

Direct contributions

Men are of course physically and intellectually as capable of doing direct work for their wives' occupations or leisure activities as the other way about. But the chances they actually routinely do so are slim. First, because very few women occupy the sorts of jobs or do the sorts of voluntary work, sports or hobbies that require or enable the direct use of a spouse's labour.[10] There are few women entrepreneurs or women in senior management and professional jobs. There are few women public figures, or politicians, or heads of state, or great artists. The division of labour in the labour market and discrimination in other parts of society thus supports the division of labour in marriage. Most women's activities outside the home neither assume nor offer the possibility of using another pair of hands.

But if a husband does get involved in his wife's occupation to the extent of becoming an 'additional worker' (that is, if her work makes such a big impact on his life), he will almost certainly take over direction from her and she will concentrate on just a part of it, for example, doing the designing while he runs the business (this applies to many successful firms founded by women, including Laura Ashley). Or he will coach and manage her if she is an athlete or a singer. Very few husbands work alongside and under their wife's direction. It is psychologically, socially or legally impossible.

A second reason why men do little for their wives' occupations is because if a married woman does become a senior manager, and even more if she becomes a head of state, her husband will have to keep well in the background if she is to stay visible – unlike a wife who can at least stand beside her husband on the platform without her status threatening his. Thus the Queen of England's Silver Jubilee had to be celebrated very much as a tribute to *her*, with incidental compliments and separate articles in magazines on Prince Philip alone, rather than as a tribute to their joint achievement – as it would have been if he had been king. In addition, a husband cannot act as a 'wife'. Consort roles are gendered: they presume their incumbents will undertake 'womanly' activities because it is presumed the position will be filled by a wife. And if men do take on tasks, they change their meaning anyway. Mr Thatcher did not act as a hostess for visiting dignitaries. He may have done some of the same *tasks* as Mrs Major, but being a host located him very differently from being a hostess.

Where husbands and wives have married spouses with similar skills, or where skills are deemed to be acquired 'over the breakfast table', it is a matter of fact that husbands give less help to wives than wives do to husbands. For example, among academic researchers, husbands almost never give as much help with interviewing and proofreading as wives do – and they absolutely never do an amount that would challenge the centrality of their own careers. Husbands *could* be general backup workers for their wives but (a third reason why they usually do relatively little) they are not as likely to have the time, or to be as well placed, or due to sex stereotyping to have the social skills to help even if they want to. Husbands usually have occupations, generally higher status occupations, and leisure pursuits of their own, so they are unlikely to be on the spot and available to take messages, to keep people away while their wives are busy, or to run errands or do some typing. (They are even less likely to be 'available' to do this, according to the evidence, if they work at home than if they have a nine-to-five job outside their house.) But even when husbands are retired and their wives are self-employed, men offer only limited help. For instance, in one couple, interviewed in 1991 as part of a French study of wives' occupational work (Delphy forthcoming), the wife had a shop and her retired husband would unload the crates once a week and come and pick her up at closing time (since he had the use of the family car). He also helped to pull down the metal shutters over the shop window, but he did not do the books and he certainly did not do the housework.

Husbands do, however, sometimes help increase their wives' earnings by 'peripheral activities'. For example, a husband's overall standing in the community may help get his wife a job (a 'woman's job' it is true, not a man's job, but it advantages his wife against other women), or a company head-hunting a man may guarantee his wife a job if he moves. Or again, being present at various dinner parties can give a woman helpful information if she and her husband work in the same area (especially since he is likely to be her senior). Or if a woman is self-employed, her husband may help her get clients or customers. And just being 'a married woman' (or even a formerly married woman) is helpful (as being married is helpful to men, though it has different nuances) in establishing normality and respectability, hence credit-worthiness, lesser liability to blackmail, etc. (All of which is collectively known to lesbians and gay men as heterosexual privilege.)

Moral support

Women workers are not seen to have the same 'need' for home comforts and a listening ear as men – and to the extent that they do need comfort and support, they are thought to be able to provide it for themselves or to get it from other people (women) rather than necessarily from their husbands. (However, continuing to rely on your mother and sister after you are married is not fully approved of. It may be regarded as a symptom of emotional immaturity, or downgraded as being 'traditional working class' behaviour.)[11] Certainly commercial companies do not vet husbands as they vet wives (on the rare occasions when women hold the sorts of job where such things happen), nor, until forced by the women's movement and equality legislation, did they see it as necessary to pay for husbands to accompany wives on trips when the wives of male executives travelled for free. Presumably any woman in a career is seen as tough enough to cope on her own.

Indeed most of the literature seems to interpret husbands' 'moral support' for wives in paid employment as being to do with men's basic acceptance of women's 'right' to have jobs at all. Even this level of support is not always forthcoming, as the Bristol, Port Talbot and French farmers material showed. One large-scale survey in Britain suggested that,

> husbands could not be described as enthusiastic supporters of their wives working . . . The overriding impression our findings give is that husbands of working wives in varying degrees tolerated their wives working though in many cases they did not want it to interfere or conflict with their own work or domestic life. Women's part-time working may be seen as an accommodation to this view of the desirable balance between paid and unpaid work. (Martin and Roberts 1984: 115)

Others have found that one wife in ten who is employed full-time, works despite her husband's disapproval or without his knowledge.[12] The nearest to support many women get is the rather small comfort of knowing that their husbands tolerate their working all day on an assembly line only because they believe 'it drives women crazy to stay at home all day.' Not surprisingly such women feel they cannot complain about anything that happens at work, nor can they ask for men's help with domestic work, because they 'chose' to work. (In this context, it is notable that none of the studies of factory workers in chapter 7 mentioned wives talking about work problems at home, although they tell us about husbands discussing, or choosing not to discuss, their employment problems with their wives.) Among professionals ('the talking classes'), a husband may well find his wife talking about her job more interesting than her talking about the neighbours (providing she does not 'go on about it' too much), and he may be an important mentor and morale booster for her – as Rosanna Hertz found in a study of high-flying couples working in large corporations in Chicago (1986). Or again, a husband who is an active Labour Party member but whose work does not allow him to become a local councillor may support his wife in getting elected and in day-to-day political activism (see Barron, Crawley and Wood 1987). But there are equally cases where husbands put down their wives' jobs and voluntary activities systematically – or whenever their wives forget to keep their heads always a little bit lower than their husbands'. Shere Hite suggests such deliberate with-holding of emotional support is an important form of male control of (and psychic violence towards) wives (Hite 1988).

Wives certainly do not seem to be owed the sexual unwinding which men 'need' so badly. Wives who have sought divorce in Britain because their husbands lost interest in sex have been refused it on the grounds that such men's behaviour is not 'unreasonable'.

Domestic labour

As we noted briefly in chapter 4, when men marry they do half the housework they did as bachelors, whereas women do twice as much. Thus having a husband substantially increases women's domestic burden even though nowadays husbands are said to 'help' with the housework. When wives have paid employment, both the proportion of husbands who do at least some housework and the amount of work they do increases – but only slightly. What they do is still clearly defined as 'helping'. The wife always has overall responsibility. And men help mainly with childcare rather than housework, and with particular aspects of childcare. Wives still do the routine care (feeding, dressing and washing, and especially changing dirty nappies) while men play with children and take them out. Employed women therefore generally end up working very long days, at the least favoured aspects of household work, having few leisure activities, and cutting down or sleep, even when they have 'good' husbands.[13]

Both men and women often feel men do more in the house than time-budgets suggest they actually do. Couples feel tasks are equally shared overall if they are equally shared when both are at home – though even this degree of sharing occurs in only one couple in four.[14] When there are young children in a household the amount of domestic work increases greatly, as it also does when there is a sick, elderly or handicapped relative needing care. Time for this work is found by women reducing their paid employment (whereas men's hours of paid work increase under such cir-cumstances, if they change at all). But again wives may feel their husbands help a lot because they expect his contribution to be limited. What they want from 'good fathers' and 'concerned' sons of elderly mothers is that the men should think and 'care about' – that is, should be emotionally involved and have pleasurable interactions with – children and the elderly, not that the men should care for them in the sense of doing the routine physical work that they require.[15]

It would seem, then, that as with moral support, to ask how much domestic help men give to facilitate women's employment or leisure time away from home is to look at the issue the wrong way round. The issue is, rather, how is it ensured that wives do not need much help? Wives are expected to look for jobs and hobbies which will enable them to continue to perform their domestic functions adequately with a minimum of support from their husbands. For example, they find work on shifts that fit with their husband's pattern of daily employment, or which (like teaching) enables them to be at home after school and in the holidays. And if they want time away from home, they have to negotiate it. It is not theirs by right. Married women will therefore rarely take on overtime or a job which involves travelling; and regular hours are important. They generally want to work not more than five days a week, finishing before 4 p.m.; or if they have children under five, they want to work in the evenings or at night. If they work part-time they prefer to reduce their hours per day rather than work fewer days per week. They cannot do shiftwork or go away for short or long periods. And they give up leisure activities such as team sports which require them to be at particular places at particular times and take up keep-fit classes (with crèches) and knitting. If they have small children or elderly relatives to care for, they may have no leisure at all.

Women can usually only be away from home, or undertake non-domestic business at home, and certainly only start up in business seriously, if they pay for some domestic help. However, few employed women do pay for help even with childcare: only about 15 per cent have nannies or baby-minders – though there is some class and ethnic variation. Most prefer kin to do the work because this is a cheaper, more flexible and more reliable arrangement, or to use nursery schools when the children are older. Others choose to work at home. But if they work at home it does not mean their husbands protect them from domestic stress. On the contrary, women 'choose' such work in order to be able to continue to deal with their home and children alongside it.

All of which shows not only what men as sellers of labour gain from being able to have wives, but also what women lose in their ability to participate freely in the labour market if they are wives and mothers.

How husbands structure their wives' lives

The social position of a woman's husband not only influences the actual tasks she performs, but also her rhythm, pattern and place of living, how hard she has to work, and her standard of living. According to Janet Finch, the geographical location of the husband's work, the pattern of his working hours, and his income, not only structure his wife's life but also 'elicit' her work. The same applies also of course to non-occupational aspects of husbands' lives.

Space

Finch points out that home and work are much less separate for many people than is suggested by the ideology of public and private spheres.

Many husbands use their home as their work base for some or all of the time. Some families live within an institutional setting dictated by the husband's work, others live in tied accommodation, and many experience regular relocation. In other cases the family is influenced by the location of the husband's activities because he is far away for short or long periods of time.

If a wife lives within the institutional setting of her husband's work, its influence on her life can be all-embracing. She may live physically in a section of their hotel or on the farm or within the confines of an army camp or a boarding school or on the campus of a national or multinational company abroad. She thus lives in housing that comes with the job, and in the latter cases may use special shops and recreational facilities, and have her social life largely determined. Something of this experience can also come on a more short-term basis, for example, through trips abroad with her husband, or accompanying him to conferences, social events or official occasions. In such circumstances a wife is subject to institutional definitions of appropriate behaviour. She is very visible and therefore vulnerable.

In the past some employers used to see it as legitimate to comment, even to have a right of veto, on potential wives. Now they (for example, the army for its officers, the Church of England for its clergy, political parties for their candidates, the Foreign Office for diplomats, and corporations for their executives) just 'look wives over' socially. Such wives must dress properly / engage in good works / be gregarious / non-boat-rocking / Christian / of a particular political party / able to fund-raise / accepting of the corporation's needs and priorities, etc., as appropriate. Some employers give wives training (for example, company wives before going abroad) and claim some authority over their life-style and behaviour (for example, diplomats' wives get lessons on protocol, and publicans' wives have to get permission from the brewery which owns 'their' pub before they take on outside employment). Such wives have their social relationships structured by their incorporation in the organizational hierarchy. Their position is defined vicariously – according to their husband's status – and their social relations with others are handled according to this definition. They can form a shadow hierarchy, with newcomers taken under the wing, and control, of the senior man's wife; and friendships are often only comfortable between women of husbands of the same rank – which is, of course, only a special, more visible, instance of the way in which a husband's social position always determines his wife's social status. There are just more opportunities for gradings to be expressed clearly in closed communities, and wives and husbands have less room for manoeuvre.

A whole series of other husbands' occupations can also affect wives profoundly. For instance, if a wife has to live in tied accommodation, her home is controlled by her husband's employer and she has to take what is given – sometimes even down to the decoration and furniture. When he leaves his job, she loses her home. Or again, some sections of the business and professional middle class regularly move house as the men 'spiral' upwards from one job to the next, while others have long or short spells abroad. Relocation is also frequent for policemen's families and those in the armed forces. For such men's dependants, moving house means changing contacts with kin and friends, especially when they move frequently and are in new places for an indefinite length of time. Putting down roots again and again is not easy, and links families establish are generally with those in the same situation – in the same company, or on the same housing estate.

The effects of frequent moves on wives' employment has been specifically recognized.[16] Wives almost always follow their husbands, even when they themselves may initially have had quite prestigious careers. Since a wife does not choose where she is going to be located, it may take her a long time to find another job. She may not speak the language. She will have no support structure and no identity and have to prove herself again and again. There is much to push her towards transferable jobs such as teaching or nursing or secretarial or catering work or cleaning. If a couple starts with two jobs in different places and one of them commutes, it becomes impractical if they have children, and it is always expensive.

There are equal (though different) repercussions for wives and children when men work at home, either all or most of the time (for example, clergy, small businessmen, hoteliers, self-employed craftsmen and writers) or some of the time (for example, senior managers, publishers, academics and civil servants), bringing work home in the evenings and using their home as an outlying office – somewhere they can be undisturbed by clients, colleagues or telephones. Working at home has been optimistically seen as the way to a new egalitarian symmetrical family, but in fact it can present real problems for dependants, whether or not they have employment themselves. Household space and routines have to be organized around the husband's needs to allow him to carry out the breadwinning activities.

The wife must keep 'the house' (that is, herself and children and visitors) quiet. She cannot listen to the radio or let the children have friends in. This is extra work, necessitated by the man treating the house as if he lived in it alone when he in fact shares it with others. If he sees people at his house – clients, sales reps, people who come by appointment or on the off-chance – at least part of the house has to be kept clean and tidy and tea and coffee supplied. The house becomes 'reconstituted as a semi-public place' (Finch 1983: 55), and the wife loses her privacy and must organize herself even more around her husband's timetable. A wife can best do the extra work this requires if she is at home all day; but even if she has a full-time outside job, she can still provide it. She can get up earlier and leave a meal to be heated up by her husband during the day and do the cleaning in the evenings.

Employers, on the other hand, may warn their employees not to let their wives get away with using the husband's presence at home to their own advantage – by for example, getting him to take her on a trip to the shops on a Friday.[17] However, it is self-employed men who work from home (as many do) who are the most demanding of their wives' (and sometimes children's) time and energy. In chapter 8 we described the variety of work wives get called on to do on farms, but it is not just a question of the wife working on the land (or in the shop or kitchen or workshop or warehouse, etc.), but of the home itself being taken over as the business premises. On farms the 'office' may be in the living room and baby lambs get reared in the kitchen. While

> during the early days of a small business in the service sector it will be virtually impossible to separate domestic activities from those of the enterprise . . . [It] may start with little more than a house, a car and a telephone . . . The spare bedroom becomes an office, the garage is converted into a workshop or stores and the family car is replaced by a van. (Scase and Goffee 1980b)

If men work absolutely regular hours outside the home or are away completely for periods of time (for example, salesmen or deep-sea fishermen), their wives can develop satisfactory coping strategies and can organize their household work as it suits them. They can do what they want in the morning, leaving the house a mess, and then rush around in the late afternoon creating order out of chaos before he gets home – and still convince their husband they have been working steadily all day. Or they can go away and stay with their mother for a few days when their husband is on a trip. But if a man works at home, his wife not only has to keep things constantly presentable, but her husband will know how she uses her time and with whom she spends it.

Time

A man's job may spill over into his non-work time to varying degrees. Some men are 'at work' physically or mentally most of the time, including some who extend their occupational relationships outside the workplace. Others escape from work into their family and use their leisure to counter the ill-effects of their paid employment. And some have jobs or voluntary activities which, whether they will it or not, colour their entire life and social persona.

Most people think about their jobs at least some of the time when they are at home (and vice versa). Some people think about them almost all the time, either because of the attractions and interest of the job, or because of its problems. When they are at home they may be thinking through office politics (and so not want to talk to their family); or they may be stressed and want to unwind *with* their family; or they may be tired and wanting peace and quiet to rest for the next day's work; or they may want to use their off-duty hours to catch up on the job. Some people are potentially always on call – not just doctors, who stereotypically get called away from their families in the midst of dinner parties and visits to the theatre, but also funeral directors, plumbers and computer managers. In such circumstances, and more generally when there are no set hours,

> the potential competition between work and family [becomes] expressed very much in a presumed dichotomy between spending time on . . . work and spending time on household work or child care. Since . . . work can be done at any time of day or night, the situation is structured so that any performance of domestic tasks appears to be an *alternative* to work; and a . . . wife who suggests that her husband might take on some of these tasks feels that she is taking him away from his work. (Finch 1983: 28 stress in original)

Most people meet some of their workmates out of work, but in some occupations it is especially marked. Railwaymen, for instance, spend most of their time off the job in the company of railwaymen, 'talking railways'. Male architects, although they operate socially as a couple with their wives, meet predominantly other architects (and their wives) at dinner parties, etc. In both cases wives have effectively married the social life as well as the man, since in general where couples have joint friends, these are more often those who were originally friends of the husband than of the wife.[18]

Some jobs affect the whole of an individual's life. Being a famous TV personality or a policeman or working on official secrets or being a headmaster 'contaminates' not only the men (or occasionally women) involved but also all the members of their families. When a man is instantly recognized on the street or has access to privileged information or must avoid favouritism, he must remain aloof from the community. His wife becomes identified with his work in almost all social contacts and she too is held at arm's length and treated with deference or hostility. Indeed she has to be even more correct and circumspect and distant than he. Caesar's wife has to be above suspicion. There can be no clergy marriage break-downs or police wives arrested for theft.

But again it is not only men's paid work which structures their wives' lives. So too may their leisure activities or their unemployment and retirement. Whether it is a question of her cooking meals for particular times to tie in with his return from drinking in the pub after work, or his trade union meetings, or golf on a Sunday morning, or his local political or masonic activities, or his train spotting, or his sport, she has to work around him. And if his preference is for doing things as a family, she has to be free to do things with him.

Standard of living

A wife's standard of living depends crucially on the level of her husband or cohabitee's income. This is an obvious truth, but it is something people often forget when they start arguing that marriage has become an equal partnership. At the level of individual couples, employed women earn on average half what men earn, and only about one in ten earns the same and one in fifty earns more than her husband.[19] Study after study has re-affirmed that for most people, the most important component of their economic well-being in the last few decades has been a change in the income earned by the men who are their household heads. State benefits and women's own earnings make a difference, sometimes quite a big difference, to a household's standard of living, but on their own they are no defence against adversity.

A wife's standard of living depends in addition not only on the level of her husband's income, but also on his goodwill. We cannot presume that members of a household share the same standard of living as the head. Indeed an important contribution to welfare policy thinking in the last 20 years has been the recognition of the continuing existence of 'secondary poverty': that even when the money going into a household seems sufficient for family needs, dependants can still be receiving less than the minimum defined as the poverty level because the man keeps a high proportion of the 'family wage' for himself.[20]

The Port Talbot study showed the consequences of various money-handling strategies for dependants, and also how family standards of living sometimes increase when men have time and a sum of money which they choose to spend on home improvements – even when one might have expected standards of living to fall because the men were unemployed. Conversely, however, pay increases do not necessarily get passed on in the housekeeping money paid to wives. In periods of rapid inflation this may mean a wife's work is greatly increased. To manage to feed everyone on the sum she has available, she has to expend an incredible amount of time and energy to save perhaps £10 a week. Or again a man trying to start his own business may reduce 'family consumption . . . in order to increase business investment: domestic living standards are squeezed in order to underwrite the costs of the business' (Scase and Goffee 1980b). Husbands' chosen spending patterns are thus shared with (read, imposed on) their dependants.

How wives structure their husbands' lives

By contrast, a wife's employment and her friendships and her hobbies should affect her husband and children as little as possible. If she has a job (and she has no automatic right to have one), its only effect should be to provide a net financial gain for the household. Even then it should not structure the household's life. A woman's earnings should not be so large as to undermine her husband's status as breadwinner. Nor should the hours she has to work change his or the children's routine. In other words, when wives have jobs – or take care of kin or neighbours outside the home, or engage in voluntary activities, or sport – they must demonstrate that their husbands and children 'do not suffer'. 'There is a rule of thumb which comes into operation when relevant issues arise . . . [namely] the work–family–work hierarchy . . . The needs of the husband's work are accorded top priority, followed by those of the family (primarily, but not exclusively, children), with the wife's own paid work, actual or potential, coming a very poor third' (Finch 1983: 134).

The relevant questions to ask are not how does a wife's employment and other activities structure her husband's life, but rather, do his work and personal needs prevent her taking *any* employment or having *any* outside interests at all? Or do his work and needs make her take less desirable employment and concentrate on hobbies or friends she is less interested in? A wife is always somewhat restricted – to employment and leisure activities which can be fitted into her husband's (work and leisure) timetable, his geography and his personal needs, and the needs of other members of the family. The latter include encouraging children's interests in whatever is appropriate for their class and gender position (football for boys and tap-dancing for girls in working class South Wales; participation by both sexes in youth orchestras and skiing in middle class Hampstead). In addition, her work and hobbies must be appropriate for the wife of her particular husband. Thus Gaynor Cohen (1978) found that in the middle class suburb she studied in south London, the wives of architects and men in marketing could not take on the jobs which were available locally (for example, cooking and serving meals in school canteens) because they were too low status. Or again Muslim households may think it better for a wife to do homework under kin control, even if this means she is socially isolated and has an extremely low wage, rather than her taking on factory work which is held to be unsuitable because it brings her into contact with unrelated men.

There is thus no symmetry between employment and leisure and family for men and women. Married women have to establish a right to employment and they have to negotiate time away from the home. They can only hope to do this when they are not needed full-time at home and if they can find appropriate employment and leisure activities. It therefore helps if their occupation is seen as worthwhile and / or as doing good for others (for example, teaching or nursing) because this helps to raise the status of the family household in the community; and / or if the job brings in a level of cash which is significant to the family. It helps if their leisure activities, too, are related to their domestic and sexual responsibilities. Studies (cited in note 22) show how they are more likely to be allowed to learn to sew, or to go swimming to keep their figures in trim, than to study for a vocational qualification or to go to the cinema or to a feminist group. In addition they are likely to be allowed to do whatever activity they choose only if it takes place where there is no chance of their meeting other men and getting involved in new relationships (a constraint never put on men's leisure).

This lack of symmetry becomes even clearer when we consider the things discussed in relation to husbands' occupations and leisure and note how these are either not aspects of women / wives' activities or do not structure women's lives outside their place of employment.

Space

Wives are supposed to find work close to home (that is, to where it is convenient for their husband to live). They are almost never employed in occupations which would require a husband to live in their institutional settings. But if a husband *were* to live with, for example, a soldier wife on her army base, he would still not be as defined by his wife as a wife would be by her husband, nor as constrained in his life-style. Equally women's occupations rarely carry tied housing for couples – and if a husband were to live in accommodation tied to his wife's job, it would probably not in any case be his place of work in the way his tied housing is hers as a housewife.

When both wife and husband have jobs with career structures they are less likely to move to further her career than his – whether for promotion, to seek new work, or because employers require it. They are certainly not likely to relocate regularly (every year or every few years) for her. Even in the minority of cases

> where both partners actively seek to facilitate the wife's career, actual decisions about moves tend most often to favour the husband. Over half the couples . . . studied [by Berger, Foster and Wallston (1978)] had developed job-seeking strategies which were initially egalitarian (operating on the basis that neither career was inherently more important than the other). However, when final decisions were made about a move, only a quarter were actually on an egalitarian basis: most decisions in the end reverted to the traditional strategy of wife following husband. This does not simply provide evidence about the strength of traditional cultural norms. The authors argue that this change was due as much to the operation of the labour market: the men got offered jobs more readily or more quickly than did the women, so the decision became a choice between accepting one job which one partner wanted, or letting it go with no knowledge of whether there was an alternative. (Finch 1983: 51)

Few men 'live over their wife's shop' (her pub, craft workshop, etc.) because few women (especially married women) head such enterprises. (If and when they do, their husbands almost never work for them.) Some employed married women certainly bring work home in the evening (teachers, civil servants, etc.) or work at home on occasional days for the same reasons as men (to be undisturbed by clients or telephone), and the majority of homeworkers are women. But the reasons for and experience of working at or from home are very different for men and for women (except in a few rare cases when the woman has a full-time servant or servants). For women working at home, the distinction between occupational and non-occupational time, space and activities is blurred – as with those professional men who are always on call, but in the opposite direction. Women usually work at home precisely so their work can be interrupted by calls from domestic duties: so that they can retain (immediate or final) responsibility for domestic work and childcare.

Where wives have jobs that are flexible in regard to time and place, they are in different occupations, and different processes are at work than when men have 'flexible' jobs. Women are, for instance, temp secretaries or copy-typists, industrial outworkers, landladies, agricultural casual workers, freelance journalists or designers or editors, or they sell toiletries or plastic ware in people's homes – so they can accept or reject work daily. Domestic responsibilities can thus overflow into time designated for possible occupational activities if necessary. This is why Cynthia Epstein suggested that if a woman wants to pursue a career, she needs a job which is outside the home and which requires her to be there every day from nine to five (Epstein 1970).

If women do non-domestic work at home they will have to find the physical space for it. Very few women have 'a room of their own' – the case is often quoted of the Brontë sisters writing on a table in a living room which had to be cleared for meals, while their (much less talented) brother wrote in his own study. And very few husbands, supposing they were present in the house during her working day, would see it as their role regularly to sort out a wife's callers and make them coffee, much less to leave her a meal to heat up as they left for outside employment.

We are reliably informed such paragons do, however, exist. They show that men are capable of such actions – which we actually did not doubt. But they are also the exceptions which prove the rule. And we suspect, cynically, that such behaviour will be more frequent early in a relationship and likely to decline as the male desire to please is less marked and the demands of his job and the lure of possible leisure activities grow.

Time

It is much less acceptable for a wife and mother than for a husband / father to be 'mentally at work' all the time: to not want to interact with her family because she has problems to sort out, or for her to be stressed or tired – or just more interested in what she has to do for her job. Nor should she use non-work time to catch up on occupational work – or even on domestic work if her husband and children want her to be with them. Whereas the family do not think she should be on call to her job, they have no compunction about taking her away from her job when they ask her to perform a domestic task, that is, about expecting her to be on call to them. Given that women rarely have work with the attractions of high income, status, intrinsic interest, attractive workplaces or moral worthiness, it is hard for them to argue against the demands of their domestic calling.

Women seldom carry over occupational work relationships into the non-employment sphere, meeting and talking shop out of work. A wife's behaviour at work is more likely to be 'contaminated' by her family role, than her family behaviour by her job.[21] The friends a woman has at work are less likely to become friends of herself and her husband as a couple than are his workmates and their wives (unless the friend's husband is a friend of her husband); and there are fewer occupation-related occasions when a woman has to produce a spouse than when a man must produce his wife – though there are some. Very few men identify themselves as 'a doctor's husband', etc. In other words, her husband (and the rest of the family) are not as closely identified with her as she is (and they are) with him. He remains an individual in his own right.

Women are certainly differently located from men when it comes to treating their family as 'an escape from work'. Domestic life may be a counter to certain of the stresses women face in employment, but families do not constitute 'leisure' for women, even when they have paid domestic help. Women do not have leisure in the strict sense of 'time other than that sold to the employer by a wage worker who owns his own labour power', because married women (and some unmarried women too) do not own their own labour power. Their time belongs to their household head – even if he has agreed to some of it being sold to an employer, and even if he is willing for the dependant to take some time off. He is still able and likely to exercise considerable control over what she does – where she goes and with whom – if she leaves the house during her 'free' time.[22]

Q. Has your leisure time changed a great deal since you've been separated?
A. Oh yes, yes.
Q. Do you think it's changed for the better?
A. Definitely, definitely (laughing).
Q. What was it like before?
A. Well I wasn't free. It was like filling a time sheet in, you had to account for every minute of your day. Even if I went shopping to town he'd be spying on me. I never went out at night then (single parent, early fifties) (Green and Hebron 1988: 45).

Standard of living

Although the money a married woman earns may be of great significance to the household she lives in – in Britain in the late 1970s it was calculated a further third of families would fall below the poverty line but for the wife / mother's earnings – a husband's standard of living is very rarely as dependent on the level and form of his wife's income as hers is on his. This applies both directly, to his actual weekly income, and also indirectly, to the credit they may be able to obtain, to the unemployment and other benefits they may receive, and to the pension they can expect.[23] Women usually marry men who are older and of higher status and higher earning capacity than themselves. If there is a chance of this order being overturned, they may deliberately keep below his level and income by forgoing promotion. If they accept a higher income to help meet the household's needs, they are likely to be unhappy with the situation and to disguise it. But in the main, wives contribute to their husbands' standard of living (and thereby to their own) not so much by their earnings as by their practical and symbolic production in building a home, and by the personalized servicing they give him.

In sum, women rarely use their occupation to challenge the 'rule of thumb' about priorities with which we opened this section. They often express this very directly and clearly. Any potential conflicts are avoided by a wife taking action to modify, adjust or change her aspirations to fit around her husband and children. If there is a conflict, her employment may be relegated to a lower priority and the man's higher earning capacity safeguarded and / or stressed. Because she constantly puts her employment in third place and forgoes promotion when it might be threatening, and gives up friends and activities outside the home 'of her own volition', a couple's continuing with what is in fact the pre-existing normative division of labour appears to be a rational and individual choice.

Concluding comments

The past chapters have shown some of the diversity in the work women do, and the extent to which they have employment and leisure outside the household. Although in each country and each locality the existing patterns seem given and inevitable, they actually vary considerably from one western country to another and within each country by region, class and ethnicity, and according to the availability and quality of state and private sector provision of support services. They are associated with differing cultural expectations of what constitutes good mothering and care of the elderly, and proper wifely behaviour.

The variations in wives' work which are far and away most often stressed are the life-course changes associated with the care of small children. This tends to be the cause of women's initial withdrawal from the labour market – and this in turn largely determines their future labour market prospects. Having children depresses a woman's lifetime earnings by 25–50 percent.[24] Childcare is also stressed because it focuses on the ideologically most 'obvious' and 'natural' difference between men and women; and because so much weight is given to the quality of maternal care in western developmental psychology. Childcare experts believe certain forms of (class and culturally specific) maternal care are good and necessary for children, and they suggest this form of care should be universal – even though in fact very different forms of maternal / parental care produce functioning adults, as cross-national studies show.

What is much less remarked is that in fact more women, especially married women, withdraw from the labour market each year to care for sick, elderly and handicapped members of their family – mainly parents or parents-in-law, but sometimes other relatives or even friends or neighbours – than now withdraw for childcare. The extent of care provided unpaid and within private homes has begun to be a matter of public issue in recent years, partly because of feminist agitation, but also because the number of people needing such care has increased dramatically with demographic changes, and because cuts in public spending have reduced the already limited public provision previously available. More than one in ten adult women in Britain have someone other than a child who 'depends on them for some sort of care', rising to over 20 per cent among women over 40.[25] Women may take on such work initially voluntarily when they are at home caring for children anyway and while the older person is still relatively hale and hearty. Indeed help may flow in both directions at the start, with the elderly relative doing some baby-sitting. It only gradually becomes a heavy burden: but it can then continue (as do women's general wifely responsibilities) beyond their husband's retirement. Those who care for confused elderly people have a mean age of 61 years and their own health is often severely impaired by the nursing involved.

In Janet Finch's analysis, it is when a husband works from home or his job requires a wife more or less institutionally that a wife has to use 'radical resistance strategies' if she is to remain uninvolved (Finch 1983: 98). But in fact it is difficult for any wife to maintain her 'independence', wherever her husband works and whatever his job. It is, for instance, a really major step for her to refuse to accompany her husband abroad or if he needs to move house, or to refuse to live in accommodation provided rent free, or not to accept the demands of his job, or his hobbies, or his friends, or even to refuse to take phone messages for him – if she wants to remain married to him. His control may be strengthened if he is at home all day, and pressures can be increased if his employer offers him incentives if his wife performs her 'proper' role, but pressures are also increased if his peers want him to be active in a trade union – or just to play football. Even when there are no direct negative sanctions if a wife refuses to do appropriate work, there are usually rewards if she is prepared to comply. And there is always the spectre of the wife who ruined her husband by not doing what was needed: who inflicted damage on his present work and seriously damaged his career prospects, or who turned him into a rapist because she refused him sexually. And beyond this there is the spectre of divorce. A wife who refuses to behave is more detrimental to a man than not having a wife at all.[26]

A married woman may initially resist having the label of assistant / subordinate / wife hung on her, and she may develop strategies to handle social relations and to minimize her 'wifely' identity – by, for instance, not changing her name, not telling people she is married, or who she is married to, or not mixing socially with others in the same situation – and she and her husband may try to stress equality. But it is then all the more poignant when she ends up bowing to circumstances (when she stops fighting her husband and the labour market) and, for instance, accepts a period of full-time motherhood and economic dependency.

There is certainly a cyclical effect: the more a wife puts into her husband, the more she is cut off from kin, friends and acquaintances, the more she has to hold on to him socially and economically. She is therefore increasingly likely to stress it is 'our job', 'our household' and 'our money', and to regard herself as part of a team, running a joint enterprise – overlooking the fact that she is the junior partner and that should they divorce, she will lose almost everything.

Notes

1 We follow the categories developed by Finch to classify wives' work and to consider the ways in which husbands' jobs structure women's lives; but our analysis obviously takes us beyond her particular concerns.

2 Nancy Reagan loved being the US President's wife, but Mary Wilson did not enjoy being married to the British Prime Minister. The autobiography of Pierre Trudeau's ex-wife Margaret (1980) is particularly illuminating.

3 These researchers have stressed the personal retainer nature of the relationship between private secretary and boss, and their accounts carry a tone of outrage that a secretary's job should require her to be personally attractive and to do things for her boss's personal life: 'half of their time is taken up with domestic tasks.' See Benet (1972: 74–5) and Vinnicombe (1980).

What is equally noteworthy, however, is how much of the work which could legitimately be that of a secretary / PA is routinely done by wives.

4 While not wanting to get entangled in the specific arguments around the Koestlers' case, we note the numbers of cases in which men actually do kill their wives before committing suicide (see Dobash and Dobash 1980: 15–17 and Cameron and Frazer 1987: 13ff).

5 See Hite 1976, 1981 and especially 1988.

6 In a sample from six cities in France (and from Pskov in the USSR) in 1966, employed wives were found to spend an average 5 hours 26 minutes (and 6 hours 55 minutes), and employed husbands 3 hours 19 minutes (and 3 hours 5 minutes) per day on household chores on their 'free' days. See Szalai (1972) and Cullen (1974). For the recent French figures see Grimler and Roy (1987).

7   See Bose (1979) and Game and Pringle (1984).
8   See Berk and Berk (1979).
9   As a topic this has been even more neglected than wives' contribution to their husbands' work, though see Epstein (1971), Platt (1976), Rapoport and Rapoport (1971; 1976; 1978) and Goffee and Scase (1985).
10 Women (or married women) are in fact specifically excluded from some of the occupations Finch considers for men – the clergy, the diplomatic service, and the armed forces and merchant services; or they have only recently been allowed in and are surviving with difficulty in less favoured sectors of the occupation, for example, women doctors, police, journalists, lorry drivers and in business.
11 A point made by Maila Stivens (1978) in her work on a suburb in Australia. Interestingly, Finch does not mention husbands' moral support for wives at all.
12 Hunt (1968) quoted in Martin and Roberts (1984).
13 See among time-budget studies especially Meissner, Humphreys, Meis and Scheu (1975) and Nissel and Bonnerjea (1982).
14 Martin and Roberts (1984). They found 'equal sharing' (defined in this way) occurred among 44 per cent of couples when the wife was in full-time employment, but only among 18 per cent when she was not employed.
15 See Oakley (1972), Ungerson (1981; 1987) and Nissel and Bonnerjea (1982).
16 See Rapoport and Rapoport (1978), Mortimore, Hall and Hill (1978), Berger, Foster and Wallston (1978), Marceau (1976; 1978) and Farris (1978).
17 Said to a (mixed sex) group attending a training course for insurance sales staff (personal communication from a member of the group).
18 On railwaymen and architects, see Salaman (1971); on friendships patterns of couples generally, see Allan (1979).
19 It is difficult to find comparisons of the incomes of individual husbands and wives, as opposed to aggregate statistics on men and women. However, Martin and Roberts (1984) found that among women aged 16–60 in GB, only 7 per cent earn as much as their male partners; while figures from the Board of Inland Revenue for GB show that where both spouses are employed or self-employed and paying tax, 9 per cent of wives earned as much or more than their husbands in 1984–5 and 13 per cent in 1985–6 (EOC 1988: 50). Meredith Edwards's study of 50 couples in Australia found only one woman earning more than her husband (Edwards 1981: 70).

Jan Pahl's survey of 102 middle income couples with at least one child under 16 in Kent in 1983, found only 50 per cent of women were employed (and in 11 per cent of couples neither partner was employed). She shows clearly the disparity between men's and women's incomes (income including here: take-home pay, child benefits, earnings from second jobs, interest on savings, gifts from relatives, loans, and gambling wins). (See table 9.1).

Table 9.1 Comparison of women's and men's incomes

Income per week (£)	Women (%)	Men (%)
up to 19	34	–
19–57	49	6
58–95	15	23
96–134	2	32
135–172	–	23
173+	–	17

Source: J. Pahl 1990, table 5.2, p. 65

Brown's national survey for the Policy Studies Institute shows that while Afro-Caribbean and Asian men and women are disadvantaged in the labour market compared to white men and women (they are more likely to be unemployed than whites, and men's median earnings may be 10–15 per cent lower), the biggest disparity is between the incomes of men and women. (See table 9.2.)

Table 9.2 Median weekly earnings of full-time employees

Ethnic origin	Men (£)	Women (£)
white	129	78
West Indian	109	81
Asian	111	73

Source: Brown 1984, from table 109, p. 212

20 See Rowntree (1902), Young (1952), Syson and Young (1974), Land (1976), Sen (1983; 1984) and review in Glendenning and Millar (1991).
21 For recent accounts see Pollert (1981) and Westwood (1984).
22 See Deem (1986), Wimbush and Talbot (1988), Green and Woodward (1988), Green and Hebron (1988) and Green, Hebron and Woodward (1990).
   These studies all report that many husbands do not like their wives or partners to go out 'alone' (that is, with friends but without their husband), and they agree to it only if their wife's activity is approved of by them. The men control the women by sulking, making the women feel guilty, by directly forbidding them, or at the limit with violence.
   These domestic controls are reinforced by the harassment and discrimination women may experience in public places while pursuing leisure activities.
23 See Hamill (1979) on the importance of women's earnings. On credit see G. Wilson (1987) and on pensions see Groves (1991).
24 This calculation was made by Heather Joshi (1989; 1991) using the same Department of Employment data as Martin and Roberts (1984). Joshi argues

that the effect of family formation is felt through women's career breaks and their subsequent reduced participation. They often work part-time and are downwardly mobile as a result.

25 Overall three times as many married as single women give care: 15 per cent of married women, 12 per cent of formerly married women and 6 per cent of single women. Over 40 there is no difference between the married and the single in the proportion giving care; though in terms of actual numbers, of course, most such care is given by married women because there are far more of them at this age. Women over 60 years old are even more likely to be carers. See Martin and Roberts (1984) and Keating and Cole (1980).

26 Women initiate three-quarters of divorces in the UK, but this is not necessarily because women more often want a divorce. It is probably because when a marriage breaks down and the couple part the man's life is less affected. His income continues and he can buy wifely services, so he does not need to seek a formal severance. The woman's life, on the other hand, particularly her income and access to resources, changes drastically. Her earning capacity has been damaged by the marriage and she needs to sort out her finances. Hence she has to initiate a legal process. See Weitzman (1985), Eekelaar and Maclean (1986) and Maclean and Weitzman (1991).

10

CONCLUSION

Feminists in the nineteenth century often argued for equality for women on the grounds that the existing situations of men and women harmed their emotional relationships. They said that if husbands and fathers had too much patriarchal power, then wives and children would obey them from fear and necessity rather than love and respect. Similarly if adult women could not support themselves economically outside the family they would have to accept proposals of marriage whatever their feelings for the individual men concerned. Even today feminists can still be found who argue for changes in family relationships in the name of love between the sexes.

What is implicit in all such arguments is an acceptance that there is a special relationship between men and women. It is assumed that whatever degree of social separation the sexes may maintain in other areas of life, individual men and women should be united with each other by love. That is to say, such arguments start from the premise that there is a 'natural' relationship between men and women which is sexual or emotional, and conversely that sexual and sentimental relationships between individuals are based on the fact that they are of opposite sexes – and any such relations between people of the same sex are 'unnatural'. They are underpinned by the theory that men and women are biologically given, distinct and complementary beings, that is, by heterosexism.

These premises can lead off in two very different directions, however, each of which has had different strategic implications for feminism in the past – though in fact both lines of argument (and the related strategies) are wrong because the theoretical premises are wrong.

Either they can lead to the assertion that precisely because women and men complement each other sexually and emotionally, inequality and 'commercial' considerations between them are harmful and shocking. Economic inequalities upset natural emotions, so women's emancipation should be sought in order to free love.

Or they can lead to a justification of the different social situations of men and women on the grounds that men will look after women. That is to say they can lead to a belief that, although the sexes cannot be equal for physical reasons, this does not matter because they are united by sexual and emotional relationships. Men's continuing dominance in the public sphere is not a problem since women benefit indirectly through their attachment to men. So women should develop their own special sphere in the domestic domain.

Second wave feminism differs from first wave feminism in that most contemporary feminists do not accept that male and female human beings relate to each other specifically or primarily sexually and sentimentally, nor that heterosexuality is more natural than other sexual practices. Rather we see 'men' and 'women' as two socially differentiated categories (two 'genders'), with one dominating the other. These two social groups are no more naturally based than any other power relations in society (they are no more natural than, for example, class or racial divisions) and the sexual and love relationships established between men and women are also seen as socially constructed and a means to the continuation of women's oppression.

Our analysis goes further than that of most present-day feminists, however, in not just differentiating 'sex' and 'gender' and rejecting hetero-sexist presumptions, but in also stressing the class-like nature of the relationship between men and women and seeing sexuality as just one (not 'the') major arena in which men use and abuse women. We see men and women as economic classes, with one category / class subordinating the other and exploiting its work. Within the family system specifically, we see men exploiting women's practical, emotional, sexual and repro-ductive labour. For us 'men' and 'women' are not two naturally given groups which at some point in history fell into a hierarchical relationship. Rather the reason the two groups are distinguished socially is because one dominates the other in order to use its labour. In other words, it is the relationship of production which produces the two classes 'men' and 'women'.

Of course western society perceives the existence of two genders as due to physiological sex differences, but this argument needs turning around. The attaching of this social meaning to physiology, that is, seeing differences in reproductive organs as resulting in two quite different sorts of human beings, is an ideology which legitimates and sustains the existence of two groups and their hierarchical relationship. The naturalization of the gender hierarchy is not unusual or surprising however, since western culture has seen, and still sees, most relations of dominance which exist within it, including those of social class and race, as (at least partly) physically and / or psychologically determined.

Relations between husbands and wives in our society certainly do usually nowadays involve a definite emotional attachment (at least at the start). But the fact that men and women love each other is neither required nor prevented by their class relationship. Conversely, the fact that men and women may be emotionally attached to each other neither requires nor prevents them having class relations. Loving women does not pre-vent men exploiting them. The link between men and women's class relationship and their sentimental attachment seems to be, rather, that because of this class relationship heterosexual relations are enjoined and all other emotional and sexual relations vilified. But it could be that people generally live in heterosexual couples and come to be emotionally attached as a result of this class relation; or it could be that the love is fostered and encouraged so that even in the presence of a wage labour system and possible independent existence, women still rush to get married. Or it could be that the love relationship is a condition of the exploitation of labour because women would not do the work or not do it as well if they did not feel love for men. Or these things may be arbitrarily correlated, with no relation of cause and effect. We may know which came first chronologically for each couple (in the West they fall in love and get married, in other parts of the world men and women get married and then may fall in love), but it is more difficult to know which is structurally primary.

Women are aware of the ambivalence in their relations with men: they recognize both the affection and support *and* the exploitation and misogyny even within intimate relations. Consequently the second wave of feminism swiftly declared oppressive the sexual division of labour within households, the hours of housework performed each week by women and the minimal amount done by men, women's isolation, loneliness and (full or partial) financial dependency in marriage, and our lack of sexual satisfaction and emotional support in heterosexual relationships. Conceptualizing women's condition as 'oppression' rather than 'difference' brought housework and female sexuality and motherhood out of the domains of the separate and 'value free' academic disciplines of psychology and sociology and law, and into the general political arena. It constituted an epistemological revolution. But theoretical analyses have developed only slowly to help our understanding of how various apparently isolated elements are related.

Our contribution in this book consists in recognizing husbands and wives (and more generally household heads and dependants) as being on opposite sides of a relationship of production, in showing the specific nature of this relationship, and in recognizing family hierarchy. We have described the mechanisms of family exploitation and the nature of the costs and benefits for the two sides. A household head / husband appropriates his wife's (and sometimes other family members') labour, and provides for their upkeep. The two have duties and obligations to each other, but these are not calculated and 'exchanged'. It *appears* as if the wife is not exploited because she is maintained, especially as she is often seen as enjoying a higher standard of living than could be purchased by any wage she personally could earn (particularly if she is a full-time housewife and has no income at all). The fact that *all* her time may be directly appropriated by her household head, along with her sexual activity and reproductive power, is remarked less than the *partial* appropriation of the wage labourer's time and energy within the capitalist system. 'He really suffers', while 'she is lucky to have someone to take care of her.'

However, other family members doing unpaid work for upkeep is nowadays less accepted in the West, which is why we have found studying work relations within the petty commodity sector, and especially in family farming, so useful in throwing light on marriage.

The exploitation of wives thus consists not in getting less than we might for the hours we work (which is to apply an inappropriate, capitalist measure to family labour), but in the appropriation of potentially all our labour and in our dependence and subordination. It matters a lot to wives that despite working long hours at whatever needs doing they have no money of their own; that men's (husband's, father's and brothers') interests are always put first and that they get given more of the family's resources; and that women and girls are supposed to look up to men and boys and to support their masculinity. This is surprisingly often overlooked in accounts of housework and family life. Wives' oppression also consists in it being seen as 'only fair' they do the work they do (including emotional and sexual servicing) because they 'contribute nothing', that is, in their work not being valued. And in its being suggested that they are responsible for their situation because they chose it, that is, in it not being recognized that as women they are positioned in an economic system not of their making in which they do not control the use of their labour. Women's oppression also consists in their being dependent on and emotionally attached to one particular person and having to please him even if he is emotionally withholding or violent (indeed especially if he is violent) because they cannot easily change to another husband. Finally, our exploitation consists in all the aspects of society which push and pressure women into marriage, femininity and heterosexuality in order that we continue to accept relationships with men.

What a husband gets from a wife is her hours of work and personal servicing. He saves money on goods produced and consumed at home, and gains time he would have had to spend on work for himself and his dependants or for the market if he did everything himself. He also gets personal support and ego-boosting, a pliant sexual partner, and children if he wants them. What men get from marriage is different, therefore, from what it costs women. Putting it crudely, what men get from marriage is 57 varieties of unpaid service, whereas the institution of marriage and the family restricts and (ab)uses (married and unmarried) women in all areas of their lives.

We have concentrated in this book on housework and the other family work done by wives (that is, on 'the family in space' – within households), only touching on gender relations within 'the family in time'. But our analysis applies not only to housework and emotional care but also to wives' sexual servicing of husbands, and to motherhood. However, while we think our analysis provides a thorough basic understanding of domestic production, we have stressed it does not fully explore gender relations even in this arena. As we said at the start, sexuality, motherhood, housework and emotional work all involve not just questions of labour but also related issues of self-identity and the construction and fulfilment of desires, etc. But since it is the labour which has up to now been most inadequately theoretically addressed and which is most basic and important, it has been on this that we have chosen to concentrate.

Although our concern has therefore not been centrally with issues of choice nor with individuals' experience and motivation, when we have touched on these areas we have always stressed that our analysis does not present women as victims or colluders in their own oppression. Women make certain decisions in households and may get great pleasure and satisfaction from family relationships. They often stand up for themselves vigorously, and keeping wives (and sisters and daughters) in their place may be a considerable problem for some husbands, brothers and fathers. In other words, women certainly contribute to the making of their own worlds. But they do so in conditions not of their own choosing. They suffer because of their situation as subordinates, though how they interpret and react to this varies. Jane Lewis has suggested, for example, that in twentieth-century Britain some (notably middle class) women have been happy with their lot and have elaborated a women's domestic culture. They have wanted men to continue as breadwinners and have sought only to reduce the risks of divorce. Other women have gone along with their wifely role less wholeheartedly, but have justified it as being necessary for various reasons, including 'for the children's sake'. Still others have been quite antagonistic to their husbands but they have reached a compromise and done their domestic duty because they accepted the importance and toughness of men's jobs and because they have not wanted to provoke male outbursts (Lewis 1984: xii). Women's resistance to domestic exploitation has in any case been hampered for most of the century by the absence of a language to explain it and a movement to offer solidarity in resisting it.

The analysis we put forward therefore does not present women as victims, and it equally does not present men as by nature, or necessarily individually, exploitative or physically abusive. It stresses that men have advantages within heterosexual couples whether they want these advantages, and work to sustain or increase them or not, whatever their politics, and however they personally treat women. They have them because of the social structure: the framework within which their interpersonal relations are set. They get them as members of a group which they did not choose to be in, but which nevertheless they are in, and which the majority of them for the majority of the time do actively seek to maintain. Men benefit from the fact that women do certain work which they are not required to do, plus they get other direct positive benefits such as women tending their needs. They also owe their occupational position, however well they personally treat their women colleagues, to the discrimination which women suffer in employment. An individual man cannot renounce his position. He can merely choose not to take active advantage of existing privileges to get more. But very few men do in practice forgo accepting promotion to enable a woman to get it, or agree to full domestic role sharing, or full sexual parity – though a few have been prepared to accept more modest moves towards equality.

Since there are stronger economic and social constraints on women to have relationships with men than on men to have them with women, marriage and 'relationships' remain 'women's concerns', and women have to accept more from men than vice versa. This asymmetry pre-exists a particular union and is a major reason why such relationships get established and why they remain unequal. Women find it hard to resist men's power within their individual couple because they need a relationship with a man, and also because, as we have said, their love and respect for a particular man veils the fact that exploitation is actually taking place. Women's work for men seems freely given: they choose to do it. So men get not only affection and support, but also work willingly done, and whatever work they individually need and want. This is characteristic of all oppressions of allegiance – of personal dependency (that is, of domestic service, slavery and serfdom as well as marriage). Personal dependants do not exchange a precise amount of a particular sort of work for wages, but rather owe their entire work capacity, devoted to whatever needs doing in exchange for protection (from other members of the dominant group) and maintenance (the dominant group having appropriated the productive resources). Despite this, they personally identify with their individual oppressor.

While contemporary feminists have insisted on the social construction of gender and heterosexuality and on the fact that men oppress women in marriage, the women's movement has had to contend with the problem that, whatever its theoretical analysis may indicate, its strategy is constrained. Heterosexual relations are experienced as natural and involuntary and desirable by most of the population, and the majority of people live in heterosexual couples most of their lives. Husbands and wives have economic *and* emotional relations simultaneously, and children are believed to need both mothers *and* fathers. What then should feminists do to struggle against male dominance, especially in relation to the family?

In trying to answer this, second wave feminism has got into real difficulties and these partly explain the decline in the women's movement in the 1980s. This decline was certainly also due to a general decline in ideology, militancy and utopianism in the West, but there is no doubt specific problems deriving from feminism's own presuppositions played a part.

In the 1970s the Women's Liberation movement made splendid use of the slogan 'the personal is political', but in the 1980s it got itself tied up in this phrase. It got caught between arguing we can and should change everything about relations between men and women, especially in our personal lives, and finding we did not seem to be able to change very much, especially in our personal lives.

'The personal is political' can be read in several ways, but it has two main aspects. First there is a theoretical aspect, which says that the division of life into public and private spheres is false; that the division is itself a social construct, an ideology. The world we live in is not divided into a sphere of public, socially constructed, work and power relations, and a private sphere of natural, non-work and non-power relations. Personal, family, sexual and love relations are all socially constructed and all involve gendered power relations. In this respect the slogan reclaimed for political analysis relations which were otherwise seen as intimate and give. It was a revolution in theory; but it did not imply much about practice.

But another aspect of 'the personal is political' was very much about action – if not about strategy. It derives from the context of the late 1960s, from the anarchist, 1968, insistence on changing life now. This reading of the slogan says, in contrast to statements by western communist parties, that it is not a question of waiting for change till after the Revolution, and meanwhile continuing to live as before. It says we should start the revolution here and now, by changing as much of society as we can. What you do in your personal life is political, so change it. This stance led some radicals in the late 1960s and early 1970s to found communal utopias which sought 'to get away from society', and gave rise to general arguments for 'politics by example'. In the case of feminism there was an increasing obligation on each and every woman to transform her life here and now. This was often not possible, or very difficult to live out – though some women could and did make changes and found they were wonderful.

There are limits to what you can do here and now. Our objective as radical feminists may be that gender divisions, the differentiation between men and women that we experience, should no longer exist – not because one has killed off the other but because the distinction between the biological sexes no longer has social significance. But this will only be achieved in the long term. Reading the 'personal is political' as saying that individuals have a responsibility to change here and now, and allying this to a truly radical vision which requires major social changes, has meant that many women have arrived at a point where they feel that to be a feminist requires them to change their lives both massively, and at once. If they do not do this they think (or they are made to think) they have to abandon the women's movement or be accused of hypocrisy. Or else they stay in the movement, but defiantly refuse to change *any* of their behaviour – some even going so far as to try to glorify some of the more dubious aspects of heterosexuality (like sado-masochist sexual practices). And the WLM has been smashing itself up over this for some time.

Many women can see intellectually that the family, for instance, is part of patriarchal society, and that by being a wife and mother, or even just living with a man, they help to maintain patriarchal society in its present form. They can also see that they are oppressed by this society, and by their father / brother / husband or lover even if their own man has a good heart and 'tries hard to help, and supports women a lot', that is, even if he's not that bad, as men go. But women want to have people whom they can love and who will love them in return, and they experience sex discrimination and low wages at work and aggression in public places which make it difficult to live or socialize alone or with other women, and homosexuality is heavily stigmatized. So their choices are not great. And not surprisingly most opt to continue relationships with their family of origin, to carry on with paid employment choosing as politically acceptable a job as they can find, and to establish or continue a sexual relationship with a man, hoping to ensure that their own particular experiences of patriarchy and heterosexuality are as unoppressive as they can make them.

Many of the current problems of the women's movement derive from underestimating the distance between the changes possible in most of our lives and the long-term changes we aim for. Obviously the women's movement is not just a utopian vision. It has personal implications and requires personal commitment and certain sacrifices. And the issue is not that feminism is (or has become) moralistic, because any political movement which is not also moralistic is in a bad way (although those that are purely moralistic are in a really bad way!). Political movements exist because moral choices are always having to be made. From the moment we make a certain analysis of society and have a notion of exploitation and oppression, there are ideas of what is good and what is bad, or rather of what is oppressive or exploitative and hurtful. We can and must have discussions and views on what are more and what are less feminist ways of behaving, and there is no getting away from this. And we should respect women who have the strength to stand up in public for their convictions and / or to change their whole lives.

But a women's movement which requires women to obey its commandments is dangerous, and some feminist arguments are too voluntaristic. They say that women can simply change their lives if they want to, and that they *must* change their lives if they are to be taken seriously politically; and that men are also personally responsible for every sexist thing they do as well as for all the advantages they have because they are men. But voluntarism has its limits. We need to recognize that there are changes women (and men) should make at once, that they can make by themselves and for which they are responsible. But we equally need to recognize that other sorts of important changes cannot be made by individuals at will or cannot be made without incurring enormous personal costs while other parts of the social structure remain unchanged.

Conversely, other feminist arguments are too deterministic. They say that there are very constraining social structures, that *society* 'makes' women do this and that, that 'the system' is to blame, and that radical change throughout society is needed to end women's oppression. There is no room for women to live differently until the whole lot is transformed.

In practice, however, one and the same individual can be found putting forward the two contradictory arguments sometimes within the course of the same discussion! She may sometimes say that marriage is a social institution and wives *have* to do this, that and the other; while at other times she will say that marriage only continues because of the choices individuals make. The latter sentiment may then lead her to argue either that women should choose not to marry, and indeed should 'give up men' and become celibate or lesbian; or to contend that 'marriage' can be changed at will and that she personally has an egalitarian relationship with the man she lives with.

If we are overly deterministic, we deny a margin for manoeuvre within relationships between women and men and we deny individual differences. Individual differences include moral differences between individuals and the fact that some are more courageous and more prepared to take risks and accept greater costs to change their lives than others. But there are limits to how far this type of moral evaluation should be applied. There are things individuals cannot change, or perhaps that others should not expect them to change, given the costs.

The women's movement thus hesitates between extreme determinism and extreme voluntarism. Which is to say no more than that feminism has not come to grips with the margin for individual action within social structures. But then, neither have philosophy and sociology and they have been addressing this issue for at least the last 100 years.

Determinism is especially marked in feminist accounts of the labour market, but voluntarism prevails in relation to the family and household relationships and issues of sexual orientation. Some women may have abandoned feminism because they felt that determinist feminist analyses did not accord with their experiences of the labour market; but far more (we believe) have left because they felt that they could not change, or did not want to risk, their own domestic or sexual lives.

It is important, therefore, to set out the structure of family relations as we have done and to stress that this structure constitutes (what the sociologist Emile Durkheim called) a social fact: it is real, external to individuals, and it constrains their behaviour.

Women enter marriage 'freely' in the West, persuaded (or pressured) largely by love for their partner – though behind that lie the social and economic advantages of conforming to the norm and of allying oneself with a member of the dominant group: sharing his income and getting his protection. But marriage (or cohabitation which is no longer very different from marriage) is not a personal relationship in the sense of being independently decided upon by each particular couple. Individuals can make choices about which partner to marry, and they choose as a couple how to organize their lives within marriage (to an extent): for example, how much to see of their respective parents and brothers and sisters, whether to have children and when, who is to dig the garden, etc. But they do not choose the nature of marriage, kinship, age divisions or heterosexual relations. These, like the language of their country, they are born into and have to 'speak'. The family as a system in space and in time is a social institution which pre-exists them and sets parameters to their choices. Their actions in relation to it are free only within a framework which ranges from social norms to coercive and penal controls.

The hierarchy within the family household and line is a social fact, not something chosen by some heterosexual couples and refused by others. Many seem to find this particularly difficult to see. What they notice is that nowadays some husbands and wives interchange tasks and spend a lot of time together, that their interactions seem informal rather than governed by etiquette, and that they love each other. This leads them to suggest that marriage has changed 'from being an institution to companionship', and to claim it is now 'symmetrical': that it exists between people who have different responsibilities and do different things but who are equal and complementary human beings. Or, alternatively, they suggest that women can avoid whatever residual male domination there may be by having children on their own or by having their intimate relationships with other women.

But neither path gets one out of patriarchy. To suggest they do is wishful thinking. Marriage is a relationship between a man and a woman who because they are men and women do different things; who because they do different things are unequal; and who because they are unequal are seen as different sorts of human being (one more fully human than the other). Individual heterosexual couples cannot get out of this. But nor can single mothers escape patriarchy; they are often poor and their situation is always difficult. Nor can lesbians escape heterosexuality: their day-to-day lives and their sexual practice are at least partially structured by it. Both single mothers and lesbians are socially stigmatized, and lesbians may be downright ostracized and even physically attacked. Women 'on their own' (alone, with children or with other women) are constantly reminded they are abnormal. This serves 'to encourage the others' to stick with men. Only by recognizing the opposition between men and women and that there is no way to escape all the effects of this opposition currently – but only various ways to work through and to struggle against it – can we understand our situation and see why change is so difficult, but also why we *must* struggle for change just the same.

We do not know what strategy feminists should adopt on the family. There is certainly no one easy answer, like 'feminists should stop getting married' or 'all feminists should be lesbians or at least stop sleeping with the enemy' – though these may be good ways of making public one's resistance to patriarchy and also helpful ways for some women to improve the quality of their own individual lives. It may be that the family and heterosexuality are not the place to start when trying to change gender relations. They are certainly not the only place to start, since women need to have a stronger public position before they give up such protection as their domestic position currently provides for them. For instance, women cannot afford to give up the right to child support after divorce while they are still so disadvantaged in the labour market and there is so little good quality non-domestic childcare available. But even if there is no simple lever to produce change, this does not mean that there should not be more feminist action around women's practical, emotional, sexual and reproductive family work.

We have to accept that some things will not change in our lifetime because they require not only goodwill and personal courage but also social transformations over which we have no immediate control. We may therefore have to accept going on living lives which we would want to see changed in the long term, and we may also have to accept various accommodations women make with the existing system. But we should certainly recognize and give credit to the many forms of resistance to patriarchy which exist now and have existed in the past. Above all we should not think there must be something wrong with our analysis of how men's power over women is exercised and reproduced, nor with feminist ideas about what we would like society to become in the long term, just because changes cannot immediately be put into operation.

BIBLIOGRAPHY

ABRAMS P and McCULLOCH A (1976) 'Men, women and communes', in D
Leonard Barker and S Allen (eds) *Sexual Divisions and Society: process and
change*, Tavistock
ADAMSON O, BROWN C, HARRISON J and PRICE J (1976) 'Women's
oppression under capitalism', *Revolutionary Communist*, no. 5
ADKINS L (1992) 'Sexual Work and Family Production: a study of the gender
division of labour in the contemporary British tourist industry', PhD thesis,
University of Lancaster
ALIBAR F and LEMBEYE-BOY P (1985) 'Le piège', *Nouvelles Questions
Féministes*, nos 9–10, Printemps
ALLAN G (1979) *A Sociology of Friendship and Kinship*, George Allen and
Unwin
ALLAUZEN M (1967) *La paysanne française d' aujourd' hui*, Gonthier
ALLEN S and WOLKOWITZ C (1987) *Homeworking: myths and realities*,
Macmillan
ALLEN S, PURCELL K, WATON A and WOODS S (eds) (1986) *The
Experience of Unemployment*, Macmillan
ALTHUSSER L (1971) *Lenin and Philosophy and Other Essays*, New Left Books
ALZON C (1973) *La femme potiche ... et la femme bonniche*, Maspero
ANYON J (1983) 'Intersections of gender and class: accommodation and resistance
by working-class and affluent females to contradictory sex-role ideologies', in
S Walker and L Barton (eds) *Gender, Class and Education*, Falmer Press
ATKINSON A B (ed.) (1973) *Wealth, Income and Inequality*, Penguin
ATKINSON A B and HARRISON A J (1978) *The Distribution of Personal
Wealth in Britain*, Cambridge University Press
ATKINSON T-G (1974) *Amazon Odyssey*, Link Books
BACHARACH M (1976) *Economics and the Theory of Games*, Macmillan
BAILYN L (1978) 'Accommodation to working life', in Rh Rapoport and
R Rapoport (eds) *Working Couples*, Routledge and Kegan Paul
BALBO L (1987a) 'The servicing role of women in the capitalist state', *Political
Power and Social Theory*, vol. 3, pp. 251–70
—— (1987b) 'Crazy quilts: rethinking the welfare state debate from a woman's
point of view', in A Showstack Sassoon (ed.) *Women and the State*, Hutchinson
BALLARD R (1982) 'South Asian families', in R Rapoport, M Fogarty and Rh
Rapoport (eds) *Families in Britain*, Routledge and Kegan Paul

BANKS O (1956) 'Continuous shift work: the attitudes of wives', *Occupational Psychology*, vol. 30(2), pp. 69–84
BARRETT M (1980) *Women's Oppression Today: problems in marxist feminist analysis*, Verso
BARRETT M and McINTOSH M (1979) 'Christine Delphy: towards a materialist feminism?' *Feminist Review*, no. 1, pp. 95–106
—— (1980) 'The family wage: some problems for socialists and feminists', *Capital and Class*, no. 11
—— (1982) *The Antisocial Family*, Verso
BARRON J, CRAWLEY G and WOOD T (1987) *Married to the council: the private costs of public service*, Bristol Polytechnic, Report to Leverhulme Trust
BARROW J (1982) 'West Indian families: an insider's perspective', in R Rapoport, M Fogarty and Rh Rapoport (eds) *Families in Britain*, Routledge and Kegan Paul
BARTHELEMY D, BARTHEZ A and LABAT P (1984) 'Patrimoine foncier et exploitation agricole', SCEES, Paris, Octobre, pp. 37–51
BARTHEZ A (1981) 'Le rapport familial dans l'agriculture', document de recherche, INRA-Dijon
—— (1982) *Famille, travail et agriculture*, Economica, Paris
—— (1983) 'Le travail familial et les rapports de domination en agriculture', *Nouvelles Questions Féministes*, no. 5
—— (1985) 'La famille et le travail dans l'agriculture, une question de méthode', note, INRA-Dijon
BASTIDE G and GIRARD A (1959) 'Le budget-temps de la femme mariée à la campagne', *Population*, no. 6
BASTIDE H (1969) 'Les rurales', *La Nef*, no. 38
BEAUVOIR S de (1949) *Le deuxième sexe*, 2 vols, Gallimard, trans 1953, reprinted 1972 as *The Second Sex*, Penguin
BECHHOFER F (1986) 'Gender and stratification: some general remarks', in R Crompton and M Mann (eds) *Gender and Stratification*, Polity Press
BECHHOFER F and ELLIOTT B (eds) (1981) *The Petite Bourgeoisie: comparative studies of the uneasy stratum*, Macmillan
BECKER G S (1965) 'A Theory of the allocation of time', *Economic Journal*, 75
—— (1976) *The Economic Approach to Human Behavior*, University of Chicago Press
—— (1981) *A Treatise on the Family*, Harvard University Press
BECOUARN M-C (1979) *Le travail des femmes d'exploitants dans l'agriculture et l'evolution des techniques. Etude de la répartition et des charactéristiques des tâches dans les exploitations agricoles spécialisées*, Université de Tours
BEECHEY V (1977) 'Some notes on female wage labour in capitalist production', *Capital and Class*, no. 3, Autumn, pp. 45–66
—— (1979) 'On patriarchy', *Feminist Review*, no. 3, pp. 66–82
—— (1985) 'Familial ideology', in V Beechey and J Donald (eds) *Subjectivity and Social Relations*, Open University Press
—— (1987) *Unequal Work*, Verso

BEECHEY V and DONALD J (eds) (1985) *Subjectivity and Social Relations*, Open University Press

BEECHEY V and WHITELEGG E (eds) (1986) *Women in Britain Today*, Open University Press

BEER U (1984) *Theorien geschlectlicher Arbeitsteilung*, Campus Verlag, Frankfurt

BELL C and NEWBY H (1976) 'Husbands and wives: the dynamics of the deferential dialectic', in D Leonard Barker and S Allen (eds) *Dependence and Exploitation in Work and Marriage*, Hutchinson

BELL C and ROBERTS H (eds) (1984) *Social Researching: politics, problems and practice*, Routledge and Kegan Paul

BENET M K (1972) *Secretary: an enquiry into the female ghetto*, Sidgwick and Jackson

BENJAMIN J (1978) 'Authority and the family revisited: or, a world without fathers?' in *New German Critique*, no. 13, Winter

BENSTON M (1969) 'The political economy of women's liberation', *Monthly Review*, vol. 21(4), September, reprinted in L Tanner (ed.) (1970) *Voices from Women's Liberation*, Signet

BERGER M, FOSTER M and WALLSTON B S (1978) 'Finding two jobs', in Rh Rapoport and R Rapoport (eds) *Working Couples*, Routledge and Kegan Paul

BERK R and BERK S F (1979) *Labor and Leisure at Home: content and organization of the household day*, Sage

BERK S Fenstermaker (ed.) (1980) *Women and Household Labor*, Sage

—— (1985) *The Gender Factory: the apportionment of work in American households*, Plenum

BERMANT C (1974) *The Walled Garden: the saga of Jewish family life and tradition*, Weidenfeld and Nicolson

BERNARD Jessie (1949) *American Community Behavior*, Holt and Co

BERTAUX D and BERTAUX-WIAME I (1981) 'Artisanal bakery in France: how it lives and how it survives', in F Bechhofer and B Elliott (eds) *The Petite Bourgeoisie*, Macmillan

BEURET K (1991) 'Women and transport', in M Maclean and D Groves (eds) *Women's Issues in Social Policy*, Routledge

BEYNON H (1973) *Working for Ford*, Penguin

BIRNBAUM B G and FERBER M A (1977) 'The "new home economics": retrospects and prospects', *J of Consumer Research*, 4, June, pp. 19–28

BLATCHFORD R (1894) *Merrie England*

BLOCH M (1964) *Feudal Society*, 2 vols, Routledge

BOSE C (1979) 'Technology and changes in the division of labor in the American home', *Women's Studies International Quarterly*, vol. 2, pp. 295–304

BOSS H (1990) *Theories of Surplus and Transfer: parasites and producers in economic thought*, Unwin Hyman

BOTT E (1957) *Family and Social Network*, Tavistock

BOURDIEU P (1972) 'Les stratégies matrimoniales dans le système des strategies de reproduction', *Annales Economies Sociétés Civilisations*, no. spécial, Famille et Société, 4–5, juil–oct, trans 1976 as 'Marriage strategies as strategies of social reproduction' in R Forster and P Ranum (eds) *Family and Society: selections from the Annales*, Johns Hopkins University Press

BOURDIEU P and PASSERON J-C (1964) *Les héritiers: les étudiants et la culture*, Editions de Minuit

—— (1970) *La Reproduction*, Editions de Minuit, trans 1977 as *Reproduction in Education, Society and Culture*, Sage

BOURGEOIS F, BRENER J, CHABAUD D, COT A, FOUGEYROLLAS D, HAICAULT M and KARTCHEVSKY-BULPORT A (1978) 'Travail domestique et famille du capitalisme', *Critique de l'Economie Politique*, Série no. 3

BRANCA P (1975) *Silent Sisterhood: middle class women in the Victorian home*, Croom Helm

BRANNEN J (1987) 'The resumption of employment after childbirth: a turning-point within a life-course perspective', in P Allatt et al. (eds) *Women and the Life Cycle*, Macmillan

BRANNEN J and MOSS P (1990) *Managing Mothers: dual earner households after maternity leave*, Unwin Hyman

BRANNEN J and WILSON G (eds) (1987) *Give and Take in Families: studies in resource distribution*, Allen and Unwin

BRITTAIN J A (1978) *Inheritance and the Inequality of Material Wealth*, Brookings Institute

BROWN C (1981) 'Mothers, fathers and children: from private to public patriarchy', in L Sargent (ed.) *Women and Revolution: the unhappy marriage of marxism and feminism*, Pluto Press

BROWN C (1984) *Black and White in Britain: the third PSI survey*, Gower

BROWN G W and HARRIS T (1978) *Social Origins of Depression: a study of psychiatric disorder in women*, Tavistock

BRUEGEL I (1979) 'Women as a reserve army of labour: a note on recent British experience', *Feminist Review*, no. 3, pp. 12–32

BURMAN S (ed.) (1979) *Fit Work for Women*, Croom Helm

BURNS S (1975) *The Household Economy*, Beacon Press

CAMERON D and FRAZER E (1987) *The Lust to Kill: a feminist investigation of sexual murder*, Polity

CAZAURANG J-J (1968) *Pasteurs et paysans béarnais*, Marimpouey

CHABAUD D and FOUGEYROLLAS D (1984) 'A propos de l'autonomie relative de la production et de la reproduction', in Collective, *Le sexe du travail*, Presses Universitaires de Grenoble

CHADEAU A (1985) 'Measuring household activities: some international comparisons', *Review of Income and Wealth*, September

CHADEAU A and FOUQUET A (1981) 'Peut-on mesurer le travail domestique?' *Economie et Statistique*, Septembre

CHADEAU A and ROY C (1986) 'Relating household final consumption to household activities: substitutability or complementarity between market and non market production', *Review of Income and Wealth*, December

CHARLES L and DUFFIN L (eds) (1985) *Women and Work in Pre-industrial England*, Croom Helm

CHARLES N (1990) 'Food and family ideology', in C Harris (ed.) *Family, Economy and Community*, University of Wales Press

CHARLES N and KERR M (1987) 'Just the way it is: gender and age differences in family food consumption', in J Brannen and G Wilson (eds) *Give and Take in Families*, Allen and Unwin

—— (1988) *Women, Food and Families*, Manchester University Press

CHESTER R (1986) 'The conventional family is alive and living in Britain', in J Weekes (ed.) *Family Directory: information resources on the family*, British Library Information Guide 1

CLARK Alice (1919) *Working Life of Women in the Seventeenth Century*, Routledge and Kegan Paul, reprinted 1982

CLARK C (1958) 'The economics of house-work', *Bulletin of the Oxford University Institute of Economics and Statistics*, 20, May, pp. 205–12

CLINE S and SPENDER D (1988) *Reflecting Men at Twice their Natural Size: why women work hard at making men feel good*, Fontana

COHEN G (1978) 'Women's solidarity and the preservation of privilege', in P Caplan and J M Bujra (eds) *Women United, Women Divided: cross-cultural perspectives on female solidarity*, Tavistock

COMER L (1974) *Wedlocked Women*, Feminist Books

CORRIGAN P (1990) 'Capitalistic relics or feudal monuments?' in his *Social Forms/Human Capacities – essays in authority and difference*, Routledge

COULSON M, MAGAS B and WAINWRIGHT H (1975) '''The housewife and her labour under capitalism'' – a critique', *New Left Review*, 89, pp. 59–71

COWARD R (1983) *Patriarchal Precedents*, Routledge and Kegan Paul

CROMPTON R and MANN M (eds) (1986) *Gender and Stratification*, Polity Press

CULLEN I (1974) 'A day in the life of . . .', *New Society*, 11 April, pp. 63–5

CURTIS R F (1986) 'Household and family in theory on inequality', *American Sociological Review*, 51, pp. 168–83

DALLA COSTA M (1972) 'Women and the subversion of the community', *Radical America*, vol. 6(1), Jan–Feb, reprinted in M Dalla Costa and S James (1972, new edition with foreword 1975) *The Power of Women and the Subversion of the Community*, Falling Wall Press, Bristol.

DAVIDOFF L (1973a) *The Best Circles: society, etiquette and the season*, Croom Helm

—— (1973b) talk to BSA Sexual Divisions Study Group

—— (1976) 'The rationalization of housework', in D Leonard Barker and S Allen (eds) *Dependence and Exploitation in Work and Marriage*, Hutchinson

—— (1979) 'The separation of home and work? Landladies and lodgers in nineteenth and twentieth-century England', in S Burman (ed.) *Fit Work For Women*, Croom Helm

DAVIDOFF L and HALL C (1987) *Family Fortunes: men and women of the English middle class 1780–1850*, Hutchinson

DAVIDOFF L, L'ESPERANCE J and NEWBY H (1976) 'Landscape with figures', in J Mitchell and A Oakley (eds) *The Rights and Wrongs of Women*, Penguin

DAVIDSON C (1982) *A Woman's Work is Never Done: a history of housework in the British Isles, 1650–1950*, Chatto and Windus

DEEM R (1986) *All Work and No Play: the sociology of women and leisure*, Open University Press

DELPHY C (1969) 'Le patrimoine et la double circulation des biens dans l'espace économique et le temps familial', *Revue français de sociologie*, vol. 10, pp. 664–86

—— (1970) 'L'ennemi principal', *Partisans*, nos 54–5, July–Oct, translated and available in mimeo 1974, reprinted in Delphy 1984

—— (1974) 'La famille et la fonction de consommation', *Cahiers Internationaux de Sociologie*, pp. 23–41, trans 1979 in C Harris et al. (eds) *The Sociology of the Family*, Sociological Review Monograph no. 28, and reprinted in Delphy 1984

—— (1976a) 'Continuities and discontinuities in marriage and divorce', in D Leonard Barker and S Allen (eds) *Sexual Divisions and Society*, Tavistock, and reprinted in Delphy 1984

—— (1976b) 'Protofeminisme et antifeminisme', *Les Temps Modernes*, no. 346, pp. 1469–500, trans in Delphy 1984

—— (1976c) 'La transmission du statut à Chardonneret', *Ethnologie Française*, vol. 4 (1–2)

—— (1977) 'Nos amis et nous', *Questions Féministes*, no. 1, trans in Delphy 1984

—— (1978) 'Travail ménager ou travail domestique?' in A Michel (ed.) *Les femmes dans la société marchande*, Presses Universitaires de France, trans in Delphy 1984

—— (1980) 'A materialist feminism *is* possible', *Feminist Review*, no. 3, also in Delphy 1984

—— (1981) 'Le patriarcat, le feminisme et leurs intellectuelles', *Nouvelles Questions Féministes*, no. 2, Oct, trans in Delphy 1984

—— (1983) 'Agriculture et travail domestique: la réponse de la bergère à Engels', *Nouvelles Questions Féministes*, no. 5, Spring

—— (1984) *Close To Home: a materialist analysis of women's oppression*, Hutchinson

—— (1989a) 'La revendication maternelle', Cahiers CRF/UQUAM, pp. 11–28

—— (1989b) 'Sex and gender', paper presented to the International Seminar on Women's Studies, National Women's Education Centre, Japan

—— (forthcoming) *Travail professionnel invisible des femmes*, report by the Centre National de la Recherche Scientifique, Paris

DELPHY C and LEONARD D (1986) 'Class analysis, gender analysis and the family', in R Crompton and M Mann (eds) *Gender and Stratification*, Polity

DEN HARTOG A P (1973) 'Unequal distribution of food within the household', *FAO Newsletter*, 10(4), Oct–Dec

DENNIS N, HENRIQUES F and SLAUGHTER C (1969) *Coal is Our Life: an analysis of a Yorkshire mining community*, Tavistock

DEX S (1985) *The Sexual Division of Work: conceptual revolutions in the social sciences*, Harvester

DHAVERNAS O (1985) *Le partage professionnel dans l'enterprise conjugale: travail familial et discours juridique*, Rapport au CNRS (ATP Recherches féministes)

DICKINSON J and RUSSELL B (1986) *Family, Economy and State: the social reproduction process under capitalism*, Croom Helm

DOBASH R E and DOBASH R (1980) *Violence Against Wives: a case against the patriarchy*, Open Books

DURAN M A (1987) *De Puertas Adentro*, Instituto de la Mujer, Ministerio de Cultura, Madrid

—— (1989) 'El dualismo de la economía española. Una approximacíon a la economía no mercantil', *Revista de Informacíon Comercial Española*, pp. 9–25

—— (1991) 'La Economía y el Tiempo', *Información Comercial Española*, Julio

DWORKIN A (1983) *Right Wing Women: the politics of domesticated females*, The Women's Press

DYHOUSE C (1989) *Feminism and the Family in England, 1880–1939*, Blackwell

EDGELL S (1980) *Middle-Class Couples: a study of domination and inequality in marriage*, George Allen and Unwin

EDHOLM F (1982) 'The unnatural family', in E Whitelegg et al. (eds) *The Changing Experience of Women*, Martin Robertson

EDHOLM F, HARRIS O and YOUNG K (1977) 'Conceptualising women', *Critique of Anthropology*, vol. 3, pp. 101–30

EDWARDS M (1981) *Financial Arrangements Within Families*, National Women's Advisory Council, Canberra

EEKELAAR J and MACLEAN M (1986) *Maintenance After Divorce*, Oxford University Press

EHRENREICH B (1983) *The Hearts of Men: American dreams and the flight from commitment*, Pluto Press

EHRENREICH B and ENGLISH D (1979) *For Her Own Good: 150 years of the experts' advice to women*, Pluto Press

EICHLER M (1981) 'Power, dependency, love and the sexual division of labour', *Women's Studies International Quarterly*, vol. 4(2), pp. 201–19

EISENSTEIN H (1984) *Contemporary Feminist Thought*, Unwin

EISENSTEIN Z R (ed.) (1979) *Capitalist Patriarchy and the Case for Socialist Feminism*, Monthly Review Press

ENGELS F (1884/1972) *Origins of the Family, Private Property and the State*, reprinted, edited and with an introduction by E B Leacock, Lawrence and Wishart

EOC (EQUAL OPPORTUNITIES COMMISSION) (1988) *Women and Men in Britain: a research profile*, HMSO

EPSTEIN C Fuchs (1970) *Woman's Place: options and limits in professional careers*, University of California Press

—— (1971) 'Law Partners and Marital Partners: strains and solutions in the dual-career family enterprise', *Human Relations*, vol. 24(6), pp. 549–64

FAGIN L and LITTLE M (1984) *The Forsaken Families, The effects of unemployment on family life*, Penguin

FAO/WHO Expert Committee (1973) *Energy and Protein Requirements*, FAO, Rome

FARRIS A (1978) 'Commuting', in Rh Rapoport and R Rapoport (eds) *Working Couples*, Routledge and Kegan Paul

FEMINIST REVIEW (1990) *Perverse Politics: lesbian issues*, no. 34, Spring

FEMINIST REVIEW COLLECTIVE (1987) *Sexuality: a reader*, Virago

FERCHIOU S (1968) 'Différençiation sexuelle de l'alimentation au Djerid (sud tunisien)', *L'homme*, ler trimestre

FERGUSON A (1989) *Blood at the Root: motherhood, sexuality and male dominance*, Pandora

FILIPPI G and NICOURT C (1987) 'Domestique-professionnel: la cohérence du travail des femmes des exploitations agricoles familiales', *Economie Rurale*, no. 178–9

FINCH J (1983) *Married to the Job*, George Allen and Unwin

—— (1989) *Family Obligations and Social Change*, Polity

FINER M and McGREGOR O R (1974) 'The history of the obligation to maintain', appendix 5 to vol. 2 of DHSS *Report of the Committee on One-Parent Families*, HMSO, Cmnd 5629

FIRESTONE S (1970) *The Dialectic of Sex: the case for feminist revolution*, reprinted Paladin 1972

FIRESTONE S and KOEDT A (eds) (1970) *Notes from the Second Year*, Notes From the Second Year Publications, New York, pp. 68–72

FLANDRIN J (1979) *Families in Former Time: kinship, household and sexuality*, Cambridge University Press

FOREMAN A (1977) *Femininity as Alienation: women and the family in marxism and psychoanalysis*, Pluto Press

FOUGEYROLLAS D (n.d.) 'Le travail domestique', Mémoire pour le Diplome d'Etudes Superieures, Unpublished thesis, University of Paris 1

FOWLKES M R (1980) *Behind Every Successful Man: wives of medicine and academe*, Columbia University Press

FOX B (ed.) (1980) *Hidden in the Household: women's domestic labour under capitalism*, The Women's Press, Toronto

FRANK A Gunder (1967) *Capitalism and Underdevelopment in Latin America*, Monthly Review Press

FRANKENBERG R (1976) ' "In the production of their lives, men(?)": sex and gender in British community studies', in D Leonard Barker and S Allen (eds) *Sexual Divisions and Society*, Tavistock

FREUDENTHAL M (1986) *Gestaltwandel der Stadtischen und Proletarischen Hauswirtschaft zwischen 1760 und 1910*, Ullstein Materialen, Frankfurt

FRIEDAN Betty (1963) *The Feminine Mystique*, Penguin

FRIEDMAN S (1982) 'The marxist paradigm: radical feminist theorists compared', mimeo, paper to BSA annual conference

FRYE M (1983) *The Politics of Reality: essays in feminist theory*, The Crossing Press

GALBRAITH J K (1973) 'The economics of the American housewife', *Atlantic Monthly*, August, which is excerpted in Galbraith (1974)

—— (1974) *Economics and the Public Purpose*, Andre Deutsch

GAMARNIKOW E, MORGAN D, PURVIS J and TAYLORSON D (eds) (1981) *The Public and the Private*, Heinemann

GAME A and PRINGLE R (1984) *Gender at Work*, Pluto Press

GARDINER J (1975) 'Women's domestic labour', *New Left Review*, no. 89, Jan–Feb

—— (1976) 'Domestic labour in capitalist society', in D Leonard Barker and S Allen (eds) *Dependence and Exploitation in Work and Marriage*, Hutchinson

—— (1978) 'Women in the labour process', in A Hunt (ed.) *Class and Class Structure*, Lawrence and Wishart

GARDINER J, HIMMELWEIT S and MACKINTOSH M (1975) 'Women's domestic labour', *Bulletin of the Conference of Socialist Economists*, vol. 4(2)

—— (1976) *On the Political Economy of Women*, CSE Pamphlet no. 2, Stage 1

GASSON R (1981) *The Role of Women in British Agriculture*, The Women's Farms and Gardens Association / Wye College

GAVRON H (1966) *The Captive Wife: conflicts of housebound mothers*, Routledge and Kegan Paul

GENOVESE E (1972) *Roll, Jordan, Roll: the world the slaves made*, Vintage Books

GERSHUNY J (1978) *After Industrial Society?*, Macmillan

—— (1983) *Social Innovation and the Division of Labour*, Oxford University Press

GERSTEIN I (1973) 'Domestic work and capitalism', *Radical America*, vol. 7(4–5)

GIDDENS A (1979) *The Class Structure of the Advanced Societies*, Hutchinson

GILLESPIE D (1972) 'Who has the power? the marital struggle', in H P Dreitzel (ed.) *Family, Marriage and the Struggle of the Sexes*, Collier Macmillan

GILLIS J (1985) *For Better, For Worse: British marriages, 1600 to the present*, Oxford University Press

GLASTONBURY Marion (1978) 'Holding the pens', in S Elbert and M Glastonbury, *Inspiration and Drudgery*, Women's Research and Resources Centre pamphlet

GLAZER-MALBIN N (1976) 'Housework', *Signs*, vol. 1(4), pp. 905–21

GLAZER-MALBIN N and WAEHRER H Y (eds) (1972) *Woman in a Man-Made World*, Rand McNally

GLENDENNING C and MILLAR J (1991) 'Poverty: the forgotten English-woman', in M Maclean and D Groves (eds) *Women's Issues in Social Policy*, Routledge

GLENDON M A (1981) *The New Family and the New Property*, Butterworth

GOFFEE R and SCASE R (1985) *Women in Charge: the experience of female entrepreneurs*, George Allen and Unwin

GOLDTHORPE J H, LOCKWOOD D, BECHHOFER F and PLATT J (1968a) *The Affluent Worker: industrial attitudes and behaviour*, Cambridge University Press

—— (1968b) *The Affluent Worker: political attitudes and behaviour*, Cambridge University Press

—— (1971) *The Affluent Worker in the Class Structure*, Cambridge University Press
GOODE W J (1981) 'Why men resist', in B Thorne and M Yalom (eds) *Rethinking the Family: some feminist questions*, Longman, NY
GOODY J (1976) *Production and Reproduction*, Cambridge University Press
—— (1983) *The Development of the Family and Marriage in Europe*, Cambridge University Press
GOODY J B, THIRSK J and THOMPSON E P (eds) (1976) *Family and Inheritance: rural society in Western Europe 1200–1800*, Cambridge University Press
GRACE J (1975) *Domestic Slavery in West Africa*, Frederick Muller
GREATER LONDON COUNCIL (1987) *Women with Disabilities*, London Strategic Planning Unit, vol. 9, LSPU
GREATER LONDON COUNCIL Women's Committee (1984) *Women on the Move*, GLC
GREEN E and HEBRON S (1988) 'Leisure and male partners', in E Wimbush and M Talbot (eds) *Relative Freedoms*, Open University Press
GREEN E and WOODWARD D (1988) 'Not tonight dear: the social control of women's leisure', in E Wimbush and M Talbot (eds) *Relative Freedoms*, Open University Press
GREEN E, HEBRON S and WOODWARD D (1990) *Women's Leisure, What Leisure?*, Macmillan
GREY A (1979) 'The working class family as an economic unit', in C Harris et al. (eds) *The Sociology of the Family*, Sociological Review Monograph no. 28
GRIMLER G and ROY C (1987) *Time Use in France in 1985–1986*, INSEE (Institut National de la Statistique et des Études Économique), Premiers Resultats, no. 100, Version anglaise, Oct
GROVES D (1991) 'Women and financial provision for old age', in M Maclean and D Groves (eds) *Women's Issues in Social Policy*, Routledge
HALL Catherine (1979) 'The early formation of Victorian domestic ideology', in S Burman (ed.) *Fit Work For Women*, Croom Helm
HAMILL L (1979) *Wives as Sole and Joint Breadwinners*, Government Economic Service Working Paper no. 15, HMSO
HAMILTON C (1912) *Marriage as a Trade*, Chapman and Hall
HAMILTON P (1985) 'Agricultural work', in R Deem and G Salaman (eds) *Work, Culture and Society*, Open University Press
HAMILTON R (1978) *The Liberation of Women: a study of patriarchy and capitalism*, George Allen and Unwin
HANMER Jalna (1978) 'Violence and the social control of women', in G Littlejohn et al. (eds) *Power and the State*, Croom Helm
HARBURY C D (1962) 'Inheritance and the distribution of personal wealth in Britain', *Economic Journal*, vol. 72, pp. 845–68
HARBURY C D and HITCHENS D (1979) *Inheritance and Wealth Inequality in Britain*, George Allen and Unwin
HARRIS C C (1983) *The Family and Industrial Society*, George Allen and Unwin
—— (ed.) (1990) *Family, Economy and Community*, University of Wales Press

HARRIS C C and MORRIS L (1986) 'Households, labour markets and the position of women', in R Crompton and M Mann (eds) *Gender and Stratification*, Polity, pp. 86–96
HARRIS C C et al. (eds) (1979) *The Sociology of the Family: new directions for Britain*, Sociological Review Monograph no. 28
—— (1987) *Redundancy and Recession*, Blackwell
HARRIS O (1981) 'Households as natural units', in K Young et al. (eds) *Of Marriage and the Market: women's subordination in international perspective*, CSE Books
HARRISON J (1973) 'The political economy of housework', *Bulletin of the C.S.E.*, Winter, pp. 35–51
HARTMAN M and BANNER L-W (eds) (1974) *Clio's Consciousness Raised: new perspectives on the history of women*, Harper Colophon Books, NY
HARTMANN H (1974) 'Capitalism and Women's Work in the Home, 1990–1930', Phd thesis, Yale University
—— (1976) 'Capitalism, patriarchy and job segregation by sex', *Signs*, 1 no. 3, part 2, Spring, reprinted 1979 in Z Eisenstein (ed.) *Capitalist Patriarchy and the Case for Socialist Feminism*, Monthly Review Press
—— (1979) 'The unhappy marriage of marxism and feminism: towards a more progressive union', *Capital and Class*, Summer, revised version reprinted 1981 in L Sargent (ed.) *Women and Revolution*, South End Press
—— (1981) 'The family as the locus of gender, class and political struggle: the example of housework', *Signs*, 6, pp. 366–94
HAYDEN D (1981) *The Grand Domestic Revolution: a history of feminist designs for American homes, neighbourhoods and cities*, MIT Press
HERNES H (1987) *Women, Power and the Welfare State*, Norwegian Universities Press
HERTZ R (1986) *More Equal than Others: women and men in dual-career marriages*, University of California Press
HIMMELWEIT S and MOHUN S (1977) 'Domestic labour and capital', *Cambridge Journal of Economics*, vol. 1(1)
HITE S (1976) *The Hite Report: a nationwide study of female sexuality*, Macmillan
—— (1981) *The Hite Report on Male Sexuality*, Alfred Knopf
—— (1988) *Women and Love: a cultural revolution in progress*, Viking
HOCHSCHILD A Russell (1983) *The Managed Heart: the commercialization of human feelings*, University of California Press
HORKHEIMER M (1936) *Studien uber Autoritat und Familie*, Felix Alcan, trans 1972 in *Critical Theory*, J Cummings, NY
HUMPHRIES J (1977) 'Class struggle and the persistence of the working class family', *Cambridge Journal of Economics*, September
HUNT Alan (ed.) (1978) *Class and Class Structure*, Lawrence and Wishart
HUNT Audrey (1968) *A Survey of Women's Employment*, HMSO
HUNT P (1980) *Gender and Class Consciousness*, Macmillan
INSEE (Institut National de la Statistique et des Études Économique) (1987) *Données Sociales 1987*, abstracts

JAGGAR A (1983) *Feminist Politics and Human Nature*, Harvester Press
JALLAND P (1986) *Women, Marriage and Politics, 1860–1914*, Oxford University Press
JÉGOUZO G (1972) 'L'ampleur du célibat en agriculture', *Économie et Statistique*, no. 34
—— (1977) *Avec qui se marient les paysans?*, INRA, Rennes
JOSHI H (1989) 'The changing form of women's economic dependency', in H Joshi (ed.) *The Changing Population of Britain*, Blackwell
—— (1991) 'Sex and motherhood as handicaps in the labour market', in M Maclean and D Groves (eds) *Women's Issues in Social Policy*, Routledge
KALUZYNSKA E (1980) 'Wiping the floor with theory – a survey of writings on housework', *Feminist Review*, no. 6
KEATING N C and COLE P (1980) 'What do I do with him 24 hours a day?: changes in the housewife's role after retirement', *Gerontologist*, vol. 20, Feb, pp. 84–9
KERGOAT D (1982) *Les ouvrières*, Le Sycomore, Paris
KERR M and CHARLES N (1986) 'Servers and providers: the distribution of food within the family', *Sociological Review*, vol. 34(1), pp. 115–57
KIRK P (1980) 'Owing to a family crisis . . .', *New Society*, 17 Jan, pp. 119–20
KITTLER G (1980) *Hausarbeit: zur geschichte einer 'Natur-Resource'*, Frauenoffensive, Munich
KLEIN V (1946) *The Feminine Character: history of an ideology*, Routledge and Kegan Paul, 2nd edn 1971
—— (1965) *Britain's Married Women Workers*, Routledge and Kegan Paul
KOMAROVSKY M (1962) *Blue Collar Marriage*, Random House, reprinted 1987 Yale University Press
KUHN A and WOLPE A-M (eds) (1978) *Feminism and Materialism: women and modes of production*, Routledge and Kegan Paul
KUSSMAUL A (1978) 'Servants in Husbandry in Early Modern England', PhD thesis, University of Toronto
LAGRAVE R-M (ed.) (1987a) *Celles de la terre*, Ecole des Hautes Etudes en Science Sociales, Paris
—— (1987b) 'L'agricultrice inclassable', in R-M Lagrave (ed.) *Celles de la terre*, Ecole des Hautes Etudes en Science Sociales
LAGRAVE R-M and CANIOU J (1987) 'Un statut mis à l'index', in R-M Lagrave (ed.) *Celles de la terre*, Ecole des Hautes Etudes en Science Sociales
LAING R D (1965) *The Divided Self*, Penguin
—— (1970) *Sanity, Madness and the Family*, Penguin
LAJUS M T (1969) 'Pour l'alimentation des veaux une agricultrice du bocage normand peut s'organiser sans grands frais', *Enterprise Agricole*, no. 6
LAND H (1976) 'Women: supporters or supported?' in D Leonard Barker and S Allen (eds) *Sexual Divisions and Society*, Tavistock
—— (1977) 'The child benefit fiasco', in K Jones et al. (eds) *The Year Book of Social Policy 1976*, Routledge and Kegan Paul
—— (1978) 'Who cares for the family?' *Journal of Social Policy*, vol. 7, part 3, July, pp. 257–84

—— (1983) 'Who still cares for the family?' in J Lewis (ed.) *Women's Welfare/ Women's Rights*, Croom Helm

LARGUIA I (1970) 'Contre le travail invisible', *Partisans*, nos 54–5, July–Oct, Maspero, Paris

LARGUIA I and DUMOLIN J (n.d. c.1973) *Towards a Science of Women's Liberation*, Red Rag pamphlet no. 1

LASLETT B (1973) 'The family as public and private institution: a historical perspective', *J of Marriage and the Family*, no. 35

LECLERC A (1974) *Parole de femme*, Grasset

LEMENNICIER B (1988) *Le marché du mariage et de la famille*, Presses Universitaires de France

LEONARD D (1980) *Sex and Generation: a study of courtship and weddings*, Tavistock

—— (1986) 'Women in the family: companions or caretakers?' in V Beechey and E Whitelegg (eds) *Women in Britain Today*, Open University Press

—— (1990) 'Sex and generation revisited', in C C Harris (ed.) *Family, Economy and Community*, University of Wales Press

LEONARD BARKER D (1978) 'Repressive benevolence: the regulation of marriage', in J Littlejohn et al. (eds) *Power and the State*, Croom Helm

LEONARD BARKER D and ALLEN S (eds) (1976a) *Sexual Divisions and Society; process and change*, Tavistock

—— (1976b) *Dependence and Exploitation in Work and Marriage*, Longman

LEONARDO M di (1987) 'The female world of cards and holidays: women, families and the work of kinship', *Signs*, vol. 12(3), pp. 440–53

LEWIS Jane (1984) *Women in England: 1870–1950*, Wheatsheaf

—— (ed.) (1986) *Labour and Love: women's experience of home and family 1850–1940*, Blackwell

LITTLEJOHN J (1963) *Westrigg: the sociology of a Cheviot parish*, Routledge and Kegan Paul

LITTLEJOHN G, SMART B, WAKEFORD J and YUVAL-DAVIS N (eds) (1978) *Power and the State*, Croom Helm

LOPATA H Z (1971) *Occupation: Housewife*, Oxford University Press, NY

LORDE A (1984) 'Age, race, class and sex', in her collection *Sister Outsider*, The Crossing Press, pp. 114–23

LUMMIS T (1982) 'The historical dimension of fatherhood: a case study', in L McKee and M O'Brien (eds) *The Father Figure*, Tavistock

LUXTON M (1980) *More than a Labour of Love: three generations of women's work in the home*, The Women's Press, Toronto

McDONOUGH R and HARRISON R (1978) 'Patriarchy and relations of production', in A Kuhn and A-M Wolpe (eds) *Feminism and Materialism*, Routledge and Kegan Paul

McINTOSH M (1978) 'The state and the oppression of women', in A Kuhn and A-M Wolpe (eds) *Feminism and Materialism*, Routledge and Kegan Paul

McKEE L and BELL C (1985) 'His employment, her problem: the domestic and marital consequences of male unemployment', in S Allen et al. (eds) *The Experience of Unemployment*, Macmillan

McKENZIE R and TULLOCK G (1975) *The New World of Economics*, Richard Irwin
MACKIE L and PATTULLO P (1977) *Women at Work*, Tavistock
MACKINNON C (1987) *Feminism Unmodified: discourses on life and law*, Harvard University Press
MACKINTOSH M (1979) 'Domestic labour and the household', in S Burman (ed.) *Fit Work for Women*, Croom Helm
——— (1981) 'Gender and economics: the sexual division of labour and the subordination of women', in K Young et al. (eds) *Of Marriage and the Market*, CSE Books
MACLEAN M and GROVES D (eds) (1991) *Women's Issues in Social Policy*, Routledge
MACLEAN M and WEITZMAN L (eds) (1991) *Counting the Cost of Divorce*, Oxford University Press
MALOS E (ed.) (1980) *The Politics of Housework*, Allison and Busby
MARCEAU J (1976) 'Marriage, role division and social cohesion: the case of some French upper-middle class families', in D Leonard Barker and S Allen (eds) *Dependence and Exploitation in Work and Marriage*, Hutchinson
——— (1978) 'Le rôle des femmes dans les familles du monde des affaires', in A Michel (ed.) *Les femmes dans la société marchande*, Presses Universitaires de France, Paris
MARCZEWSKI J (1976) *Comtabilité nationale*, Dalloz, Paris
MARSDEN D and DUFF E (1975) *Workless: some unemployed men and their families*, Penguin
MARTIN J and ROBERTS C (1984) *Women and Employment: a lifetime perspective*, HMSO
MARTIN R and WALLACE J (1984) *Working Women in Recession: employment, redundancy and unemployment*, Oxford University Press
MARX K (1867/1970) *Capital*, vol. 1, Lawrence and Wishart
MASPÉTIOL R (1946) *L'ordre éternel des champs*, Librairie Médicis
MASS OBSERVATION (1957) *The Housewife's Day*, Bulletin no. 42, May / June
MAUSS M (1954) *The Gift: forms and functions of exchange in archaic societies*, trans I Cunnison 1954, Cohen and West, repub 1970, Routledge
MEAD M (1928) *Coming of Age in Samoa*, repub 1943, Penguin
——— (1930) *Growing Up in New Guinea*, repub 1942, Penguin
——— (1935) *Sex and Temperament in Three Primitive Societies*, William Morrow, NY
——— (1950) *Male and Female*, repub 1962, Penguin
MEILLASSOUX C (1975) *Femmes, greniers et capitaux*, trans 1981 as *Maidens, Meal and Money: capitalism and the domestic economy*, Cambridge University Press
MEISSNER M, HUMPHREYS W, MEIS S and SCHEU W (1975) 'No exit for wives: sexual division of labour and the cumulation of household demands in Canada', *Canadian Review of Sociology and Anthropology*, vol. 12(4), part 1

MELHUISH E and MOSS P (eds) (1991) *Day Care for Young Children: international perspectives*, Routledge

MENDRAS H (1976) *Sociétés paysannes*, A Colin, Paris

MICHEL A (1959) *Famille, industrialisation, logement*, CNRS

—— (1960) 'La femme dans la famille française', *Cahiers internationaux de sociologie*, no. 111, March–April

—— (1972) *Sociologie du mariage et de la famille*, Presses Universitaires de France, Paris

—— (1974) *The Modernization of North African Families in the Paris Area*, Mouton, Paris

—— (ed.) (1977) *Femmes, sexisme et sociétés*, Presses Universitaires de France, Paris

—— (ed.) (1978) *Les femmes dans la société marchande*, Presses Universitaires de France, Paris

MIDDLETON C (1974) 'Sexual inequality and stratification theory', in F Parkin (ed.) *The Social Analysis of Class Structure*, Tavistock

MIES M (1986) *Patriarchy and Accumulation on a World Scale: women in the international division of labour*, Zed Books

MIKES G (1983) 'Arthur and Cynthia', *Observer Review*, 7 August, p. 21

MILHAU J and MONTAGNE R (1968) *Economie rurale*, Presses Universitaires de France, Paris

MILLWARD N (1968) 'Family status and behaviour at work', *Sociological Review*, vol. 16(2), pp. 149–64

MINCER J and POLOCHEK S (1974) 'Family investment in human capital: earnings of women', in T Schutz (ed.) *Marriage, Family Human Capital, and Fertility*, University of Chicago Press

MITCHELL Juliet (1966) 'Women: the longest revolution', *New Left Review*, no. 40

—— (1975) *Psychoanalysis and Feminism*, Penguin

MITCHELL J and OAKLEY A (eds) (1976) *The Rights and Wrongs of Women*, Penguin

—— (eds) (1986) *What is Feminism?*, Blackwell

MOLYNEUX M (1979) 'Beyond the domestic labour debate', *New Left Review*, no. 16

MONTAGUE A (1952) *The Natural Superiority of Women*, Macmillan, NY

MORRIS Lydia (1984a) 'Patterns of social activity and post redundancy labour market experience', *Sociology*, vol. 18(3)

—— (1984b) 'Redundancy and patterns of household finance', *Sociological Review*, vol. 32(33)

—— (1984c) 'Responses to redundancy: labour-market experience, domestic organisation and male social networks', *Int J Soc Economics*, vol. 12(2), pp. 5–16

—— (1984d) 'Renegotiation of the sexual division of labour: a research note', *BJS*, vol. 35(4), pp. 606–7

—— (1985a) 'Local social networks and domestic organisation: a study of redundant steel workers and their wives', *Sociological Review*, vol. 33(2), May, pp. 327–42

—— (1985b) 'Renegotiation of the domestic division of labour in the context of male redundancy', in H Newby et al. (eds) *Restructuring Capital*, Macmillan
—— (1990) *The Workings of the Household*, Polity
MORRIS L D with RUANE S (1989) *Household Finance Management and the Labour Market*, Gower
MORRIS W (1890) *News From Nowhere*, 2nd edn 1924
MORTIMORE J, HALL R and HILL R (1978) 'Husbands' occupational attributes and constraints on wives' employment', *Sociology of Work and Occupation*, vol. 5(3), pp. 285–313
MORTON P (1970) 'A women's work is never done', *Leviathan*, vol. 2(1), pp. 32–7
MOSCOVICI M (1960) 'Le changement social en milieu rural et le rôle des femmes', *Revue française de sociologie*, 3, pp. 314–22
MOSER C A (1950) 'Social research: the diary method', *Social Service*, 24, pp. 80–4
MOSS P and FONDA N (1980) *Work and the Family*, Temple Smith
MURCOTT A (1982) '"Its a pleasure to cook for him": food, mealtimes and gender in some South Wales households', in E Gamarnikow et al. (eds) *The Public and the Private*, Heinemann
MYRDAL A and KLEIN V (1956) *Women's Two Roles: home and work*, Routledge and Kegan Paul
NAVA M (1983) 'From utopian to scientific feminism? Early feminist critiques of the family', in L Segal (ed.) *What is to be Done About the Family?*, Penguin
NEWBY H (1972) *The Deferential Worker*, Allen Lane
—— (1979 repub 1985) *Green and Pleasant Land? social change in rural England*, Wildwood House
NEWBY H, BELL C, ROSE D and SAUNDERS P (1978) *Property, Paternalism and Power*, Hutchinson
NEWBY H, ROSE D, SAUNDERS P and BELL C (1981) 'Farming for survival: the small farmer in the contemporary rural class structure', in F Bechhofer and B Elliot (eds) *The Petite Bourgeoisie*, Macmillan
NEWBY H, BUJRA J, LITTLEWOOD P, REES G and REES T L (eds) (1985) *Restructuring Capital: recession and reorganization in industrial society*, Macmillan
NISSEL M and BONNERJEA L (1982) *Family Care of the Handicapped Elderly: who pays?*, Policy Studies Institute, London
N.Y. RADICAL FEMINIST MANIFESTO (1970) in S Firestone and A Koedt (eds) *Notes From the Second Year*, Notes From the Second Year Publications
OAKLEY A (1972) 'Are husbands good housewives?' *New Society*, 17 Feb, pp. 337–40
—— (1974a) *Housewife*, Allen Lane
—— (1974b) *The Sociology of Housework*, Martin Robertson
O'BRIEN M (1983) *The Politics of Reproduction*, Routledge and Kegan Paul, Boston
OLAH S (1970) 'The economic function of the oppression of women', in S

Firestone and A Koedt (eds) *Notes From the Second Year*, Notes From the Second Year Publications

OREN L (1974) 'The welfare of women in laboring families: England 1860–1950', in M Hartman and L Banner (eds) *Clio's Consciousness Raised*, Harper Torchbooks

PAHL J (1983) 'The allocation of money and the structuring of inequality within marriage', *Sociological Review*, vol. 13(2)

—— (1990) *Money and Marriage*, Macmillan

PAHL R (1984) *Divisions of Labour*, Blackwell

—— (ed.) (1988) *On Work*, Blackwell

PATEMAN C (1988) *The Sexual Contract*, Polity

PERKINS GILMAN C (1903) *The Home: its work and influence*, reprinted 1972 by University of Illinois Press, Urbana

—— (1915) *Herland*, reprinted 1979 edited A Lane, Pantheon Books

—— (1966) *Women and Economics: a study of the economic relation between men and women as a factor in social evolution*, Harper Torchbooks

PHIZACKLEA A (1982) 'Migrant women and wage labour: the case of West Indian women in Britain', in J West (ed.) *Work, Women and the Labour Market*, Routledge and Kegan Paul

PHOENIX A (1987) 'Theories of gender and Black families', in G Weiner and M Arnot (eds) *Gender Under Scrutiny*, Hutchinson

PLATT J (1969) 'Some problems in measuring the jointness of conjugal role relationships', *Sociology*, December, pp. 287–97

—— (1971) *Social Research in Bethnal Green*, Macmillan

—— (1976) *The Realities of Social Research*, University of Sussex Press

—— (1984) 'The *Affluent Worker* revisited', in C Bell and H Roberts (eds) *Social Researching*, Routledge and Kegan Paul

PLECK J (1977) 'Husbands' participation and family roles: current research issues', in H Lopata and J Pleck (eds) *Research in the Interweave of Roles: families and jobs*, JAI Press, Greenwood

POLLACK R A (1985) 'A transaction cost approach to families and households', *J of Economic Literature*, 23, June, pp. 581–608

POLLERT A (1981) *Girls, Wives, Factory Lives*, Macmillan

PORTER M (1978a) 'Consciousness and secondhand experience: wives and husbands in industrial action', *Sociological Review*, vol. 26(2), May

—— (1978b) 'Worlds apart: the class consciousness of working class women', *Women's Studies International Forum*, vol. 1, pp. 175–88

—— (1982) 'Standing on the edge: working class wives in the labour market', in J West (ed.) *Work, Women and the Labour Market*, Routledge and Kegan Paul

—— (1983) *Home, Work and Class Consciousness*, Manchester University Press

POSTER M (1978) *Critical Theory of the Family*, Pluto Press

POULANTZAS N (1975) *Classes in Contemporary Capitalism*, New Left Books

PYUN Chong Soo (1972) 'The monetary value of a housewife', in N Glazer-Malbin and H Waehrer (eds) *Women in a Man-Made World*, Rand McNally

QUERSHI H and SIMONS K (1987) 'Resources within families: caring for elderly people', in J Brannen and G Wilson (eds) *Give and Take in Families*, Allen and Unwin

QUERSHI H and WALKER A (1989) *The Caring Relationship: elderly people and their families*, Macmillan

RAPOPORT Rh and RAPOPORT R (1971) *Dual-Career Families*, Penguin

—— (1976) *Dual-Career Families Re-examined*, Martin Robertson

—— (eds) (1978) *Working Couples*, Routledge and Kegan Paul

RATTIN S (1987) 'La place des femmes dans l'agriculture', *Economie Rurale*, no. 5, Mars–Juin, pp. 178–9

RAYMOND J (1986) *A Passion For Friends*, The Women's Press

REICH W (1969) *The Sexual Revolution*, Farrar, Strauss and Giroux

REX J and TOMLINSON S (1979) *Colonial Immigrants in a British City: a class analysis*, Routledge

RILEY D (1983) *War in the Nursery*, Virago

ROBERTS E (1984) *A Woman's Place: an oral history of working-class women 1890–1914*, Blackwell

ROBINSON J J (1977) *How Americans Use Time*, Praeger

ROGERS B (1988) *Men Only: an investigation into men's organisations*, Pandora

ROWBOTHAM S (1981) 'The trouble with "patriarchy"', in Feminist Anthology Collective (eds) *No Turning Back: writings from the Women's Liberation Movement 1975–1980*, The Women's Press

ROWNTREE B S (1902) *Poverty: a study of town life*, Macmillan

RUBIN G (1975) 'The traffic in women: notes on the "political economy" of sex', in R Rapp Reiter (ed.) *Toward an Anthropology of Women*, Monthly Review Press

—— (1984) 'Thinking sex: notes for a radical theory of the politics of sexuality', in C Vance (ed.) *Pleasure and Danger: exploring female sexuality*, Routledge and Kegan Paul

RUSHTON P (1979) 'Marxism, domestic labour and the capitalist economy: a note on recent discussions', in C C Harris et al. (eds) *The Sociology of the Family*, Sociological Review Monograph no. 28

RUSSELL G (1983) *The Changing Role of Fathers*, Open University Press

SALAMAN G (1971) 'Two occupational communities: examples of a remarkable convergence of work and non-work', *Sociological Review*, vol. 19, pp. 389–407

SARGENT L (ed.) (1981) *Women and Revolution: a discussion of the unhappy marriage of marxism and feminism*, South End Press, Boston

SAYERS J (1986) *Sexual Contradictions*, Tavistock

SCASE R and GOFFEE R (1980a) 'Home life in a small business', *New Society*, 30 October pp. 220–2

—— (1980b) *The Real World of the Small Business Owner*, Croom Helm

SCHUTZ T (ed.) (1974) *Marriage, Family, Human Capital, and Fertility*, University of Chicago Press

SCHWARTZ COWAN R (1983) *More Work for Mother: the ironies of household technology from the open hearth to the microwave*, Basic Books, NY

SECCOMBE W (1974) 'The housewife and her labour under capitalism', *New Left Review*, no. 83, pp. 3–24

—— (1975) 'Domestic labour – reply to critics', *New Left Review*, vol. 94, pp. 85–96

SEGAL L (1983) 'Smashing the family? Recalling the 1960s', in L Segal (ed.) *What is to be Done About the Family?* Penguin

SEGALEN M (1983) *Love and Power in the Peasant Family: rural France in the nineteenth century*, Blackwell

SEN A K (1982) *Choice, Welfare and Measurement*, Blackwell

—— (1983) 'Economics and the family', *Asian Development Review*, 1

—— (1984) 'Family and food: sex bias in poverty', in his *Resources, Values and Developments*, Blackwell

SHAMMAS C, SALMON M and DAHLIN M (1987) *Inheritance in America: from colonial times to the present*, Rutgers University Press

SHORTER E (1975) *The Making of the Modern Family*, Collins

SMART C (1989) *Feminism and the Power of the Law*, Routledge

SMITH D (1973) 'Women, the family and corporate capitalism', in M Stephenson (ed.) *Women in Canada*, New Press, Toronto

SMITH D J (1977) *Racial Disadvantage in Britain: the PEP report*, Penguin

SMITH P (1978) 'Domestic labour and Marx's theory of value', in A Kuhn and A-M Wolpe (eds) *Feminism and Materialism*, Routledge and Kegan Paul

SNELL M (1979) 'Equal pay and the sex discrimination acts: their impact in the workplace', *Feminist Review*, no. 1

Social Trends, HMSO, annually

SPENDER D (1980) *Man Made Language*, Routledge and Kegan Paul

STACEY M (1981) 'The division of labour revisited or overcoming the two Adams', in P Abrams et al. (eds) *Practice and Progress: British sociology 1950–1980*, Allen and Unwin

STAFFORD R, BACKMAN E and DIBONA P (1977) 'The division of labor among cohabiting and married couples', *J of Marriage and the Family*, 39, pp. 43–57

STEPHEN B (1980) 'What is a wife really worth?' *San Francisco Chronicle*, 25 Aug, p. 21

STIEHM J (1976) 'Invidious intimacy', *Social Policy*, March–April, pp. 12–16

STIVENS M (1978) 'Women and their kin: kin, class and solidarity in a middle-class suburb of Sydney, Australia', in P Caplan and J Bujra (eds) *Women United, Women Divided*, Tavistock

STONE K (1983) 'Motherhood and waged work: West Indian, Asian and white mothers compared', in A Phizacklea (ed.) *One Way Ticket: migration and female labour*, Routledge and Kegan Paul

STRASSER S (1982) *Never Done: a history of American housework*, Pantheon Books, NY

STROBER M H (1977) 'Wives labor force participation and family consumption habits', *Am. Economic Review*, vol. 67(1), pp. 410–17

SUMMERFIELD P (1984) *Women Workers in the Second World War*, Croom Helm

SYSON L and YOUNG M (1974) 'Poverty in Bethnal Green', in M Young (ed.) *Poverty Report 1974*, Temple Smith

SZALAI A (1972) *The Use of Time: daily activities of urban and suburban populations in twelve countries*, Mouton
TANNER L B (ed.) (1970) *Voices from Women's Liberation*, Signet
THOMPSON E P (1963) *The Making of the English Working Class*, Penguin
TILLY L and SCOTT J (1978) *Women, Work and Family*, Holt, Rinehart and Winston
TOLSON A (1977) *The Limits of Masculinity*, Tavistock
TRUDEAU M (1980) *Beyond Reason*, Arrow Books
UNGERSON C (1981) 'Women and caring; skills, tasks and taboos', in E Gamarnikow et al. (eds) *The Public and the Private*, Heinemann
—— (1987) *Policy is Personal: sex, gender and informal care*, Tavistock
VAN GELDER L (1979) 'The dollar value of a housewife: experts strive to figure it out', *New York Times*, 10 Dec, p. D12
VANEK J (1974) 'Time spent in housework', *Scientific American*, pp. 116–20
VAUGH C (1976) 'Growth of the fast food industry', *Cornell Motel and Restaurant Administration Quarterly*
VINNICOMBE S (1980) *Secretaries, Management and Organization*, Heinemann
VOGEL 1 (1973) 'The earthly family', *Radical America*, July–Oct
WAERNESS K (1978) 'The invisible welfare state: women's work at home', *Acta Sociologica*, pp. 193–207
WALBY S (1986) *Patriarchy at Work*, Polity
—— (1990) *Theorizing Patriarchy*, Blackwell
WALKER K E (1978) 'La mesure de temps consacré aux activitiés domestiques des familles américaines', in A Michel (ed.) *Les femmes dans la société marchande*, Presses Universitaires de France
WALKER K E and GAUGER W H (1973) *The Dollar Value of Household Work*, Cornell University Information Bulletin no. 60, Ithaca NY
WALKERDINE V and LUCEY H (1984) *Democracy in the Kitchen: regulating mothers and socialising daughters*, Virago
WALTER P (1986) 'The financing of childcare services in France', in B Cohen and K Clarke (eds) *Child Care and Equal Opportunities*, HMSO for the EOC
WARING M (1989) *If Women Counted: a new feminist economics*, Macmillan
WEBER M (1947) *The Theory of Social and Economic Organization*, ed. by T Parsons, Collier Macmillan
WEINBAUM B and BRIDGES A (1976) 'The other side of the paycheck: monopoly capital and the structure of consumption', *Monthly Review*, vol. 28, part 3, pp. 88–103
WEITZMAN L (1985) *The Divorce Revolution: the unexpected social and economic consequences for women and children in America*, Free Press, NY
WEST J (ed.) (1982) *Work, Women and the Labour Market*, Routledge and Kegan Paul
WESTWOOD S (1984) *All Day Everyday: factory and family in the making of women's lives*, Pluto Press
WESTWOOD S and BHACHU P (1988) *Enterprising Women: ethnicity, economy and gender relations*, Routledge
WHEELOCK J (1990) *Husbands at Home: domestic economy in post-industrial society*, Routledge

WHITEHEAD A (1976) 'Sex antagonisms in Herefordshire', in D Leonard Barker and S Allen (eds) *Dependence and Exploitation in Work and Marriage*, Hutchinson
—— (1981) 'I'm hungry mum: the politics of domestic budgeting', in K Young et al. (eds) *Of Marriage and the Market*, CSE Books
WILSON A (1974) *Finding a Voice: Asian women in Britain*, Virago
WILSON E (1977) *Women and the Welfare State*, Tavistock
—— (1985) *Adorned in Dreams: fashion and modernity*, Virago
WILSON G (1987) *Money in the Family: financial organisation and women's responsibility*, Avebury
WIMBUSH E and TALBOT M (eds) (1988) *Relative Freedoms: women and leisure*, Open University Press
WOLFELSPERGER A (1970) *Les biens durable dans la patrimoine du consommateur*, Presses Universitaires de France
WOOD S (1981) 'Redundancy and female employment', *Sociological Review*, vol. 29(4), pp. 649–83
WOODCOCK G and AVAKUMOVIC I (1950) *The Anarchist Prince*
WYNN ALLEN P (1988) *Building Domestic Liberty: Charlotte Perkins Gilman's architectural feminism*, University of Massachusetts Press
YOUNG I (1981) 'Beyond the unhappy marriage: a critique of dual systems theory', in L Sargent (ed.) *Women and Revolution*, South End Press
YOUNG K, WOLKOWITZ C and McCULLAGH R (1981) *Of Marriage and the Market: women's subordination internationally and its lessons*, CSE Books
YOUNG M (1952) 'The distribution of income within the family', *British Journal of Sociology*, vol. 3(4)
YOUNG M and WILLMOTT P (1973) *The Symmetrical Family: a study of work and leisure in the London region*, Routledge and Kegan Paul
ZARETSKY E (1976) *Capitalism, the Family and Personal Life*, Pluto Press
ZWEIG F (1961) *The Worker in an Affluent Society*, Heinemann

INDEX

advertising, 45, 50
Afro-Caribbean origin families, 14,
    19, 20, 114, 118, 127 n6, 162 n15
    income, 255 n19
    proportion with women heads,
        113–15, 127 n4
    see also Black families; ethnic
    minority families
age, 129–30, 133–6, 200, 251
agricultrices (women farmers), 207–8,
    216–17, 218, 224 n8, 225 n17
    co-farmers/ collaborators, 214–16
aides familiaux (family helpers), 198,
    212–13, 217, 224 n8
alienation, 61, 66, 71 n21, 39–40, 45
Allauzen, M., 201
alternative household structures, 7–8,
    14, 263
Althusser, L., 70
Alzon, C., 48
anarchism, 12, 263
appropriation of women's family
    work, 16, 29, 45–6, 63–7, 84, 89,
    96, 118–21, 159, 259–60, 262
Asian origin families, 14, 114
    income, 255 n19
    proportion with woman heads,
        113–4, 127 n4
    see also Black families; ethnic
    minority families
ateliers hors-sol, 199, 203
Atkinson, T.-G., 16
au pairs, 236; see also servants
authority, legitimacy of men's,
    137–42, 160 n4, 199

see also delegation; patriarchy

Barker, R., 25
Barrett, M., and McIntosh, M., 223
Barron, J., Crawley, G., and Wood,
    T., 239
Barthez, A., 197–220
Bastide, H., 201
Beauvoir, S. de, 10–11
Becker, G. S., 103, 161, n9
Bell, C., and Newby, H., 137–8
Benston, M., 87–8
Benyon, H., 193 n8
Berger, M., Foster, M., and Wallston,
    B. S., 248
biology, 15, 30, 34, 257–8
    biologistic explanations, 46–7, 48,
        58–60, 68
    see also naturalistic explanations
birth order, 155, see also heirs;
    hierarchy
Black
    families, 19–20, 65, 138, 139, 227,
        234, 255 n19
    feminism, 13–14, 134
    Power, 12
    women heads of household,
        113–15, 127 n5
    see also Afro-Caribbean families;
    Asian families; ethnic minority
    families
Blatchford, R., 7
body, women's work as specifically
    concerning, 22–3, 30, 257
Bott, E., 194, n19